How Greek Philosophy Corrupted The Christian Concept of God

How Greek Philosophy Corrupted The Christian Concept of God

Richard R. Hopkins

Copyright © 1998 By
HORIZON PUBLISHERS & DISTRIBUTORS, INC.

---

*All rights reserved.
Reproduction in whole or any parts thereof in any form
or by any media without written permission is prohibited.*

First Printing: April 1998

International Standard Book Number:
0-88290-607-0

Library of Congress Catalog Card Number:
98-071162

Horizon Publishers' Catalog and Order Number:
1035

Printed and distributed
in the United States of America by

& Distributors, Incorporated

Mailing Address:
P.O. Box 490
Bountiful, Utah 84011-0490

Street Address:
50 South 500 West
Bountiful, Utah 84010

Local Phone: (801) 295-9451
WATS (toll free): 1 (800) 453-0812
FAX: (801) 295-0196

E-mail: horizonp@burgoyne.com
Internet: http://www.horizonpublishers.com

Contents

1. The True Foundation For the Christian Concept of God ... 11
Sola Scriptura: An Unheeded Battle Cry, 11; The Early Church Fathers, 14; The Ante-Nicene Fathers, 14; Table 1, 17; An Apostasy at the Hands of the Apologists, 19; Greek Philosophy Inspires the Apostasy, 19; The Influence of Greek Philosophy on Orthodox Christianity Is Well Known, 21; The Greek Influence on Present-day Criticism of Mormon Theology, 22; A Classical Theist's Idea of Mormon Theology, 23; Greek Elements in the Fundamental Tenets of Classical Theism, 24; A Summary of the Orthodox View of God, 24; Orthodox Christian Differences With Biblical Doctrine Are Significant, 27; The Breadth and Challenge of This Study, 27; Restrictions on the Scope of This Study, 27; A Summary of Contents and Direction, 28; The Nature and Goal of The Study, 29; This Book Is a Tribute As Well As a Critique, 30.

Part I
How God Prepared the Gentiles to Receive Christianity: The Rise of Greek Philosophy

2. The Revolutionary Theology of the Greek Philosophers ... 34
Theology Begins Among the Greeks, 35; Pythagoras Discovers God by the Numbers, 36; Heraclitus Discovers God in Opposition, 37; The Greek "*Logos*," 37; Parmenides Reinvents God and Reality, 38; Anaxagoras Sees God as Pure Mind, 40; Plato Fashions Greek Theology, 40; Plato's World of Forms As the Agents of God, 42; Plato's Alternative Concept of God and the Creation, 43; Aristotle Places the Capstone on Greek Theology, 44; Aristotle's Use of the Term "Ousia," 45; Aristotle and the Greek Love of Logic, 47.

3. The Problem of Evil and the Development of Hellenism ... 50
The Stoics Espoused a Monistic View of the Universe, 50; Stoic Idealism Had a Profound Influence on Ethics, 52; The Platonists Advocated a Dualistic View of the Universe, 52; Influence of the Problem of Evil on Greek Theology, 53; The Book of Job and the Problem of Evil, 54; The Platonistic Response to the Problem of Evil, 56; The Stoics Found an Ethical Solution to the Problem of Evil, 57; Greek Gnosticism and Its Strange Theology, 57; The Problem of Evil and the Free Agency of Man, 59; Understanding the Problem of Evil, 60; Modern Revelation and the Problem of Evil, 61; Philo of Alexandria Forged the Path to the Theological Apostasy, 63.

4. The Greek Education System and the Spread of Hellenism . 68
Greek Education—the Model for Modern Education Systems, 68; Greek Education Emphasized Literature, Philosophy and Argument, 70; Greek Education Spread Quickly to Rome, 71; Jewish Education and Culture Remained Strictly Separate, 72; The Nature of Jewish Education, 73; A Deep Rift Between the Jews and the Gentiles, 73; The Skeptics and the Appeal of Christianity, 74; The Greek Fascination for Christianity Did

6   How Greek Philosophy Corrupted the Christian Concept of God

Not Include the Scriptures, 75; Greek Methods of Interpretation Were Used to Distort the Scriptures, 75; Philo and the Greek Method of Allegory, 76; The Apologists Adopted Allegorical Interpretations of the Scriptures, 76; The Greek Love for Sophistry Infects the Early Church, 77; The Development of Neoplatonism, 78; Christianity and Greek Culture Mutually Affected Each Other, 79; Jewish Commandments vs. Greek Ethics, 80; Jewish Inspiration vs. Greek Teaching, 81; Changes to the Gospel Were Inevitable, 81.

Part II
How Greek Philosophy Influenced Early Christianity: The Theological Apostasy

5. Foundations of the Theological Apostasy 84
Evidence of the Apostasy, 84; Signs of the Apostasy: Lack of Unity, 85; Signs of Apostasy: Adoption of Greek Philosophy, 86; Signs of Apostasy: Behavior of Church Leaders, 87; Causes of Apostasy: Heresy, 90; Causes of Apostasy: Early Persecution, 90; Beginnings of Apostasy: Writings of the Apostolic Fathers, 94; Clement of Rome, 94; Ignatius of Antioch, 96; Polycarp of Smyrna, 100; Papias of Hierapolis, 102; Hermas' Shepherd, 102.

6. The Apologists and the Theological Apostasy 106
Criticism of the Early Church, 106; Justin Martyr, The "First" Apologist, 108; Irenaeus, the Most Renowned of the Greek Apologists, 111; Lack of Information About the Gospel at the Time of Irenaeus, 111; No Clear Biblical Canon, 113; Greek Exegesis Resulted in Inaccurate Interpretation, 114; Confusion Interjected by Heretics and False Teachers, 115; Another Example of Irenaeus' Errors: the Age of Christ, 116; The Apologists Tackled Tough Questions, 117; The Apologists Responded to Jewish As Well As Greek Criticism, 118; Hellenization of the Early Church, 119; Renewed Persecution, a Catalyst for Apostasy , 120; Apologies Addressed to Marcus Aurelius, 120; The Impact of Stoic Philosophy, 121; The Boldness of the Early Apologists Offended Rome, 123; Apologetic Writings After 161 A.D., 124; Christian Descriptions of God Before 161 A.D., 124; Justin Martyr's View of God the Father, 129; Tatian Embraces the Hellenized God with Enthusiasm, 131; Melito Introduces Metaphysics to Christian Theology, 132; Athenagoras Teaches the Platonistic God, 134; Irenaeus Becomes the Father of Co-Substantiality, 136; Theophilus Introduces the Term "Trinity," 138; Minucius Felix Concurs in Latin, 140; Summary of the New Doctrine Developed by the Apologists, 141; Justin Martyr—A Heretic, or Simply Misunderstood?, 143; Presenting a United Front to Rome, 143; The Apologists Were Glorified by Their Deaths, 145; The Rise of Catholicism Advanced the Apostasy, 147.

7. Heresies and Heretics 153
Heretical Jewish Sects Clung to the Law of Moses, 154; The Judaizers, 154; Cerinthus and Gnostic Ebionism, 154; The Essenes or Clementines, 155; Ebionites Described by Epiphanius, 156; The Elkasaites, 157; Docetism Denied the Suffering of Christ, 157; Christian Gnosticism Began in Infamy, 158; Simon Magus, 158; Menander, 158; The Nicolaitans, 159; The Ophites, the Cainites and the Sethites, 159; Carpocrates, 159; The Syrian Gnostics Followed Platonistic Dualism, 159; Satornilus, 160; Tatian, 160;

Bardesanes, 161; The Egyptian Gnostics Were Monistic, 162; Basilides, 162; Valentinus, 163; Ptolemy, Heracleon and Mark, 164; Marcion, 165; Errors Made While Opposing Heretics, 167; Creation Out of Nothing, 167; A Residue of Gnosticism Remained in Orthodox Christianity, 168; Monarchianism, the Foundation of Arianism, 170; Montanism Claimed Endless New Revelations, 170; The Defeat of Montanism Ended the Concept of Ongoing Revelation, 172; The End of the Battles Against Heresy and Its Effect on the Early Church, 172.

8. The Arian Controversy: Cementing the Theological Apostasy 176

How Roman Persecution Was Triggered, 177; Roman Trials Preceded the Condemnation of Christians, 178; Christian Reactions Bewildered Roman Authorities, 179; Roman Persecution After Marcus Aurelius, 180; The Persecution by Decius, 181; A Controversy Arises Over Treatment of the "Lapsed," 182; The Baptism of Heretics Is Accepted by the Early Church, 183; Roman Persecution Continues, 184; The Final Battle, Diocletian's Persecution, 184; The Rise of Constantine and the Edict of Milan, 187; The Untimely Rise of the Arian Controversy, 188; Monarchianism the Great Heresy of the Third Century, 188; Modalism Under the Hand of Sabellius, 190; The Conflict Between Dionysius of Rome and Dionysius of Alexandria, 191; Subordination of the Son to the Father, 193; Paul of Samosata, The Forerunner of Arius, 193; Lucian Takes the Next Step Toward Arianism, 195; The Tenets of Arianism, 195; The Controversy Begins With the Excommunication of Arius, 196; Differences Between Arianism and Mormonism, 196; The True Nature of the Arian Controversy, 198; How the Controversy Came to Nicaea, 199; Arianism After Nicaea, 200; Systematizing the Theological Apostasy, 201.

Part III
The Influence of Greek Philosophy On Classical Theism Today: What Are the Attributes of God?

9. Understanding the Attributes of God 206

The Importation of Greek *A Priori* Assumptions Into Christianity, 206; The Danger of Using *A Priori* Assumptions to Learn About God, 208; Unbiblical Assumptions About God Must Be Rejected, 208; Examples of False *A Priori* Assumptions in Aristotelian Physics, 209; False *A Priori* Assumptions About Metaphysics, 211; Classical Theism Recognizes Some of Its Own Assumptions, 213; Dogmatism, 214; The Danger of Relying on Greek Terminology, 216; The Attributes of God, 217; A Note About the History of Theology After the Fourth Century, 217.

10. The Personal God 220

Greek Philosophy and Christianity Merged, 220; The Philosophers' View of God as a Person, 221; The Classical Attempt to Define the Personal God: The Trinity, 223; The Modern Expression of an Unsolvable Enigma: The Trinity As Three Separate Persons, But One Individual, 225; The Separateness of the Persons in the Trinity, 227; Justin and the Separateness of the Father and the Son, 228; Metaphysics, the Cradle of the Trinity, 230; What Does the Bible Say About "Co-substantiality"?, 231; Justin Martyr's Teachings About the Genesis of Christ, 232; Christ, the "Beginning of the Creation of God," 233; Rejection of Pre-Mortal Birth As the Means for the Genesis of Christ, 233; Rejection of Pre-Mortal Creation as the Means for the Genesis of Christ, 234; The Idea of

8 How Greek Philosophy Corrupted the Christian Concept of God

"Emanation" and the Rejection of "Division" as the Means for the Genesis of Christ, 235; What's Wrong With Being Created by God?, 238; The Orthodox Answer to the Genesis of Christ, 239; The Timing of Christ's Genesis, 240; The Biblical View of the Genesis of Christ, 241; The True Origin of Christ, 242; God's True Nature as an Individual, 242; Was the Godhead Different in the Old Testament?, 243; Biblical Evidence for Three Separate Centers of Consciousness, 244; Separate Knowledge Dictates Separate Centers of Consciousness, 245.

11. The Corporeal God 250

False Assumptions About Corporeality, 250; "Face to Face" With the Biblical God, 251; "Theophanies" and "Anthropomorphisms" in Bible Passages, 253; Does the Bible Say That God Has Wings?, 253; Is God Only a Spirit?, 255; God's Resurrected Body is Different From That of Mortal Men, 257; Numbers 23:19 As Proof That God Is Corporeal, 259; The Invisible God, 260; Greek Origins of Incorporeality as a Supposed Attribute of God, 262; The Classical Doctrine of a Transcendent God Is Based on Greek Metaphysics, 263; The Greek Notion of a Transcendent, Incorporeal God, 264; Transcendence and Incorporeality in Hellenized Judaism, 266; Earliest Christian Views on the Transcendency and Corporeality of God, 267; Early Christian Belief in a Corporeal God, 268; The Apologists Imported the God of Greek Philosophy Into Christianity, 268; Not All the Apologists Agreed That God Was Incorporeal, 271; What Does the Bible Teach About the Transcendency of God?, 271; Classical Attempts to Defend the Transcendence of God From the Bible, 272; Incorporeality, an Idolatrous Doctrine, 273; The Real God Contrasted With Idols, 274.

12. God, The Creator 278

The Classical Doctrine of Creation, 278; What "Things" Did God Create?, 279; No Biblical Support for the Idea that God Created Reality, 279; "All Things" Does Not Include Space and Time, 281; Space and Time Are Not "Things," 281; A Theological Argument Against the Creation of Time and Space, 282; God Is Not Confined, or Limited by Space or Time, 282; Being "In" Time Does Not Give God a Beginning or an End, 284; "Eternity" Is Not the *Pleroma*, 284; Straining the Scriptures Provides No Biblical Support, 284; Being "In" Time Does Not Make God Dependent on Time or Space, 285; Philosophical Problems With the Creation of Time and Space, 286; Vacuum and Quantum Theory, 286; Irenaeus Missed an Important Argument, 287; Biblical Creation of the Heavens and the Earth, 288; Renovation of the Earth Appears in the Original Hebrew, 288; What Is Included in "The Heavens and the Earth?," 289; God's Additional Creations Told in Modern Revelation, 289; Ineffective Efforts to Support the *Ex Nihilo* Doctrine From the Bible, 290; Passages Used to Support *Ex Nihilo* Creation Actually Refute Metaphysics, 291; Romans 4:17 and "Being," 292; Hebrews 11:3 and "Phenomenon," 293; *Ginomai* Does Not Teach Creation Out of Nothing, 294; Development of the *Ex Nihilo* Doctrine in the Early Church, 295.

13. The Omnipotent God 304

How Powerful Is Omnipotence?, 304; Problems with the Classical View, 306; Omnipotence and Corporeality, 307; Einstein and the Power of Corporeality, 308; Mormonism Teaches that God Is Omnipotent, 309.

14. The Omniscient God 311
Classical Theism's Position on God's Omniscience, 311; Can God Know the Future?, 311; Mormon Theology On God's Omniscience, 313; Classical Theism's Idea of How God Knows the Future, 315; How Does God Really Know the Future?, 316; Greek Barriers to Understanding the Omniscience of a Corporeal God, 319; Modern Advances in Knowledge Support the Corporeality of God, 320; Power of the Human Brain, 321.

15. The Omnipresent God 324
Understanding Omnipresence, 324; Classical Theism's Notions of God's Omnipresence, 325; God Has a Specific Location in Space and Time, 327; The Personal God and the Dilemma of Omnipresence, 328; Classical Reactions to the Dilemma of Omnipresence, 329; Is God's Omnipresence an Irrational Paradox?, 330; Mormons Believe God's Omnipresence is Rational, 331; Biblical Omnipresence, 332; Where Is God? Not in Temples Made With Hands, 332; Unworthy Temples, 334; Omnipresence as a Consequence of Omniscience, 335; Immanence and Transcendence, 337; God's Ability to Travel as an Aspect of Omnipresence, 337; God's Nearness as an Aspect of Omnipresence, 338; Communication as an Aspect of Omnipresence, 339; A Modern Analogy to Biblical Omnipresence, 340; Some Insights on the Nature of God's Telecommunication System, 342.

16. The Immutable and Eternal God 345
Scriptural References to God's Immutability, 345; Immutability an Essential Attribute of God, 346; The Static Versus the Dynamic View of God, 346; In What Way Does God Remain Unchanged?, 347; In What Ways Does God Change?, 349; Changes in Knowledge and Wisdom, 349; Changes in Bodily Characteristics, 350; Changes In Office, Title or Position, 350; Origin of the Classical View of Immutability, 354; The Idea of God As a Necessary Being, 354; Origin of The "Necessary God" Concept, 355; The Biblical Doctrine of God's Necessity, 355; What If God Did Not Exist?, 356; Has God Always Been "God?", 357; From Everlasting to Everlasting, 358; Christ's Exaltation to the Office of "God," 359; Christ Was Exalted to the Godhead *Because* of His Immutable Righteousness, 361; Joseph Smith's Teachings About God's History, 362; Joseph's Teachings Are Compatible With God's Immutability, 363; Eternal Progression and Immutability, 364; Was the Father Exalted?, 365; Does Christ's "Creation" as a Spirit Refute His Immutability?, 366.

17. The Plural and Only God 371
Classical Theism's Position: One God "by Nature," 371; The Scriptures and "the Only God," 372; God's Oneness is Figurative, 373; The Principle of Agency in the Godhead, 374; Who Are the Agents of God?, 375; The Origin of Angels, 376; Special Agents of God, 377; Understanding Passages in Isaiah, 378; Christ's Submission To The Father, 379; Paul and the Oneness of "Many Gods," 380; Corporate Aspects of the Godhead's Functionality, 383; Other Passages Confirm the Father's Authority as Singular, 384; Is Biblical Theology Monotheistic?, 384; Failure of the Greek Mind to Grasp the Godhead's Functionality, 385; The Confused Doctrine of Subordination, 387.

10 How Greek Philosophy Corrupted the Christian Concept of God

Part IV
Classical Theism Reacts to the Biblical Concept of God: Philosophical Problems With Eternal Progression

18. Man and the Infinite 393

An Ontological Look at God and Man, 393; The Classical Doctrine of Man's "Finiteness," 395; The Biblical Response to the Orthodox Doctrine of Man's "Finiteness," 397; The Principle of Progression, 398; An Infinite Number of Gods, 399; A Finite Look at Infinity, 401; Infinity in Mormon Theology, 405; Beginnings in Mormon Theology, 405; The Number of Gods in the Universe, 406; Logical Requisites For Eternal Progression, 407; The Function of Free Agency, 408.

19. Answering Philosophical Objections to The Doctrine of Eternal Progression 413

The Problem of an Infinite Number of Past Events: Can an Infinite Number Be Traversed in a Real Universe?, 414; Can an Infinite Number Be Traversed?, 416; If Not Men, Hasn't God Traversed an Infinite Number?, 417; Conclusion On the Problem of an Infinite Number of Past Events, 418; The Problem of Eternal Progression With an Infinite Past, 419; Segment One of Eternal Progression: The Intelligence, 420; Greek Notions About The Intelligence, 422; Segment Two of Eternal Progression: The Spirit, 422; Segment Three of Eternal Progression: Mortality, 423; An Adjunct to Segment Three: The Spirit World, 424; Segment Four of Eternal Progression: Resurrection and Eternal Life, 424; An Overview of God's Creative Cycles, 426; The Duration of God's Eternal Rounds, 428; Was There a Beginning of Time?, 429; Greek Beliefs About the Cycle of Eternal Progression, 429; The Problem of Achieving Omniscience by Eternal Progression, 430; Man's Knowledge in Pre-Mortality, 432; Obtaining Omniscience, 433; How Man Gains Knowledge, 435; Man Can Become Omniscient!, 436; The Coherent Concept of God, 436.

20. A Summary of Greek Influences on the Christian Concept of God 441

Erroneous Greek Philosophical Concepts Incorporated into Early Christian Doctrine, 442; *1.* Strict Monotheism: The Numerically Singular God, 442; *2.* The "Logos": Embodiment of the Metaphysical God's "Reason," 443; *3.* Dualism: The Absolute Distinction Between Mind and Created Things, 444; *4.* The Metaphysical Universe: Man's Universe Is an Illusion, 444; *5.* Metaphysical Theism: God Exists in the Pleroma, the World of "Forms," 444; *6.* God As Transcendent: Existence Outside Time and Space, 445; *7.* The Supposed Inferiority of Created Things, 446; *8.* The Supposed Incomprehensible and Unknowable God, 446; *9.* The Supposed Incorporeality of God: Mind Without Matter, 446; *10.* Creation and Some Distorted Beliefs About God's Omnipotence and Omniscience, 446; *11.* Distorted Ideas About the Omnipresence of God, 447; *12.* God As The "Unmoving Mover": God Differs From Men Because He Never Changes, 447; *13.* The Origin of Christ: No Pre-Mortal Birth for the Firstborn Son of God, 448; *14.* Rationalism: Reason Rather than Revelation, 448; *15.* Logic More Important Than Empirical Truth, 448.

Scripture Index 451

Subject Index 457

The True Foundation For the Christian Concept of God

One of the most inspiring expressions of the Protestant Reformation was found in its battle cry, *sola Scriptura* ("only the Scriptures"). To the Reformers, these watchwords meant not only that God had revealed Himself through the Bible, but that "Scripture can and does interpret itself to the faithful from within . . . so that not only does it not need Popes or Councils to tell us, as from God, what it means; it can actually challenge Papal and conciliar pronouncements, convince them of being ungodly and untrue, and require the faithful to part company with them."[1]

Yet today, that historic phrase is but a vague memory. Neither Protestants nor Catholics actually base their beliefs about the nature of God on the Bible. Though this may surprise some Christians, to believe otherwise is more than naive—it is a failure to apprehend the very essence of what is known as "Christian orthodoxy."

Sola Scriptura: An Unheeded Battle Cry

One of the holds the Roman Catholic Church had on its membership prior to the Protestant Reformation was the belief that only the Pope was able to communicate the will of God and interpret the scriptures for the people. At the Council of Trent (1545-1563) the Roman Church expressed the following statement as the attitude of Roman Catholicism toward the scriptures:

---

[1] J. I. Packer, "'Sola Scriptura' in History and Today," in *God's Inerrant Word*, ed. John Warwick Montgomery (Minneapolis: Bethany Fellowship, 1975), 44-45.

> The sacred and holy, ecumenical, and general Synod of Trent, ... following the example of the orthodox fathers, receives and venerates with an equal affection of piety and reverence all the books both of the Old and of the New Testament—seeing that one God is the author of both—*as also the sacred traditions*,[2] as well those pertaining to faith as to morals, as having been dictated, either by Christ's own word of mouth or by the Holy Ghost, and preserved in the Catholic Church by a continuous succession.[3]

Thus, the Roman Church openly declared its reliance on Catholic tradition as being of equal stature with the scriptures as a basis for theology and ethics.

The Reformers countered this view with the doctrine of *sola Scriptura*, the belief that Man[4] is able to ascertain the will of God by reading and interpreting the Bible for himself, without the official pronouncement of Catholic leaders. The Protestant concept, intended to counter the lingering pull of Catholic tradition and ecclesiastical authority, firmly rejected tradition and Church office as a factor in determining doctrine. The Reformers believed that the Bible interprets itself, and that no outside source is authorized by God to interpret it or introduce other doctrines as coming from God (2 Pet. 1:20). In their view, all Christian teaching on faith and morals was to be based on the truth and inerrancy of the Bible.[5]

Sadly, however, that objective has never been realized by any Protestant group—Evangelicals, Pentacostals, or any others who claim to be "orthodox." "Christian orthodoxy" goes far beyond the teachings of the Bible in its definition of the nature and attributes of God. While it pretends not to do so, tradition is at its very foundation—the tradition

---

[2] Emphasis added. The author will, from time to time, emphasize portions of the passages cited by him by placing the emphasized words in italics. Hereafter, that will be done without further use of the notation, "emphasis added." Occasionally, similar emphasis appears in the original quotations. Where emphasis is added by the original author, the emphasis has been removed to avoid confusion. Where emphasis from the original has been left in the text, the author will indicate that fact by the notation, "emphasis in original."

[3] John Miley, *Systematic Theology* (Peabody: Hendrickson Publishers, 1989), 2 vols., 1:13.

[4] The words "Man" or "Men," as used in this book, refer to mankind generally, both male and female.

[5] J. D. Douglas, Walter A. Elwell and Peter Toon, *The Concise Dictionary of the Christian Tradition* (Grand Rapids: Zondervan Publishing House, 1989), s.v. "Sola Fide, Sola Gratia, Sola Scriptura."

of theology established during the second century A.D., long after the close of the New Testament canon.

Some Protestant theologians justify this by pointing out that oral traditions that came directly from the Apostles of Christ's day were a proper basis for Christian faith and morals. This was a point of instruction by Paul (2 Thess. 2:15). The problem is that in the early second century, the only reliable traditions available from the Apostles were found in their writings. Very little else had been passed on to the survivors of the early persecutions. Therefore, the question is, what traditions actually came from the Apostles and which came from other sources? Also, how long did tradition, in the form of early Christian writing, remain reliable after the death or disappearance of the Apostles (approximately the end of the first century A.D.)?

Contrary to the Protestant battle cry of *sola Scriptura*, it is the position of most orthodox Christian theologians that the writings of the "earlier fathers" are reliable as a source of accurate teaching about God. Thus, John Miley, a noted Protestant theologian, writes as follows:

> Within a proper limitation of time and under favorable conditions even oral tradition may be of value. It was so in apostolic times and even after. So Paul exhorted the Christians of Thessalonica to observe the traditions received from him, whether by word or epistle, and to withdraw from any who refused this observance [2 Thess. 2:15, 3:6]. *The earlier fathers appealed to apostolic traditions, and might do so with safety and profit.*[6]

Unfortunately, this excerpt is unclear as to who might be included among the "earlier fathers."

Most Protestant theologians assert that the time when believers in *sola Scriptura* may cease to include tradition as a factor in their faith is approximately "the commencement of the third century." That is the opinion asserted by Miley following the statement above. He explains:

> *After the commencement of the third century*, when the first teachers of the apostolic churches *and their immediate successors* had passed away and another race came on, *other doctrines and forms were gradually introduced, which differed in many respects from apostolical simplicity*. And now these innovators appealed more frequently than had ever been done before to apostolical tradition, in order to give

---

[6] Miley, *Systematic Theology*, 1:13.

currency to their own opinions and regulations. *Many at this time did not hesitate, as we find, to plead apostolical traditions for many things at variance not only with other traditions, but with the very writings of the apostles, which they had in their hands.* From this time forward tradition became naturally more and more uncertain and suspicious.[7]

This excerpt acknowledges that significant doctrinal errors were made in the writings of Christian leaders after approximately 200 A.D. However, writings from the second century A.D. are given a status essentially equal with scripture, consistent with the Catholic position stated by the Council of Trent. Indeed, the Church fathers of the late second century provided the foundation for all current interpretation of the Scriptures pertaining to the nature of God by those who call themselves "orthodox." Their opinions and interpretations, which often run contrary to the Bible, provide the real foundation for the concept of God held by the majority of both Catholics and Protestants today.

The pivotal question is this: Are the writings of these early Church fathers entitled to the same reverence as those of the Apostles? Should they be excluded from the concern about erroneous tradition expressed in the fervent cry of *sola Scriptura*?

This book will demonstrate that the second century Church fathers known as the Apologists embraced gross doctrinal error regarding the nature and attributes of God. The cutoff date selected by Protestants who call themselves "orthodox Christians" is nearly a century too late. The theological horse was already out of the stable by the time they shut the door on tradition as a factor in faith. It was these Church fathers of the late second century who led the Church away from the biblical truth about God and allowed Greek philosophy to corrupt the Christian concept of God.

The Early Church Fathers

The early Church fathers are usually divided into two major groups, the **Ante-Nicene** and the **Post-Nicene Fathers**. Those, like Athanasius, who span the Nicene period are sometimes included in a third group, the **Nicene Fathers**. Within the two major groups are several subgroups.

The Ante-Nicene Fathers

The earliest of the Ante-Nicene Fathers is the group called the **Apostolic Fathers**. They lived in the era of Church history immediately

---
[7] *Ibid.*, 1:13-14.

following Christ's Apostles and learned from them. Those counted in this group include very few:

1. **Clement of Rome**, the third bishop of Rome, lived from approximately 30-100 A.D. and wrote his *Epistle to the Corinthians* shortly before his death.[8]

2. **Ignatius of Antioch** lived between 30 and 107 A.D., and is traditionally believed to have been the child Christ placed in the midst of the apostles in Matthew 13:2.[9]

3. **Polycarp of Smyrna** was likely ordained bishop of that city by the Apostle John. He lived from 65 to 155 A.D.[10]

4. **Papias of Hierapolis** wrote five books,[11] of which only fragments now remain. He is thought to have lived from 70 to 155 A.D., but may have died in 163 A.D. in Rome.

Of these four, only Polycarp and Papias survived the persecutions inflicted by the Roman Emperor Trajan, which ended in 117 A.D.

Sometimes counted among them because of the spirit of his writings, if not because of his association with the Apostles, is **Hermas**.

The Apostolic Fathers were followed in the mid-second century A.D. by a group that includes the real pioneers of orthodox Christian theology. "Apology," in Greek rhetoric, is the verbal defense of ideas. Thus, the men who first used Greek methods of reasoning to defend Christianity were known as the **Apologists**.

This group includes, primarily, the following individuals:

1. **Aristides**, who wrote an apology to the Emperor Hadrian in 125 A.D.

2. The author of the ***Epistle to Diognetus***, written circa 130 A.D., who identifies himself only as ***Mathetes***, meaning "disciple."

3. **Justin**, known as Justin Martyr, who lived from circa 100 A.D. to approximately 163 A.D.

---

[8] Alexander Roberts and James Donaldson, eds., *The Ante-Nicene Fathers: Translations of The Writings of the Fathers down to A.D. 325* (Grand Rapids; Wm. B. Eerdmans Publishing Company, reprinted 1986), 1:1.

[9] *Ibid.*, 1:45.

[10] *Ibid.*, 1:31.

[11] Irenaeus, *Against Heresies*, 5:33:4. (The numbers used in classical references, such as the foregoing, are the modern equivalent of the Roman numbers used anciently to divide the work into book:chapter:paragraph.)

4. Justin's pupil, ***Tatian***, who wrote from about 150 A.D., and was in turn a teacher of Clement of Alexandria.[12] After the death of Justin, Tatian became a heretic.[13]

5. ***Melito of Sardis***, who wrote an apology to Marcus Aurelius about 170 A.D. of which only fragments remain.[14]

6. ***Athenagoras***, who wrote his apology to Marcus Aurelius in 177 A.D.

7. ***Theophilus***, bishop of Antioch until about 180 A.D.

8. ***Irenaeus***, undoubtedly the most revered of the Greek Apologists, who lived from approximately 130 A.D. to circa 200 A.D.

8. ***Minucius Felix***, the first of the Latin Apologists. There is a controversy about his writings. Kidd places them circa 180 A.D.[15], but others claim they were written in 210 or later.[16]

9. ***Tertullian*** (c. 155-222 A.D.), who was a famous Roman lawyer before his conversion, and is considered second only to Augustine among the Latin Apologists. He left the Roman Church in the late second century to join the Montanist sect.[17]

10. ***Hippolytus***, who lived from 170[18] to 236 A.D. was among the last Apologists.

11. ***Clement of Alexandria*** (c. 150 to c. 215 A.D.) was one of two prolific Apologists known as the Alexandrian Fathers.

12. ***Origen*** (c. 185 to c. 254 A.D.) was the other of the two Alexandrian Fathers. He was perhaps the most voluminous of the early Christian writers.

Some historians include *Barnabus* (not the companion of Paul, but the author of the apocryphal *Epistle of Barnabus*), *Quadratus, Claudius Apollonaris*, and *Cyprian* as Apologists. However, of the writings of Quadratus and Claudius Apollonaris only fragments remain, and Cyprian lived in the third century. He was not so much an innovator as

---

[12] *Encyclopaedia Britannica* (Chicago: William Benton, Publisher), 1960 ed., s.v. "Tatian."

[13] Irenaeus, *Against Heresies,* 1:28.

[14] *The Ante-Nicene Fathers*, 8:751.

[15] B.J. Kidd, *A History of the Church to A.D. 461* (Oxford:Clarendon Press, 1922), 1:84.

[16] *The Ante-Nicene Fathers*, 4:169; Henry Melvill Gwatkin, *Early Church History to A.D. 313* (London: MacMillan and Co., 1909), 1:177.

[17] Kidd, *History of the Church*, 1:297; see also, *Encyclopaedia Britannica*, 1960 ed. and *Ante-Nicene Fathers* under the headings of the various men named.

[18] 155 A.D. according to Kidd, *History of the Church* 1:154.

a defender of the doctrines developed between 150 and 200 A.D. A list of the most notable among the Ante-Nicene Fathers is contained in Table 1.

Table 1
The Ante-Nicene Fathers
(All Dates are A.D.)

Name	Born	Died (Wrote)	Principle Work(s)
The Apostolic Fathers			
Clement of Rome	30	100	Epistle to the Corinthians
Barnabus[19]		(100)	Epistle of Barnabas
Polycarp	69	155	Epistle to the Philippians
Ignatius	30	107	Epistles to Polycarp, the Ephesians, and the Romans[20]
(anonymous)		(150)	Second Letter of Clement to the Corinthians
Papias	70	155	Exposition of the Oracles of the Lord (fragments)
Hermas[21]		160	The Shepherd
The Apologists, including the Anti-Gnostic and Alexandrian Fathers			
Aristides		(125)	Apology
Quadratus		(126)	(fragments)
Mathetes[22]		(130)	Epistle to Diognetus
Justin Martyr	110	165	First Apology, Second Apology, Dialogue with Trypho[23]
Tatian	110	172	Address to the Greeks
Melito of Sardis	160	177	Apology
Athenagoras		(177)	A Plea for the Christians
Irenaeus	120	202	Against Heresies
Theophilus of Antioch	115	181	To Autolycus

---

[19] The name here is uncertain. Most scholars agree that this was not Barnabus, the companion of Paul. Many include this writer among the Apologists. Eusebius considered his epistle to be spurious.

[20] There are a number of other writings by Ignatius, but these three are the only ones acknowledged by the vast majority of scholars.

[21] Not generally thought to be a true Apostolic Father, Hermas is included because of the character of his writing.

[22] The true name of this author is unknown, and he is often counted among the Apostolic Fathers.

[23] Several other writings are attributed to Justin, but these three are the only ones on which scholarship agrees.

Name	Born	Died (Wrote)	Principle Work(s)
Minucius Felix		(180 or 210)[24]	The Octavius
Clement of Alexandria	153	217	Exhortation to the Heathen, Miscellanies (Stromata)
Tertullian	145	220	The Apology, To Scapula, An Answer to the Jews, A Treatise on the Soul, The Prescription Against Heretics, Against Marcion, Against Hermogenes, Against the Valentinians, On the Resurrection of the Flesh, Against Praxeas, De Fuga in Persecutione
Origen	185	254	De Principiis, Against Celsus, plus other works too numerous to mention
Hippolytus	170	236	The Philosophic Refutation of All Heresies

Minor Writers: Caius, Aristo of Pella, Hegesippus, Maximus of Jerusalem, Claudius Apollinaris, Polycrates, Dionysius of Corinth, Theophilus of Caesarea, Serapion, Apollonius, Pantaenus, pseudo-Irenaeus.

Fathers of the Third Century

Name	Born	Died (Wrote)	Principle Work(s)
Commodianus		(240)	Instructions on Christian Discipline
Cyprian	200	258	Epistles, Treatises, Seventh Council of Carthage (minutes)
Novatian	210	280	Treatise Concerning the Trinity
Gregory Thaumaturgus	205	265	The Oration and Panegyric, Four Homilies
Dionysius of Alexandria	200	(265)	Against Sabellius (fragments), Epistle to Dionysius of Rome (fragments)
Dionysius of Rome		(269)	Against the Sabellians
Julius Africanus	200	245	Epistle to Aristides, Chronography (fragments)
Archelaus		(277)	Acts of the Disputation with the Heresiarch Manes
Alexander of Lycopolis		(301)	Of the Manichaeans
Peter of Alexandria	260	311	The Genuine Acts of Peter, The Canonical Epistle
Alexander of Alexandria	273	326	The Deposition of Arius

---

[24] The controversy boils down to whether Tertullian copied Minucius or Minucius copied Tertullian.

Name	Born	Died (Wrote)	Principle Work(s)
Methodius	260	312	*Banquet of the Ten Virgins, Concerning Free-Will*
Lactantius	260	330	*The Divine Institutes, The Epitome of the Divine Institutes, On the Workmanship of God, or the Formation of Man*
Arnobius	297	303	*Against the Heathen*

Minor Writers: Anatolius, Alexander of Cappadocia, Theognostus, Pierius, Theonas, Phileas, and Pampilus, Venantius, Asterius Urbanus, Victorinus.

The Post-Nicene Fathers

Of the **Post-Nicene Fathers**, the greatest is unquestionably *Augustine*, but he, too, was a justifier of doctrine, not an innovator of it. He systematized the doctrines of the Apologists and provided the intellectual rationale for "classical theism," the orthodox theology which has been accepted by the Christian world for eighteen hundred years. Because it is the Apologists whose influence is most strongly felt in classical theism, it is this group that will be the primary focus of this book. It is to their era that the theological apostasy can be traced.

An Apostasy at the Hands of the Apologists

What orthodox Christians do not appreciate is that a significant apostasy from true biblical doctrine about the nature and character of God occurred at the hands of the Apologists during the latter half of the second century. The reason this notion is so difficult for them to grasp is quite simple. The Apologists were diligently engaged at the time in combating the very apostasy into which they fell.

Many of their writings are a defense of the faith against the heresies that were daily cropping up in the early Church. Those heresies were grossly erroneous. By comparison, the subtle influence of Greek philosophy introduced by the Apologists went largely unnoticed by the early Church, which had been deprived of knowledgeable and respected leaders for many years.

Greek Philosophy Inspires the Apostasy

The true fountain of theological apostasy was not found in the wild theories of the Christian Gnostics and other heretics whose notions were so obviously non-biblical that even the unlearned could see their errors. Rather, it was found in the more subtle background of Hellenism that pervaded the Gentile world at the time of Christ. Christ and His Apostles had warned the early Church against false prophets and false teachers (Matt. 7:15, 24:11, 24; Mark 13:22; 2 Pet. 2:1; 1 John 4:1). Their warnings did not relate to some distant future threat. They were immediate and urgent. The Savior's warning in Matthew 7:15 was in the present tense. The warning in 2 Peter 2:1, written in 66 A.D., was in the future tense, but the similar warning issued by John in 1 John 4:1, written more than 25 years later, indicates that Peter's prophecy was already being fulfilled.

The Apologists were aware of these warnings and believed they were aimed at heretics, especially the Jewish and Christian Gnostics and other groups that ignored the Bible to import an almost paganistic theology into Christianity. Thanks to the Apologists, these heretical groups were ultimately put down by the end of the second century, but their own errors have proved far more difficult to excise.

In his second epistle to Timothy (2 Tim. 4:2-4, 67 A.D.) Paul issued a warning that was easy to accept as a reference to the Gnostic heretics. He said:

> Preach the word; be instant in season, out of season; reprove, rebuke, exhort with all longsuffering and doctrine.
>
> For the time will come when they will not endure sound doctrine; but after their own lusts shall they heap to themselves teachers, having itching ears;
>
> And they shall turn away their ears from the truth, and shall be turned unto fables.

The word "fables" in this passage is translated from the Greek word, muthos, which can also be rendered "myth," "legend" or "cleverly devised story."[25] It is a specific reference to one of the popular Greek styles of writing in Paul's time. Didactic fables were made famous by Aesop, who lived in Samos, Greece, from about 620 to 560 B.C. Fables of this nature had become a distinctly Hellenistic form of expository writing by the first century A.D.[26] This word describes perfectly the kind of myth-like fables imported into the Church by the Gnostics with whom Paul was then struggling.

---

[25] Walter Bauer, *A Greek-English Lexicon of the New Testament and Other Early Christian Literature*, 2d ed., William F. Arndt and F. Wilbur Gingrich, trans., (Chicago: University of Chicago Press, 1979), s.v. $\mu\nu\theta o\varsigma$.

[26] *Encyclopaedia Britannica*, 1960 ed., s.v. "Aesop."

But Paul's admonition to Timothy was part of a broader warning he had issued years before. That warning clearly identified the direction from which the early Church could expect the most dangerous false teaching to arise—the popular Greek theology and culture of the time. In Colossians 2:8 (NASB), written circa 60 A.D., Paul gave his explicit warning in these words: *"See to it that no one takes you captive through philosophy and empty deception, according to the tradition of men, according to the elementary principles of the world, rather than according to Christ"* (emphasis added).

The "tradition of men" at the time Paul wrote this letter was Hellenism. The "elementary principles" that prevailed in the "world" were those taught by the Greeks. Though they avoided many "fables," the Apologists were susceptible to Hellenistic assumptions, and it is from that direction apostasy ultimately came. Greek philosophy and education were pervasive at the time, and the principles taught by the classical Greek philosophers were the foundation of all theological consideration—for the Apologists as well as the heretics. The scriptures were written on a different set of assumptions, namely those of the Hebrew prophets. This made them susceptible to misinterpretation by those with an orientation in Greek philosophy.

Paul's predictions and warnings about the future of teaching in the early Christian Church should make every student of the Bible skeptical about any theological development that occurred in the years following the death of the Apostles, especially if it had a Hellenistic orientation. Yet most Christian churches today accept without question the teachings of the early Church Fathers, primarily the Apologists, as if they had a weight equal to, and sometimes greater than, the biblical canon. That acceptance must now be questioned if orthodox Christianity is to recover its lost understanding of God.

The Influence of Greek Philosophy on Orthodox Christianity Is Well Known

Surprisingly, the influence of Greek philosophy on the early Christian Church has been widely recognized for centuries and is well documented by Bible scholars and theologians.[27] Yet classical theism remains blind to the difference between the Hellenistic teachings

---

[27] "Platonism After Plato: Influence on Christian Thought," *Encyclopaedia Britannica*, 1960 ed., s.v. "Plato."

adopted by the Apologists and the original theology taught in the Bible. It is unlikely that most Christian believers today are even aware of the extent to which the admixture of Greek philosophy and Christianity has affected their fundamental beliefs about God.

This situation first became evident to the author in 1995, when he had a weekly radio program in Los Angeles. While interviewing Dr. Charles Morgan, an astute Bible scholar thoroughly trained in the classical tradition, it became obvious that the origins of non-biblical theology accepted by orthodox Christianity were well known to him. But he refused to accept the idea that there was any difference between the doctrines taught by the Apologists and those taught in the Bible. Instead, he felt that the writings of the early Church fathers provided a deeper insight and understanding of biblical theology. He and other classical theists have blessed the marriage of ancient Christianity with the philosophy against which Paul so vehemently warned.

This book is written to document the departure of early Christian theology from its biblical roots in favor of Greek philosophy and religion. It will show that the orthodox reverence for the writings of the Apologists must be reexamined. Using the Greek scholarship of the time, these early writers filled the gaps in their understanding of God with many distinctly Greek notions that have no foundation in the Bible at all. It will also show that LDS theology provides a rational and entirely biblical alternative to these notions.

The Greek Influence on Present-day Criticism of Mormon Theology

That this is no dry and ancient inquiry is apparent from modern criticism of Mormon theology by classical theists. A prime example is found in an article recently written by Dr. Francis J. ("Frank") Beckwith, formerly a Lecturer of Philosophy at the University of Nevada Las Vegas and now a professor at Whittier College in Southern California. It is entitled "Philosophical Problems with the Mormon Concept of God" (Irvine: Christian Research Institute, 1994) and was taken from a book entitled *The Mormon Concept of God: A Philosophical Analysis* (Edwin Mellen Press, 1991) co-authored by Dr. Stephen E. Parrish. The article has appeared on the Internet and has received wide dissemination through the Journal of the Christian Research Institute.

In it, Dr. Beckwith states what he believes to be Mormon doctrine about God, with the qualification that it is "in effect" what Mormon's teach.[28] This means that his version has undergone a kind of Hellenistic transformation that may be difficult for LDS readers to understand without the background provided in this book. He states his erroneous summary of LDS teachings from the perspective of an orthodox Christian. That view is enlightening to anyone interested in proselyting those of that faith. Indeed, this statement of Mormon theology is not just interesting. It was in many respects the impetus for this book.

A Classical Theist's Idea of Mormon Theology

Dr. Beckwith writes as follows:

> Though there is certainly disagreement among Mormon scholars concerning some precise points of doctrine, I submit that the church currently teaches that God is, in effect, (1) a contingent being, who was at one time not God; (2) finite in knowledge (not truly omniscient), power (not omnipotent), and being (not omnipresent or immutable); (3) one of many gods; (4) a corporeal (bodily) being, who physically dwells at a particular spatio-temporal location and is therefore not omnipresent like the classical God (respecting His intrinsic divine nature—we are not considering the Incarnation of the Son of God here); and (5) a being who is subject to the laws and principles of a beginningless universe with an infinite number of entities in it.
>
> No doubt there are individual Mormons whose personal views of God run contrary to the above five points. But since both the later writings of Joseph Smith and current Mormon orthodoxy clearly assert these five points, Mormons who dispute them are out of step with their church.[29]

Of course, not only are there "individual Mormons whose personal views of God run contrary to the above five points," but, with the exception of one or two statements, the entire Mormon Church would stand in disagreement with Dr. Beckwith's summary of its teachings. It will be a point of this book to correct the errors made by Dr. Beckwith in his analysis of Mormon doctrine. Another will be to

---

[28] Francis Beckwith, "Philosophical Problems with the Mormon Concept of God," *Christian Research Journal,* CRI document number CJR0100A, character set US-ASCII, page 5, when printed on 8$^{1}/_{2}$x11 paper.
[29] *Ibid.,* 5.

address his conclusions based on those errors. This, however, will require some background before the effort is undertaken.

Greek Elements in the Fundamental Tenets of Classical Theism

The points that must be understood in order to respond to Dr. Beckwith are found in the seven basic attributes of God taught by Christian orthodoxy, which he contrasts with the supposed points of Mormon doctrine listed above. These attributes of God are the ones on which the Apologists led the early Church astray. They provide the basic subject of inquiry for this book, and are quoted below in Dr. Beckwith's own words and using his own citations (with one limited omission).

Truth and error are subtly mixed in these doctrines of Christian orthodoxy. Therefore, the elements that will be shown to have a Greek origin are identified in an italic typeface lest readers suppose that Mormonism disagrees with everything taught in orthodox theology. Anything that is not in italics is a reasonably accurate statement of biblical doctrine and therefore consistent with Mormonism. Even the parts that are in italics should not be taken as entirely false or non-biblical. Sometimes there is an element of truth in these concepts, but they are derived from Greek theology. When true ideas about God are derived from that source rather than the Bible, they invariably have an erroneous twist that must be identified and analyzed.

The italic portions are not comprehensive. There are additional points of doctrine in classical theism that relate to the attributes of God. Not all of them have been identified in Dr. Beckwith's brief summary. However, all the significant departures from biblical theology that have occurred in classical theism will be examined in Part 3.

A Summary of the Orthodox View of God

Dr. Beckwith's summary of classical theism, with italic typeface highlighting the concepts that have a Greek origin appears below. To avoid confusion, all of Dr. Beckwith's original italics have been removed.

> **1. Personal and Incorporeal.** According to Christian theism, God is a personal being who has all the attributes that we may expect from a perfect person: self-consciousness, the ability to reason, know, love,

communicate, and so forth. This is clearly how God is described in the Scriptures (e.g., Gen. 17:11; Exod. 3:14; Jer. 29:11).

God is also incorporeal. Unlike humans, God is not uniquely associated with one physical entity (i.e., a body). This is why the Bible refers to God as Spirit (John 4:24).

2. The Creator and Sustainer of Everything Else that Exists. In classical theism, *all reality is contingent on God—that is, all reality has come into existence and continues to exist because of Him. Unlike a god who forms the universe out of preexistent matter, the God of classical theism created the universe ex nihilo (out of nothing).* Consequently, it is on God alone that everything in the universe depends for its existence (see Acts 17:25; Col. 1:16, 17; Rom. 11:36; Heb. 11:3; 2 Cor. 4:6; Rev. 4:11).

3. Omnipotent. God is also said to be omnipotent or all-powerful. This should be understood to mean that God can do anything that is (1) logically possible (see below), and (2) consistent with being a personal, incorporeal, omniscient, omnipresent, immutable, wholly perfect, *and necessary* Creator.

Concerning the latter, these attributes are not limitations of God's power, but perfections. They are attributes at their infinitely highest level, which are essential to God's nature. For example, since God is perfect, He cannot sin; because He is personal, He is incapable of making Himself impersonal; because He is omniscient, He cannot forget. All this is supported by the Bible when its writers assert that God cannot sin (Mark 10:18; Heb. 6:18), cease to exist (Exod. 3:14; Mal. 3:6), or fail to know something (Job 28:24; Ps. 139:17-18; Isa. 46:10a). Since God is a perfect person, it is necessarily the case that He is incapable of acting in a less than perfect way—which would include sinning, ceasing to exist, and being ignorant.

* * *

4. Omniscient. God is all-knowing, and His all-knowingness encompasses the past, present, and future. Concerning God's unfathomable knowledge, the psalmist writes: "How precious to me are your thoughts, O God! How vast is the sum of them! Were I to count them, they would outnumber the grains of sand. When I awake, I am still with you" (Ps. 139:17, 18). Elsewhere he writes, "Great is our Lord and mighty in power; his understanding has no limit" (147:5). The author of Job writes of God: "For he views the ends of the earth and sees everything under the heavens" (Job 28:24). Scripture also teaches that God has total knowledge of the past (Isa. 41:22). Concerning the future, God says: "I make known the end from the beginning, from ancient times, what is still to come. I say: 'My purpose will stand, and I will do all that I please,'" (Isa. 46:10). Elsewhere Isaiah quotes God as saying that knowledge (*not opinion or highly probable guesses*) of the future is essential for deity (Isa. 41:21-24), something that distinguished God from the many false gods of Isaiah's day.

5. Omnipresent. Logically following from God's omniscience, *incorporeality*, omnipotence, and role as creator and sustainer of the universe is His omnipresence. Since God *is not limited by a spatio-temporal body*, knows everything immediately *without benefit of sensory organs*, and sustains the existence of all that exists, it follows that He is in some sense present everywhere. Certainly it is the Bible's explicit teaching that God is omnipresent (Ps. 139:7-12; Jer. 23:23-24).

6. Immutable and Eternal. When a Christian says that God is immutable and eternal, he or she is saying that God is unchanging (Mal. 3:6; Heb. 6:17; Isa. 46:10b) and has always existed *as God*, throughout all eternity (Ps. 90:2; Isa. 40:28; 43:12b, 13; 57:15a; Rom. 1:20a; 1 Tim. 1:17). *There never was a time when God was not God.*

Although God certainly seems to change in response to how His creatures behave—such as in the case of the repenting Ninevites—His nature remains the same. No matter how the Ninevites would have responded to Jonah's preaching, God's unchanging righteousness would have remained the same: He is merciful to the repentant and punishes the unrepentant. Hence, a God who is responsive to His creatures is certainly consistent with, and seems to be entailed in, an unchanging nature that is necessarily personal.

7. Necessary and the Only God. The Bible teaches that although humans at times worship some beings as if these beings were really gods (1 Cor. 8:4-6), there is only one true and living God *by nature* (Isa. 43:10; 44:6, 8; 45:5, 18, 21, 22; Jer. 10:10; Gal. 4:8; 1 Cor. 8:4-6; 1 Tim. 2:5; John 17:3; 1 Thess. 1:9). And since the God of the Bible possesses all power (see above), *there cannot be any other God, for this would mean that two beings possess all power. That, of course, is patently absurd, since if a being possesses all of everything (in this case, power) there is, by definition, nothing left for anyone else.*

Moreover, since everything that exists depends on God, and God is unchanging and eternal, *it follows that God cannot not exist. In other words, He is a necessary being, whereas everything else is contingent.*[30]

---

[30] *Ibid.*, 2-4.

Orthodox Christian Differences With Biblical Doctrine Are Significant

It will probably surprise classical theists, and even some Mormons, that the points on which Mormon theology differs from Christian orthodoxy are so few. They are, however, fundamental points, and LDS disagreement on these issues has made it difficult for classical theism to accept the idea that Mormon theology teaches the points of doctrine that are not in italics. It will be necessary, therefore, to include in this book an explanation of how Mormon theology on these points is consistent with its rejection of the other points of classical orthodox theology.

The Breadth and Challenge of This Study

The primary focus of the discussion that follows will be the biblicity of those points of classical theism with which Mormons disagree. This will not be a simple task. It will be necessary to provide a background in Greek philosophy and early Church history to understand how the pure Gospel of Jesus Christ delivered to the Gentile world by the Apostles was transformed into the Hellenistic doctrines taught by the Apologists.

Adding to this difficulty is the fact that the errors of classical theism have been cemented by repetition and inclusion in creeds for almost eighteen hundred years, during which they have been rationalized by some of the brightest men in history. Though, over the ages, many Christian scholars have been dissatisfied with the conclusions of the Apologists, they have been unable to convince the mainstream of Christianity to review or reconsider its understanding of God. Therefore, the explanations contained in this book are aimed at individuals, not at churches. Personal study and prayer are essential, and investigators should be cautious in weighing the opinions of those with vested interests in the current institutions of Christianity.

Restrictions on the Scope of This Study

This inquiry is restricted to theological issues (i.e., the study of God and His attributes). That is both necessary (because of space limitations) and appropriate. The Prophet Joseph Smith said, "It is the first principle of the Gospel to know for a certainty the character of God."[31] Solomon

---

[31] *Teachings of the Prophet Joseph Smith*, comp. Joseph Fielding Smith, (Salt Lake City: Deseret Book Company, 1970), 345.

expressed the same truth as follows: "The fear of the Lord is the beginning of knowledge" (Prov. 1:7).

The same view has been expressed repeatedly by Hank Hanegraaff, a prominent spokesman for the Evangelical establishment and President of the Christian Research Institute. On "The Bible Answerman," a national Christian radio broadcast, he has frequently used words to this effect: "All truth begins with a correct understanding of God."

The point is well taken from whatever source. An understanding of God lies at the heart of the Gospel of Jesus Christ, as will be demonstrated in Part 4. The better Man understands his Father, the more he will understand the process of becoming like Him.

A Summary of Contents and Direction

Part 1 of this book will examine the development of Greek philosophy and religion (*Hellenismos*) as it changed from the gross practices and beliefs of paganism and idolatry to the ethical standards and monotheistic beliefs that characterized the major philosophical schools at the time of Christ. **Part 2** will review early Christian Church history and the overwhelming influence of Greek philosophy and education on the early Church, amplified by the pressure of Roman persecution. It will trace these influences through their progress, beginning in the first century A.D. and ending at the Council of Nicaea in 325 A.D.

Part 3 will analyze the specific doctrines of Christian orthodoxy relating to the attributes of God listed above. It will discuss Greek and biblical sources for classical theism based on the information provided in Parts 1 and 2, and compare Mormon doctrine with each point. It will also harmonize what classical theists have assumed to be conflicts between the Bible's literal teachings about God and the assumptions of Greek logic, showing, for example, how the infinite attributes of God are consistent with His corporeal nature as taught throughout the Old and New Testaments.

The Apologists assumed that God could not possess infinite attributes, such as omnipresence, omniscience and omnipotence, if the Bible's testimony that He is a perfect, resurrected human being were taken literally. Their assumptions were based on the level of scientific knowledge and the common understanding of God that prevailed in the Hellenized world at the time. In the centuries that followed, many scientific beliefs of the Greeks have proven to be erroneous. The deficiencies found by the scientific community in the Aristotelian thinking of the past will occasionally be applied to theology to show that the truths taught in the Bible are far more compatible with modern scientific knowledge than are the teachings of classical theism.

Lastly, **Part 4** will examine why it is important for Men to have a true understanding of their Heavenly Father. It will refute the philosophical criticisms directed at the distinctly Mormon doctrine of eternal progression in the article by Dr. Beckwith cited above. That analysis will show how the methods of false teaching rampant in the days of the early Church are still at war with the truth today.

The Nature and Goal of The Study

This book is intended to help LDS members and missionaries explain the Gospel in its simplicity to individuals who believe the orthodox Christian concept of God. Few Evangelicals today recognize that their understanding of God, rather than being Bible-based, is a derivative of Greek philosophy and religion, and even approaching the issue can engender a heated reaction. That is not the intent of this study, but, like the Pharisees of Christ's time, many orthodox Christians feel they are listening to blasphemy when anyone disagrees with their concept of God. That reaction must be treated with kindness and consideration if emotional barriers to the truth are to be overcome.

This analysis is meant to reveal the origins of the basic tenets about God contained in Christian orthodoxy. It will show which are embodied in the Bible and are worthy of acceptance, and which are based only on Greek philosophy and are worthy of rejection. The intent is to encourage orthodox Christians to follow the advice of Justin Martyr, who argued that, if the "opinion of the ancients" should "prove to be worthless," all Men should "refuse to follow" it.[32]

This should be agreeable to all Christians, for the true God of the Bible is the one who deserves Man's veneration, whether He be the God described by Latter-day Saints or the God described by orthodox Christians. No Christian should take offense if the truth differs from what is currently taught in orthodox Christianity. The only question should be, How is God really described within the pages of the Bible?

---

[32] Justin, *First Apology*, 2. (Single numbers identify the paragraphs that divide the work, originally in Roman numerals.)

One must examine these issues *without* jumping to conclusions about whether or not it is possible for God to be the way He is described in scripture. A theologian must be very cautious about rationalizing God's attributes. It is bad hermeneutics to argue, "the Bible says such-and-such about God, but we know that is impossible, so it must mean something else." The theologian's job is to find out *how* God can be the way He is described in the Bible without rationalizing His attributes as they are described in holy writ.

This book does not substitute Greek attributes for God in place of the ones described in the Bible. Instead, it shows how God, though He is not the metaphysical paradox described by the Apologists and the Nicene Creed, can, in fact, be possessed of such infinite characteristics as perfection, omnipotence, omniscience, omnipresence, immutability, eternity and oneness. The understanding this effort provides may surprise classical theologians and perhaps some Latter-day Saints.

This Book Is a Tribute As Well As a Critique

The biblical doctrine taught by The Church of Jesus Christ of Latter-day Saints differs from the Greek doctrines of classical theism adopted by the Apologists. However, it should never be forgotten that the Gentiles, the Hellenized men and women who joined the early Church in the first three centuries after Christ, at the risk of great personal peril, preserved many principles of Christianity through centuries of intellectual chaos and political turmoil. Were it not for them, Christ's teachings could have been lost completely when the House of Israel rejected its Messiah.

An immense debt of gratitude is owed to the early Church fathers, many of whom gave their lives for the Faith. The hand of Man may be visible in the mistakes they made, but the hand of the Lord is visible in the events that led up to the "times of the Gentiles" discussed in the chapters that follow, and it doubtless remained with the early Church long after its theology departed from biblical truth. Perhaps the greatest testimony this book bears to Latter-day Saints is that they should not be critical or disparaging of these outstanding and well-meaning early leaders as they become acquainted with them in the pages that follow.

THE TRUE FOUNDATION FOR THE CHRISTIAN CONCEPT OF GOD

Summary

1. Contrary to the Protestant battle cry of *sola Scriptura*, Evangelicals and other orthodox Christians do not base their beliefs about God solely on the Bible.
2. The orthodox Christian concept of God is founded primarily on the writings of the Church fathers of the second century, particularly the Apologists.
3. The Church fathers of the second century are among the Ante-Nicene Fathers. The Ante-Nicene Fathers include the Apostolic Fathers, the Apologists and the Fathers of the Third Century (see Table 1).
4. While they combated heresy, the Apologists slipped gently into apostasy.
5. By embracing Greek philosophy, the Apologists ignored the warnings of Paul and opened themselves up to error.
6. The influence of Greek philosophy on early Christianity is well known, but differences between biblical teachings and Hellenistic theology have not been acknowledged as apostate.
7. Greek thinking still affects modern theologians and philosophers, the "classical theists" of today.
8. Seen through the eyes of a classical theist, Mormonism is generally misrepresented and misunderstood.
9. The elements of Greek philosophy in classical theism can be specifically identified.
10. The majority of orthodox teachings about God are biblical and agree with Mormon theology.
11. The differences between Mormonism and orthodox Christianity, though relatively few, are very significant.
12. A background in Greek philosophy and early Church history is essential to understanding the apostasy.
13. A sound knowledge of the Gospel begins with a correct understanding of God.
14. This study is divided into a review of Greek philosophy, an examination of early Church history through the fourth century to show the factors and influences that resulted in the theological apostasy, a comparison of the teachings of classical theism and the Bible in

regard to the attributes of God, and a response to philosophical objections made to the Mormon concept of God and the eternal progression of Man.
15. The purpose of this study is to show which doctrines about the nature of God came from the Bible and which are founded only in Greek philosophy.
16. Though they made some errors, the world owes a huge debt of gratitude to the early Church fathers who preserved many of the teachings of Christ after the Jews rejected their Messiah.

Part I

How God Prepared the Gentiles to Receive Christianity: The Rise of Greek Philosophy

—Clement of Alexandria

"Indeed philosophy has been given to the Greeks as their own kind of Covenant, their foundation for the philosophy of Christ."

Miscellanies, 6:8

The Revolutionary Theology of the Greek Philosophers

According to prophecies in the Old Testament (e.g., Isa. 11:10), New Testament (e.g., Rom. 11:25), and the Book of Mormon (e.g., Jacob 5:7-17), the Gentiles (*Hellens*) were to be drawn to Christ following His mortal ministry when Israel would reject Him (Isa. 53). The Gentiles were expected to take from the Jews the mantle of the Gospel and be grafted into the house of Israel until the last days when the fulness of the Gentiles would come in and the "times of the Gentiles" would be "fulfilled" (D&C 45:25).

At the time Isaiah announced this prediction, reasonable men could have seen it as ludicrous. How could a pagan, polytheistic society of depraved idolaters be brought to a point where they would even be interested in the Gospel, let alone supplant the House of Israel as its chief proponent? What could possibly have predisposed the Gentiles to accept Christ in such numbers that Christianity would become the dominant religious system of the Gentile world in less than three hundred years after His death? The answers to these questions are essential to an understanding of what happened to the early Church as it made the transition from Jewish exclusivity to Gentile dominance. They will also aid in understanding the changes that accompanied that transition, for the influence that prepared the Gentiles to be the standard bearers of the Gospel also bore the poisoned fruit that led them to apostasy.

The transition to a largely Gentile Church began as early as the middle of the first century (c. 50 A.D.), and the doctrinal transition was complete by the end of the second century (200 A.D.). Historically, this may seem a swift and profound change in God's development of mankind. The foundation for the change, however, began more than 500 years earlier. In fact, it started very shortly after the first prophecy of its occurrence was given through the prophet Isaiah. That was when a major shift in Gentile worship began through the medium of the classical Greek philosophers.

It was the theory of Justin Martyr[1] (c. 100 A.D.-c. 165 A.D.) and Clement of Alexandria[2] (c. 150 A.D.-c. 215 A.D.) that every truth derived by the philosophers during the Classical Period of Greek history came from Moses and the Hebrew prophets—men who lived long before the Greek writers. Some have criticized this view as naive,[3] but it cannot be denied that the philosophers derived many truths that are very close to doctrines taught in the Old Testament. There is not enough resemblance between Greek theology and Judaism to conclude that the philosophers derived very many of their ideas from the Old Testament, but there are several similarities. These similarities ultimately caused the Gentiles to be both attracted to the full truth of the Gospel and confused by the erroneous elements that remained in Hellenism.

Theology Begins Among the Greeks

The word "theology" was invented by Plato.[4] It comes from two Greek words, theos and logia, which literally mean "God-learning" or "discourse-about-the-divine." Only a brief introduction to Hellenism, the philosophy and religion of the Greeks at the time of Christ, is possible here, and there is no space to discuss the political aspects of these developments. It should be remembered, however, that the ideas of the Greek philosophers were truly revolutionary. They contradicted the prevailing views of the pagan system, and the men who advanced them waged the same battle for religious liberty fought by reformers in every age. The movement even had its own martyrs, Heraclitus and Socrates being among the most noted.

Hellenism is founded primarily on the ideas of six Greek thinkers. These men include ***Pythagoras***, who was active around 530 B.C., ***Parmenides*** and ***Heraclitus***, contemporaries in the next generation (around

---

[1] Justin, *First Apology*, 44.
[2] Clement of Alexandria, *Miscellanies*, 5.14.
[3] James Shiel, *Greek Thought and the Rise of Christianity* (London: Longmans, Green and Co., Ltd, 1968), 51.
[4] Shiel, *Greek Thought*, 20.

500 B.C.), and ***Anaxagoras***, who lived in the succeeding generation (approximately 500 to 428 B.C.). The fundamental concepts derived by these four were dissected and refined by ***Plato***, who lived from 428 B.C. to about 347 B.C., and his star pupil, ***Aristotle***, who died in 322 B.C.

Over the centuries that followed, the distinctive ideas of these six men grew into various schools of thought. The beliefs of those schools were gradually syncretized in the minds of the Greek public so that, by the time of Christ, they were viewed by most of the Gentile world as a single monotheistic system of beliefs distinct from the polytheism and pantheism of the older, though still popular, pagan religions.

What follows is a brief introduction to these six men, focusing on the philosophical contributions each one made to the foundations of Greek thought that so profoundly influenced both the Gentile world and early Christianity. It is hoped that this introduction will spark some interest in the reader to examine more closely the ideas of these six thinkers. Even cursory reading in most modern encyclopedias will provide some enlightening amplification of the essential concepts presented here.

Pythagoras Discovers God by the Numbers

Pythagoras was a pioneer in geometry, astronomy and music, and is generally lauded as the first pure mathematician. He was fascinated with numbers, and in them he saw God. He was not, himself, a religious reformer, however. In fact, he was an avowed and practicing pagan. The mathematician Apollodorus states that Pythagoras sacrificed oxen, in the pagan tradition, when he discovered that the hypotenuse of a right triangle has a square equal to the sum of the squares of the other two sides.[5] Nevertheless, he was the inspiration for the entire religious reform that followed him.

He demonstrated that the visible universe functions in such perfect order that numerical formulae can be used to predict the movements of the heavens with perfect accuracy. The realization of this orderliness in the natural world inspired him and the philosophers after him to postulate the concept of monotheism, the idea that a single power dominates the entire universe.[6] This was the beginning of the philosophic departure from pagan polytheism that resulted in the strict monotheism

---

[5] Diogenes Laertius, *Lives of the Philosophers*, 8:12.
[6] Cf. Edwin Hatch, *The Influence of Greek Ideas and Usages upon the Christian Church* (1891; reprint, New York: Lenox Hill Pub. & Dist. Co., 1972), 171-172.

common to Greek philosophy at the time of Christ.

Heraclitus Discovers God in Opposition

Heraclitus, an Ionian philosopher, was extremely critical of the pagan rituals of his time. Inspired by Pythagoras, he saw a unity in the cosmos, and where Pythagoras numbered the movements of the stars, Heraclitus tried to explain how and why they moved. He saw motion and change as the result of an underlying connection between opposites, and observed a harmony in such opposition. For example, he saw that sea water was harmful for men but beneficial for fish, and believed that a similar hidden attunement could be found in all things. He believed in a coherent system in which changes in one direction were ultimately balanced by corresponding changes in the opposite direction.

He formulated a theory of universal change, teaching that "all things flow,"[7] and that everything comes into existence through opposition. "The urge in opposites towards generation he [Heraclitus] calls war or strife, the urge which leads to destruction he calls harmony and peace; change is a way up and a way down, and according to it the world is made."[8] God, he postulated, is eternal and completely wise, the one who brings, or is, order in these opposites. He alone knows "how all things are steered through all."[9]

His theories were attempts to explain the real universe as he observed it around him. Because the universe is complex, Heraclitus' view of it suggested a complexity that was disquieting to most philosophers of the time. If the universe were in constant flux, they argued, knowing anything about it would be impossible, especially given Man's limited ability to observe. Hence, the views of Heraclitus were not favored as the ultimate explanation of reality among the Greek philosophers of his time.[10] However, his conclusions had wide-reaching influence.

The Greek "*Logos*"

Heraclitus was the first to use the term "*Logos*" in philosophical discussion. The word has many connotations in Greek. Specifically, it means "word" (see John 1:1, 14) but it can also be translated "thought,"

---

[7] Shiel, *Greek Thought*, 8.
[8] Diogenes Laertius, *Lives of the Philosophers*, 9:7.
[9] *Encyclopaedia Britannica*, 1960 ed., s.v. "Heraclitus."
[10] Cf. Shiel, *Greek Thought*, 9.

means "word" (see John 1:1, 14) but it can also be translated "thought," "speech," "discussion," "mathematical calculation," "proportion," "dramatic utterance," "public oration," "treatise" or "thinking."[11] To the ancient Greeks, the term most commonly meant "reason." Eventually, the word came to be used to imply a kind of metaphysical embodiment of that mental activity, as though "Reason" were an actual being endowed with personality and will.

By his use of this term, Heraclitus simply meant the law that determines the movements observed in all reality.[12] Yet he was the first to identify Destiny, or fate, with *Logos* or Reason, implying that what Men perceive as fate or destiny actually occurs because of the reasoned will of God.

Parmenides Reinvents God and Reality

The Italian philosopher, Parmenides, a contemporary of Heraclitus, proposed an alternative theory of reality that appealed powerfully to the philosophical minds of his day. Instead of looking at the universe empirically, as Heraclitus did, he viewed it from the perspective of pure abstract thought. Using this approach, he deduced several fundamental and significant principles.

He reasoned that whatever exists must be eternal and uncreated, because that which exists could not have been derived from something that does not exist.[13] He also concluded that, since there was a distinct and demonstrable unity to the universe, all reality must be composed of a single substance, which he called "being."

In this respect, Parmenides adhered to the view known as "**Monism**," the idea that thought or force is part of and incorporated in Matter. "Thought," he said, was not a separate substance from Matter, but an *activity* of "being." "Thought and being are the same. Thought and that for the sake of which thought is are the same. For you will never find thought without the existent in regard to which it is expressed. Nothing exists or will exist outside of being."[14]

The Ionian philosophers, like Heraclitus, explained the visible universe on the theory that it was composed of only one type of substance.

---

[11] Shiel, *Greek Thought*, 7.
[12] Paul Tillich, *A History of Christian Thought* (New York: Harper & Row, 1968), 7.
[13] Parmenides, *"Truth" in Nature*, fr. 16.
[14] Parmenides, *Nature*, fr. 5d, 7d.

Parmenides adopted that position as an ultimate truth. Then showed that, in such unity, accounting for the existence of the movement and change that occur in the observable universe was impossible.[15]

This established a conflict between the unity of the universe seen by Pythagoras and the diversity found in the movement and change observed by Heraclitus. Parmenides' resolution of that conflict profoundly influenced all Greek philosophic thought after him, and in many ways laid the foundation for the theological apostasy that occurred in the early Christian Church.

He insisted that, since the universe is in perfect unity, making motion and change impossible, the entire observable universe is an illusion. What Man sees as reality is nothing but appearance, not "being." He explained the fact that all men are observing the same appearance by postulating that a singular reality is generated by the sum of Man's opinions. These opinions result in a "plenum of light" that fills the universe (comparable in function to Heraclitus' "*logos*") and causes what Man sees as current reality.

"Thus," Parmenides concludes, "according to opinion, were the things of our world generated, and are now, and shall hereafter grow and come to an end."[16] In other words, the visible, or apparent, universe ("the phenomenal world," as Plato later called it) is the figment of the collective imaginations of all Men!

This notion caused philosophers after Parmenides to question the validity of human sensation and knowledge. They turned to speculation on ultimate reality and became fascinated with questions about what really exists as opposed to what only seems to exist, what permanently exists in contrast to what temporarily exists, and what exists independently and unconditionally rather than what exists dependently and conditionally.[17] Quite appropriately, Parmenides is known as the father of **metaphysics**.[18]

---

[15] *Encyclopaedia Britannica*, 1960 ed., s.v. "Anaxagoras."
[16] Parmenidies, "Opinion" in *Nature*, fr.16; *Encyclopaedia Britannica*, 1960 ed., s.v. "Parmenides."
[17] Shiel, *Greek Thought*, 4; *Encyclopaedia Britannica*, 1960 ed., s.v. "Ontology" and "Parmenides."
[18] *Encyclopaedia Britannica*, 1960 ed., s.v. "Parmenides."

Anaxagoras Sees God as Pure Mind

A generation after Parmenides and Heraclitus, Anaxagoras, perhaps the greatest of the Ionian philosophers, proposed an alternative to the single-substance theory of the universe that had led Parmenides to metaphysics. He suggested that the universe is composed out of an infinite number of different basic substances. Inspired by Anaxagoras, Democritus, in the next generation, postulated the existence of "atoms," individual particles of a small but fixed size, from which all matter is constructed. Anaxagoras, however, was focused on compounds, and believed that there was something of every element in every different type of thing. A larger proportion of some elements over others was his explanation for the existence of different substances.[19]

Anaxagoras' theories were consistent with "**Dualism**," which views thought or force as separate from and entirely outside Matter. Given a choice between Thought and Matter, he proposed that *nous* (which means "mind") created the universe. The method of creation supposedly involved two major stages. At first, all Matter, all elements, were mixed together, and nous caused this mixture to start revolving. In the second stage, also controlled by nous, like things were drawn to like in the whirling mixture until distinct substances large enough to be significant were formed. The heavenly bodies were stones that formed in the eddies of the swirling mass, and animals and plants came into being from "seeds" that already existed in the original mixture. In the completed world, he believed that it was through the power of *nous* in living things that they were able to draw from other substances the foods required for their growth.[20]

Anaxagoras described *nous* as the "thinnest" of all things, not an ingredient in the mixture from which the universe was created, but that which controlled the mixture and determined what changes occurred. According to Anaxagoras, *nous* knows all things and has power over all things.[21]

Plato Fashions Greek Theology

Unquestionably the greatest of the Greek philosophers, Plato is the man whose views, more than any other, became the norm of Greek thinking on the subjects he explored. He accepted and rejected ideas

---

[19] *Encyclopaedia Britannica*, 1960 ed., s.v. "Anaxagoras."
[20] *Ibid.*
[21] *Ibid.*

from the pioneers discussed above and added others of his own. Yet his theology remained the most enigmatic.

On ethics, Plato rejected Relativism, holding instead that there are absolute and unchanging standards of truth, goodness and beauty.[22] Correspondingly, he recognized that there are both good and bad pleasures. He declined to follow the Hedonists, who taught that good and pleasure are identical.[23]

Plato clearly accepted the monotheism that had prevailed among Greek philosophers since the time of Pythagoras. As arguments for God, he cites "the soul—that it is the noblest and divinest of all . . . things . . . ," and "the order inherent in the motion of the stars and those bodies subject to a controlling intelligence which sets the whole in order."[24]

He adopted the metaphysics of Parmenides, rejecting Empiricism and Naturalism, and maintained that it is impossible for the senses to bring human beings to knowledge.[25] Rather, he believed in Rationalism, the idea that *Men can only obtain knowledge by reason.*[26]

He accepted the existence of an immaterial or ideal world that exists independent of the physical or material world in which the bodies of Men reside,[27] and believed that the visible world of concrete individuals and things was a transitory phenomenon. Only the invisible world of intelligible essences was real and permanent. The first, the phenomenal world or world of the senses, was genesis or "becoming." The second, the invisible world where God exists, often called the *Pleroma*, was *ousia*, or "being."[28]

Plato followed Anaxagoras, however, in his Dualism.[29] He believed that mind is separate from matter and acts upon it. While he took from

---

[22] Ronald H. Nash, *Christianity & the Hellenistic World* (Grand Rapids: Zondervan Publishing House, 1984), 31.
[23] *Ibid.*
[24] Plato, *Laws*, 966d. (The numbers and letters used to cite Plato's works are a convention commonly used in English translations. They are derived from the page and column numbers of Stephanus' 1578 edition of Plato's works edited and printed by Henri Estienne.)
[25] Nash, *Hellenistic World*, 31.
[26] *Ibid.*
[27] *Ibid.*
[28] Hatch, *Influence of Greek Ideas*, 271.
[29] *Ibid.*, 17.

Parmenides the metaphysical idea of a universal distinction between the supposedly real metaphysical world and the phenomenal or sensory world in which Men live,[30] he did not accept Parmenides' explanation of the existence of that world. Rather, he viewed the sensory world as a state of flux in the process of becoming real *through the action or direction of God*. He believed that human beings participate in both worlds, one through the bodily senses and the other through the mind.[31]

According to Plato, while Men can have an opinion about the changing world, they can only *know* about things that are unchanging. By this he meant the unchanging "Forms" which Plato imagined to exist in the Pleroma. "Plato held that . . . sense objects [things perceived with the human senses] are always in flux [as Heraclitus taught] and so there can be no real knowledge of them."[32] Men could only know the Forms.

Plato's World of Forms As the Agents of God

A critical part of Plato's idea of the universe involved the Forms or Ideas (which he also called *ousia*). These were objects of thought, perfect embodiments or archetypes of the things that compose the observable world. Some of these Forms were mathematical and geometrical figures, such as the perfect eternal circle. Others, however, were the unchanging absolutes of Goodness, Justice, Truth, and Beauty.[33] Plato suggested that the ideal world of immaterial and eternal essences included Forms for everything that exists in the material world. Everything that exists in this, the world of bodies, he taught, is a copy or imitation of the perfect Form of that thing in the ideal, nonspatial world of the Pleroma.[34]

These Forms were not just spiritual conceptions to Plato. They had an objective existence outside the mind and pre-existed the formation of

---

[30] *Ibid.*

[31] Nash, *Hellenistic World*, 32.

[32] Aristotle, *Metaphysics*, 987a. (References are keyed to Immanuel Bekker's 1831 edition of the Greek text. The numbers refer to the pages and the letters to the columns in Bekker. They are commonly used to index Aristotle's works in most English translations.)

[33] Nash, *Hellenistic World*, 33.

[34] *Ibid.*; see also, Plato, *Republic*, 597d. This notion is amazingly close to the truth that God made all things spiritually before he made them physically (see Pearl of Great Price, Moses 3:5), which supports the claim of Justin Martyr and Clement of Alexandria that the Greek philosophers learned from the Hebrew prophets.

human minds.35 The ability of men to conceive of them was attributed by Plato to remembrance (*anamnesis*) of knowledge obtained in a pre-existent non-temporal state. "Since . . . the soul [of a man] has already learned everything, there is nothing to prevent a man from proceeding from the remembrance—or, as people say, the knowledge—of one thing to the discovery of all other things, provided the man is brave and does not tire in his search."36

In some of his writings, Plato ranks the Forms in a kind of hierarchy, identifying the *Form of Good* as the highest. The Good, he has Socrates say in *Republic*, is the ultimate end of human life, the necessary condition of human knowledge, and the creative and sustaining cause of all else. "With objects of knowledge you can say that not only the fact of their being known [to men] comes from the Good but their existence and essence come from it as well. And the Good is not the same as their essence; it is beyond essence, because of its superior nobility and power."37

Why "superior nobility and power" should place this Form "beyond essence [*ousia*]," Plato does not explain. This unsupported reasoning on his part is typical of many assumptions in Greek philosophy that were accepted without examination because they seemed self-evident. This one demonstrates the Greek acceptance of what was generally an oriental feeling of antipathy toward the physical world.

Plato's Alternative Concept of God and the Creation

In the *Timaeus*, Plato presents a myth about the creation of the world. In it, he concludes that the world was not eternal but created. It had a beginning.38 In telling how it came to be, Plato describes the creation as the work of a divine Craftsman, or "Demiurge," whom he calls "the god," who fashioned the world out of pre-existing matter using the patterns found in the world of Forms.39

"He took over all that was visible, all that was not at rest, all that was moving out of tune and in disorder, and he reduced it from disorder to order, thinking the latter to be by far the better state."40 The order

---

35 *Ibid.*
36 Plato, *Meno*, 81d. This is obviously another idea for which Plato may have looked more to the prophets than the philosophers.
37 Plato, *Republic*, 509b.
38 Plato, *Timaeus*, 28b.
39 *Ibid.*, 28c.
40 *Ibid.*, 29e.

established by this god involved a three-level composition and left the universe itself a living thing. Plato explains:

> Consideration showed him that of the things which by nature are visible one which lacks mind will never be in all respects better than one which possesses mind; and further, that mind can never come to anything except in the company of soul. Because of this consideration he put mind into soul and soul into body and thus fashioned the universe, aiming to produce a work which would be by nature the fairest and best. And so we must use the most likely description and say that this universe is a living thing, a creature which really possesses mind, and that it came to be such through the foresight of the god.[41]

The similarity of these teachings to the LDS understanding of the intelligence (cp. mind), spirit (cp. soul), and body, and the many references in the Old Testament to the Earth having the attributes of a living thing (see, e.g., Deut.31:28; 32:1; Job 12:8), suggest either an inordinate degree of inspiration in Plato's writings or some knowledge of Jewish scriptures, as Justin and Clement claimed. It could also be that the truths about Man's pre-existence are not buried so deeply by the veil of forgetfulness that Men cannot conceive or imagine the truth through the exercise of reason and imagination (cf., Wordsworth's *Intimations on Immortality*).

Unfortunately, whether or not the god of *Timaeus* is the same as the Form of Good from *Republic* was never resolved by Plato. Neither did he clarify the relationship between these two and the various beings he describes as intermediaries between God and the world in *Symposium* 202e. Thus, Plato left many questions about theology open to the speculation of his pupils. It was the Platonists, the school of Greek thought that developed in the centuries that followed Plato, who concluded that God was the Form of the Good, and that the intermediary or intermediaries between God and the world constituted the Logos or "Reason" of God, the Demiurge who acted on behalf of the Good to create the earth.

Aristotle Places the Capstone on Greek Theology

The most influential of Plato's pupils was Aristotle. He rejected many of Plato's dualistic ideas, especially the separation between the

---
[41] *Ibid.*

world of the Forms and the sensible world in which Men live. In this respect, Aristotle sided with monism.

Though Aristotle continued to believe in the Forms, he postulated that they exist in this earthly world as a metaphysical part of each thing that constitutes the physical world.[42] That is, he taught that everything is composed of Form *and* Matter (with one notable exception—God), all of which, either separately or together, he called *ousia*.

Aristotle distinguished between the soul and the mind of Man, but used the term "soul" very differently than did Plato. Plato used the word to designate the essential and immaterial part of a human being which survives independently of the body. Thus, Plato's view was dualistic. Consistent with his monism, Aristotle used the term as a synonym for the life of the human being, the spirit and body combined.[43] He did, however, make a distinction between two aspects of the human mind, one the "passive intellect," and the other the "active intellect." The passive, he taught, receives information from the senses, and the active acts on what is thus received. Aristotle believed that the active intellect was "separable and immortal,"[44] much like the spirit or intelligence of Man in Mormon theology.

Aristotle's View of God: The Unmoving Mover

As to the nature of God, Aristotle reasoned that there had to be an uncaused and unchanging being who was the ultimate cause of everything else that exists. If this Ultimate Cause moved or changed in any way, it could not really be the ultimate cause, since it would be necessary to ask why it changed and what changed it. Hence, Aristotle derived the concept of the Unmoving Mover, the ultimate being who neither changes nor moves, but causes all else to change and move. Since, to Aristotle, Matter implied the possibility of change (based on the theories of Heraclitus), and since change was viewed as an imperfection, this Unmoving Mover had to be Pure Actuality, or in other words, pure Form without Matter.[45]

Aristotle's Use of the Term "Ousia"

Aristotle used *ousia* in three distinct senses. Because this word lies at the base of Trinitarian doctrine, it is important to understand its

---

[42] Nash, *Hellenistic World*, 44-45.
[43] *Ibid.*, 49-50.
[44] Aristotle, *On the Soul*, 430a.
[45] Nash, *Hellenistic World*, 51.

origin in Greek philosophy. First, it was used synonymously with *hylê* to designate the physical or material part of a thing, that is, the particular material from which the thing was made.[46] For example, a desk is a specific Form, but it can be composed of several different types of Matter, e.g., metal, wood or stone. The word was used in this sense most commonly by the Stoics, a major school of Greek thought at the time of Christ. To the Stoics, the Matter out of which the world was made by God, was the *ousia* of God.[47] Each separate thing was a "rational seed" or *logoi* ("reason") of God. The totality of all these *logoi* composed the whole—God.

Aristotle also used the word "*ousia*" to refer to matter embodied in a specific form, i.e., Matter and Form combined as a specific thing. He focused on the combination of Form and Matter in each individual thing, animal or mineral, and saw the nature of each thing as a potentiality that is moving through a process of development toward its true, final and perfect form or *ousia*. For Aristotle, the perfect *ousia* was what each thing is when Form and Matter are fully developed.

Lastly, he used the word to refer to the Form itself, the set of essential properties that makes a specific thing the kind of thing it is, the ideal essence or common element identifying it as a member of a particular class of things into which sensible objects can be grouped or classified. It was used in this form most commonly by the Platonists, the other major school of Greek thought at the time of Christ.

Although the latter usage was the form in which the word *ousia* was employed in the Nicene formula and the sense in which it is used today by classical theists, it is not surprising that, because of the various uses of the word in Greek philosophy, there is some confusion as to its usage in orthodox Christian theology. That confusion reared its head in the latter half of the third century as the word was used by the Alexandrian fathers in a way that ultimately led to the Arian controversy.

Ousia is what classical theists mean when they use the term "essence." Aristotle's belief that God is Form without Matter, is equivalent to the orthodox belief that He is pure "essence." The word must be studied in Greek philosophy because that is its origin, and its use in the Nicene formula to describe the Trinity has no parallel in the Bible.

---

[46] *Ibid.*, 46.
[47] *Ibid.*, 269.

Orthodox Christians who use the word "essence" are not always able to define it because many are unaware of its philosophical derivation.

In its most fundamental sense, *ousia*, or "essence," is the description of a thing. The classical Greeks, however, looked on that description as much more than a list of characteristics. They imagined it as one of Plato's Forms. Thus, *ousia* was used to mean the common essence that exists outside the individual members of a class by participation in which they are identifiable as members of that class. For example, the mental image of the quintessential embodiment of species *homo sapiens* would have been called the *ousia* of Man in Aristotle's time.

Later, the word was used in a wider sense to include a broader classification of things—in biological terms, the genus or family of animals in which Man is grouped. Ultimately, the Platonists used the word to distinguish between the *"ousia"* of God, the perfect essence of what Plato called "being," and the substance, nature or essence of all created things, which they called the *"summum genus."* The *summum genus* was believed to be the farthest thing from perfect *ousia*. It was "not being," decomposable Matter, the seed of all visible creation.

Aristotle and the Greek Love of Logic

Besides his theological and scientific contributions, rational analysis of logic began with Aristotle, who developed the basic logical form known as the *syllogism*. Several fundamental syllogisms defining the basic methods of logical analysis were proposed by Aristotle. The first of these is familiar to most school children today. As Aristotle originally formulated it, it read: "For if A is predicated of all B and B of all C, it is necessary for A to be predicated of all C."[48] In modern terms this is usually expressed as follows: "If A equals B, and B equals C, then A equals C."

The systematic analysis of logic was one of Aristotle's greatest contributions to modern thought. Unfortunately, the beauty and symmetry of his syllogisms became almost an object of worship in their own right. His students fell in love with the form itself and failed to recognize that, although truth is always logical, that which is logical, symmetrical and beautiful is not always true.

---

[48] *Encyclopaedia Britannica*, 1960 ed., s.v. "History of Logic."

By the fourth or fifth century, the early Church was as enamored of logical symmetry as those who had worshiped at the feet of Aristotle. Instead of measuring a premise on the basis of its greater or lesser probability of truth, it was judged on the basis of its logical symmetry and the perceived certainty of the conclusions that followed from that symmetry. Symmetry, rather than reality, was often used as the test of truth,[49] and form became preferred over substance in logical analysis.

Aristotle was never so adoring of his own discoveries. Had his notes not been lost for nearly two hundred years following his death, Greek philosophy and religion might have taken a different course, continuing its development from the point at which Aristotle stopped. Instead, Greek thinking, for the most part, ceased to progress after Aristotle, whose death marks the end of what is known as the Classical Period in Greek history. Thereafter, the Greeks became satisfied with dissecting the ideas that had developed up to that time and spreading them throughout the known world.

Summary

1. Isaiah prophesied that the Gentiles would take the leadership of God's church.
2. Concurrently, God began preparing the Gentiles for that role.
3. Pythagoras' discovered unity in the cosmos, suggesting that the universe obeys one lawgiver.
4. Heraclitus used the term "*Logos*" to describe the law by which all things are governed.
5. The theory of Heraclitus was that the universe is in constant flux.
6. Heraclitus postulated that God (or "Mind") and the Universe (or "Matter") are composed of the same substance, a concept known as Monism.
7. Parmenides invented metaphysics with the notion that what Man sees as reality is actually an illusion.
8. God is the only true reality according to Parmenides, and He exists outside of the reality Men observe.
9. Anaxagoras described God as Pure Mind ("*Nous*"), and postulated the idea that God is an entirely different substance from Matter, out

---
[49] Hatch, *Influence of Greek Ideas*, 136-137.

of which He composed the universe. This concept is called Dualism.
10. Plato postulated the World of Forms, and taught that the "phenomenal" world was patterned after these Forms.
11. Plato said that Men can only have true knowledge of what is real. Hence, he concluded that they must have known the World of Forms in a prior existence.
12. The Form of the Good, according to Plato, was the highest of the Forms. That Form, he said, transcends "essence" (*ousia*).
13. Later, Plato taught of a "Demiurge" ("*Demiurgus*") who created the "phenomenal" or sensory world by acting upon existing matter, first placing mind into soul then soul into body, using the pattern of the Forms.
14. Plato taught of other intermediaries who helped to fashion the universe, but never indicated who he thought God was, the Form of the Good or the Demiurge.
15. Aristotle combined Form and Matter, and spoke of them, either separately or together, as substance (*ousia*).
16. Aristotle taught that God alone was perfect Form *without* Matter.
17. The body and soul of Man were combined in one *ousia* according to Aristotle.
18 Aristotle believed that Man is composed of an "active" and a "passive" intellect, which are separable. The active intellect Aristotle believed to be immortal.
19. Aristotle's Supreme God was the Unmoving Mover, the ultimate uncaused causation of everything else in the Universe.
20. By the time of Christ, the Platonists taught that the Form of the Good was the Supreme God and the Demiurge was His "*Logos*" through whom He acted upon Matter to bring the universe into existence.
21. The term "*ousia*" was used to distinguish the substance or "essence" of God from the substance or "essence" of created things, called the "*summum genus.*" This "*Summum genus*" was considered to be vastly inferior to "*ousia*." Created things were considered imperfect, "becoming" as opposed to "being." They were illusory as opposed to real.

The Problem of Evil and the Development of Hellenism

Following the death of Aristotle, the theological notions introduced by the Greek philosophers evolved into the widespread culture known as Hellenism. Two major schools of Greek thought arose in the centuries that followed—the *Stoics* and the *Platonists*. The latter were by far the most popular. Many smaller schools enjoyed varying degrees of popularity as well, e.g., the *Peripatetics*, *Pythagoreans* and *Skeptics*, but the theological beliefs of the two major schools had the most profound influence on the early Church. Two other groups are of special interest as sources of heresy and error within the early Church. These include the *Gnostics*, which some believe to be a purely Christian development, and the *Hellenized community of Jews in Alexandria* led by Philo.

The Greek schools were not churches with any formal system of dogma or ecclesiastic hierarchy. They were more akin to educational systems, schools at which a particular philosophy was taught. As in secular education today, there were often as many variations on the concepts being taught as philosophers to teach them. The teachings of all these schools had grown together in the minds of a largely pagan public until, by the time of Christ, a kind of syncretism of all their beliefs constituted what was viewed as the theology of the Greek philosophers.

The Stoics Espoused a Monistic View of the Universe

The Stoics followed the Ionians in the belief that the universe is composed of a single substance. Like Heraclitus, they believed that movement and change in the universe are the result of an active force that works intelligently on its passive nature, Matter. The active elements of this intelligence were frequently called the *logoi,* or "reasons."

Matter was regarded by the Stoics as a "mode" of God. That is, Matter was believed to be a particular form or manner in which God expresses Himself. It was sometimes referred to as an "emanation" of Deity. God, they believed, was the sum of an infinite number of rational forces or "seeds" which continually strove to express themselves through the Matter with which they were in union. God was through them and in them working to realize an end so that the totality of these seeds, forces or *logoi* were God.[1]

To the Stoic, God, in His purest essence, was the highest form of mind in union with the most attenuated form of Matter. In the lowest form of His essence, He was the cohesive force that holds together the atoms of a stone. Between these two poles were infinite gradations of being. Nearest to the pure essence of God was the human soul, which the Stoics believed was made in God's image. To the Stoics, the soul was, in a special sense, God's offspring—an emanation or outflow from God, like a sapling that is separate from the parent tree, but remains connected with it.[2] Thus, the Stoics were among the first of the ancient Greeks to teach the universal brotherhood of Man.[3]

The world was viewed by Stoics as the ever-changing self-evolution of God. There was no concept of a beginning for the Stoic. Creation was an eternal process of differentiation and change, having a kind of rhythmic or cyclical pattern that was believed to end in fire.[4] God was the soul of the world, and the world was the body of God.[5] This notion was originally pantheistic, but the later Stoics (by the time of Christ) had differentiated themselves from pantheism by investing God with a personality.

---

[1] Hatch, *Influence of Greek Ideas*, 176, 182, 192, 260-261.
[2] *Ibid.*, 176-177.
[3] Shiel, *Greek Thought*, 31.
[4] Nash, *Hellenistic World*, 72. This belief is not unlike that described in the Book of Mormon (e.g., 1 Nephi 10:19) and the Doctrine and Covenants (e.g., D&C 3:2), which state that "the course of the Lord is one eternal round" (see also, Chapter 19).
[5] *Ibid.*, 69.

Stoic Idealism
Had a Profound Influence on Ethics

Perhaps the greatest contribution of the Stoics is found in their ethical ideals. They were the precursors of Calvin in the belief that nothing in the world ever happens because of chance or of the free will of men. Man, they believed, was like a dog tied to a cart. *Where* the dog is going is not up to the dog, only *how* it gets there—pleasantly and cooperatively, or kicking and screaming. To the Stoic, Man's highest duty is to live according to nature, that is, to cooperate with the natural order of things. If evil comes, it is not just to be tolerated, but accepted with joy as part of the will of God.[6]

The best statements of these ethical principles are contained in the writings of the two most noted late Stoic writers, *Epictetus*, a Roman slave born about 50 A.D., who incorporated many Christian teachings and concepts in his writing, and, surprisingly, *Marcus Aurelius Antoninus*, the Roman Emperor who lived from 121 A.D. to 180 A.D. These writers were highly respected moralists, a fact that proved to be a great stumbling block for the early Church, as will be seen in Chapter 6.

The Platonists Advocated
a Dualistic View of the Universe

The approach of the Platonists to universal truth about God was dualistic, following Anaxagoras in the belief that Mind is separate from Matter. The Platonists, however, went beyond him, following Plato's distinction (based on Parmenides) between the so-called real world, where God dwells, and the phenomenal world, the world of the senses.

God, who was identified with Plato's Form of the Good, was regarded by the Platonists as existing totally outside the "phenomenal" or sensory world. Using intermediaries, He fashioned the world from Matter as a carpenter shapes wood or a potter molds clay. In so doing, God acted with reason. His Reason (*Logos*) or Mind (*Nous*) was sometimes spoken of as itself being the fashioner of the world.[7]

Each thought of God was believed to have shown itself in a particular group of material objects. To the extent these objects had definable characteristics, they were viewed as imitations or embodiments

---

[6] *Ibid.*, 71.
[7] Hatch, *Influence of Greek Ideas*, 178.

of particular Forms that existed either as thoughts in God's mind or as forces proceeding from His mind and acting outside of it.

Gradually, the idea of the Forms as external forces became more developed, until by the time of Christ these cosmic forces were treated not just as qualities, ideas, or patterns, but as personifications having the power to impress themselves upon Matter. They became less the form and more the cause of the phenomenal world. They were intermediaries or agents of God working on the rude materials of the universe to bring them into the unchanging perfection of the invisible world.[8] These forces were grouped into a vast array of gradations. The higher types were seen as the most powerful and active forces, the highest being the Form of Perfection.

The Platonists, by stressing the distinction between the creative force of God and the Forms in the mind of God, introduced a third element to the creative process. It became common to speak of God, Matter, and the personified Forms as three separate and distinct principals, thus going beyond dualism to a form of pluralism, though God and the Forms were never really considered separate from each other. Ultimately, all the Forms came to be viewed as the multifaceted expression of a single agent, the "*Logos*."[9]

Influence of the Problem of Evil on Greek Theology

The Greeks were a highly cultured people, and among them was a growing sense of ethics. As the influence of the new monotheistic theology grew, so did the desire to test it against the standards of this growing sense of morality and ethics. Thus arose an ethical and philosophical problem that had a profound influence on the development of Hellenism, as well as on the early Church itself. It is called the problem of evil, and is considered by many to be the ultimate test of any theological system.[10]

The problem of evil is this: *if God is all-powerful, the Creator of all things, and the source of all good, how can evil exist in His universe?* Some answered this question with the argument that evil has a

---
[8] *Ibid.*
[9] *Ibid.*, 181-182.
[10] Harold Kushner, *When Bad Things Happen to Good People* (New York: Schocken Books, 1981), 6.

beneficial effect on Men, providing them a challenge against which they can develop traits of character that have eternal value. The answer to that response, however, is quite simple. If God is in fact able to do anything, and He is perfectly good, and He is the sole creator of Men, why didn't He create them so they already possessed all the traits of character He wanted them to have?

Obviously, careful thought is required about the premises on which the problem of evil is based. Since the Greeks, and later the early Church, struggled with this problem, and in many respects shaped their theology around it, the problem will be considered further at this point to show how Mormonism provides a more complete answer to it than any other system of theology.

The Book of Job and the Problem of Evil

The Old Testament dealt with the problem of evil long before the Greek philosophers even considered it. It is confronted head-on in the oldest book in the Bible, the Book of Job, which, by most estimates, dates from the time of Abraham. The fact that the earliest recorded scripture in the Old Testament was written primarily to address this very problem is an indication of its pivotal importance in a systematic theology.

Rabbi Kushner, in his book *When Bad Things Happen to Good People*, discusses the problem of evil as it is presented in the Book of Job, and provides the following analysis:

> Let us take note of three statements which everyone in the book [of Job], and most of the readers, would like to be able to believe:
> A. God is all-powerful and causes everything that happens in the world. Nothing happens without His willing it.
> B. God is just and fair, and stands for people getting what they deserve, so that the good prosper and the wicked are punished.
> C. Job is a good person.
> As long as Job is healthy and wealthy, we can believe all three of those statements at the same time with no difficulty. When Job suffers, when he loses his possessions, his family and his health, we have a problem. We can no longer make sense of all three propositions together. We can now affirm any two only by denying the third.[11]

---

[11] Kushner, *Bad Things Happen*, 37.

The Problem of Evil and the Development of Hellenism 55

Rabbi Kushner goes on to point out that Job's friends rationalized the problem of evil by denying Proposition C. They accused Job, saying that he must have been doing something wrong to have suffered so. Job, however, denied any wrongdoing, and the defense of his own virtue would put most religious men of today to shame (see, e.g., Job 31). Therefore, Job placed the blame for his suffering on Injustice. Essentially he denied Proposition B. The Lord, when He enters the discussion in chapter 38, makes it clear that both approaches were wrong.

Kushner's Proposition A was also effectively upheld by the Lord's reply, but it was never really questioned by the protagonists in the Book of Job. That omission is used by the good Rabbi for his answer to the problem of evil—a denial of God's omnipotence. For Rabbi Kushner, Proposition A is the one that is incorrect. Men can importune God for help, on the off chance that He can do something about the problems in their lives, but according to Rabbi Kushner, He cannot guarantee anything.

This is not the orthodox approach, nor is it the teaching of Mormonism. As will be shown in Part 3, all three of Kushner's Propositions are, in essence, confirmed in scripture. True, God has certain limitations on His power by virtue of His being who He is, i.e., God. For example, He is powerless to do evil. But scripture clearly shows that He is not powerless to prevent evil, as Rabbi Kushner suggests. Rather, He sometimes chooses not to interfere. There are even instances when the scriptures suggest He encourages action that some would view as evil, such as the destruction of Jerusalem and the subjugation of Israel by Babylon in approximately 580 B.C. (Ezra 5:12; Jer. 27:8; 28:14).

How is the problem of evil resolved in Job? The answer is that it is not! God doesn't give any direct explanation in the Book of Job. Instead, He asked Job a series of enlightening questions. The gist of his queries was, "Do you have enough knowledge to counsel Me on how to run the Universe?" He then gave Job a vision that thoroughly convinced him that God knows what He is doing and that he, Job, is wholly inadequate to the task of second-guessing God (Job 42:5). The point thus made was that Man, at least in Old Testament times, did not have sufficient knowledge to see the Universe from God's perspective. Without that knowledge and perspective, he could not understand why God allows evil a certain amount of leeway in the universe, even using it to His advantage at times.

The Book of Job was sufficient for the children of Abraham for thousands of years. But the Greek mind-set by the time of Christ was very different. The philosophers wanted to have definitive answers to every inquiry, and they did not recognize any limitations on their ability to understand the universe. Neither they nor the Apologists could be dissuaded from their fretful examination of this problem.

Ethical reasoning among the Greeks had progressed from the belief that all things happen by necessity (an outgrowth of the Pythagorean observation of order in the universe), to the claim that all things happen by destiny (a kind of fatalistic view of the effects of that order), and finally to the notion that all things happen by the will of God, i.e., because of His Reason or Providence. Fundamental to this notion was the assumption that God is good and that His will is beneficent toward Men. The problem of evil, for them, could not be ignored or left untouched until later revelation gave Men a deeper insight into the knowledge and perspective of God.

The Platonistic Response to the Problem of Evil

For the Greeks, the problem of evil had both an ethical and a cosmological aspect. Ethically, the question related to how a Good God could allow evil to exist. Cosmologically, the question was, How did evil come into existence in the first place in a universe created by a beneficent deity? Because of their dualistic view of the universe, the Platonists dealt primarily with the second problem.

One of the most respected authorities on the subject, Professor Edwin Hatch, whose lectures at Oxford in the late 19th century were published in *The Influence of Greek Ideas and Usages upon the Christian Church*, explains the Platonistic view of creation as follows:

> The creative energy of God is spoken of as the *Demiurgus*, who himself made an ideal world, and employed subordinate agents in the construction of the actual world. The matter upon which the Demiurgus or his agents work is sometimes conceived as potential being, the bare capacity of receiving the qualities and forms, and sometimes as chaotic substance which was reduced to order. The agents were gods who, having been themselves created, were bidden to create living beings, capable of growth and decay. The distinction [was made] between the two spheres of creation, that of a world in which nothing was imperfect since it was the work of a Perfect Being, and that of a

---

[12] Hatch, *Influence of Greek Ideas*, 179-180.

world which was full of imperfections as being the work of created beings . . .[12]

Thus, the Platonists conceived the idea that the agents of God were inferior beings whose existence, as authors of evil, was either permitted or overlooked. They reasoned that these intermediaries were inferior because they were created by God rather than being God. Being inferior, they made mistakes in the creation of the world. For them, this explained the presence of evil in the universe.

The Stoics Found an Ethical Solution to the Problem of Evil

The Stoics had a very different view of the problem of evil. By simply denying that the vicissitudes of life are evil, they dealt with the ethical and the cosmological problems together. They viewed Matter as a passive extension of God, and therefore it too had to be good, including all its manifestations in mortality. On this theory, what looked like evil was treated as nothing more than the will of a benevolent Providence whose plans differ from those of Men. All appearances of evil, according to the Stoics, were either forms of good, or incidental to the operation of good in the lives of Men and, indeed, essential to that operation.[13] This view is similar to the ideas of Christian Science, which insists that evil is an illusion.

One obvious response to this approach is hard to refute. There certainly appears to be evil in this world. It is especially evident in the way Men treat each other. Therefore, to claim that God says, "This may look like evil, but it's really not," is to postulate that He is involved in a kind of deception.

The Stoic answer, though in some ways similar to that given in the Book of Job, was not an entirely satisfying explanation for the existence of misery. The Greeks, in their typically probing manner, wanted more understanding of the necessity and cause of suffering in a world administered by a perfect being. So the search for an ethical solution continued, giving rise, among other ideas, to the heretical notions of Christian Gnosticism, which will be discussed in Chapter 7.

Greek Gnosticism and Its Strange Theology

Gnostic philosophy is believed by some to have begun as a school of Greek theology, or perhaps a syncretism of Greek and oriental

---

[13] Epictetus, *Discourses*, 2:5:24; 2:10:5.

schools.[14] There were many sects among the Gnostics, but generally, they were elitists professing special knowledge obtained in some mystic way so that only the initiated could receive it and thus obtain whatever was viewed as the ultimate goal of the group, whether it was true happiness, ultimate wisdom, or salvation.

Gnostic theology was strongly influenced by a fundamental belief in the evil nature of Matter. Any god who could bring a material world into existence could not, in the theology of Gnosticism, be the supreme Good God, who would have nothing to do with Matter. This was more extreme than the Platonists, who reasoned that whatever contact the Good God had with the evil material world must have taken place through intermediary beings but did not imagine Matter as antagonistic to God.[15]

The following excerpts from the *Corpus Hermeticum* give a picture of the fantastic details of early Gnostic theology. Its foundation in the paganism of Greek mythology is obvious, as is its purpose, to explain the simultaneous existence of an evil material world and a supreme Good God:

> God Nous, being male-female, being life and light, gave birth by reason to another demiurge Nous, who as god of fire and spirit fashioned seven governors who enclosed in circles the sensible universe; their government is called fate.[16]
>
> Nous, father of all, being life and light, brought forth Man, equal to himself, whom he loved as his own child. For he was very beautiful, having the likeness of his father. In all truth God was enamoured of his own image and handed over to his offspring all the tasks of creation.[17]

The early Gnostics believed in an eternal god/being, manifested as a radiant light diffused throughout space and emanating from the Pleroma. Mosheim, the famous eighteenth-century church historian, explains their beliefs as follows:

> The eternal nature, infinitely perfect and infinitely happy, having dwelt from everlasting in a profound solitude, and in a blessed

---

[14] Kidd, *History of the Church*, 1:193.
[15] Nash, *Hellenistic World*, 39-40.
[16] *Corpus Hermeticum*, 1:1:9.
[17] *Ibid.*, 1:1:12.

tranquility, produced at length from itself, two minds of a different sex, which resembled their supreme parent in the most perfect manner. From the prolific union of these two beings, others arose, which were also followed by succeeding generations; so that in process of time a celestial family was formed in the Pleroma. This divine progeny, immutable in its nature, and above the power of mortality, was called, by the philosophers, *Aeon*–a term which signifies, in the Greek language, an eternal nature. How many in number these Aeons were was a point much controverted among the oriental sages.[18]

These notions, with their focus on a kind of family dwelling in the celestial realms of the Pleroma, have parallels in the teachings of the Bible about Man, his pre-existence, and the heavenly family to which Man belongs (see, e.g., Eph. 3:14-15). The latter doctrines are now taught only by The Church of Jesus Christ of Latter-day Saints. For that reason, there is a tendency for classical theists familiar with Gnostic ideas to mistakenly equate Mormonism with Gnosticism. But there is only a hint of similarity between LDS teachings and the Gnostic beliefs described above, as will be seen in Chapter 7.

The Problem of Evil and the Free Agency of Man

Ultimately, a more satisfying answer to the problem of evil was arrived at by the Greek philosophical schools. It came from the Stoics, but it was one that could also be found in the writings of Homer, and was even quoted as a tenet of the Pythagoreans. It was that Men are the authors of their own misery. They are free to do right or wrong and accordingly to be happy or miserable.

This is a fundamental truth about the nature of justice in the universe and a just God, and it is, of course, taught in the Bible. It was taught with great power by Alma in the Book of Mormon (see, e.g., Alma 42), and is part of Mormonism's answer to the problem of evil. Man has Free Agency and is free to choose right or wrong, with resulting consequences, either immediate or ultimate. God does not give Man the gift of Free Agency and then abrogate the consequences of his evil

---

[18] John Lawrence Mosheim, *Ecclesiastical History* (Philadelphia: Stephen G. Ustick, 1798), Cent. I, Part II, Ch. 1:7, quoted in James E. Talmage, *The Great Apostasy Considered in the Light of Scriptural and Secular History* (Salt Lake City: Deseret Book Company, 1964), 98-99.

acts so they will not affect others. Therefore, evil things happen in God's creation. But this does not solve the problem of evil entirely.

The Greeks had no understanding of the Fall of Man. The idea of imperfect intermediaries was hardly satisfying, and without that element, their philosophy did nothing to explain the origin of evil in the first place. Accordingly, theirs remained essentially an ethical explanation of evil. It did nothing to explain, for example, why God allows evil to befall the innocent and the righteous, especially children. Why are some people born into evil circumstances while others are born into good? These questions plagued not only the philosophers but also the Apologists, who were no more successful at solving the problem than Job and his friends.

Understanding the Problem of Evil

To understand why evil befalls the righteous, it is necessary, as the Book of Job implies, to see things from God's perspective. As will be demonstrated below, two basic concepts are essential to that perspective. They are (1) a sufficient understanding of *the pre-mortal existence of Man*, and (2) a knowledge of *Man's ultimate goal*, the true purpose of his creation.

Without some understanding of Man's pre-existence, the circumstances of Man's birth into this life can appear arbitrary and unjust. If God created Men out of nothing at the instant of birth, as orthodox Christianity asserts, the presence of evil in the world must be charged to God Himself. With no understanding of Man's pre-existence, the problem of evil cannot be resolved except through the fatalistic theology espoused by the Stoics.

As noted in the previous chapter, the Greek philosophers, from the time of Plato, believed in Man's pre-existence. However, although that concept is compatible with the Old and New Testaments, the idea of Man's pre-mortal existence as spirit children of God was never accepted by the Apologists. Origen, one of the later Apologists, was the sole exception, and he expressed some insights into the problem of evil that went far beyond the mainstream of Christian thought at the time. His comments follow Greek thinking in many ways, and are fraught with error, but he did perceive some aspects of the truth in his resolution of the problem of evil. Addressing the question of why some individuals are born into good circumstances and others into poor, he wrote:

They were created absolutely equal; for, on the one hand, God had no reason in Himself for causing inequalities; and, on the other hand, being absolutely impartial, He could not give to one being an advantage which He did not give to another. . . . Every created rational being is thus capable of both good and evil; . . . consequently also of happiness and misery; of the former if it chooses holiness and clings to it, of the latter if by sloth and negligence it swerves into wickedness and ruin. . . . In the temporal world which is seen, as well as in the eternal worlds which are unseen, all beings are arranged according to their merits; their place has been determined by their own conduct. . . . The present inequalities of circumstance and character are thus not wholly explicable within the sphere of the present life. But this world is not the only world. Every soul has existed from the beginning . . . *Its place in this world as a vessel appointed to honor or to dishonor is determined by its previous merits or demerits.*[19] (Emphasis added.)

Origen went on to teach a doctrine of universal salvation that was consistent with many schools of Greek and oriental thought at the time. It involved a series of progressive incarnations involving remedial punishment for sins. Mormons, as well as orthodox Christians, reject such teachings as non-biblical. However, his suggestion that Men made errors in the pre-existence for which they reap the consequences in this life goes a long way toward taking the blame for evil off the shoulders of the Lord. Orthodox Christianity did not accept this idea. That lack of acceptance leaves some serious issues relating to the problem of evil unresolved for orthodox theologians.

Modern Revelation and the Problem of Evil

A full understanding of the presence of evil in a Universe created by a perfect, all-powerful and loving God was greatly aided by revelation reserved for this, the last dispensation of the Gospel of Jesus Christ. The crucial information is that, contrary to Origen's teachings, God never created the basic personalities of Men. If He had created Men "absolutely equal," as Origen claims, they would be clones, and God would be responsible for any evil committed by them.

From modern revelation (D&C 93:29), Mormons understand that God merely brought Man's eternal, independent intelligence into

---

[19] Origen, *On First Principles [de principiis]*, 2:9:6; 1:8:4; 1:5:2, 5; 3:3:5; 3:5:3; 3:1:20, 21.

spirit and, ultimately, into physical form. The basic personality of each person, with his or her characteristics and predispositions, is, in its fundamental sense, an independent, self-conscious, eternal, uncreated entity. Therefore, Men are, and have always been, independent agents, personally responsible for their own good or evil choices, and their circumstances are the just and beneficent result of those choices.

As noted above, an understanding of Man's ultimate goal to become like God is also important to a satisfying resolution of the problem of evil. Mormons believe the New Testament when it teaches that, if Men follow God's laws, they can become like Him, just as a son can become like his father (see, e.g., John 17:3, 21-22; 1 John 3:2-3; Rev. 3:21). This suggests a broader view of Man's purpose in this life than is shared by any theological system outside Mormonism, and it puts some flesh on the bones of the Stoic notion that God's plan is greater than Man's limited view of it.

God is not engaged in an easy work. He runs the Universe, and the best preparation for anyone planning to follow in His footsteps must necessarily include some experience in overcoming great obstacles and difficulties. God, knowing each of His children perfectly from their eternal pre-existence with Him, provides in this life the circumstances that will best aid them to attain their goal. Thus, the circumstances in which individuals find themselves in this life are not the result of arbitrary decisions by God or a plan that has no relation to Man's needs. Nor should they be considered a punishment for past mistakes, as Origen supposed. They are the combined result of Man's own choices and the beneficent aid of a loving Father.

In a very complex way, what Men do in their pre-mortal life affects them in this life, but not always in a way that is obvious to Men on earth. Circumstances of birth and other vicissitudes that fall upon the righteous are individually suited to the personality of each man and woman and are related to the choices and progress each has made during his or her eternal existence. They are designed to help each individual become the person he or she has always wanted to be, a righteous son or daughter of the Eternal God.

Without a full understanding of these two principles, principles that allow Men to view the universe from a point of view that is just a little closer to God's perspective, the problem of evil is essentially unsolvable. Since this information was not available to the Greek philosophers or the Apologists, the enigma of evil proved to be an impetus for many doctrinal variations, both in Hellenism, in Christian Gnosticism, and in the Christian world today.

Philo of Alexandria Forged the Path to the Theological Apostasy

The last theological movement that had a significant influence on the early Church was the Hellenization of Judaism, predominantly through the writings of Philo of Alexandria (c. 20 B.C. to c. 50 A.D.). Philo wrote in Greek, the language used by most of the Jews at the time of Christ, and used Greek philosophy and rhetoric to interpret the Old Testament. Because the early Church had its roots firmly planted in Judaism, the Apologists were often influenced by Philo's reasoning and exegesis, even though they opposed some of his tenets.

Philo believed that the universe was created by God because "the Father and Maker is good, and . . . being good He did not grudge the best kind of nature to matter (*ousia*) which of itself had nothing excellent, though it was capable of becoming all things."[20] About God, he taught: "In the one really existing God there are two chief and primary faculties, Goodness and Power, . . . by Goodness He begat the universe, and by Power He governs it."[21]

With the philosophers, he taught that God is Mind, and from Him, as from a fountain, proceeded all forms of Mind and Reason. To Philo, Reason, whether unconscious in the form of natural law or conscious in the form of human thought, is like a river that flows from God to fill the universe.[22]

Of Man's creation, he wrote:

> *The soul came from nothing that is created, but from the Father* and Leader of all things. For what He breathed into Adam was nothing else than a divine breath, *a colony from that blissful and happy nature*, placed here below for the benefit of our race; so that granting man to be mortal in respect of his visible part, *yet in respect of that which is invisible he is the heir of immortality.*"[23]

---

[20] Philo, *On the Creation*, 5.
[21] Philo, *On the Cherubim*, 9.
[22] Hatch, *Influence of Greek Ideas*, 183-184.
[23] Philo, *On the Creation*, 46.

Thus, he believed that the soul of Man came from God, existing from the moment He breathed it into Man. Yet, of God's relationship to Man, Philo taught that "He Himself is more than life, being the ever-flowing fountain of life."[24]

As to the manner of creation, Philo taught a doctrine that sounded very much like that of Plato. According to Philo, God was transcendent and acted upon matter that was outside Himself. "It was in itself without order, without quality, without soul, full of difference, disproportion, and discord: it received a change and transformation into what was opposite and best, order, quality, animation, identity, proportion, harmony, all that is characteristic of a better form."[25] Thus, Philo retained the Platonistic idea, consistent with Genesis 1:2, that the heavens and the earth were created from preexisting, unorganized substance.

However, he went on in the Platonist vein as follows: "Out of it God begat all things, Himself not touching it: for it is not right that the all-knowing and blessed One should touch unlimited and confused matter: but He used the unbodied Forces whose true name is the Forms (ideai), that each class of things should receive its fitting shape."[26]

While, in this passage, he calls the "unbodied Forces" used by God in His creation by the Platonistic name, "Forms," he sometimes referred to them in Stoical language as "Reasons" (*logoi*, plural of *logos*), in Pythagorean language as "Numbers" or "Limits," in Old Testament language as "Angels," and even in the popular language of Greek mythology as "Daemons."[27] In each case, Philo explained that God made the world, and these Forces acted strictly as His agents, intermediaries in the Platonistic sense. The visible world was "no other than the mind of the architect, planning to realize in a visible city the city of his thought."[28]

As to God, Himself, Philo taught that He was a being absolutely bare of any qualities. He had no body or soul and was not composed of elements, or of matter or form. According to Philo, no "limitations" could be ascribed to God, who was eternal, unchangeable, substance ("ousia"), free, self-sufficient, and better than the good and

---

[24] Philo, *On Flight and Finding*, 36.
[25] Philo, *On the Creation*, 5.
[26] Philo, *On the Sacrifices of Abel and Cain*, 13.
[27] Hatch, *Influence of Greek Ideas*, 185.
[28] Philo, *On the Creation*, 4.

the beautiful. He was absolutely transcendent, so that, to describe God would be to reduce Him to the sphere of finite existence.

Philo was among the first to apply the Greek idea of *incomprehensibility* (see, e.g., Maximus of Tyre, "we cannot apprehend His essence"[29]) to the God of Abraham, Isaac and Jacob. He spoke of Him as follows:

> He is incomprehensible: not even the whole universe, much less the human mind, can contain the conception of Him:[30] we know *that* he is, we cannot know *what* He is:[31] we may see the manifestations of Him in His works, but it were monstrous folly to go behind His works and inquire into His essence.[32] He is hence unnamed: for names are the symbols of created things, whereas His only attribute is to *be*.[33] [Emphasis in original.]

Thus, in many respects, Philo was an antecedent to the doctrines of classical theism later adopted by the Apologists, and was occasionally cited as authority for them. He put the final touches on the Hellenistic theology that so profoundly affected early Christianity under the leadership of the second-century Apologists.

Summary

1. After Aristotle, Greek philosophy developed into several schools or theological systems of teaching.
2. The two major Greek philosophical schools at the time of Christ were the Stoics and the Platonists.
3. The Stoics adhered to the philosophical concept of "monism," the idea that Mind and Matter are composed of the same substance or essence (*ousia*).
4. The Stoics believed Man's soul was nearest to the essence of God, and that Men are, in a special sense, offspring of God and hence brothers and sisters.

---

[29] Maximus of Tyre, *Dissertations*, 8, 9.
[30] Philo, *On Abraham*, 1:224, 281, 566; 2:12, 654.
[31] Philo, *On Rewards and Punishments*, 7.
[32] Philo, *On the Posterity and Exile of Cain*, 48.
[33] Philo, *On the Change of Names*, 2.

5. To the Stoics, there was no beginning in the sense of a singular act of creation. Creation was an ever-evolving process of change that had a kind of rhythmic or cyclical pattern ending in fire.
6. According to the Stoics, creation was carried out by the "reasons," (*logoi*) of God, "rational seeds" that gave Matter its appropriate form. These *logoi* were in all things, making all things the sum and substance of God. (This idea was very much like the idea of the "Force" in the *Star Wars* trilogy.)
7. The Stoics believed in being obedient to the will of Nature (i.e., God).
8. They taught that all things happen according to God's benevolent will, and that men can either fight the inevitable or learn to go along with it pleasantly.
9. The Platonists championed the philosophy of "dualism," the idea that Mind is an entirely different substance or essence (*ousia*) from Matter.
10. According to the Platonists, the "phenomenal" world, or world of the senses, in which Men exist, was fashioned after the perfect Forms that exist in the celestial realm where God dwells as pure mind.
11. The sensory or "phenomenal" world, the Platonists taught, is in the process of "becoming," while the celestial realm, the "Pleroma," is a state of "being," and is therefore true reality.
12. The Platonists taught that the Forms, or "ideas" of God, acted as his agents to create the sensory world.
13. Both the Stoics and the Platonists taught that God is transcendent. That is, according to them, He exists entirely outside of the sensory universe, outside of space and time.
14. By the time of Christ, the *Ideai* or "Forms" were viewed as a single agent of God, the "*Logos*," meaning the Mind, Reason or Word of God.
15. The problem of evil strongly affected the development of Greek systems of theology.
16. The problem of evil is the question of why a perfect, all-good and all-powerful God would allow evil to exist.
17. The Book of Job addressed the problem of evil long before the Greek philosophers lived.

The Problem of Evil and the Development of Hellenism 67

18. The problem of evil presented in the Book of Job can easily be resolved by denying either that (a) God is all-powerful, (b) God is benevolent, or (c) Job was righteous. If all three of these statements are true, as the Bible teaches, there must be something Men do not understand in the basic premises of the problem of evil.
19. The Book of Job answers the problem of evil with questions that suggest Men cannot comprehend the answer to the problem of evil without a fuller understanding of God and the universe. Though the Jews accepted that answer, the Greeks did not.
20. The Platonists tried to solve the problem of evil by teaching that evil was the work of intermediaries, inferior beings who acted as agents of God to create an inferior world.
21. The Stoics solved the problem of evil by denying that the vicissitudes of life are evil. They claimed that "evil" was merely part of God's beneficent plan for Man and necessary to its fulfillment.
22. Eventually the Greek answer to the problem of evil centered on the agency of Man. He could choose right or wrong and accordingly be happy or miserable.
23. The idea that Man's free agency causes all evil does not resolve the problem of evil as presented in the Book of Job.
24. The Gnostics tried to resolve the problem of evil by postulating a strange story about the Good God creating a progeny of lesser gods, or Aeons, who became progressively more material until they were able to create the evil world of Matter.
25. None of the philosophical solutions to the problem of evil was fully satisfying, and hence the problem remained largely unresolved, as the Lord predicted in the Book of Job.
26. A belief in the pre-mortal existence of Men brought Origen to a better understanding of the problem of evil.
27. Modern revelations, which teach that the fundamental personalities of Men are uncreated and that Man's ultimate goal is to become like God, have helped to unravel the problem of evil.
28. The Hellenization of Judaic theology by Philo of Alexandria strongly affected the Apologists in their development of classical theism.

ΩΣ4ΣΩ

The Greek Education System and the Spread of Hellenism

The last great element that prepared the Gentiles to receive the Gospel of Jesus Christ was the educational system that dominated Gentile society at the time of Christ. While Greece had been losing political power for hundreds of years, it had been gaining in literary supremacy. By the Christian era, though Greece was a subject of Rome, she reigned supreme in the domain of letters, spreading her culture throughout the Gentile world.

Greek Education—
the Model for Modern Education Systems

Except for the physical sciences, education in the known world during the first three centuries after Christ was much like that in any well-developed modern country today. In fact, it was not so much similar as it was the forerunner of modern education, at least until approximately the middle of the twentieth century when the study of Greek and Latin—the Classics—all but disappeared from American public schools.[1]

Before Plato, there were no public schools in Greece. Instead, boys from leading families were taken to professional teachers by slaves called *paidagogoi*, or "boy-leaders" (from which the English word "pedagogue" is derived). Education was divided into three fields, (1) grammar, i.e., reading, writing and sometimes arithmetic, (2) music and singing, and (3) gymnastics, including wrestling, boxing and other forms of physical education. Boys from seven to fourteen studied

---
[1] Cf. Hatch, *Influence of Greek Ideas*, 27-28.

grammar and music. From twelve to eighteen, they learned gymnastics at a private *"palaestra"* or gymnasium. Literature was studied as part of grammar, especially in the music classes, where Homer and other early poets were memorized.

Around 450 to 400 B.C., the Sophists, especially Socrates, helped to develop something like a secondary education system. It was unorganized, with no systematic curriculum, but there were added to the subjects noted above some lectures on the natural sciences, divinity, mathematics, ethics and law. The education of girls was always in domestic training only.

Plato and Aristotle were strong advocates of state control over the education system. In *Republic* and *Laws*, Plato advocated dissolving family life and family ties entirely in favor of state education of all future citizens. Aristotle was less extreme in his theorizing, but both advocated compulsory public education controlled by the state, and taught that it should be uniform, at least at the early stages. Plato devised a curriculum to be used in such a system, a three- to four-year course, which he offered free at the Academy in Athens.

In the years that followed Aristotle's death, a real public education system began to develop. Boys at the age of fifteen or sixteen left their private *palaestra* for public gymnasiums such as the one maintained at public expense at Plato's Academy. There they took a course patterned essentially after that developed by Plato, until at approximately eighteen, as "ephebes," they were admitted to citizenship and underwent two years of compulsory training in the military regiments on the frontier. After this service, they were required to remain in training, and many returned to the gymnasiums.

Additional training at this point was not at public expense, so only the wealthy could continue their education. Gradually, the Academy developed into a fashionable lounge where the Platonic and other schools were born. Logic and ethics, built on a foundation of geometry and mathematics, were the principal subjects taught at the higher levels in the Academy. Aristotle established a similar public gymnasium when he set up his own school, the Lyceum. There he lectured twice a day, in the morning to the elite, and in the afternoon to the public.[2]

---

[2] *Encyclopaedia Britannica*, 1960 ed., s.v. "Schools, Ancient."

Another element that influenced Greek education was the rise of sophistry—expository speaking—which was vainly opposed by Plato and Aristotle. In a democratic state, oratory was fast becoming the quickest path to influence and power, not unlike the study of law in today's society. More and more young men were attending Sophist schools to learn rhetoric, argument and extemporaneous speaking which they could use to advance their personal ambitions. This tendency resulted in a gradual increase in the emphasis on intellectual pursuits, especially rhetoric. Under Philip of Macedonia and his son Alexander the Great, higher education became purely intellectual, and its relationship to political and social life grew increasingly remote.[3]

Secondary education, meanwhile, was also increasing in public domination. The Alexandrians, particularly Antiodorus and Eratosthenes (c. 250 B.C.) advanced grammar, which included literary criticism and scholarship, to a science, and fathered the "grammar school."[4] In approximately 120 B.C., Dionysius Thrax wrote the first existing Greek grammar. It was translated into Latin and remained the foundation text for all subsequent grammatical instruction through the nineteenth century.

Greek Education Emphasized Literature, Philosophy and Argument

By the time of Christ, the Greek educational curriculum was complex and rigorous in the following fields: Grammar (the study of literature), Rhetoric (the study of literary expression and argument), and Philosophy, including Logic, especially in the form of Dialectic (the Socratic method of questions and answers aimed at uncovering the truth).

The main subjects of literary education were the Greek poets, especially Homer, who was regarded by the majority of Greeks much as Christians regard the Bible. Large portions were often committed to memory. There are records dating from the fourth century A.D. that indicate a high percentage of the common populace, even in remote Greek colonies, knew the entire *Iliad* by heart.[5]

---
[3] *Ibid.*, s.v. "Education, History of."
[4] *Ibid.*, s.v. "Schools, Ancient."
[5] Hatch, *Influence of Greek Ideas*, 30.

The Greeks loved to argue, discourse, reason, talk and listen to talks. They belittled cultures, groups and individuals who could not defend their ideas with detailed proofs and carefully devised rhetoric. They were "almost the slaves of cultivated expression."[6] They were seen as the seat of learning, culture and knowledge (that knowledge being Hellenism), making their education and scholarship almost irresistible to the cultures that surrounded them.

Greek Education Spread Quickly to Rome

In Rome, schooling was originally accomplished in the home. The father had unlimited power over his son's life, and was open to public censure if he failed to train him in the ordinary moral, civic and religious duties. Later, when Greek culture was imported to Rome, the first instrument of education was Greek literature. In 272 B.C. Livius Andronicus was brought to Rome as a slave. He eventually became a freeman, teaching Greek and Latin. Among other accomplishments, he translated the *Odyssey* into Latin.

The first grammar school was opened in Rome by Spurius Carvilius about 230 B.C., and others soon followed. These were of the nature of elementary schools, and were dominated by Greek teachers and lecturers as late as Cicero's time (first century B.C.). They were not available to the working class, but were more like the English prep schools of the nineteenth century. Schools of rhetoric, like Greek secondary schools, were also established, and in 92 B.C., Latin rhetoric schools began.

In 91 B.C., the first Roman public schools were started by Fabius Quintilianus who wrote the classic Roman curriculum known as *Institutio oratoria*. Pliny the younger, a pupil of Quintilianus, established an endowed school and by the early second century A.D., public elementary (grammar) and secondary (rhetoric) schools were common. The emperor Antoninus Pius, who figured positively in the history of Christian persecution by Rome, assigned offices and salaries for rhetoricians throughout the provinces of the Roman Empire. Alexander Severus, one of his successors, established schools for poor boys, provided they were free-born.

By the time of Christ, education was no longer in the hands of private tutors who worked in the houses of great families. "Grammar

---

[6] *Ibid.*, 27.

schools" were established in almost every town, where all youths received the first part of their education. Secondary education was in rhetoric, and supplementing this education by attending lectures of eminent professors was common. Children progressed from grammar school through what would today be called the University in much the same way they do now. By then, the school Aristotle established at the Lyceum in Athens was one such university. Plato's Academy was another. Students at these institutions received a well-rounded higher education by attending lectures and participating in sports and the theater.

Jewish Education and Culture Remained Strictly Separate

Unlike the rest of the known world at this time, the Jews resisted all inroads from outside influences that might affect their education or culture. The most notorious of these efforts came from Antiochus Epiphanes in 169 B.C. He attempted to Hellenize the Jews by desecrating the Temple in Jerusalem. The result was the Maccabean revolt, which established in the minds of all subsequent conquerors of the region the necessity of leaving the Jewish practice of their religion and education strictly alone if it did not impose on political issues.[7]

However, Greece was not without its inroads into Jewish culture. In approximately 270 B.C., Ptolemy Philadelphus commissioned the translation of the Hebrew Old Testament into Greek. The work was called the *Septuagint*. The project took centuries, but by the time of Christ, a form of Greek that was in many ways unique to the Jewish culture was not only the language of the Old Testament but the common language of the region.

This form of Greek was sometimes called "koine" Greek, a term derived from the Greek *koinós* meaning "common, vulgar or profane," in contrast to classical Greek. It included words that had no Greek origin at all, such as the word translated "paradise" in the Old Testament, which comes from a Persian word for "garden." The Greek *Septuagint* was the source of most quotations by Christ from the Old Testament. Other than this concession to the

---

[7] *Encyclopaedia Britannica*, 1960 ed., s.v. "Jews."

prevailing world civilization, however, the inroads of Greek education and culture were largely excluded from Israel.

The Nature of Jewish Education

Education in the Jewish state consisted primarily of studying Hebrew poetry and the Law of Moses as well as the writings of the prophets and respected rabbis. Since Hebrew had been a dead language among the Jews from the time of the Babylonian exile, this teaching was accomplished primarily through a study of the Septuagint and what was known as the Oral Law, consisting of interpretations and applications of Old Testament writings. Between 10 and 220 A.D., the Oral Law was finally reduced to writing in the form now known as the *Talmud*.

A Deep Rift Between the Jews and the Gentiles

Though they shared a common language, the Greek and Jewish cultures could not have been more divergent at the time of Christ. Except among the elite in Jerusalem and the Hellenized Jews of Alexandria, the practice of Greek rhetoric and oratory were largely eschewed by the Jews. The complexities of unreal reality accepted by the Greek philosophers in their metaphysical machinations were entirely foreign to those raised on the absolutes taught by Moses and the prophets. This condition reflected the general attitude of the Jews toward the Gentiles, and posed a major problem for the Church when the Gospel was eventually opened to all nations.

This rift had immense significance for the early Church. The Gospel and the scriptures were originally and historically Hebrew. The setting, form, style, context and foundation of the Bible are distinctly Jewish. This required the message of the Old Testament, though written in Greek at the time of Christ, to be translated into the context of Hellenistic thinking using a Hebrew rather than a Greek mind set.

The crucial difficulty was the interpretation of the figurative language used by the prophets in their statements about God. The Hebrews had absolutely no idea of metaphysics. If they spoke of two separate persons, they really meant two entirely separate individuals. The Jews used strong figurative language to put across the notion that two entirely separate persons were in such perfect sync that they could be called "one," but the metaphysical idea of two separate persons actually being one person is not present in the Bible.

This difference in usage made interpretation of the Old Testament prophets and the Jewish writers of the New Testament difficult for men like the Apologists who were trained in Greek schools. To understand the Bible, it is necessary to think like an ancient Hebrew, not like an ancient Greek, but their natural tendency was to view the figurative language of the scriptures in a metaphysical light. It is the transition from a figurative interpretation of literal facts to a metaphysical interpretation of those facts that most clearly marks the theological apostasy to be discussed in Part 2.

The Skeptics and the Appeal of Christianity

The Greek education system was not entirely desirable by the time of Christ. In many ways the Greeks had created a type of life that was so artificial they were unable to recognize its artificiality. The established schools, instead of being laboratories for obtaining the knowledge of the future, had become "forges in which the chains of the present were fashioned from the knowledge of the past."[8]

As a result, a school of Greek philosophers called the Skeptics had become quite influential. Skepticism took a negative view of every philosophical and religious theory, exposing every flaw and belittling every position to the point that there were many who felt a strong dissatisfaction with life in general. They needed some new doctrine to revitalize their intellectual interests.

Into this environment, the message of the Gospel came with great force. The vibrant truths preached by the Apostles revived intellectual activity among the Gentiles, and the new ideas of Christianity fascinated them and soon enjoyed a predominant influence. The similarity of Christian doctrines to the immensely popular teachings of Plato did not go unnoticed. The distinctly Greek need for an understanding of the utmost detail of the new theology was stimulated, provoking questions not previously asked by Jewish Christians. As Paul so perfectly described it in 2 Timothy 4:3, the "ears" of the Gentile world were "itching" to hear and dissect the truths of the Gospel.

---

[8] Hatch, *Influence of Greek Ideas*, 49.

The Greek Fascination for Christianity Did Not Include the Scriptures

Just as the Jews eschewed Hellenism, the Greeks of this era had a general distaste for the Semitic style of writing. It sounded barbarous, awkward, and unmusical to them. This was not as great a problem in the second century as it became by the fourth century A.D., but from the beginning, it created a tendency among Church scholars trained in Greek rhetoric to avoid scripture study. By the fourth century, the Church had become so steeped in Greek culture that reading the Bible was difficult for converts, and references to its passages became less frequent among Christian writers.

For example, Father Basil, writing to his old teacher, Libanius, in the fourth century, said, "I must apologize for the style of this letter. The truth is, I have been in the company of Moses and Elias, and men of that kind, who tell us no doubt what is true, but in a barbarous dialect, so that your instructions have quite gone out of my head."[9] Augustine is said to have hated reading the scriptures because of their "barbarous dialect." However, he was pushed into reading the Old Testament by Saint Ambrose, and he is said to have enjoyed the writings of Paul.[10]

Greek Methods of Interpretation Were Used to Distort the Scriptures

To make matters worse, beginning in the second century A.D., interpretation of the scriptures was strongly influenced by the methods of rhetoric and exegesis commonly taught in the Greek education system. As the attitude toward pagan polytheism changed during the revolution that produced Hellenism, the Greek philosophers had developed a new way to interpret the pagan poets. It was a method used to find themes of goodness and virtue consistent with the new monotheism in the old pagan stories. The methods involved very creative use of allegory.

The technique was attributed to Anaxagoras, but it actually predates him. For example, Heraclitus held that Homer was speaking allegorically when he wrote "Ocean, the birth of gods, and Tethys their mother." What Homer meant, supposedly, was that all things are the offspring of

---

[9] *Ibid.*, 29.
[10] Shiel, *Greek Thought*, 48.

flow and movement.[11] The Platonists held that when Zeus reminded Hera of the time when he had hung her trembling by a golden chain in the vast concave of heaven, it was God speaking to Matter, which He had taken and bound by the chains of law.[12] Some Greek exegetes became almost indifferent to the original meaning of the writer, interpreting all passages allegorically to suit their pet theories.

Philo and the Greek Method of Allegory

The allegorical form of exegesis was applied with great artistry to the Old Testament by Philo of Alexandria. He and Aristobulus (c. 170 B.C.-150 B.C.) before him, taught, for example, that references to God's body in the Old Testament were to be explained allegorically. To them, the "hand" of God meant His power, and His "feet" were the stability of the world. A complete listing of such interpretations was later made by the Apologist Melito of Sardis in his work, *The Key*.[13] In that work, for example, the phrase, "feet of the Lord," was incongruously interpreted as a reference to "His immoveableness and eternity."[14] Some of Philo's allegorical interpretations are so fanciful as to be almost amusing.[15]

The Apologists Adopted Allegorical Interpretations of the Scriptures

Allegorical methods of exegesis had a strong influence on the early Church, especially the Apologists. They used them not only to interpret scripture, but to argue that the Greek poets taught Christian truths. For example, Clement of Alexandria interpreted the withdrawal of Oceanus and Tethys in Homer's *Iliad* to mean the separation of land and sea spoken of in the Old Testament. He also argued that Homer, when he made Apollo ask Achilles, "Why fruitlessly pursue him, a god," meant to show that Divinity cannot be understood by bodily powers.[16] It is said of Simon Magus, one of the earliest Christian Gnostic heretics, that he

---

[11] Plato, *Theaetetus*, 9:152d, quoting Homer *Iliad* 14:201-302.
[12] Origen, *Against Celsus*, 6:42, referring to Homer *Iliad* 15:18, et seq.
[13] Fragments of this work are available in *Ante-Nicene Fathers*, 8:760-762.
[14] Melito, *The Key*, in *Ante-Nicene Fathers*, 8:761.
[15] See, e.g., Philo, *On Dreams*.
[16] Hatch, *Influence of Greek Ideas*, 70 (see also, fn. 3).

"interpreted in whatever way he wished both the writings of Moses and also of the [Greek] poets."[17] Thus, the scriptures were frequently subjected to the most strained interpretations. The result was to impress on scripture the views of the interpreter, rather than the reverse process intended by God.

An anonymous contemporary of Tertullian, quoted by Eusebius, lamented the situation that prevailed in the early Church as follows:

> These men have fearlessly perverted the divine Scriptures, and set aside the rule of ancient faith, and have not known Christ, seeking as they do, not what the divine Scriptures say, but what form of syllogism may be found to support their godlessness; and if one advances any express statement of the divine Scripture, they try to find out whether it can form a conjunctive or a disjunctive hypothetical."[18]

The Greek Love for Sophistry Infects the Early Church

The early Church was also deeply influenced by the cultural taste of the Greeks for professional teachers and preachers. Teaching was held in high regard at the time of Christ and was a profitable profession. Many professional philosophers and teachers enjoyed a kind of celebrity status. A "sermonette" from one of these philosophers after dinner was as much in fashion then as a piece of vocal or instrumental music performed by a famous artist was in nineteenth-century England.

Many such speakers traveled around giving talks as a form of entertainment. These were the Sophists, whose field of expertise has been described as rhetorical philosophizing. They were looked down on by the more serious philosophers, but the more famous among them were in great demand. They often received money and even political office as a result of their public speaking abilities.

The tendency to follow this pattern in the early Church was as irresistible as the other aspects of Greek culture that flowed from the predominant education system. Preaching soon replaced teaching in the Church and became increasingly structured, so that the effort to entertain eventually overwhelmed the effort to change lives. Dio

---

[17] Hippolytus, *Philosophical Refutation of All Heresies*, 6:14.
[18] Eusebius, *Ecclesiastical History*, 5:28:13. It is speculated that the author was Hippolytus.

Chrysostom, writing in the fourth century, lamented this development in the following words:

> There are many preachers who make long sermons: if they are well applauded, they are as glad as if they had obtained a kingdom: if they bring their sermon to an end in silence, their despondency is worse, I may almost say, than hell. It is this that ruins churches, that you do not seek to hear sermons that touch the heart, but sermons that will delight your ears with their intonation and the structure of their phrases, just as if you were listening to singers and lute-players. And we preachers humor your fancies, instead of trying to crush them. We act like a father who gives a sick child a cake or an ice, or something else that is merely nice to eat—just because he asks for it; and takes no pains to give him what is good for him; and then when the doctors blame him says, "I could not bear to hear my child cry." . . . That is what we do when we elaborate beautiful sentences, fine combinations and harmonies, to please and not to profit, to be admired and not to instruct, to delight and not to touch you, to go away with your applause in our ears, and not to better your conduct. Believe me, I am not speaking at random: when you applaud me as I speak, I feel at the moment as it is natural for a man to feel. I will make a clean breast of it. Why should I not? I am delighted and overjoyed. And then when I go home and reflect that the people who have been applauding me have received no benefit, and indeed that whatever benefit they might have had has been killed by the applause and praises, I am sore at heart, and I lament and fall to tears, and I feel as though I had spoken altogether in vain, and I say to myself, What is the good of all your labors, seeing that your hearers don't want to reap any fruit out of all that you say? And I have often thought of laying down a rule absolutely prohibiting all applause, and urging you to listen in silence.[19]

It is interesting to note that the modern Church, The Church of Jesus Christ of Latter-day Saints, has instituted the very rule suggested here by Chrysostom in its meetings.

The Development of Neoplatonism

Ultimately, the reaction of the philosophical schools to Christianity was an attempt to revitalize Hellenism. This effort was championed by

---

[19] Chrysostom, *Homily 30 On the Acts of the Apostles* 3:9:238.

Plotinus, the chief author of Neoplatonism. While it professed to be genuine Platonism, Neoplatonism assimilated many doctrines belonging to other schools and to both Greek and oriental religions as well as some Christian ideas.

It taught of an incomprehensible deity, absolutely transcendent, but the source out of which all things originally flowed. These emanations dispersed and thus decreased in "reality" until they reached the current state of the sensory universe. Plotinus taught that all things, having derived from God, long to return to their origin. This return, he taught, takes place in Man through "ecstasy," a state achieved by asceticism and prayer.[20]

Though respected for its beauty of form and high ethical standards, Neoplatonism was no match for Christianity. The Roman Emperor, Julian, in 361 A.D., who attempted a return to Hellenism by establishing Neoplatonism as a church, failed miserably in that effort. Neoplatonic asceticism and devotion, however, were ultimately absorbed in the monastic movement within the Christian Church.

Christianity and Greek Culture Mutually Affected Each Other

Through its pervasive education system, Hellenism invaded Christianity with the same force Christianity invaded Hellenism. The time of Christ was an age of moral reformation. There was a growing interest in higher religious morality and a belief that God was pleased by moral action rather than by pagan sacrifice. The people of the time were reacting negatively to the vices of the great centers of population, and there was a recognition among the populace that life requires "amendment" (what is called in the Gospel, "repentance").[21]

But the Gentile soil, though fertile, included a negative side. The Greeks loved metaphysics and argument. They dissected ideas in a way that was completely foreign to the Jewish mind, which had been firmly grounded in reality. The Greeks had to have reasons for everything and a definition or label for every idea. Every position had to be supported by proofs that were carefully formulated using the rules of rhetoric taught in the Greek schools.

---

[20] Plotinus, *Enneads*, 6.9.7; see also 5.1.6 and Porphyry, *Life of Plotinus*, 23.
[21] Hatch, *Influence of Greek Ideas*, 140-141.

Until the second century, the Church was primarily composed of Jews. It had few leaders who expressed themselves in the Greek mode. Unfortunately, by the time such men were ready to be an influence in the Gentile world, the Church was bereft of its principal leaders, men like the Apostles, who thoroughly understood the Gospel and the truths taught in the Bible. Paul and John made efforts to address the Greeks in their own style. However, due to the lethal Roman, Jewish and pagan persecutions, they were not available by the end of the first century to answer the new questions that were being asked.

These new questions were especially difficult to answer because of the deep rift between the Hebrew and Greek cultures noted above. Greeks and Jews came to the conversation with an entirely different set of assumptions and an entirely different view of the real world. The Gospel was Jewish, not Greek, but it was easy for the Greeks to give the figurative style of Hebrew writing a metaphysical twist. Because figurative passages in the Hebrew scriptures almost had to be translated, not into another language, but into another mind set, preserving the purity of Gospel truths from the metaphysical assumptions of Hellenistic thought was essentially impossible.

Jewish Commandments vs. Greek Ethics

One very simple example of this problem is found in the rules of ethical behavior. In the Judeo-Christian tradition, these rules were introduced as commandments of God, and obedience was seen as a requirement of holiness. For the Greeks, there had to be a rational, humanistic basis for all rules of conduct, and there was no element of retribution in their ethics. Though the Greeks spoke of godly behavior and the perfection of God as something ultimately to be attained, they had no absolute standards of godly perfection that applied to them. The idea of aesthetic denial was often nothing more, in practice, than avoiding the extreme excesses of paganism. While their minds were in the heavens, their behavior was often in the gutter. As the Greek view became more popular in the early Church, it led to a greater laxity in adherence to the commandments.[22]

---

[22] *Ibid.*, 158-159.

Jewish Inspiration vs. Greek Teaching

Another difference was that the Greek approach to theological issues did not respect the role of inspiration as much as did the Semitic approach. The Greeks believed that their own poets and philosophers were inspired in a sense.[23] They even referred to their more respected teachers as "saviors," because they saved their students from ignorance and bondage to false ideas. The need for a Savior from sin was a Semitic understanding. The idea of absolute reliance on the Word of God was completely foreign to the Greek mind.

Changes to the Gospel Were Inevitable

As will be seen, these are minor discrepancies compared to the differences that arose when Greek metaphysics was applied to scriptural teachings about God. The Gospel was delivered to the Gentiles in sublime perfection, without metaphysical assumptions and without endless dialectic proofs, but it did not long remain so. The result of Gentile dominance in the early Church was, as classical historians admit, completely predictable. As Professor Hatch put it, "It was impossible for Greeks, educated as they were with an education which penetrated their whole nature, to receive or to retain Christianity in its primitive simplicity."[24]

Thus, despite their preparation and readiness for the pure, "primitive" Gospel of Jesus Christ, the education, scholarship and metaphysical thinking of the Greeks led the early Church into theological apostasy. Greek notions about the true nature and characteristics of God have deluded orthodox Christianity to this day. The mechanism of that momentous change will be examined in Part 2.

Summary

1. As early as the fourth century B.C., Plato and Aristotle advocated uniform compulsory education for all boys.
2. The Greeks had a rigorous, full-scale public education system by the third century B.C.
3. The same public education system was imported to Rome by the beginning of the first century B.C.

---

[23] *Ibid.*, 51.
[24] *Ibid.*, 49.

4. Through the Maccabean revolt in 169 B.C., the Jews were allowed to remain aloof from Hellenistic influences.
5. Jewish curriculum was the written and oral law. The latter ultimately became embodied in the Talmud.
6. Greek education included music, grammar (the study of literature), rhetoric (the study of composition and argument), and philosophy (including logic and extemporaneous speaking).
7. Greek culture and education at the time of Christ had hardened into an unrealistic system that welcomed the infusion of new Christian ideas.
8. The Greeks had no respect for the Jewish and Christian scriptures, but were anxious to dissect Christian concepts.
9. Christian orthodoxy overwhelmed Hellenism, and, by the second century, was itself overwhelmed by the assumptions and thinking of the philosophers.
10. Greek intellectuals reacted to Christianity with an effort to revitalize Hellenism. They established Neoplatonism which was championed by Plotinus.
11. Greek techniques of allegorical interpretation affected the Apologists, who followed Philo and Aristobulus in asserting that Old Testament references to the physical attributes and activities of God were allusions to what they thought were metaphysical characteristics.
12. The Greek love for speeches turned teaching into preaching in the early Church fueled by the applause of the congregation.
13. The historic rift between the Jews and the Gentiles kept the Jews from adopting metaphysics. This made it difficult to communicate the Gospel to Greeks without their putting a metaphysical slant on the literal and figurative teachings of the Hebrew scriptures.
14. Jewish commandments were merely ethical standards to the Greeks; likewise, Jewish revelations from God were nothing more than skillful teachings to the Greeks.
15. Because of their culture and education, it was impossible for the Greeks to leave Christianity in the pure form delivered to them by Jewish Christians.

Part II

How Greek Philosophy Influenced Early Christianity: The Theological Apostasy

Paul

*Beware lest any man spoil you
through philosophy and vain deceit,
after the tradition of men,
after the rudiments of the world,
and not after Christ.*

Colossians 2:8

Foundations of the Theological Apostasy

It may seem incongruous that, following the lengthy preparation of the Gentiles for their role as standard bearers of the Gospel, apostasy should occur so quickly at their hands. Yet that very turn of events was predicted by Isaiah, the same prophet who foretold the coming of the Gentile era in the first place (Isa. 60:2; see also Amos 8:11). Among Bible scholars, prophesies of an apostasy from the teachings of Christ are well known. The issue for them is not whether it would occur, but when.

Mormonism teaches that it has already occurred. The next four chapters will explore when and how the truth about God was lost by the early Christian Church.

Evidence of the Apostasy

Until recently, it would have been unnecessary to prove to Protestant theologians that prophesies of a great apostasy were fulfilled during the Dark Ages, when the Church was under Roman rule. Today, however, many Evangelical Christian scholars deny that any such apostasy occurred. They still look to the future for those prophecies to be fulfilled. But there are many clear signs that the original Protestant position, which taught that the apostasy has already taken place, was correct.

That the great apostasy prophesied in scripture has already occurred can be seen from several changes in Christ's Church that are observable today with the aid of 20-20 hindsight. The most significant evidence, however, comes from the early Church history and writings that will be reviewed below and in the chapters that follow. That review will demonstrate that an apostasy in regard to the central points of biblical theology was complete by the end of the second century A.D.

The downhill progress of the early Church in the centuries that followed its rise to power is merely the outward evidence of what was a subtle beginning—the assimilation of Greek culture and thought. While widespread and significant, this subtle beginning was almost undetectable against the prevailing background of extreme heresies that confronted the early Church. As will be seen in Chapter 7, the heretics taught doctrines so far afield from biblical truth that their errors were obvious even to those who were toying with the issues that would lead the Church into theological apostasy.

With the profusion of heresies that bombarded the early Church, and with the gradual loss of biblical truths to the inroads of Hellenism, confusion infected even the finest of the early Christian scholars. Tertullian, for example, first converted to Christianity, then gravitated toward one of the heretical sects as the early Church slid further into error. Given the pressures brought to bear on the young Church, what is really amazing is not that the apostasy occurred, but that it did not result in an even greater departure from the truth.

Signs of the Apostasy: Lack of Unity

The Apostle Paul said there is "one Lord, one faith, one baptism, one God and Father of all" (Eph. 4:5-6). He referred to the Church as "one body in Christ" (Rom. 12:5), and admonished the members to "be of one mind" (2 Cor. 13:11). Likewise, Christ prayed earnestly to the Father that all who would believe in Him would be one, as He and the Father are one (John 17:20-21). Yet today, thousands of denominations claim to be Christian. This diversity differs significantly from the condition of the Church in the first centuries after Christ. Then a single Christian Church could be identified despite the fact that it was pitted against a myriad of heretical sects. Today, there is diversity even among the groups acknowledged to be following Christian orthodoxy.

Some argue that churches established during or after the Protestant Reformation, including those that make claims to new or different revelations of Christianity (e.g., Christian Science), do not detract from the unity of the Christian Church because they are not a part of it. They say that these churches departed from Christianity and, therefore, are cults with no claim to the original Church. Technically, that argument would not apply to The Church of Jesus Christ of Latter-day Saints, which claims to be the original Church established by Christ, restored to the earth today through divine intervention. Those who claim a direct connection to their church by historical descent from Christ's original Church are not united either. They include both the Roman Catholic and Greek Orthodox Churches, which have been at odds for centuries.

Others argue that belief in certain theological doctrines associated with Christian orthodoxy is enough to satisfy the biblical demand for unity in the Lord's Church. They minimize the differences between sects, claiming that their differences only relate to points of doctrine on which disagreement does not affect one's salvation. Believing in the right God and the right method of salvation are the real necessities of Christian unity, according to this group.

The truth is that the level of diversity found in orthodox Christian denominations today directly controverts the prayers, admonitions and teachings of Christ and His Apostles cited above. Heretical groups may be that divergent, but, a more perfect unity was always a characteristic of Christ's Church (see, e.g., Rom. 12:5; 1 Cor. 1:10; 2 Cor. 13:11; Philip. 1:27; 1 Pet. 3:8). Whether the Mormon claim of being the restored Church (Acts 3:20-21) is accepted or not, there can be no question that something changed the Church Christ established after He and His Apostles died, just as the New Testament foretold (see, e.g., Matt. 7:15; 24:11, 24; Mark 13:22; 2 Tim. 4:2-4; 2 Pet. 2:1; and 1 John 4:1). That change involved a significant level of departure from the Bible's teachings, and a loss of the perfect unity the Apostles admonished.

Signs of Apostasy: Adoption of Greek Philosophy

Professor James Shiel, Lecturer in Classical and Medieval Studies at the University of Sussex in England and himself a great fan of Hellenism, describes a macroscopic change in early Christianity in his introduction to *Greek Thought and the Rise of Christianity*. The transformation he describes from the perspective of a non-Christian is indicative of more than a change in culture. It is a sign of the apostasy. He writes as follows:

> The student of Greek thought wonders what to make of the New Testament. The book is printed in the same Greek alphabet as his other texts and he is aware that among papyrus discoveries fragments of this

book have appeared alongside those of the pagan Greek literature, written in the same style of handwriting and obviously belonging to the same ancient world. Yet when he attempts to read this document of the ancient mind he is surprised. Its style of expression is not that of the Greek he knows. *It feels rather like a veneer of Greek over a Semitic mode of expression.* Though the book deals with wisdom and morality he sees little hope of finding in it the congenial and lucid thoughts of the Greek thinkers. *And that little hope will vanish if he happens to notice in Saint Paul's letters a severe warning against Greek philosophy as a dangerous deception.*

If from here he moves forward to the Christian Greek writing of only a few generations later he comes upon a reversed situation. The religious message is now framed in philosopher's language, reminiscent at every turn of Heraclitus or Plato or Aristotle or Cleanthes or Epictetus. Indeed, the Christian religion is now occasionally called a philosophy and its founder described as a philosopher. One Christian bishop, Phileas, on trial before the Roman magistrate Cucianus in A.D. 303, says that Paul himself was the greatest of the Greeks and a finer philosopher than Plato.[1]

So dramatic a change does not go unnoticed by historians. Orthodox theologians have recognized the Greek influence on Christianity for centuries, but their claim has always been that Greek thought merely aided in the development of the rudimentary concepts revealed in the New Testament. In their opinion, Greek philosophy and rhetoric allowed the early Church to arrive at a better understanding of the deeper truths about God that were only intimated in the Bible, but are now embodied in their fullness in Christian orthodoxy.

Were that the case, there would have been no need for Paul's warning in Colossians 2:8. In the light of that warning, this clearly detectable change is patent evidence of the apostasy. The failure of the early Church to heed Paul's words resulted in significant departures from biblical truth. These departures relate precisely to the observations made by Dr. Shiel—the adoption of Greek thinking by Church leaders.

Signs of Apostasy: Behavior of Church Leaders

Perhaps the most telling evidence of the apostasy is found in the horrors of the Dark Ages perpetrated in the name of Christianity. The

---

[1] Shiel, *Greek Thought*, 1.

behavior of men who occupied the papal see is exactly what Protestant writers in past centuries associated with the apostasy or falling away prophesied in scripture.

Paul, writing to the Thessalonians in 51 A.D., prophesied of an apostasy that would precede the Second Coming, and described a notable change in the behavior of the head of the Church as one sign of that apostasy. In 2 Thessalonians 2:1-4 (NASB), he said:

> Now we request you, brethren, with regard to the coming of our Lord Jesus Christ, and our gathering together to Him,
>
> that you may not be quickly shaken from your composure or be disturbed either by a spirit or a message or a letter as if from us, to the effect that the day of the Lord has come.
>
> Let no one in any way deceive you, for *it will not come unless the apostasy comes first,* and the man of lawlessness [KJV: "sin"] is revealed, the son of destruction,
>
> *who opposes and exalts himself above every so-called god or object of worship, so that he takes his seat in the temple of God, displaying himself as being God.*

The last two verses of this passage have traditionally been interpreted by Protestant theologians as a reference to the papacy.[2] In discussing this passage, Dr. MacKnight, a noted Protestant commentator, states:

> As it is said, the man of sin was *to be revealed in his season*, there can be little doubt that *the dark ages*, in which all learning was overturned by the irruption of the northern barbarians, *were the season allotted to the man of sin for revealing himself.* Accordingly we know, that in these ages, the corruptions of Christianity, and the usurpations of the clergy, were carried to the greatest height. In short, the annals of the world cannot produce person and events to which the things written in this passage can be applied with so much fitness as to the bishops of Rome [some emphasis in original].[3]

Today many Evangelical Christians deny that Roman Catholicism, with which they disagree in many respects, ever lost the fundamental beliefs of Christian theology. Surprisingly, that position actually

---

[2] Adam Clarke, *Bible Commentary*, quoted in Talmage, *The Great Apostasy*, 37-38, 50.

[3] Quoted from Talmage, *The Great Apostasy*, 149.

Foundations of the Theological Apostasy

strengthens their claim to be a true part of the body of Christ. To admit the occurrence of apostasy undermines not only the Roman Catholics but all whose theology is derived from their tradition.

Papal behavior during the Dark Ages, however, supports Dr. McKnight's conclusions. It so contrasts with the behavior of Christ and His Apostles one can hardly argue that there was any vestige of Christ's Church left by 1000 A.D. The actions of just two Popes who lived during that period, John XII (956 A.D.) and Benedict IX (1033 A.D.), are described in the following excerpt from J. W. Draper's *Intellectual Development of Europe* as an example of the behavior in question:

> John was only nineteen years old when he thus became the head of Christendom. His reign was characterized by the most shocking immoralities, so that the Emperor Otho I was compelled by the German clergy to interfere. A synod was summoned for his trial in the Church of St. Peter, before which it appeared that John had received bribes for the consecration of bishops; that he had ordained one who was but ten years old, and had performed that ceremony over another in a stable; *he was charged with incest with one of his father's concubines, and with so many adulteries that the Lateran Palace had become a brothel; he put out the eyes of one ecclesiastic, and castrated another, both dying in consequence of their injuries; he was given to drunkenness, gambling and the invocation of Jupiter and Venus.* . . . [H]e was deposed, and Leo VII elected in his stead, A.D. 963; but subsequently getting the upper hand, he seized his antagonists, cut off the hand of one, the nose, finger, and tongue of others. His life was eventually brought to an end by the vengeance of a man whose wife he had seduced.
>
> . . . It seemed impossible that things could become worse: yet Rome had still to see Benedict IX, A.D. 1033, a boy of less than twelve years, raised to the apostolic throne. Of this pontiff, one of his successors, Victor III, declared that *his life was so shameful, so foul, so execrable, that he shuddered to describe it. He ruled like a captain of banditti rather than a prelate.* The people at last, unable to bear his adulteries, homicides, and abominations any longer, rose against him. In despair of maintaining his position, *he put up the papacy at an auction.* It was bought by a presbyter named John, who became Gregory VI, A.D. 1045.[4]

---

[4] J. W. Draper, *Intellectual Development of Europe*, 1:12:378-381, quoted in Talmage, *The Great Apostasy*, 144-147.

These horrors from the Dark Ages are not denied by Roman Catholics, nor are they cited here to cast aspersions on that division of Christianity today. They merely demonstrate what many non-Mormon theologians have long recognized, namely that something went terribly wrong in the early Church of Jesus Christ, as prophesied by Paul and others. Just why and how this occurred can be seen from a close examination of the events that occurred during the first few centuries after Christ.

Causes of Apostasy: Heresy

In the two centuries that followed Christ's death, early Church writers documented 156 heretical Christian sects, of which 32 were significant movements.[5] With so many points of doctrine being misunderstood or misrepresented, it is amazing that more error was not introduced into the early Church. The major heresies will be reviewed in a later chapter, but the effect of these heresies was magnified by the evident lack of training in the fundamentals of the Gospel that prevailed among Church leaders in the second century A.D. That lack of training was largely the result of the widespread and extensive persecution of the early Church by Rome.

Causes of Apostasy: Early Persecution

For nearly three hundred years after the Church's inception, Christians were subjected to lethal persecution at the official hands of the Roman Empire and other groups. This persecution was often inflamed or perpetrated by sources within the Jewish community. Christ Himself was put to death under such circumstances—sentenced under Roman authority at the insistence of Jewish leaders. John's brother, James, suffered martyrdom in about 47 A.D. under Herod Agrippa. James, the Lord's brother, was stoned to death in Jerusalem in 62 A.D. by order of the high priest Ananus, who took advantage of the death of Festus, the Roman procurator, to have James sentenced by an irregular court.[6]

The Lord's brother was devout in his practice of both Christianity and the Law of Moses, and was widely respected by both Christians and Jews, many of whom called him "the just man." Until his murder there

---

[5] Kidd, *History of the Church*, 1:193.
[6] Gwatkin, *Early Church History*, 1:85.

was a kind of uneasy peace between the two groups, the Christians of that era being primarily Jewish. Many Christian Jews continued to observe the Law of Moses, remaining devout in their Judaism as they lived the Gospel of Christ. Christianity was viewed by many as true Messianic Judaism. The death of James the Just marked a point when coexistence was no longer tolerated. After the death of the Lord's brother in 62 A.D., one could be either a Jew or a Christian, but not both.

This was the turning point in the transition from Jewish to Gentile dominance of the Church. It was at this time that some Apostles and other leaders moved to Asia Minor, John to Ephesus and Philip to Heirapolis. Andrew is believed to have lived in that vicinity as well.[7] Thereafter, greater efforts were made to proselyte the Gentiles and the focus of missionary efforts turned away from the Jews.

The Jews suffered terribly following the stoning of James, and many among them attributed their subsequent fate to that act. Jerusalem fell and the Temple was destroyed by Rome in 70 A.D., and the Jews were banished from the Holy Land on pain of death. After that, their influence on the early Church began to diminish. Still, they aided in fomenting persecution for many years and have been accused of inciting the persecutions that resulted in the martyrdom of Polycarp and other Christian leaders at Smyrna in the mid-second century.[8]

Peter and Paul were put to death in Rome during the persecutions under Nero that lasted from 64 to 68 A.D.[9] Nero's actions set a precedent in the annals of history. The law he established was one of annihilation. He decreed that "it is not lawful for you [Christians] to exist."[10] During these persecutions, Christians were nailed on crosses, sewn up in the skins of wild beasts and exposed to the fury of dogs, or smeared with flammable materials and lit up like torches.[11]

John was banished to the Isle of Patmos during the persecutions under Domitian that began in approximately 93 A.D. One naturally wonders why John was simply banished while the other Apostles were put to death. According to Tertullian, John's banishment followed an attempt to kill him by immersing him in burning oil, from

---

[7] Gwatkin, *Early Church History*, 1:61.
[8] E.g., *Ibid.*, 1:148.
[9] *Ibid.*, 1:81-82.
[10] Kidd, *History of the Church*, 1:58.
[11] Tacitus, *Annals*, 15:44, quoted in Talmage, *The Great Apostasy*, 69.

which, as Tertullian put it, he "took no hurt."[12] It was on Patmos that he wrote the Book of Revelation in approximately 95 A.D. After the death of Domitian, John left Patmos and returned to Ephesus.

Persecution also arose under Roman declaration during the reign of Trajan, who ruled from 98 to 117 A.D. During these persecutions, as with each of the ten official Roman persecutions,[13] the law originated by Nero was revived, so that failure to renounce their faith meant Christians would be put to death.[14]

Many historians believe John was put to death in Ephesus during the Trajan persecutions (sometime between 100 and 105 A.D., after the completion of the Fourth Gospel).[15] However, there is no authoritative account of his death. Irenaeus says John lived up to the time of Trajan and published his Gospel in Ephesus during the rule of that Emperor, while the Book of Revelation was written earlier, during the reign of Domitian.[16] Mormons teach that John did not die, but was preserved alive to see the coming of the Lord. Nevertheless, there is no question that his ministry to the early Church ended sometime before 117 A.D.

It is likely that the remainder of the original Twelve met their fate during the persecutions under Trajan, if not earlier. Tradition has it that Andrew was crucified at Patras in Achaea on an X-shaped cross. Bartholomew, which is likely the surname of the Apostle Nathanael, is said to have been either beheaded or flayed alive and crucified. Simon, the brother of the Lord, was martyred in 107 A.D., clearly a victim of Trajan's persecution. There is no reliable information about the fate of the other Apostles, but their ages at the time Christ selected them suggest that by 100 A.D. they had all passed away of natural causes or were martyred.

---

[12] Tertullian, *On the Prescription of the Church Against Heresies*, 36. This story is discounted by Kidd, *History of the Church*, 1:62.

[13] The ten, and the approximate dates (A.D.) of their persecutions are: Nero, 64-68, Domitan, 93-96, Trajan, 98-117, Marcus Aurelius and his son Commodus, 161-185, Septimus Severus, 202-211, Maximin, 235-238, Decius, 249-251, Gallus, 251-253, Valerian, 257-261, Diocletian, 303-313.

[14] Letter of Trajan to Pliny, from Joseph Milner, *History of the Church of Christ*, 1810 ed., Cent. II, ch. 1, quoted in Talmage, *The Great Apostasy*, 80-81.

[15] Kidd, *History of the Church*, 1:59; see also *Encyclopaedia Britannica*, 1960 ed., s.v. "John, Gospel of St."

[16] *Encyclopaedia Britannica*, 1960 ed., s.v. "John, Saint."

Despite their severity, these persecutions did not hinder the spread of Christianity. Many early Church members looked upon martyrdom as a blessing. Justin Martyr argued forcefully in his *First Apology* (written to the Roman Emperor, Titus, in about 150 A.D.), "You can do no more, as I have already said, than put us to death, which to us indeed involves no loss, but to you, and to all who persecute us unjustly, and do not repent, brings eternal punishment by fire."[17]

Similar sentiments were expressed by Ignatius, who was the bishop of Antioch in Asia Minor until about 107 A.D. when he was martyred during Trajan's persecutions. On his way to be fed to lions in Rome, he wrote these poignant words to the early Church members:

> I write to the churches, and I declare to all, that willingly I die for God, if it be that you hinder me not. I beg of you, do not become to me an unseasonable love. Let me be of the beasts, by whose means I am enabled to obtain God. I am God's wheat, and by the teeth of the beasts am I ground, that I may be found God's pure bread. Rather entreat kindly the beasts that they may be a grave for me, and may leave nothing of my body; that not even when I am fallen asleep, I may be a burden upon any man. Then I shall be in truth a disciple of Jesus Christ, when the world seeth not even my body. Supplicate our Lord for me, that by these instruments I may be found a sacrifice to God.[18]

Despite Justin's arguments and Ignatius' willing march to martyrdom, and despite the futility of the first three Roman persecutions in hindering the spread of Christianity, they had one very profound effect on the early Church. With but two known exceptions, they resulted in the death or banishment of *all* the knowledgeable and experienced leadership of the early Church. The leadership of the Church were the most notorious of Christians, so they were the first to fall when persecution began. Reliable historical sources indicate that Peter and Paul were martyred on the very first day of Nero's decree.[19]

This left the early Church essentially rudderless. Of those who were known to have received instruction directly from the Apostles, few survived the beginning of the second century. Seven years after the end of the first century, the original Apostles were in their graves and only two of the Apostolic Fathers are known to have remained alive: Polycarp of

---

[17] Justin, *First Apology*, 45.
[18] Ignatius, *Epistle to the Romans*, 4.
[19] Kidd, *History of the Church*, 1:58-59.

Smyrna and Papias of Hierapolis. These men, though revered for their age were not respected for their scholarship and so had little influence on the Church as it attempted to rebuild in the early second century.

Beginnings of Apostasy: Writings of the Apostolic Fathers

The Apostolic Age in early Church history is usually measured by the lives of the Apostles and the Apostolic Fathers, the early Church leaders who knew the Apostles and learned directly from them. Their era ended in approximately the middle of the second century with the deaths of the last, Polycarp and Papias, at the hands of pagan persecutors. Their writings are regarded as extremely important, especially by those who argue that they show early support for the non-biblical doctrines later adopted by the Apologists. In fact, there is little basis for that claim. A review of their teachings is essential to an understanding of the foundations of the theological apostasy.

Clement of Rome

Probably the earliest document written by an Apostolic Father is the *First Epistle to the Corinthians*, written by Clement of Rome, who is believed to have died in 101 A.D. during the Trajan persecutions. It is filled with quotations from the scriptures, and calls the Corinthians to repentance, citing their pride, division and error in following after numerous heretical sects. Nothing Clement writes is inconsistent with the Bible, as is readily apparent from the passages of scripture he quotes frequently in support of his advice.[20]

The writings of the Apostolic Fathers were characterized by instructions encouraging members to follow their local leaders faithfully. This was clearly part of an effort to maintain order while the Church hierarchy was under lethal attack. At the time Clement wrote his epistle, the failure to heed duly ordained leaders of the early Church in Corinth had become so severe that a bishop had actually been thrown out of office by the local congregation. Regarding that situation, Clement wrote the following wise words that reveal the extent to which the local churches were even then starting to fall from correct practices:

---

[20] George P. Fisher, ed., *Early Church Literature Primers* (New York: D. Appleton and Company, 1884), 1:27, et seq.

And our apostles also knew, through our Lord Jesus Christ, that there would be strife on account of the office of the bishop. For this reason, therefore, inasmuch as they had obtained a perfect foreknowledge of this, they appointed those [ministers] already mentioned, and afterward they laid down a rule that when these should fall asleep, other approved men should succeed them in their ministry. We are of opinion therefore, that those appointed by them, *or afterwards by other eminent men, with the consent of the whole Church*, and who have blamelessly served the flock of Christ in a humble, peaceable, and disinterested spirit, and have for a long time possessed the good opinion of all, cannot be justly dismissed from the ministry. For our sin will not be small, if we eject from the bishopric those who have blamelessly and holily presented the offerings [of that office]. Blessed are those elders who, having finished their course before now, have obtained a fruitful and perfect departure [from this world]; for they have no fear lest any one deprive them of the place now appointed them. But we see that ye have removed some men of excellent behavior from the ministry, which they fulfilled blamelessly and with honor.[21] [Brackets are fillers for gaps in the original text.]

Roman Catholics argue that this part of Clement's epistle supports their claim to supremacy in the papal see, but that interpretation is strained at best. The phrase appearing in italics ("or afterwards by other eminent men") is from the translation of Roberts and Donaldson in *The Ante-Nicene Fathers*, 1:17. It has been broadly interpreted by Roman Catholics as justification for their practice of electing the Bishop of Rome through the College of Cardinals. The Lightfoot translation reads "men of repute" (*Early Church Literature*, 1:9). It is possible that the Greek word so translated was meant to refer to men holding a specific calling in the early Church. In any case, the phrase no doubt refers to faithful men who held the priesthood authority necessary to ordain ("appoint") new bishops.

The language obviously does not specify the current arrangement for electing the Pope in the Roman Catholic Church, and that body makes no claim that their election method is the result of revelation, as is the case in Mormonism. Therefore, the LDS practice regarding the calling and ordination of bishops is, at the very least, equally worthy of support from these words. This is especially true in light of the phrase

---

[21] Clement, *First Epistle to the Corinthians*, 44.

that follows, "with the consent of the whole church." That phrase suggests that the practice in the early Church, as in The Church of Jesus Christ of Latter-day Saints today, was to obtain the sustaining vote of all members of the Church in favor of their leadership, not just a select group of leaders.

Ignatius of Antioch

In his epistles, written largely while en route to Rome in 107 A.D. where he was to be executed, Ignatius of Antioch also exhorted early Church members to follow their local leaders so as not to be led astray by false teachers. Regarding Church government, he said "It is not lawful apart from the bishop to baptize or to hold a love-feast."[22] The "love-feast," or *Agapé*, was a Sunday evening meeting at which the Sacrament of the Lord's Supper was regularly practiced in the early Church (until about 150 A.D. when the Sacrament was moved to the Sunday morning meeting).[23]

The letters attributed to Ignatius have caused great controversy among scholars over the centuries. Clearly, eight of the fifteen letters originally attributed to Ignatius are spurious. Of the seven that remain there are fragments of both a long and a short Greek version. Of these, it is unknown which, if either version, is the original. Only three of these seven (the ones to Polycarp, the Ephesians and the Romans) are found in the Syriac version, which is considered by many to be the most accurate.[24]

It is claimed that Ignatius wrote the following in chapter 7 of his epistle to the Church in Smyrna (short Greek version): "The heretics abstain from Eucharist [the Sacrament of the Lord's Supper] because they do not allow that the Eucharist is the flesh of Christ." This letter is not found in the Syriac version,[25] which may not be considered determinative, but the quoted language is missing entirely from the long Greek version, which makes its authenticity even more suspect.

Ignatius appears to have understood the benefits of having a physical body—of flesh being combined with spirit permanently, as will be

---

[22] Ignatius, *Epistle to the Smyrnaeans*, 8. Ignatius' epistles clearly indicate that in his day a bishop was like the pastor of a local church, just as is the case in the Mormon Church today.
[23] Gwatkin, Early Church History, 1:254-256.
[24] *Ante-Nicene Fathers*, 1:46-48.
[25] *Ibid.*, 47.

the case for Man in the resurrection and as was the case for Christ following His resurrection. This appears from the following statement in the Syriac version of his letter to Polycarp:

> For this reason thou art [composed] of both flesh and spirit, that thou mayest deal with those things which are visible before thy face, and mayest ask, as to those which are concealed from thee, that they [too] may be revealed to thee, in order that thou be deficient in nothing, and mayest abound in all gifts.[26]

This is strong evidence that early Christianity believed God was corporeal. Later writers clearly adopted the Greek and oriental distaste for the flesh and attributed to God a purely spiritual form. If Ignatius had recognized the efficacy of a body composed of both flesh and spirit, it is likely he recognized it as a characteristic of God. The idea that God has a body is clearly tied to the resurrection of Christ, and Ignatius firmly taught the Church at Smyrna that Christ had been physically resurrected and was, in his opinion, still possessed of a physical body in his day (107 A.D.).[27]

As for his theological understanding of the relationship between the Father and the Son, a spurious letter to the Antiochians has Ignatius saying, "He also that confesseth Christ, yet not as the Son of the Maker of the world, but of some other unknowable being, different from Him whom the law and the prophets have proclaimed, this man is an instrument of the devil."[28] This language contradicts the idea of an incomprehensible God, and implies that such a notion is contrary to the way God is described in the Bible. Incomprehensibility is a characteristic of God that was regularly attributed to him by the Greek philosophers in part because their metaphysical theories about Him could not be rationalized with the problem of evil.

The context of this phrase in the Antiochian letter suggests an attempt to counter heresies that were importing Greek metaphysical notions about the Father and the Son into the teachings of the Church. The ideas being countered in this passage are contrary to those that later bore sway in the writings of the Apologists, as will be seen in the next chapter.

---

[26] Ignatius, *Epistle to Polycarp*, 2 (Syriac Version).
[27] *Epistle to the Smyrnaeans*, 3 (both short and long versions); *Ante-Nicene Fathers*, 1:87.
[28] Ignatius, *Epistle to the Antiochians*, 5. *Ibid*, 1:111.

The spurious nature of the *Epistle to the Antiochians*, however, is evident from a reference in a later section of the letter to Church officers that had no existence until much later in Church history (e.g., "confessors"). Yet if any portion of it was actually written by Ignatius, it would suggest an effort consistent with that of Paul to counter the inroads of Greek philosophy that were even then beginning to appear in the early Church.

That conclusion, on the other hand, appears to be contradicted by a statement in Ignatius' letter to Polycarp in the Syriac version. In that letter he appears to confuse the persons of the Father and the Son in the following language:

Syriac version:

> Be discerning of the times. Look for Him that is above the times, Him who has no times, Him who is invisible, Him who for our sakes became visible, Him who is impalpable, Him who is impassible, Him who for our sakes suffered, Him who endured everything in every form for our sakes.[29]

Here Ignatius describes God as "above the times," and as having "no times." Notably, his reference is in the plural and is made in context with a reference to "the times," which Ignatius wants Polycarp to discern. This suggests that he is speaking figuratively about something that is real, i.e., the evil times then befalling the Church. It is not phrased strictly as a reference to the metaphysical idea that God is above time. The New Testament clearly describes God the Father as invisible (Col. 1:15), and explains that, in a figurative sense, He "for our sakes became visible" through the incarnation of Christ. All Men can know what the Father is like by looking to Christ (John 14:7-9; Col. 1:15; Heb. 1:1-3, et al.).

But the words "impalpable" and "impassible" appear nowhere in sacred writ. The Apostolic Fathers in general followed the scriptures. They were not innovators. The term "impalpable" means "untouchable," incapable of being perceived through the sense of touch. But Christ was clearly palpable after His resurrection. Indeed, He invited His Apostles to touch Him in the upper room (Luke 24:39). If He had his body in Ignatius' day, as Ignatius testified to Polycarp (see above),

---

[29] Ignatius, *Epistle to Polycarp*, 3. Ante-Nicene Fathers, 1:99.

He could hardly be described as "impalpable," as the above passage does.

"Impassible" means without passions, emotionless or unaffected by emotion. This is not a term used in the Bible or implied by any of its passages. It is a purely Greek concept, describing the Immovable Mover Aristotle envisioned. Scriptural references to the "wrath" of God show clearly that the God of the Bible is definitely "passable" (righteously, of course). The word "impassible" is, therefore, incongruous coming from the pen of an Apostolic Father.

Because of these discrepancies, it will be useful to compare the short and long Greek versions of this passage with the Syriac version quoted above.

The short Greek version:

> Look for Him who is above all time, eternal and invisible, yet who became visible for our sakes; impalpable and impassible, yet who became passable on our account; and who in every kind of way suffered for our sakes.[30]

The long Greek version:

> Look for Christ, the Son of God; who was before time, yet appeared in time; who was invisible by nature, yet visible in the flesh; who was impalpable, and could not be touched, as being without a body, but for our sakes became such, might be touched and handled in the body; who was impassible as God, but became passable for our sakes as man; and who in every kind of way suffered for our sakes.[31]

These versions contain distinct references to the metaphysical idea of God being transcendent in the sense of being above and outside of time. However, there is greater clarity with respect to the persons of the Father and the Son in the long version. That version seems focused on one person, "Christ, the Son of God." The short version does not make that distinction and so could be viewed as a reference to the Trinity.

The inconsistencies and contradictions between these three versions make any attempt to use them as a guide to the actual thinking of Ignatius in 107 A.D. next to impossible. It would be pure guesswork to accept the theological implications of any one of these three versions as

---

[30] *Ante-Nicene Fathers*, 1:94.
[31] *Ibid.*

an indication of the earliest Christian beliefs about the issues they raise. As will be shown later, it was not uncommon in the second and third centuries to change the writings of earlier Church fathers to make them appear consistent with whichever theory was then being espoused. This may have been the fate of Ignatius' original writings.

What is clear from his epistles is that Ignatius was firm in upholding the literal resurrection of Christ against the heresies of the docetes (to be discussed in Chapter 7), and in rejecting the return to Judaistic ritual recommended by the Judaizing Ebionites of his day (their doctrines will also be discussed in Chapter 7). His writings in this regard are consistent both internally and with the Bible.

Ignatius is the most respected and oft quoted of the Apostolic Fathers. However, his focus was not on theology but on preserving order in the early Church through difficult times. His letters were not in the style of the later writings of the Apologists, which were clearly influenced by Greek rhetoric and style. Philosophical buzzwords adopted from Greek rather than sacred writings were not used extensively by Ignatius as far as scholars can determine. That is about all that can be concluded from the writings of Ignatius available today. The controversy over the authenticity of his letters makes it difficult to draw any other conclusions about his theology.

Polycarp of Smyrna

During the season of relative peace that followed the Trajan persecution, greater communication and freedom of expression fostered the apologetic developments that began in approximately 130 A.D. and flourished during the latter half of the second century. The largest and most influential population center of the time was Rome, and there the Church both flourished and grew lax. Of the two Apostolic Fathers who survived Trajan's persecution, neither lived at Rome, and while Rome respected these men, it did not demonstrate that respect by following their precepts.

This period of transition, from apostolic teaching to apologetic philosophizing, was observed, almost from beginning to end, by one man, Polycarp, whose lengthy service in the early Church bridged the gap between the Apostolic Age and the age of the Apologists. He was the bishop of Smyrna from at least the time of Ignatius' martyrdom in 107 A.D. until his own murder at the hands of a pagan mob in 155.

Foundations of the Theological Apostasy   101

During his life, he became sick almost to death of the heresies developing within the Church. On one occasion, he wrote:

> For every one who shall not confess that Jesus Christ is come in the flesh is antichrist; and whosoever shall not confess the testimony of the Cross is of the devil; and whosoever shall pervert the oracles of the Lord to his own lusts and say that there is neither resurrection nor judgment, that man is the firstborn of Satan. Wherefore let us forsake their vain doing and their false teaching and turn unto the word which was delivered unto us from the beginning.[32]

The progress of apostasy in spite of all opposition by the Apostolic Fathers was apparently a cause of deep sorrow for Polycarp. In the last years of his life, these words are said to have been constantly on his lips: "Oh good God, to what times hast thou spared me, that I must suffer such things!"[33] These are not the words of a leader who is pleased with the status and progress of the Church in which he served. They are further evidence of the progress of apostasy.

Nor was Polycarp happy with the leadership of the Church in his age. Not long before his martyrdom, he traveled to Rome to visit Anicetus, who was then the bishop in that city. He went to discuss various problems, among them being a disagreement about the correct time of the Easter festival. Though he is said to have converted some from the heretic sects known as the Marcionites and Valentinians during his visit, he was no more successful than any of the Apostolic Fathers before him in stemming the tide of apostasy.

As Polycarp was one of the few still living who had learned directly from the Apostles, Anicetus honored him and promised to stay in communion with him, but he refused to change the custom of the Roman Church regarding the time of the Easter festival.[34] Polycarp, not wanting to undermine the authority of a fellow Church leader, was cordial and did not condemn the man, but promised to remain in close contact. It appears from his writings that he was holding his tongue.

When Polycarp returned to Smyrna, he found new pagan persecutions of Christianity sweeping Asia Minor. At a great festival in 155 A.D., the crowd, unsatisfied with the slaughter of eleven Christians mostly from Philadelphia, raised the cry, "Away with the atheists. Let

---

[32] Polycarp, *Epistle to the Philippians*, 7.
[33] *Encyclopaedia Britannica*, 1960 ed., s.v. "Polycarp."
[34] *Ibid.*

search be made for Polycarp." When he was found, the offer was made to spare his life if he would "revile Christ." To this offer he courageously responded: "Eighty and six years have I served Him and He has done me no wrong. How then can I speak evil of my King who saved me?" Having thus refused to renounce his faith, the last of the Apostolic Fathers was put to death before a mob who proclaimed "This is the teacher of Asia . . . the father of the Christians: this is the destroyer of our gods: this is the man who has taught so many no longer to sacrifice and no longer to pray to the gods."[35]

Papias of Hierapolis

The only Apostolic Father who may have survived Polycarp was Papias, the bishop of Hierapolis.[36] He is believed to have died in 155 A.D. possibly as part of the same pagan persecution that claimed the life of Polycarp. He too made every effort, yet in vain, to keep the early Church in line with the teachings and traditions of the Apostles (whom he called "the Elders," a title that will be familiar to Mormons, who use it to refer to the Apostles of this era). At the end of his life, a new day dawned for the early Church, in which Greek philosophy took the helm of a rudderless vessel and forged a new theology in the seas of unrest that were buffeting the young Church.

Hermas' Shepherd

In the midst of those seas, a notable voice cried out for repentance. It is embodied in one of the earliest documents from the second century, *The Shepherd [or "Pastor"] of Hermas*, an alleged revelation, written by Hermas, the brother of Pius (bishop of Rome from 140 to 154 A.D.). The author of the *Shepherd*, who describes himself as a prophet, recites five "Visions," and provides a segment on "Commandments," and one on "Similitudes." The longest of the visions (Vision 3) uses, as an analogy, the construction of a church out of stones. Some stones fit well, while others were cast aside. These "visions" were seen as a call to the early Church to repentance, self-mastery and righteousness.[37]

For many members of the Church in Rome at this time, Christianity had come by birth but not by conviction. Peace abounded and the

---

[35] *Encyclical Epistle of the Church at Smyrna Concerning the Martyrdom of the Holy Polycarp*, 9, 12. Ante-Nicene Fathers, 1:39-44.

[36] *Encyclopaedia Britannica*, 1960 ed., s.v. "Papias."

[37] *Encyclopaedia Britannica*, 1960 ed., s.v. "Hermas, Shepherd of"; Fisher, *Early Church Literature*, 1:101, et seq.

conditions were ripe for intellectual pursuits. Church members finally had the freedom to indulge in philosophical rhetoric and inquiry, and they found themselves divided between a recognition of the spiritual good and a desire for worldly pleasures. Some were inclined to ask, "The Christian ideal may be glorious, but is it practicable?"

To this inquiry Hermas reported the Shepherd's response in terms similar to many scriptural passages. Asking if He who made Man "to rule over all things under heaven" would give him commandments beyond his ability, the Shepherd states that, if a man "hath the Lord in his heart," he "shall know that there is nothing easier nor sweeter nor gentler than" the Lord's commandments.[38] This message is consistent with the inspired writings of James, John, and the other Apostles, as well as the Book of Mormon, and reflects an effort to help the Church overcome the trials of the early second century.

Irenaeus believed the *Shepherd* to be inspired scripture. It was similarly revered by Clement of Alexandria and Tertullian.[39] At the very least, it is of historical value for its account of the internal pressures on the Church in the early second century, and the need for repentance among its worldly members.

Still, a seed of misunderstanding and error seems to flaw one of its passages. Commandment First of Book Second begins with a sentence that could be translated as follows: "First of all, believe that there is one God who created and finished all things, and made all things out of nothing."[40] This statement was later used by the Apologists as authority for the *ex nihilo* doctrine of creation. It contradicts, however, the first Apologist, Justin Martyr, whose teachings were contemporaneous with the *Shepherd*, but Justin's teachings were consistent with both the Bible and some schools of Greek philosophy on this point.

It may be that the *Shepherd* has been mistranslated here. That possibility will be examined later. The way it was interpreted, however, provided a foundation for the swift progress of apostasy that marked the latter half of the second century, a progress that will be examined in depth in the next chapter.

---

[38] *Ibid.*
[39] Kidd, *History of the Church*, 1:141.
[40] Quoted from the translation contained in *Ante-Nicene Fathers*, 2:20.

Summary

1. The apostasy prophesied in the Bible has already occurred.
2. Lack of unity among the orthodox Christian churches of today is one evidence of the apostasy.
3. Another evidence of apostasy is the adoption by the early Church of Greek philosophical terminology and assumptions, contrary to the admonitions of Paul.
4. A third evidence of apostasy is seen in the gross misbehavior of Church leaders during the Dark Ages.
5. Extensive heresy and a lack of training in the principles of the Gospel caused confusion on doctrine in the early Church.
6. The top leaders of the early Church who died in Roman, pagan and Jewish persecutions were:
    a. James, the son of Zebedee, martyred in 47 A.D. under Herod Agrippa.
    b. James, the Lord's brother, martyred in 62 A.D. by the Jews.
    c. Peter and Paul, put to death in Rome in 64 A.D. by Nero.
    d. John the Beloved, banished to Patmos after an attempt to boil him in oil.
    e. Andrew, crucified at Patras on an "X"-shaped cross.
    f. Nathanael, surnamed Bartholomew, either beheaded, or flayed alive and crucified.
    g. Simon, the brother of the Lord, martyred in 107 A.D.
7. By 100 A.D. only a few men, known as the Apostolic Fathers, were alive who had learned from the Apostles. Only two survived past 107 A.D.
8. Clement of Rome, one of the Apostolic Fathers, documented serious departures from proper Church government in Corinth.
9. Clement of Rome taught that Peter and Paul had left instructions for authorized men to replace bishops when necessary, with the consent of the whole church.
10. Ignatius of Antioch, another of the Apostolic Fathers, upheld the authority of bishops who presided over the individual churches.
11. The writings of Ignatius of Antioch about God are shrouded in controversy over their authenticity. They do not agree completely with those of the Apologists, but they show indications of the entry of

Greek philosophical concepts about God that were not commonly thought until their era.

12. Polycarp survived Trajan's persecution to see the Church's transition from apostolic teaching to apologetic philosophizing.
13. Polycarp was bishop of Smyrna from Ignatius' martyrdom in 107 A.D. until his own martyrdom in 155 A.D.
14. Anicetus, the bishop of Rome, refused to acquiesce in Polycarp's admonitions concerning the date on which Easter was to be celebrated.
15. Papias of Hierapolis admonished adherence to the teachings of the "Elders." He was also martyred in 155 A.D.
16. Sometime between 130 and 140 A.D., Hermas' *Shepherd* raised a strong cry for repentance in the early Church, which was then becoming lax.
17. The *Shepherd* contains a possible reference to the idea of creation out of nothing, which indicates that false doctrines about God and His creation were beginning to enter the mainstream of accepted Church teachings.

6

The Apologists and the Theological Apostasy

Following the death of Trajan in 117 A.D., the Emperor Hadrian changed Roman policy toward the Church dramatically with his *Epistle on behalf of the Christians*, which restrained any action against Church members, except on the basis of adjudicated violations of the law.[1] The period of peace that followed, however, did not stem the tide of criticism or false charges against Christians, but it did provide an atmosphere conducive to intellectual exchange—circumstances ideal for the rise of the Apologists.

Criticism of the Early Church

The prevailing criticism of Christians in the second century, like that engendered against Mormons in the nineteenth century, was ill-informed and calculated to foment hatred. It was born of rumor and innuendo. Between 165 and 170 A.D., a writer named Lucian, the ancient equivalent of a tabloid journalist, amused his readers with gossip about the Christians.[2]

Among the many charges made against Christians by Lucian and others of his ilk, three were more common than any others. The most significant of these was atheism. Christians were accused of being atheists, just as Mormons are now accused of being polytheists, not because the label fit, but because it drew negative attention

---

[1] Kidd, *History of the Church*, 1:241.
[2] *Ibid.*, 1:228-229.

to the difference between the God they worshiped and the popular gods of the Gentile world.

The other two common charges were Thyestean banquets or cannibalism (more precisely ritual child-murder followed by drinking of the blood), and incest or "Oedipodean intercourse."[3] These claims were groundless and ignorant, of course, but, like modern false charges of sexual misconduct in LDS temples, they arose because knowledge about early Christian ordinances (such as the Sacrament of the Lord's Supper) was veiled from the unbaptized just as temple ordinances in The Church of Jesus Christ of Latter-day Saints are today.[4]

In time, more sophisticated critics of the early Church picked up on these themes and others. The writings of certain men were especially inflammatory. The situation cried out for a response from intelligent and educated Christians. One example of this criticism came from the noted anti-Christian writer, Celsus, who wrote a stinging criticism of Christianity in about 178 A.D. Most of his work was quoted and then refuted by Origen in his work, *Against Celsus*. The following is an example of this critic's brand of taunting denunciation. Celsus claimed "the following are the rules laid down by Christians":

> Let no one come to us who has been instructed, or who is wise or prudent (for such qualifications are deemed evil by us); but if there be any ignorant, or unintelligent, or uninstructed, or foolish person, let them come with confidence. By which words, acknowledging that such individuals are worthy of their God, they manifestly show that they desire and are able to gain over only the silly, and the mean, and the stupid, with women and children.[5]

As demonstrated in Part 1, Greek thinking was the respected form of scholarship at that time. Therefore, Celsus' attack suggests that, until at least the first half of the second century the early Church had been following Paul's admonition to avoid debates involving Greek philosophy. But, because of criticism like that from Celsus and the continuing ridicule cast upon Church members from the Hellenized world, it is not surprising that champions of Christian theology eventually tried to use Greek methods to defend the Gospel. The adoption of Greek methods to defend the Gospel became the definitive trend of the second century.

---

[3] *Ibid.*, 1:229-231.
[4] *Ibid.*, 1:231.
[5] Origen, *Against Celsus*, 3:44.

Early in the reign of Emperor Hadrian, Church members began to believe that rational philosophy was an item of pagan culture they could take as their ally in opposing popular mythology and the philosophical sects.[6] Unfortunately, with Greek methods of analysis came a way of thinking about ultimate truths that was radically different from the thinking of the Hebrews to whom the scriptures had been revealed. Misunderstanding and misinterpretations were inevitable as the early Church grew more neglectful of Paul's admonitions against Greek philosophy.

Justin Martyr, The "First" Apologist

The lives of all the Christian Apologists are worthy of a thorough study, but space does not permit more than a brief look at two of them, Justin and Irenaeus—the "first," and the most renowned, respectively. Justin, to whose name the title Martyr is commonly appended, was called the first Apologist by many historians. There are earlier apologetic writings than those of Justin Martyr, but most were of unknown authorship. Aristides, who is actually the earliest known Apologist, wrote his *Apology* in about 125 A.D., but it was not rediscovered until the last century. So, Justin has long been deemed the first. He was certainly the epitome of the ideal theologian-philosopher of his age.

He was a convert to Christianity at Ephesus, after having made a thorough study of the philosophies of the Peripatetics (the school of Aristotle), the Pythagoreans, the Stoics and the Platonists. This study convinced him that the Greek scholars had not found the truth. He was impressed, however, with the Old Testament prophets and the life and death of Jesus Christ.

After his conversion he continued to wear his philosopher's cloak, the distinctive badge of the wandering professional teacher of philosophy in that day. He went from place to place, discussing Christianity in an effort to bring educated pagans to Christ through the reasoning and analysis of the Greeks philosophers. In Rome, he gave lectures in a classroom of his own where he was frequently opposed by his fellow teachers.[7]

---

[6] Shiel, *Greek Thought*, 51.
[7] *Encyclopaedia Britannica*, 1960 ed., s.v. "Justin Martyr."

The Apologists and the Theological Apostasy

Late in his life, he wrote his famed *Apology*, now called the *First Apology* (c. 147-150 A.D.) to distinguish it from his *Second* (c. 159 A.D.). His *Dialogue with Trypho* was written near the time of his death (c. 159-165 A.D.).[8] In his *Second Apology* Justin tried to argue, from the trial of a Christian that had recently been held in Rome, that the innocence of the Christians was proven by the very persecutions they were suffering. Unfortunately, he did not convince the Roman authorities and had to flee Rome. He was himself martyred in approximately 163 A.D.[9]

Justin's writings include frequent references to the Old Testament and the inspired writings later assembled into the New Testament. His brilliant exposition of Isaiah to the Roman Emperor, Antoninus Pius, is an excellent example of his work:

> That the land of the Jews, then, was to be laid waste, hear what was said by the Spirit of prophecy. And the words were spoken as if from the person of the people wondering at what had happened. They are these: "Sion is a wilderness, Jerusalem a desolation. The house of our sanctuary has become a curse, and the glory which our fathers blessed is burned up with fire, and all its glorious things are laid waste: and Thou refrainest Thyself at these things, and hast held Thy peace, and has humbled us very sore" [Isa. 66:10-12]. And ye are convinced that Jerusalem has been laid waste, as was predicted. And concerning its desolation, and that no one should be permitted to inhabit it, there was the following prophecy by Isaiah: "Their land is desolate, their enemies consume it before them, and none of them shall dwell therein" [Isa. 1:7]. And that it is guarded by you lest any one dwell in it, and that death is decreed against a Jew apprehended entering it, you know very well [referring to the decree of Hadrian, which The Antonines refused to annul].[10]

In his *Dialogue With Trypho*, Justin describes himself as a young philosophy student, trusting in the philosophers until he meets a wise man who proves the unreliability of the philosophers as sources of knowledge about God, whom they never saw or claimed to have seen. Justin, the student, asks, "Should any one, then employ a teacher? Or

---

[8] Dates estimated by author based on Charles Cruttwell, *A Literary History of Early Christianity: Including the Fathers and the Chief Heretical Writers of the Ante-Nicene Period* (London, 1893; reprint, New York: AMS Press, 1971) 2:322.

[9] *Encyclopaedia Britannica*, 1960 ed., s.v. "Justin Martyr."

[10] Justin, *First Apology,* 47 (quoted from the translation in *Ante-Nicene Fathers*, 1:178).

whence may anyone be helped, if not even in them there is truth?" The answer underscores Justin Martyr's great respect for and reliance on the scriptures:

> There existed, long before this time, certain men more ancient than all those who are esteemed philosophers, both righteous and beloved by God, who spoke by the Divine Spirit, and foretold events which would take place, and which are now taking place. They are called prophets. These alone both saw and announced the truth to men, neither referencing nor fearing any man, not influenced by a desire for glory, but speaking those things alone which they saw and which they heard, being filled with the Holy Spirit. Their writings are still extant, and he who has read them is very much helped in his knowledge of the beginning and end of things and of those matters which the philosopher ought to know, provided he has believed them. For they did not use demonstration in their treatises, seeing that they were witnesses to the truth above all demonstration, and worthy of belief; and those events which have happened, and those which are happening, compel you to assent to the utterances made by them, although, indeed, they were entitled to credit on account of the miracles which they performed, since *they both glorified the Creator, the God and Father of all things, and proclaimed His Son, the Christ [sent] by Him:* . . . But pray that, above all things, the gates of light may be opened to you; for these things cannot be perceived or understood by all, but only by the man to whom God and His Christ have imparted wisdom.

Justin used the learned language of the Greeks and their philosophy to explain the extensive biblical passages he quotes. He gave lucid commentary on the symbolic language used by Isaiah and other early prophets to demonstrate the fulfillment of their prophesies in Christ and the events preceding and following His time. Later apologetic writing tended more to Greek methods of exegesis.

Some believe Justin may have studied under the Apostles and would count him among the Apostolic Fathers were it not for the apologetic style of his writing. However, though he was from Ephesus, it is unlikely that he learned anything from the Apostle John. He was converted, at the earliest, in his late teens, and was most likely born about 100 A.D.

Irenaeus, the Most Renowned of the Greek Apologists

Born about 120 A.D.,[11] Irenaeus was brought up in Asia Minor, where he studied at the feet of Polycarp. He spent part of his prime in Rome, where Hippolytus attended his lectures. He then became a presbyter (elder) at Lyons in southern France. When persecution broke out in that city, he was sent to Rome with letters of protest. Upon his return, in 177 A.D. after the bishop of the city had been martyred, he was made bishop of Lyons. He wrote in Greek, and so is included among those referred to as the Greek Apologists (though he never actually wrote an "Apology" to the Roman authorities).

He was diligent in missionary labor and is credited with converting most of the residents of Lyons to Christianity.[12] He sent out missionaries to much of Gaul (now France), and is highly revered for his efforts to spread Christianity throughout that region.

His principal writing is the *Refutation and Overthrow of Gnosis, falsely so called*, which has become known as *Against Heresies*. It consists of five Books that provide an extensive summary of the various Gnostic heresies then rampant in the Church. It includes his refutation of those heresies, and his explanation of the Gospel to the extent he understood it.

It is evident throughout this work that Irenaeus tried too hard to defeat the heretics on their own ground. They were essentially pagan groups whose notions were absurd, and their claims of scriptural support were obviously flawed. Rather than simply turning to scripture to prove the truth, Irenaeus used extensive philosophical arguments to overwhelm them with logic. In so doing, he made many errors of his own.

Lack of Information About the Gospel at the Time of Irenaeus

Though he received training from Polycarp as a young boy, Irenaeus was not well grounded in Gospel fundamentals. This was not because of any lack of intelligence on his part. Rather, it was a natural result of the persecutions the Church had so long endured. Polycarp was

---

[11] Kidd, *History of the Church*, 1:317. According to Gwatkin, he was born in 130. A.D. Gwatkin, *Early Church History*, 2:370.

[12] *Encyclopaedia Britannica*, 1960 ed., s.v. "Irenaeus."

one of the few who had known the Apostles, but he was not acknowledged by his contemporaries as a brilliant theologian. He was a bishop, not a philosopher, and undoubtedly he did the best he could in that capacity under the trying circumstances of the time.

In his *Letter to Florinus*, Irenaeus expresses his gratitude for all that he learned from Polycarp, but complains about his recollection of Gospel principles and rues his failure to write down the teachings of his master as follows:

> And everything that he had heard from them [the Apostles] about the Lord, about His miracles and about His teaching, Polycarp used to tell us as one who had received it from those who had seen the Word of Life with their own eyes, and all this in perfect harmony with the Scriptures. To these things I used to listen at the time, through the mercy of God vouchsafed to me, noting them down, *not on paper but in my heart*, and constantly by the grace of God *I brood over my accurate recollections.*[13]

Unfortunately, a better written record of Polycarp's teachings was not made. Indeed, written knowledge of Christ in the early second century was limited almost entirely to the four Gospels. As the noted Church historian, Henry Melvill Gwatkin, explains, "almost all other memory of Christ seems to have perished early. The scraps of genuine tradition otherwise preserved are astonishingly meager."[14] As a result, the principal difficulty faced by the Apologists was not their facility with Greek rhetoric, nor the genuineness of their devotion to Christ, but their limited knowledge of the Gospel they endeavored to defend.

This lack of information and understanding was evident, in part, from the reaction of the Church to the open apostasy of many early Church leaders. Some of the greatest of the Apologists went astray, some grossly. Tatian, for example, became a radical Gnostic after the death of his teacher, Justin Martyr. Tertullian departed from the Church around the turn of the century on what he thought were sound doctrinal grounds. Yet, their writings are still relied upon for many fundamental aspects of the concept of God embraced by classical theists, and they remain among the most eminent Christian teachers of the time. Instead,

---

[13] *Encyclopaedia Britannica*, 1960 ed., s.v. "Polycarp."
[14] Gwatkin, *Early Church History*, 2:98-99.

No Clear Biblical Canon

their writings deserve some scholarly criticism, in light of their defections from biblical Christianity.

Compounding the lack of a "genuine tradition" on which the Apologists could rely was a substantial degree of uncertainty about what was really scripture. Marcion and other heretical teachers of the time (see Chapter 7) denied the validity of many crucial New Testament texts. It is easy now to look back and see that these men were heretics. Polycarp immediately recognized Marcion as "the firstborn of Satan,"[15] but he was thought by some of his contemporaries to have been harsh in that judgment. The fact that Marcion, Valentinus and other heretics were not immediately identified as apostates and excommunicated is another sign of the confusion and lack of understanding that prevailed then.

An indicator of this problem is found in the fact that, after Tatian became a heretic, he compiled a comprehensive harmony of the Gospels from which he excluded those portions that discredited or disagreed with his heretical doctrines.[16] Despite the fact that he was branded a heretic by Irenaeus in the late second century, his harmony of the Gospels (called the *Diatessaron*) was widely used in the Church for decades. In fact, during the entire third century, it was the only text from which the Gospel narrative was read in many Syriac-speaking branches of the early Church.[17]

In addition to the effort by some to discredit valid scripture, many questionable texts were being given canonical status. Hermas' *Shepherd* is one example. Another is the *Didaché*, known commonly as *The Teaching of the Apostles*.[18] Written in approximately 120 A.D.,[19] the latter was a manual of instruction and worship commonly used at the time, much as handbooks of priesthood instruction are used by LDS bishops today. The *Epistle of Barnabus* and several other apocryphal works were also in circulation at the time, and many believed them to be scripture.

---

[15] Kidd, *History of the Church*, 1:182.
[16] *Ante-Nicene Fathers*, 2:63.
[17] Kidd, *History of the Church*, 1:200-201.
[18] Full title: *The teachings of the Lord to the Gentiles by the Twelve Apostles*. Lightfoot, *Apostolic Fathers* (abridged edition), 215-35.
[19] *Ante-Nicene Fathers*, 7:375.

The books of the New Testament that were ultimately accepted as inspired were also widely circulated then, but the lack of a defined canon caused confusion. Specifically, it encouraged a willingness to look outside scriptural sources, to philosophical reasoning, in the effort to resolve questions on doctrine.

Greek Exegesis Resulted in Inaccurate Interpretation

In addition to their uncertainty about the New Testament canon, the Apologists had problems interpreting inspired writing. The common Greek tools of interpretation relied too heavily on allegory. These methods were imported into the early Church by the Apologists, as noted in Chapter 4.

Referring to the use of these methods by the Apologists, Gwatkin says, "it turned the Old Testament into a book of pious riddles, and parts of the New fared little better."[20] Thus, the written scriptures were of little help in preventing the Apologists from giving the Gospel their own preferred twist.

This was especially problematical as the Apologists turned their attention to interpreting figurative passages in the Hebrew scriptures about God the Father and His relationship to Christ. The Hebrews knew nothing of metaphysics and made no metaphysical assumptions in their writings (except the Alexandrian Jews at the time of Philo, to whom no scripture was revealed). For the Israelites, to whom the scriptures were addressed, if a prophet spoke of two persons, it could be reliably assumed that he really meant two real, separate individuals!

Likewise, the men who wrote the New Testament had no metaphysical assumptions in mind when they described the relationship between the Father and the Son. That their figurative language was susceptible to such interpretation, especially using the broad stroke of allegorical exegesis, is certainly true, but such an interpretation was not justified. The basic assumptions of the Hebrews were different from those of the Greeks. The Apologists, like all Greek exegetes of the time, failed to understand the significance of the fact that the scriptures were revealed to the Jews, not the Greeks.

Thus, when Christ made statements regarding His relationship to the Father, such as "I and my father are one" (John 10:30), the Apologists failed to acknowledge that He was speaking as a Jew to Jews.

---

[20] Gwatkin, *Early Church History*, 2:101.

Reality was assumed by the Jews to be real. Therefore, Christ's statements should have been seen as figurative language intended to express forcefully the perfection of unity that exists between two very real and separate persons. He would not have been speaking of two persons who were *literally* one individual, one "substance," or one *ousia*, because that notion is metaphysical and the Jews had no concept of metaphysics.

Metaphysics had no solid rules. Reality was not real, so almost anything could exist in the supposedly "real" world and be explained simply as beyond the understanding of humans who occupy the "unreal" (phenomenal) world. A kind of general logic was employed in metaphysical interpretation, but the result of this "logical" analysis did not, itself, have to be logical.

It was easy for men with the background of the Apologists to transition from a proper Hebrew interpretation of passages such as John 10:30 to a totally erroneous Greek metaphysical interpretation. That they, in fact, made that transition will be demonstrated below.

Often, Irenaeus and Athenagoras used phrases from scripture merely to support their philosophical conclusions, which they reasoned out using Greek rhetorical techniques. Though they were insightful in their analysis of Gospel principles, they did not derive their theological conclusions from the scriptures using the perspective of the Hebrews to whom those sacred writings had been revealed. Theological error was, therefore, inevitable.

Confusion Interjected by Heretics and False Teachers

Along with apocryphal writings and problematic interpretation, the Church was being presented with the writings of some very intellectual heretics. Men like Basilides (see Chapter 7) were claiming secret knowledge of the mysteries of God and some were quite astute in their presentation of that "knowledge." Basilides is credited by historians with introducing the *ex nihilo* doctrine of creation, which was subsequently developed by Tatian.[21] Heretical writings were often opposed by some Apologists and accepted by others. The net result was the introduction of new and false doctrines into the mainstream of the Church.

The views of the Apologists were greatly influenced by their opposition to anti-Christian critics as well as Christian heretics. Volumes of material were written by Irenaeus, Tertullian, Hippolytus and Origen,

---

[21] Hatch, *Influence of Greek Ideas*, 194-197.

among others, refuting the strange notions and teachings of various critics of the early Church. Though much of it is an accurate, even brilliant, defense of biblical truths, especially Old Testament passages, errors crept in simply because of the effort to oppose so much heresy. The writings of the Apologists became a patchwork of truth and error. Sometimes the source of their teachings is completely unknown.

One example is found in Irenaeus' *Against Heresies* 3:22:4. There he is ably defending the Gospel against the docetes (see Chapter 7) when he makes the following curious statement about Eve that appears to be his own fabrication:

> And even as she, having indeed a husband, Adam, but being nevertheless as yet a virgin (for in Paradise "they were both naked, and were not ashamed," [Gen. 2:25] inasmuch as they, having been created a short time previously, had no understanding of the procreation of children: *for it was necessary that they should first come to adult age, and then multiply from that time onward*), having become disobedient, was made the cause of death, both to herself and to the entire human race; so also did Mary, having a man betrothed to her, and being nevertheless a virgin, by yielding obedience, become the cause of salvation, both to herself and the whole human race. . . . And thus also it was that the knot of Eve's disobedience was loosed by the obedience of Mary. For what the virgin Eve had bound fast through unbelief, this did the virgin Mary set free through faith.

This curious doctrine regarding the age of Adam and Eve in the Garden of Eden and their physical immaturity has no basis in any currently available scripture and is a puzzle to scholars. Likewise, the doctrine of Mary's involvement in an atonement for Eve's "sin" has no scriptural foundation. Perhaps it was an allegory that occurred to Irenaeus as he cited the fact of Mary being Christ's physical mother in his effort to combat the docetic belief that Christ was never actually born into a human body. See Chapter 7.

Another Example of Irenaeus' Errors: the Age of Christ

Irenaeus' most obvious acknowledged error was his belief that Christ was nearly fifty years old before he was crucified.[22] Classical

---

[22] Irenaeus, *Against Heresies*, 2:22:4-6.

theists find this error surprising,[23] but it is entirely consistent with the prevailing conditions of ignorance about the Gospel. They refuse to accept the implications of this ignorance and Irenaeus' other errors, even though he went so far as to claim that the doctrine about Christ's age was taught by the Apostle John! [24]

Such errors would not have been so significant if they had been made by someone else, someone other than the Apologist whose renown was based in large part on his connection with the Apostolic Fathers through Polycarp. It is sobering to consider that none of the Apologists were on a more familiar basis with the truths originally taught by the Apostles than Irenaeus.

The Apologists Tackled Tough Questions

The Apologists faced many questions that had complex new dimensions.[25] Some of these questions were not directly addressed in the existing canon, but resulted from the kind of probing the Greeks enjoyed. The most significant were directed toward the nature of God.

These questions arose from an entirely different mind set than that of the Hebrews to whom the scriptures had been revealed. The answers were in the sacred writings available at the time, but the Church was without a guide to point them out (a "preacher" as Paul put it in Romans 10:14).

The Apologists were largely in the dark as they began to lay the foundations of modern orthodox theology. No one was then alive who could tell them with authority, "The Greeks are right about the pre-existence of the soul and God's creation of the heavens and the earth out of pre-existing matter, but they are wrong about the incorporeality and transcendency of God." Instead, they were left simply to follow their own conclusions on each issue they addressed. It is amazing that they did not make more mistakes. Their writings are filled with many penetrating and biblical responses to the issues of the time, but in the crucial area of theology they frequently erred.

The greatest problem of the time was the belief of the Church in one God, namely the Father, side-by-side with its worship of Christ, His Son, as "Lord" (1 Cor. 8:6). The Greeks could never comprehend the simple

---

[23] *Ante-Nicene Fathers*, 1:392. Fns. 2, 6.
[24] Irenaeus, *Against Heresies*, 2:22:5.
[25] Gwatkin, *Early Church History*, 2:101-102.

explanation that Christ, though an equal, voluntarily submitted Himself to the authority of His Father, the source of all authority and power. That doctrine was clearly taught in the scriptures (e.g., John 5:30; 8:25-29) and acknowledged by the early Church, but it was always misunderstood by the Greeks, as will be seen in subsequent chapters. In the latter half of the second century, the failure to provide a satisfactory philosophical answer to this question lay at the foundation of the charge of "atheism," which had for decades been leveled at Christians.

That failure was the impetus for much of the criticism and ultimately some of the most severe persecution the Church ever endured. Ultimately, it nearly split the Church apart in the Arian controversy. The answer developed by the Apologists became popular through a series of events that will be described below, and it was adopted as the official doctrine of the early Church at the Nicene Council. By then, however, the early Church had no appreciation for the difficulties and lack of knowledge noted above, and no realization that their theology rested on Greek rather than Hebrew foundations.

The Apologists Responded to Jewish As Well As Greek Criticism

Part of the reason for this failure was the attitude of many in the early church toward the Jews. The directions from which the threat of persecution came in the latter half of the second century were well known to the Apologists as being Jewish as well as Roman. The Jews were religiously motivated in their opposition to Christianity, while the Romans were driven primarily by a kind of misguided patriotism. They believed that the prosperity of the state depended upon appropriate worship of the god or gods of that state. Jewish opposition carried a greater antipathy, and though they were not a political power, their influence was still considered dangerous, for they vigorously sought to inflame Roman and other pagan persecutions.

Thus, besides writing pleas directed at the Roman Emperors of their time and pamphlets (as they might be called today) responding to anti-Christian critics, the Apologists wrote works responding to Jewish criticism. Justin Martyr wrote *Dialogue with Trypho*, a Jew; Tertullian wrote *Against the Jews*; and Cyprian wrote *Three Books of Evidence Against the Jews*, all as means for turning back the tide of Jewish persecution during the second and third centuries.

Hellenization of the Early Church

Greek methods of rhetoric and analysis had thoroughly pervaded the early Church by the latter half of the second century. Evidence of this invasion can be seen as early as 180 A.D. in the verbal assault on Apelles mounted by Rhodon, who had been a student of Tatian and was a noted Christian controversialist. Apelles was also one of Tatian's pupils, but he had apparently resisted the new areas of inquiry. Instead, he was trying to follow the admonition of Paul not to be drawn into Greek philosophy.

Rhodon's remarks, reported by Eusebius, reflect the Greek obsession with proofs, and the extent to which the Church had been Hellenized in violation of Paul's warnings. They are as follows:

> He [Apelles] was often refuted for his errors, which indeed made him say that we ought not to inquire too closely into doctrine; but that as every one had believed, so he should remain. For he declared that those who set their hopes on the Crucified One would be saved, if only they were found in good works. But the most uncertain thing of all that he said was what he said about god. He held no doubt that there is One Principle, just as we hold too: but when I said to him, "Tell us how you demonstrate that, or on what grounds you are able to assert that there is One Principle," ... he said that he did not know, but that was his conviction. When I thereupon adjured him to tell the truth, he swore that he was telling the truth, that he did not know how there is one unbegotten God, but that nevertheless so he believed. Then I laughed at him and denounced him, for that, giving himself out to be a teacher, he did not know how to prove what he taught.[26]

The problem Rhodon refers to in this statement is the very question noted above. Like many of the Greek Christians of his time, Apelles was unable to explain how there could be only "One Principle" (i.e., one ultimate authority), when at least two persons are mentioned in the New Testament as "God." He simply accepted it, without introducing Greek analysis into the equation and without supporting the explanation the Apologists developed.

As Rhodon's response makes clear, the Gentile Church of the late second century was no longer willing to follow Paul's advice and accept

---

[26] Eusebius, *Ecclesiastical History*, 5:13.

the truth without the introduction of philosophical analysis. This attitude contributed to the adoption of the Apologist's theological doctrines by the early Church.

Renewed Persecution, a Catalyst for Apostasy

The importation of the Trinity doctrine into Christian theology was greatly expedited by the untimely and unexpected resumption of Roman persecution under Marcus Aurelius Antoninus, who reigned from 161 to 180 A.D. When he took the throne, Marcus Aurelius was already one of the great Stoic philosophers. He was a man of ethics, respected for his high moral character, who fancied himself the fulfillment of Plato's vision of the ideal "philosopher-king." His merciful nature was renowned, so it was likely a great surprise to the Apologists to find in him a deadly adversary.

The Roman Empire was then in its decline, and Marcus, with many other Romans, viewed the Christians as atheists and the source of God's wrath upon them. To him their refusal to worship in some way appropriate to Roman citizenship was a serious charge. The Christians, especially Justin Martyr in his *First Apology*, had scorned the worship of Rome and Caesar. As this was "the very core of Roman public life,"[27] Marcus saw no reason that the Christians should not suffer for it by death, the penalty for treason. His persecution was unquestionably one of the most severe ever suffered by the Church.

The reputation of Marcus Aurelius was especially intimidating. The Apologists could not accuse him of being another Nero. The feeling of the Roman public was that if Marcus Aurelius persecuted someone, they deserved it. As a result, the Apologists were anxious to approach him with their reasoned defenses of Christianity,[28] especially those addressed to the charge of atheism.

Apologies Addressed to Marcus Aurelius

Miltiades addressed an apology to Marcus and his brother Lucius Verus sometime between 161 and 169 A.D., but the text of that writing has not survived to the present. Justin's *Dialogue with Trypho* was probably written about the same time. Claudius Apollinaris addressed his *Defense of the Christian Faith* to Marcus in 172, but that document

---

[27] Kidd, *History of the Church*, 1:247.
[28] *Ibid.*

too has been lost. About the same time, Melito of Sardis submitted his *Defense of the Christian Faith*. Fragments of that defense are available today and will be reviewed below. In 177 A.D., Athenagoras, a contemporary of Irenaeus, made his defense of Christianity in *A Plea for the Christians*, which he sent to Marcus and his son Commodus. Theophilus of Antioch wrote his *To Autolycus* in 180 A.D., and Minucius Felix most likely wrote his Latin series, the *Octavius*, in the same year. All of the latter documents are available today.

The approach of the Apologists in these efforts was to point out the similarities of Christian theology to that of the Greek philosophers. Their question was, How could Marcus call Christians atheists, when biblical teachings about God are similar in so many ways to the teachings of the philosophers? The problem was not the viability of this argument, as far as it went, but the Apologists' lack of knowledge about the Gospel, coupled with their Greek education. In their zeal to compare Christian theology to Greek philosophy and defend the Church against the charge of atheism, their philosophical background overwhelmed their knowledge of God. The similarities between Greek philosophy and biblical theology were allowed to consume the differences between the two, and the metaphysics of the Greeks was allowed to assimilate the figurative language of the Hebrews. In the short time embraced by the apologies cited above (approximately 161 to 180 A.D.), the God of Christianity was transformed into the God of Greek philosophy.

The Impact of Stoic Philosophy

Stoicism, the philosophy of Marcus Aurelius, cannot be ignored as a factor in his persecution and the reaction of the Apologists to it. The Platonists were dualistic, making their theology more like that of Christianity with its belief in a Father and a Son. The Platonists believed in a Supreme God and a lesser Demigod or *Logos* consisting of God's thoughts, which were seen almost as independent of God and therefore able to act upon evil Matter.

The Stoics, however, were strict monists. With the Platonists, they believed in one Principle, or one Law, but their view of the *Logos* was not compatible with any view of the Father and the Son as separate persons. The processes of nature were seen by the Stoics as the result of numerous active forces, containing within themselves the law of the form in which they were ultimately seen. These forces were called *logoi* or Reasons and, according to Stoic philosophy, they acted as self-developing seeds that brought forth the material universe. They were viewed as part of one *Logos*, which runs through the whole universe.[29]

The two systems, Stoicism and Platonism, had been growing closer together over the years, so that, by the time of Christ, the *logoi* of the Stoics was sometimes hard to distinguish from the *Logos* of the Platonists. But the conception was never really independent of the Supreme God. They were only viewed in a metaphysical sense as acting separately.

This concept had enough similarity to Christian theology that the Apostle John had used the word "*Logos*" (translated "Word" in English Bibles) in approximately 105 A.D. to describe Christ (John 1:1-3, 14). Undoubtedly he was trying to communicate to Greek minds a testimony of the truth that lay behind the myths they had developed. Unfortunately, the reference was often used as an excuse to ignore Paul's warnings and apply metaphysical interpretations to the scriptures. Tatian, for example, was obsessed with the word. He and other heretics used it as an excuse for the wholesale importation of Greek notions into Christianity.

While the Platonists found the similarity between their doctrine and that of Christianity fascinating, the Stoics had no patience for Christians. First, the Christians seemed to worship two separate persons, the Father and the Son, each as though He were "God," while they simultaneously averred a belief in only one God. This violated their sense of logic. More importantly, Christians refused to accept their lot in the natural order of things. Rather than comply with Roman rules of worship, they were so obstinate as to allow themselves to be killed. This was an even greater source of annoyance to the Stoics, as it gave them the oft-unpleasant job of carrying out the verdict.

That theological differences between Christians and Greeks were a critical motivation in the persecution under Marcus Aurelius is evident from the question routinely put to the martyrs at the time. In 177 A.D. the Christians in Southern France were brutally tortured and murdered. To Pothinus, the ninety-year-old bishop of Lyons at the time, the Roman

---

[29] See Hatch, *Influence of Greek Ideas*, 180, et seq. for further clarification.

court put this question, "Who is the god of the Christians?" His reply was, "If you are worthy, you shall know." On the way back from this appearance, he was set upon by the crowd and beaten so badly that he died two days later.[30]

The Boldness of the Early Apologists Offended Rome

During the lengthy respite from Roman persecution that followed the reign of Trajan, the early Apologists had waxed bold in their defense of the faith. Their approach before 161 A.D. is typified by the following excerpts from the introduction given by Justin Martyr to his *First Apology*, written in approximately 150 A.D.:

> To the Emperor Titus Ælius Adrianus Antoninus Pius Augustus Caesar, and to his son Verissimus the philosopher, and to Lucius the philosopher, . . . and to the sacred Senate, and to the whole people of Rome, in favor of those men of all nations who are unjustly hated and oppressed, I, Justin, . . . have composed this address and petition.
>
> Reason directs that all who are really pious and philosophical should honor and love that alone which is true, and refuse to follow the opinion of the ancients, should they prove to be worthless; . . . the lover of truth ought, even if threatened with death, to choose to speak and to do what is right.
>
> You everywhere, then, hear yourselves termed pious, and philosophers, and guardians of justice, and lovers of learning; it shall [now] be seen whether you are indeed such. For we have not come to flatter you by these writings of ours, nor to bespeak favor; but to make our claim to be judged after a strict and searching inquiry; so that neither by prejudice, nor desire of popularity from the superstitious, nor by an unthinking impulse of zeal, nor by that evil report which has so long kept possession of your minds, you may be urged to give a decision against yourselves. For it is our maxim that we can suffer harm from none, unless we be convicted as doers of evil, or proved to be wicked: you may indeed slay us, but hurt us you can not.[31]

The Romans, especially those who were Stoics, simply did not comprehend this approach. It was an offense to them, and was actually counterproductive for the Church. The Apologists tried in their letters to demonstrate logically and philosophically that the Church posed no

---

[30] Gwatkin, *Early Church History*, 1:159-160.
[31] Justin, *First Apology*, 1-2.

threat to the Roman culture and rule of the time. Christians, they said, made excellent citizens of any country, and believed in God. The Roman authorities saw this as anything but a statement of strict loyalty to Rome. While these apologetic writings were ultimately influential in combating the charges of atheism, ritual child-murder and oedipal intercourse, as will be seen, they did not prevent or stop any persecution. Justin's frank and forceful language, especially in his *Second Apology*, and his brave defense of the separateness of the Father and the Son (see below and Chapter 10) had only a negative effect.

When persecution resumed under Marcus, Justin was one of its first and most noted victims. His *Second Apology* had made him unpopular in Rome, so he had moved to Ephesus, but in approximately 163 A.D. he was returned and beheaded by Rusticus, prefect of Rome. Notably, Rusticus was also a Stoic philosopher of great distinction, and a teacher of Marcus Aurelius.

Apologetic Writings After 161 A.D.

The exact progress of the theological apostasy can be traced in the writings of the early Church Fathers before 161 A.D. Though it is not certain that Marcus Aurelius paid any attention to the apologies sent to him after 161 A.D., the tone and progression of these later writings suggest that there was a determined and organized effort to appease Roman authorities on the charge of atheism. It is almost as if someone in the Roman hierarchy was demanding greater and greater clarity in the Apologists' descriptions of God, until, by 177 A.D., they had taken a position that was unmistakably metaphysical and hence acceptable to the Hellenized Romans.

Christian Descriptions of God Before 161 A.D.

Written about 100 A.D., the *Epistle of Barnabas* is one of the earliest Christian writings of the second century. It is thought by some to have been written by Paul's companion, hence the name, but the best authorities now concede that it was not,[32] though that concession does not diminish the importance of the work as an indicator of early Church teachings. It contains no reference to Christ as the *Logos* nor any other metaphysical concepts. It does not even discuss the relationship between

---

[32] *Ante-Nicene Fathers*, 1:133-135.

the Father and the Son. However, it clearly identifies both and treats them as entirely separate persons. For example, after quoting Genesis 1:28, it states, "These things were spoken to the Son."[33]

Another of the early writings of the second century mentioned above was the *Teaching of the Twelve Apostles*. As it is a book of instructions, and not a treatise on theology, there is only a limited reference to the relationship between the Father and the Son within its passages. Often, however, it prescribes prayers for the use of the Church in various ordinances. Those prayers are addressed to God the Father and refer to "Jesus Thy Servant."[34] This language recognizes two separate persons, the Father and the Son, and suggests an agency relationship between the two.

The *Apology* of Aristides was recovered late in the nineteenth century. There are two versions—one in Greek and the other in Syriac. The Syriac was discovered in 1889, whereupon it was noted that an ancient version of the Greek had been available for centuries. It had not been recognized as belonging to Aristides, however, because it was incorporated in an early Christian romance entitled *The Life of Barlaam and Josaphat*.

The two versions, Greek and Syriac, differ markedly in their description of God, the Syriac version being very similar to the descriptions of God written after 161 A.D. Since Aristides was an Athenian philosopher,[35] he wrote in Greek. The Syriac, therefore, had to be a translation. Accordingly, it is most likely of later origin and of questionable accuracy.

The Greek version describes God thus:

> The self-same being, then, who first established and now controls the universe—him do I affirm to be God who is without beginning and without end, immortal and self-sufficing, above all passions and infirmities, above anger and forgetfulness and ignorance and the rest.[36]

This description agrees with biblical descriptions of God. It can be argued that the reference to God being "above all passions" is not biblical, but it would appear from the context that the author is merely saying that God is above negative or unwarranted passions, and that would certainly be biblical, since God's wrath is always shown in scripture to

---

[33] *Epistle of Barnabas*, 6.
[34] *Teaching of the Twelve Apostles*, 9 and 10.
[35] *Ante-Nicene Fathers*, 10:259.
[36] Aristides, *Apology*, 1 (Greek version).

be fully justified. Aristides nowhere refers to Christ as the *Logos* or alludes to any other metaphysical ideas, nor does he make any comparisons of the Christian God to the God of the Greek philosophers.

The earliest apologetic writing of which a clearly genuine copy is available today is the *Epistle to Diognetus*, written in about 130 A.D. The author and addressee of this letter are completely unknown. Internal evidence suggests that it was written by someone who lived at the beginning of the second century. He describes himself as follows: "having been a disciple of the Apostles, I am become a teacher of the Gentiles." If this is true, the writer would be properly included among the Apostolic Fathers, though the style of writing is definitely an apology, a verbal defense of the Gospel apparently addressed to a friend whom the writer sought to convert. That is uncharacteristic of most Apostolic Fathers, and the letter was, for a long time, attributed to Justin.

The *Epistle* contains statements that are completely consistent with biblical Mormonism. The author repeatedly refers to the Father and the Son as entirely separate individuals and at one point describes their relationship as follows: "*As a king sends his son, who is also a king, so sent He Him; as God.*"[37] This understanding of the relationship between the Father and the Son—as of a King and His Prince—is a clear and accurate expression of biblical theology. It recognizes the complete separation of the individual who is King from the individual who is Prince, while it explains the filial relationship between the two that allows the Son to be called God without violating the authority of His Father, the King.

The writer, often called "Mathetes," which means "disciple," also demonstrates a clear understanding of the principles of eternal progression and Man's relationship to the Father in the following statement:

> If you also desire to possess this faith, you likewise shall receive first of all the knowledge of the Father. *For God has loved mankind, on whose account He made the world*, to whom He rendered subject all the things that are in it, to whom He gave reason and understanding, to whom alone He imparted the privilege of looking upwards to Himself, *whom He formed after His own image*, to whom He sent His only-begotten Son, *to whom He has promised a kingdom in heaven,*

---

[37] *Epistle to Diognetus*, 7.

and will give it to those who have loved Him. And when you have attained this knowledge, with what joy do you think you will be filled? Or, how will you love Him who has first so loved you? And if you love Him, you will be an imitator of His kindness. *And do not wonder that a man may become an imitator of God. He can, if he is willing.*[38]

So likewise does The Church of Jesus Christ of Latter-day Saints today invite all Men, having been "formed after His own image," to be "imitators of God," so they can reap the promise of a "kingdom in heaven."

Though it cannot be said that Polycarp wrote any theological or apologetic works, there are indications in his *Epistle to the Philippians*, written after 107 but before 150 A.D., that he understood the complete separateness of the Father and the Son. This view appears from such passages as the following:

> I have greatly rejoiced with you in our *Lord Jesus Christ, because ye have followed the example of true love as displayed by God*, and have accompanied, as became you, those who were bound in chains, the fitting ornaments of saints, and which are indeed the diadems of the true elect of God and our Lord . . .[39]

> *His blood will God require of those who do not believe in Him. But He who raised Him up from the dead* will raise up us also, if we do His will, and walk in His commandments, and love what He loved, . . .[40]

> *But may the God and Father of our Lord Jesus Christ, and Jesus Christ Himself, who is the Son of God, and our everlasting High Priest, build you up in faith and truth,* . . . and may He bestow on you a lot and portion among His saints, and on us with you, and on all that are under heaven, *who shall believe in our Lord Jesus Christ, and in His Father, who "raised Him from the dead."*[41]

In these writings, nothing describes Christ as anything like the Greek *Logos*. That is notable not because it contrasts with John's reference, but because it shows that the earliest writers did not emphasize that description of Him. Nor do any of these writings use metaphysical language to describe either the Father or the Son or the relationship

---

[38] *Ibid.*, 10.
[39] Polycarp, *Epistle to the Philippians*, 1.
[40] *Ibid.*, 2.
[41] *Ibid.*, 12.

between them. The same philosophical void is apparent in all Christian writings before 150 A.D.

In his *First Apology*, written in 150 A.D., Justin is emphatic in defending the total separateness of the Father and the Son, and the role of the pre-mortal Christ as the God of the Old Testament. He wrote:

> The Jews, always thinking that *the Father of all things spoke to Moses, he who spoke to him being the Son of God*, who is called both Angel and Apostle, are rightly upbraided both by the Spirit of prophecy and by Christ himself, as knowing neither the Father nor the Son. *For they who say that the Son is the Father are proved neither to know the Father, nor that the Father of all things has a Son, who, being moreover the first-born Word of God, is also God.*[42]

His doctrine of separation between the three members of the Godhead was such that he placed the Father, the Son and the Holy Ghost in order of hierarchy as follows:

> Our teacher of these things is Jesus Christ, who also was born for this purpose, and was crucified under Pontius Pilate, procurator of Judea, in the times of Tiberius Caesar; and that we reasonably worship Him, having learned that *He is the Son of the true God Himself, and holding Him in the second place, and the prophetic Spirit in the third, we will prove.*[43]

Justin does call Christ the *Logos* ("Word") of God, but in no different sense than did the Apostle John. This usage contrasts markedly with the philosophical usage made of that title by Tatian, Justin's former pupil, as will be noted below.

In his defense of the charge of atheism, also contained in the *First Apology*, Justin did not try to compare the God of the Bible with the Greek or pagan gods, as did the later Apologists. Rather, he disclaims any belief in the Greek gods, and simply asserts a belief in the true God and His Son as the ultimate proof that Christians are not atheists. His words are as follows:

> Hence it is that we are even termed atheists. And we confess ourselves atheists as regards such beings if they be esteemed as gods, *but not with respect to the most true God and Father of righteousness and sobriety, and all other virtues, and who partakes not of evil; but both*

---
[42] Justin, *First Apology*, 63.
[43] *Ibid.*, 13.

him and his son, who came from him, and taught us these truths, and the host of the other good angels who follow and imitate him, *and the Spirit of prophecy, we reverence and worship*, honoring him in reason and truth, and fully instructing every one who wishes to learn as we are taught ourselves.[44]

Justin Martyr's View of God the Father

Despite his understanding of the separate identity of God the Father and His Son, Jesus Christ, Justin shows signs of a transition to Greek philosophy in his *First Apology*. It is evident from his references to God the Father as the "unbegotten God," in the citation below.

Nowhere in the scriptures is the word "unbegotten" found, and nothing like it is used to describe the Father. Apparently, this was a word Justin adopted to contrast Christ, the "only begotten" Son of God (John 1:14, 18; 3:16, 18), with His Father, whom Justin, and all the Apologists after him, assumed to be "unbegotten." This adjective does not appear in association with the Father in any authentic writings that predate the *First Apology*. Justin's willingness to ascribe attributes to God the Father that are not mentioned in the scriptures will be seen as a growing trend in the writings of the Apologists.

Justin's *First Apology* was addressed to Antoninus Pius. Marcus Aurelius was also an Antonine, and could easily have become aware of Christian teachings about the Father and the Son through that letter. The clear separation of the Father and the Son taught in his writings appears to have been the tenet of Christian theology that most irritated Marcus, inspiring the question that later became the hallmark of his persecution: "Who is the god of the Christians?"

Justin may have been trying to clarify his position on that issue in *Dialogue with Trypho*, written in Ephesus sometime between 158 and 163 A.D. There he adopted a distinctly Hellenistic view of God the Father. After citing the actions of God described in the Old Testament, he distinguishes between the Father and the Son as follows:

> These and other such sayings are recorded by the lawgiver and by the prophets; and I suppose that I have stated sufficiently, that wherever God says, "God went up from Abraham," or, "The Lord spake to Moses" and "The Lord came down to behold the tower which the sons

---

[44] Justin, *First Apology*, 6.

of men had built," or when "God shut Noah into the ark," *you must not imagine that the unbegotten God Himself came down or went up from any place. For the ineffable Father and Lord of all neither has come to any place, nor walks, nor sleeps, nor rises up*, but remains in His own place, wherever that is, quick to behold and quick to hear, *having neither eyes nor ears*, but being of indescribable might; and He sees all things, and knows all things, and none of us escapes His observation; and He is not moved or confined to a spot in the whole world, for He existed before the world was made.[45]

Justin understood correctly that (after the Fall) it was the Son who acted in each instance that describes action by God in the Old Testament. However, he apparently did not understand the reason for that arrangement. He may have taken the position quoted above in reliance on the writings of Philo of Alexandria, whose description of God is very similar (see Chapter 4). No scriptural language anywhere disclaims the movements of God the way Justin does here, nor is there any biblical language that agrees with his description of God. In fact, it is in direct conflict with passages like Deuteronomy 4:28 and Revelation 9:20.

The description of God Justin gives, however, is very close to Aristotle's Unmoving Mover, the ultimate cause whom that philosopher envisioned as the creator of all things. Justin had received training in the Peripatetic school, which based its precepts on the teachings of Aristotle. The adoption of Aristotle's view of the ultimate God would have been a natural progression for him in the absence of a better understanding.

Unlike his other explanations of theology, Justin cites no scriptural passages to support his description of God the Father. He discusses events in the Old Testament (God's appearances on Sinai and in the tabernacle Moses built, and the occasion of Solomon's placing the ark in the Temple) where Christ's or the Father's glory could not be seen by Men, and claims that these instances are evidence for his statements about the Father's physical characteristics.[46] But there is nothing in the passages he cites that confirms his description, and he ignores all the passages that describe an appearance by God to the Jews that *was* visible to them (see Chapter 11).

---

[45] Justin, *Dialogue with Trypho*, 127.
[46] *Ibid.*

Notably, Justin does not mention the repeated statements made by New Testament writers after the resurrection of Christ to the effect that the Son is the express image of the Father (2 Cor. 4:4; Col. 1:15; Heb. 1:3). From these statements it could readily be surmised that the Father also has a physical, resurrected body. To overlook so obvious a conclusion suggests a predisposition in favor of a Supreme God who is like the God of the Greek philosophers.

Tatian Embraces the Hellenized God with Enthusiasm

Writing in the middle of the second century, just after the *First Apology* was written by his master, Justin Martyr, Tatian presents a Hellenized view of God in his *Address to the Greeks*. No earlier writings contain so extreme a view of God as those of Tatian, and it is likely that his views strongly influenced the Apologists in their progressive adoption of a Greek slant on the scriptural teachings about God. He states:

> God is a Spirit, not pervading matter, but the Maker of material spirits, and of the forms that are in matter; He is invisible, impalpable, being Himself the Father of both sensible and invisible things. . . .[47]

> God was in the beginning; but the beginning, we have been taught, is the power of the *Logos*. For the Lord of the universe, who is Himself the necessary ground (*hupostasis*) of all being, inasmuch as no creature was yet in existence, was alone; but inasmuch as He was all power, Himself the necessary ground of things visible and invisible, with Him were all things; with Him, by *Logos-power*, the *Logos* Himself also, who was in Him, subsists. And by His simple will the *Logos* springs forth; and the *Logos*, not coming forth in vain, becomes the first-begotten work of the Father.[48]

Tatian nowhere refers to Christ in this address except by the word "*Logos*." Compared with Christian writings before his, this was an extreme, even obsessive, use of the term. Not long after this address was written, Tatian fell into heresy. Orthodox Christian historians try to suggest that this was a lapse due to the infirmities of old age and ascetic living,[49] but it would be more accurately viewed as the natural result of his progressively apostate theology, of which the above is but one example. This address was merely the foundation on which Tatian later built an

---
[47] Tatian, *Address to the Greeks*, 4.
[48] *Ibid.*, 5.
[49] *Ante-Nicene Fathers*, 2:61-63.

entire superstructure of Gnostic foolishness (see Chapter 7). As will be seen, it contains the seeds of more than one apostate notion.

It is notable that Tatian does not try to support his views with specific scriptural quotations. Even more significant, he uses a Greek word, *hupostasis*, to describe God. This word is not used anywhere in the scriptures in the context in which Tatian uses it. It was commonly used in this context, however, by Aristotle, Philo and other philosophic writers.[50]

Melito Introduces Metaphysics to Christian Theology

The next available apologetic writings of the time were those of Melito of Sardis, who wrote sometime between 169 and 172 A.D. He was the first to use distinct metaphysical references to God in his *Apology* addressed to Marcus Aurelius. He states:

> There "is" that which really exists, and it is called God. He, I say, really exists, and by His power doth everything subsist. This being is in no sense made, nor did He ever come into being; but He has existed from eternity, and will continue to exist for ever and ever. *He changeth not, while everything else changes. No eye can see Him, nor thought apprehend Him, nor language describe Him;* and those who love Him speak of Him thus: "Father, and God of Truth."[51]

The reference here to God being "that which really exists" is a clear reference to the Greek metaphysical belief in real and unreal worlds. Melito's reference to everything else changing, except God, was drawn from Heraclitus and his theories (see Chapter 2). Also introduced for the first time in early Christian literature is the notion that comprehending God is impossible (*"nor thought apprehend Him, nor language describe Him"*). This notion is practically word-for-word from the writings of Philo (see Chapter 4). No scriptural passage is so extreme in its statement of God's incomprehensibility, nor does Melito cite a single passage in support of his ideas.

In his description of Christ, Melito introduced words that were familiar to the Greeks, raising a subtle comparison between the true God of the Bible and the god of Greek philosophy, as follows:

---

[50] Joseph Thayer, *Greek-English Lexicon of the New Testament* (Grand Rapids: Baker House, 1977), s.v. ὑπό-στασις.
[51] *Ante-Nicene Fathers*, 8:751.

The Apologists and the Theological Apostasy   133

> We have made collections from the law and the prophets relating to those things which are declared concerning our Lord Jesus Christ, that we might prove to your love that he is the perfect Reason, the Word of God; who was begotten before the light; who was Creator together with the Father; who was the Fashioner of man; who was all things in all; who among the patriarchs was Patriarch; who in the law was Law; among the priests, Chief Priest; among kings, Governor; among the prophets, Prophet; among the angels, Archangel; among voices, the Word; among spirits, Spirit; in the Father, the Son; in God, God, the King for ever and ever.[52]

Here Melito is the first to make a direct reference to the Platonistic theory of God by using terms that specify the sense in which he intends the word "*Logos*" to be understood. He refers to Christ as "the perfect Reason, the Word (*Logos*) of God" and the "Fashioner of man." This goes further than the Apostle John's identification of the Son as the Word (*Logos*) in John 1:1-14. It identifies the "Word" with God's "Reason," suggesting the same relationship between the Father and the Son as that which the Greeks envisioned between the Platonistic God and his *Logos*.

It doesn't actually say that the Father and the Son are the same Being, as the Platonists believed their Supreme God and his *Logos* to be, however. So, it could have been viewed as nothing more than an analogy to the Platonistic theory of God, an attempt to mislead Roman authorities by using the right words without intending the same meaning. Melito's writings consistently referred to the Father and the Son as distinctly separate beings, which conflicts with Greek theology. For example, he refers to Christ in one passage as follows:

> Thou has not known, O Israel, that *this was the first-born of God*, who was begotten before the sun, who made the light to shine forth, who lighted up the day, who separated the darkness, who fixed the first foundations, who poised the earth, who collected the ocean, who stretched out the firmament, who adorned the world. . . . *This is He who made the heaven and the earth, and in the beginning, together with the Father, fashioned man;* who was announced by means of the law and the prophets; who put on a bodily form in the Virgin; who was

---

[52] Melito, *On Faith*, in Jackson, *The Apostolic Fathers and the Apologists of the Second Century*, Vol 1 of *Early Christian Literature*. See also *Ante-Nicene Fathers*, 8:756-757.

hanged upon the tree; who was buried in the earth; who rose from the place of the dead, and ascended to the height of heaven, and *sitteth on the right hand of the Father*.[53]

The idea of Christ sitting "on the right hand of the Father," was inconsistent with the theology of the philosophers. It is unlikely, therefore, that Melito's *Apology* convinced the Romans that belief in the Christian God was anything but atheism. To them it would have looked like the same theology they had heard from Christians for decades, thinly veiled in Hellenistic terminology. If the Romans were to be convinced that the Christian God really was like the God of the philosophers, as the Apologists were trying to claim, it would be necessary for the early Church to "clarify" its view even further.

Athenagoras Teaches the Platonistic God

A few years later, that needed clarification was provided concurrently by Athenagoras and Irenaeus. The description of God provided by Athenagoras in his 177 A.D. plea addressed to Marcus and his son is clearly Platonistic. He adopts the dualistic view espoused by the Platonists in the following language:

> But to us, who distinguish God from matter, and teach that *matter is one thing and God another*, and that they are separated by a wide interval *(for that the Deity is uncreated and eternal, to be beheld by the understanding and reason alone, while matter is created and perishable)*, is it not absurd to apply the name of atheism?[54]

Thus, Athenagoras has incorporated not only dualism into Christianity, but the Platonistic notion of a distinction between that which is uncreated and that which is created. Later in the same chapter, he explains that what is created "does not come to be," while that which is not created does come to be. This is a reference to Plato's metaphysical distinction between the world of the forms, which is "being," and the phenomenal world, or world of the senses, which is not real but merely "becoming" (see Chapter 2).

From this argument, Athenagoras goes on as follows:

---

[53] Melito, *On Faith*. The portion containing this statement is numbered as 5 "v" in *Ante-Nicene Fathers*, 8:757-758.
[54] Athenagoras, *A Plea for the Christians*, 4.

If, therefore, *Plato is not an atheist for conceiving of an uncreated God, the Framer of the universe, neither are we atheists who acknowledge and firmly hold that he is God who has framed all things by the Logos, and holds them in being by his Spirit.* . . .[55]

He goes on to mention the Aristotelian view of one God and points out that, though the Stoics believe that matter is permeated by the Spirit of God, they consider God to be one. He then complains that "against us a law lies in force, though we are able to demonstrate what we apprehend and justly believe, namely *that there is one God*, with proofs and reason accordant with truth."[56] Athenagoras then asserted more clearly than any before him that the Father and the Son are not truly separate. He wrote:

That we are not atheists, therefore, seeing that *we acknowledge one God*, uncreated, eternal, invisible, impassible, incomprehensible, illimitable, who is apprehended by the understanding only and the reason, who is encompassed by light, and beauty, and spirit, and power ineffable, *by whom the universe has been created through his Logos,* and set in order, and is kept in being—I have sufficiently demonstrated.[57]

This description of God lacks only the words "incorporeal" and "transcendent" for it to state the essential doctrine of orthodox Christian theology today. The language is Greek in character, not biblical, and openly portrays the Son as having the same basic relationship to the Father as the *Logos* of the Platonists had to their Supreme God. In fact, Athenagoras went on as follows:

But the Son of God is the Logos of the Father, in idea and in operation; for after the pattern of Him and by Him were all things made, *the Father and the Son being one*. And, *the Son being in the Father and the Father in the Son, in oneness and power of spirit*, the understanding and reason of the Father is the Son of God. But if, in your surpassing intelligence, it occurs to you to inquire what is meant by the Son, I will state briefly that *He is the first product of the Father, not as having been brought into existence (for from the beginning, God, who is the eternal mind (nous), had the Logos in Himself*, being from eternity

---

[55] *Ibid.*, 6.
[56] *Ibid.*, 7.
[57] *Ibid.*, 10.

instinct with *Logos*); but inasmuch as He came forth to be the idea and energizing power of all material things, . . .[58]

Athenagoras included the Holy Ghost in his formula as follows: "*The Holy Spirit Himself also, which operates in the prophets, we assert to be an effluence of God, flowing from Him, and returning back again like a beam of the sun.*"[59] This directly contradicted earlier statements made by Justin Martyr (see Chapter 10). Clearly, the separateness ascribed to the members of the Godhead by that early Apologist had been supplanted by an entirely new doctrine. It cannot even be said that the Holy Ghost, under this definition, is an individual. The notion is pure Platonism in its false teaching that the Holy Ghost is merely one emanation of a Platonistic god and his Demiurge who has no separate reality except in some metaphysical sense.

Irenaeus Becomes the Father of Co-Substantiality

The clearest statement of this new doctrine, later referred to as "co-substantiality," came from Irenaeus, who wrote at or about the same time as Athenagoras, approximately 177 A.D. Referring to Christ as "*Logos*," "Mind" and "the mind of God," he taught the following:

> But God being all Mind, and all *Logos*, both speaks exactly what He thinks, and thinks exactly what He speaks. *For His thought is Logos, and Logos is Mind, and Mind comprehending all things is the Father Himself*. He, therefore, who speaks of the mind of God, and ascribes to it a special origin of its own [as certain Gnostics did], declares Him a compound Being, *as if God were one thing, and the original Mind another.*[60]

Here Irenaeus does more than just compare the Father and the Son to Plato's Supreme God and His *Logos*, or *Nous* (Mind). He states unequivocally that the Father and the Son are the same being. His explicit statement is that they are not "a compound Being," by which he means that the Father's thoughts, which he identifies as the being known as Christ, are not separate from the Father who thinks them. In Platonistic fashion, he is speaking of the Father's thoughts as if they were a separate being, while claiming always that they are not. To him

---
[58] *Ibid.*
[59] *Ibid.*
[60] Irenaeus, *Against Heresies*, 2:28:5.

they are not even a compound being—two beings in one. The two separate persons are no more than a single individual.

Such an idea could only arise in the mind of a person who was immersed in metaphysics. By 177 A.D. the set of assumptions that come with a metaphysical mind set had been completely accepted by the Apologists without any concern for the fact that metaphysics was entirely foreign to the Hebrew mind to whom the holy writ was revealed.

Irenaeus did not even attempt to show how his Greek-based doctrine correlates with anything the scriptures say about God. He did no more to justify it than contrast it with an equally false and heretical gnostic idea. He did, however, spend most of Book 4 in his *Against Heresies* in an argument against the false teachings of Marcion, in which he tried to show how much the doctrine of co-substantiality fits the scriptures that prove Marcion wrong.

In that argument, he emphasized the separate identities of the Father and the Son, and correctly defended the biblical fact that the Son actually took on a physical body contrary to the docetic teachings of Marcion and many other Gnostics (see Chapter 7). This seeming defense of Christ as a separate person from the Father is easily misconstrued by those who read excerpts of Irenaeus' writings out of context. The true nature of Irenaeus' co-substantiality becomes clear from such statements as the following:

Christ Himself, therefore, together with the Father, is the God of the living, who spake to Moses, and who was also manifested to the fathers.[61]

The Father therefore has revealed Himself to all, by making His Word visible to all; and conversely, the Word has declared to all the Father and the Son, since He has become visible to all.[62]

And through the Word Himself who had been made visible and palpable, was the Father shown forth, although all did not equally believe in Him; but all saw the Father in the Son; for the Father is the invisible of the Son, but the Son the visible of the Father.[63]

---

[61] *Ibid.*, 4:5:2.
[62] *Ibid.*, 4:6:5.
[63] *Ibid.*, 4:6:6.

Wherefore, then, in all things, and through all things, *there is one God, the Father, and one Word, and one Son, and one Spirit,* and one salvation to all who believe in Him.[64]

These phrases are part of Irenaeus' exposition on the verse, which he quoted as follows: "No man knoweth the Son, but the Father; nor the Father, save the Son, and those to whomsoever the Son shall reveal Him" (Matt. 11:27; Luke 10:22). They only hint subtly at the metaphysical problem he created, and seem almost consistent with a figurative explanation of the relationship between two literally separate individuals. But when one realizes that Irenaeus is not even talking about "a compound Being," that, using the strange and invalid notions of metaphysical philosophy, he is referring to two persons who may be separate in the unreal world of the senses but are not separate in the "real" realm of God, it becomes apparent that his view of God represented a radical change from the view that prevailed from the time of the Apostles until approximately 161 A.D.

For Irenaeus, the Son was a projection or emanation from the Father consisting of the Father's thoughts embodied for the sake of Mankind in a physical body that made the Father seem more real to them. Irenaeus, of course, did not for one second entertain the idea that God the Father was a separate being who actually possessed a physical body of flesh and bones like the one Christ had while He was "the visible of the Father." None of the Apologists were willing to take the passage cited above and carry it to that logical and intended conclusion.

Theophilus Introduces the Term "Trinity"

It appears that by 180 A.D., the merger of the Christian doctrine of God with Greek metaphysics was commonly accepted among the Apologists. When the term first appeared in the early Christian writing of Theophilus, he referred to the "Trinity" casually, as though it were a well-known term by then. He used the word as follows in connection with the creation: "In like manner also the three days which were before the luminaries, *are types of the Trinity, of God* [meaning the Father], and *His Word* [the Son], and *His wisdom* [a reference to the Holy Ghost]."[65] Here the Holy Ghost is seen as the embodiment of a

---

[64] *Ibid.*, 4:6:7.
[65] Theophilus, *To Autolycus*, 2:15.

third aspect of God, His wisdom. Wisdom is the more passive aspect of thought, namely its subject. This is typical of the Greek tendency to embody mental attributes.

The following is a description of God given by Theophilus in his work *To Autolycus*. What he describes is a totally singular God. He does not even mention the Son here. This is the God whom the Apologists arrived at in answering the question, "Who is the God of the Christians?" to the satisfaction of their Roman persecutors:

> The appearance of God is ineffable [too sacred to utter] and indescribable, and cannot be seen by eyes of flesh. For in glory He is incomprehensible, in greatness unfathomable, in height inconceivable, in power incomparable, in wisdom unrivaled, in goodness inimitable, in kindness unutterable. For if I say He is Light, I name but His own work; if I call Him Word, I name but His sovereignty; if I call Him Mind, I speak but of His wisdom; if I say He is Spirit, I speak of His breath; if I call Him Wisdom, I speak of His offspring; if I call Him Strength, I speak of His sway; if I call Him Power, I am mentioning His activity; if Providence, I but mention His goodness; if I call Him Kingdom, I but mention His glory; if I call Him Lord, I mention His being judge; if I call Him Judge, I speak of Him as being just; if I call Him Father, I speak of all things as being from Him; if I call Him Fire, I but mention His anger. . . .
>
> And He is without beginning, because He is unbegotten; and He is unchangeable, because He is immortal. And he is called God on account of His having placed all things on security afforded by Himself; and on account of *théein*,[66] for *théein* means running, and moving, and being active, and nourishing, and foreseeing, and governing, and making all things alive. But he is Lord, because He rules over the universe; Father, because He is before all things; Fashioner and Maker, because He is creator and maker of the universe; the Highest because of His being above all; and Almighty, because He Himself rules and embraces all.[67]

The Son is later described by Theophilus as follows:

> The God and Father, indeed, of all cannot be contained, and is not found in a place, for there is no place of His rest; but *His Word, through*

---

[66] This word is not in any Greek-English lexicon so it appears in the text in the original Greek, untranslated. Fortunately, Theophilus provides his own definition of the word in the phrase that follows.

[67] Theophilus, *To Autolycus*, 1:3-4.

whom He made all things, being His power and His wisdom, assuming the person of the Father and Lord of all, went to the garden in the person of God, and conversed with Adam. For the divine writing itself teaches us that Adam said that he had heard the voice. But what else is this voice but the Word of God, who is also His Son? Not as the poets and writers of myths talk of the sons of gods begotten from intercourse with women, but as truth expounds, the Word, that always exists, residing within the heart of God. For before anything came into being He had Him as a counselor, being His own mind and thought.[68]

The errors contained in these descriptions have been incorporated in modern day classical theism. They will be examined in Part 3, so they will not be further addressed here. What is important to note is the difference between these statements about the Father and the Son and those contained in the earlier Christian writings cited above. This difference marks the second century as a time of major theological transition.

Minucius Felix Concurs in Latin

Minucius Felix, writing in Latin at or about the same time,[69] concurs in Theophilus' description of God as follows:

> The bees have one king; the flocks one leader; among the herds there is one ruler. Canst thou believe that in heaven there is a division of the supreme power, and that the whole authority of that true and divine empire is sundered, when it is manifest that God, the Parent of all, has neither beginning nor end—that He who gives birth to all gives perpetuity to Himself—*that He who was before the world was Himself to Himself instead of the world?*[70]

As though quoting the language of Philo of Alexandria, Minucius Felix gives the following description of this singular and co-substantial God:

> He can neither be seen—He is brighter than light; nor can be grasped—He is purer than touch; nor [can He be] estimated; He is greater than all perceptions; infinite, immense, and how great is known to Himself alone. But our heart is too limited to understand Him, and

---
[68] *Ibid.*, 2:22.
[69] *Ante-Nicene Fathers*, 4:169-171.
[70] Minucius Felix, *The Octavius*, 18.

therefore we are then worthily estimating Him when we say that He is beyond estimation.... He who thinks that he knows the magnitude of God, is diminishing it; he who desires not to lessen it, knows it not.[71]

Humble acknowledgment of the greatness of God is one thing, but this language goes far beyond humility. It declares, as a characteristic of God, His utter incomprehensibility. This Hellenized view of God is not consistent with the scriptures, as will be explained in Part 3.

Summary of the New Doctrine Developed by the Apologists

The Apologists adopted Greek theology and metaphysics in an effort to arrive at a solution to the problem of how the scriptures can speak of three persons as "God" while simultaneously teaching that there is but "one God." Theirs was a metaphysical solution, which required that they assume the existence of unreal reality. That assumption is not only false as a matter of science, it is entirely contrary to Hebrew thinking and hence incompatible with the Hebrew scriptures.

Given their background and training, it is likely the Apologists did not even recognize the extent of their concession to Greek philosophy in arriving at their new doctrine. Indeed, they regularly contrasted their views of God with the views of the "philosophers," but in making such distinctions they rarely noted their points of agreement. For centuries after them, their work has been seen by those similarly trained in Greek philosophy as nothing more than a clarification or restatement of biblical doctrine. But that is not the case. The Apologists clearly followed Platonism in its metaphysical view of a Supreme God and His *Logos*, fusing the Father and the Son into a single "substance," whose separateness, though openly acknowledged, was contradicted in the same breath.

The doctrine of co-substantiality caused immense confusion in the decades that followed, spawning numerous heresies and eventually the Arian controversy before it became established as the cornerstone of classical theism. The elements of this doctrine are directly contradictory in a real space-time universe, but each was considered essential. They are (1) *the Father, the Son and the Holy Spirit are three entirely sepa-*

---

[71] *Ibid.*

rate persons; and (2) *the Father, the Son and the Holy Spirit are one singular substance (ousia)*.

This notion, confirmed in the writings of Theophilus quoted above, cannot be comprehended except by abandoning all rules of reality, or at least denying that they apply to God. The Greeks were used to doing that, but the Hebrews were not. This made the doctrine of co-substantiality difficult for many in the early Church to accept.

For example, a man named Callistus is described by Hippolytus in the early third century as having supported a heresy to the effect that the Father suffered along with the Son on the cross (see Chapter 7 for more about this heresy). Callistus' doctrine was as follows:

> Callistus alleges that the *Logos* Himself is Son, and that Himself is Father; and that though denominated by a different title, yet that in reality He is one indivisible spirit. And he maintains that the Father is not one person and the Son another, but that they are one and the same; and that all things are full of the Divine Spirit, both those above and those below. And he affirms that the Spirit, which became incarnate in the virgin, is not different from the Father, but one and the same. And he adds, that this is what has been declared by the Savior: "Believest thou not that I am in the Father, and the Father in me?" For that which is seen, which is man, he considers to be the Son; whereas the Spirit, which was contained in the Son, to be the Father. "For," says Callistus, "I will not profess belief in two Gods, Father and Son, but in one. For the Father, who subsisted in the Son Himself, after He had taken unto Himself our flesh, raised it to the nature of Deity, by bringing it into union with Himself, and made it one; so that Father and Son must be styled one God, and that this Person being one, cannot be two."[72]

This doctrine is a logical extension of Theophilus' language, but it does not comport with the idea of co-substantiality stated by Athenagoras and most carefully expounded by Irenaeus. Those writers *insisted* on a separation between the Father, the Son and the Holy Ghost, at least in the "unreal" world of the sensory universe which Man inhabits, but denied the possibility of any actual separation among the three in the "real" world where God dwells. That is the essence of co-substantiality. It assumes the existence of the Pleroma of Greek philosophy and adopts the conclusions of Parmenides about unreal reality to explain teachings

---

[72] Hippolytus, *Philosophic Refutation of All Heresies*, 9:7.

that should have been recognized as figurative statements explaining a relationship between three absolutely real and separate individuals.

Justin Martyr—A Heretic, or Simply Misunderstood?

The first tenet of the co-substantiality doctrine, cited above, allowed the Apologists to make an appearance of resolving the teachings of Justin Martyr with those of the new doctrine. Justin had clearly and emphatically taught that the Father and the Son were separate individuals. His words seemed to have triggered Marcus Aurelius' persecution. So, resolving his writings with the new doctrine may well have been a major project of the later Apologists, as will be seen below. There can be no doubt that it was very important in the battle against the charge of atheism.

Were it not for Justin's writings, the separateness of the Father and the Son could, perhaps, have been glossed over, as Callistus and many others did (though only by doing great injustice to the scriptures). As a respected martyr, the later Apologists could not ignore Justin. Therefore, they included the first element of the co-substantiality doctrine, the separateness of the members of the Godhead, and emphasized certain teachings of Justin to reconcile his teachings with the doctrine of co-substantiality (see Chapter 10).

Thus, the transition from a biblical understanding of God to the version embodied in current Christian orthodoxy was complete. It appears to have taken less than twenty years, encompassing the rise of Marcus Aurelius to the Emperor's seat and the resumption of lethal persecution under his reign based on the charge of atheism.

The theological changes instituted by the Apologists during the late second century were very successful in combating that charge. By the end of the second century, no one seriously contended that Christians were atheists. However, that did not stop persecution against the Christians on other grounds.

Presenting a United Front to Rome

There is evidence strongly suggesting that the writings of Justin Martyr and other early Apologists, whose statements seemed contradictory or inconsistent with the new co-substantiality doctrine, were rehabilitated by later Christian writers. As noted earlier, the *Apology* of Aristides was discovered toward the end of the nineteenth century, after which it was quickly noticed that a previous version, in Greek, had been available all along in an ancient Christian romance. The following is the **Syriac version**:

> And it is manifest that that which causes motion is more powerful than that which is moved. But that I should make search concerning this same mover of all, as to what is his nature (for it seems to me, he is indeed unsearchable in his nature), and that I should argue as to the constancy of his government, so as to grasp it fully,—this is a vain effort for me; for it is not possible that a man should fully comprehend it. I say, however, concerning this mover of the world, that he is God of all, who made all things for the sake of mankind. And it seems to me that this is reasonable, that one should fear God and should not oppress man.
>
> I say, then, that God is not born, not made, an ever-abiding nature without beginning and without end, immortal, perfect, and incomprehensible. Now when I say that he is "perfect," this means that there is not in him any defect, and he is not in need of anything but all things are in need of him. And when I say that he is "without beginning," this means that everything which has beginning has also an end, and that which has an end may be brought to an end. He has no name, for everything which has a name is kindred to things created. Form he has none, nor yet any union of members; for whatsoever possesses these is kindred to things fashioned. He is neither male nor female. [For that which is subject to this distinction is moved by passions.] The heavens do not limit him, but the heavens and all things, visible and invisible, receive their bounds from him. Adversary he has none, for there exists not any stronger than he. Wrath and indignation he possesses not, for there is nothing which is able to stand against him. Ignorance and forgetfulness are not in his nature, for he is altogether wisdom and understanding; and in Him stands fast all that exists. He requires not sacrifice and libation, nor even one of things visible; He requires not aught from any, but all living creatures stand in need of him. (The portion in brackets appears in an Armenian version of this passage.)[73]

The **Greek version**, which was quoted previously, is repeated here with some additional material that corresponds with the beginning and end of the version quoted above:

---

[73] Aristides, *Apology*, 1 (Syriac version), in *Ante-Nicene Fathers*, 10:263-264.

For everything which causes motion is stronger than that which is moved, and that which controls is stronger than that which is controlled.

The self-same being, then, who first established and now controls the universe—him do I affirm to be God who is without beginning and without end, immortal and self-sufficing, above all passions and infirmities, above anger and forgetfulness and ignorance and the rest. Through Him too all things consist. He requires not sacrifice and libation nor any one of the things that appear to sense; but all men stand in need of Him.[74]

Not only is the description, written to Hadrian around 125 A.D., much closer in the Syriac version to the Apologists' teachings from 177 A.D., but it is greatly expanded over the Greek. The only reference in the Greek to the metaphysical is the statement that God has no need for "any one of the things that appear to sense." Though this terminology is that of a Greek philosopher, it does not ascribe any metaphysical characteristic to God. It is an expression of His self-sufficiency in the language of a philosopher. The Syriac, however, is filled with references to metaphysical qualities, especially the statement that God is "altogether wisdom and understanding."

This is strong evidence that the additional material in the Syriac was added to Aristides' *Apology* no earlier than the latter half of the second century. The only reason for adding this material would have been to present a united front to Roman authorities on the question of "Who is the God of the Christians?" Such forgeries were not uncommon then,[75] and may be the cause of the confusion in Ignatius' writings (though some of his spurious letters are believed to have been modified by Arians in the later third or early fourth centuries). Modifications of this nature reveal the extent to which the later Apologists went to satisfy Rome on the charge of atheism, and advance the cause of Church unity.

The Apologists Were Glorified by Their Deaths

The Apologists were devoted followers of Christ who preserved many great truths of the Gospel from the errors of heretics and the disbelief of the Jews. Unfortunately, at the same time, they tapped Greek

---

[74] *Ibid.* (Greek version).
[75] See e.g., *Early Christian Fathers*, Cyril Richardson, ed. (New York: Collier Books, 1970), 81, for one explanation of the changes to Ignatius' epistles.

philosophy to supplant their lack of understanding about God and to preserve the Church from the charge of atheism. There is no question that they were operating under great disadvantages and horrendous peril.

It should come as no surprise that they made theological errors under these circumstances. That they did so should not be condemned, but it should be recognized so their doctrines can be reexamined in the light of the Bible with greater objectivity.

Instead, the doctrine of co-substantiality grew in acceptance until it became etched in the stone of Nicaea. One reason for this result may be hard to comprehend today, but it is entirely understandable within the context of the times. Their deaths, many by martyrdom, greatly increased the stature of the Apologists in the early Church, lending greater credibility to their opinions. The situation is expressed by the noted Church historian, B. J. Kidd, as follows:

> It was natural that Christians should treasure both the memories and the remains of those who so nobly gave their lives for the Faith. They procured and edited the *Acta* or minutes of the Courts; and they wrote *Passions* as well. Into these documents, editors or authors introduced a miraculous element–visions, a supernatural voice, and parallelisms with the Passion of the Lord. This does not necessarily mean that the originals were altered, but that the incidents were so viewed–no doubt, under stress of exalted feeling. A similar reverence led the Christians to collect, entomb, and care for the relics of the martyrs, and to offer the Holy Sacrifice at their sepulchers, as often as their Natalitia came around.[76]

Thus, in death the Apologists claimed a far greater authority than they might ever have had if their ideas had been more carefully examined by objective and unpressured scholars in a subsequent generation. Now antiquity as well as reverence make it very difficult to open the eyes of orthodox Christians to the mistakes these men made. Honest and able scholarship, however, will support the conclusions drawn above.

---

[76] Kidd, *History of the Church*, 1:255-256.

The Rise of Catholicism Advanced the Apostasy

Another factor in the theological apostasy was the rise of catholicism in the early Church. As they dealt with heresy, the Apologists influenced the Church to adopt a universal set of opinions. After the death of the Apostles, there were differences, primarily in tradition but also in doctrine, between different branches of the Church. One such difference was the timing of the Easter festival with which Polycarp was concerned.

The writings of the Apologists caused the Church to unite doctrinally. Normally, this would be viewed as a positive goal, but in the early Church it led to universal adoption of the errors as well as the truths these men taught. Thus, it did as much to spread apostasy as it did to correct false teaching.

In the last twenty-five years of the second century, Irenaeus perceived the Church as strongly united on doctrinal issues, and expressed his feelings about its teachings as follows:

> The Church having received this belief preached by the Apostles carefully preserves it, and though she is dispersed throughout the world she preserves it as if she lived in one house. She believes the same doctrines everywhere, as if she had a single heart and soul, and she teaches them harmoniously everywhere as if she had but one tongue. The languages of the world may be different, but the message handed on by the Church is one and the same.[77]

Unfortunately, this unity of doctrinal teaching eventually grew into orthodoxy, a normative form of Christianity where the "truth" was not judged by what the scriptures taught, but by the popularity of opinions among the various bishops and influential teachers. The doctrinal and philosophical views that were most commonly embraced in the Church became the accepted and mandatory interpretations of scripture.[78] This led to the adoption of creeds in the third century, and, in the early fourth century, to the determination of doctrinal issues and issues of policy and discipline through conferences of bishops, such as the Nicene Council.

The adverse aspects of this development are best illustrated in the following decree issued by Constantine early in the fourth century:

---

[77] Irenaeus, *Against Heresies*, 1:10:2.
[78] See Arland J. Hultgren, *The Rise of Normative Christianity* (Minneapolis: Fortress Press, 1994).

> *I, as Emperor, cannot determine what Christian doctrine is, but I will take the opinion of the majority*, and will so far recognize that opinion that no one shall have the privileges of Christians, a right to hold property and an exemption from civil burdens, who does not assent to that opinion.[79]

Though he relented from this position during the Arian controversy (see Chapter 8), it reflects the catholicism or "universality" that came to dominate the early Church as a result of the Apologists' efforts. This urge to catholic agreement on doctrine and dogma sealed the errors of the Apologists into the doctrines of Christian orthodoxy to this day.

Summary

1. During the respite from persecution offered by Emperor Hadrian following the death of Trajan in 117 A.D., the Church continued to suffer criticism, false charges and assaults from uninformed and hostile critics.
2. Three charges were commonly made against the Church: atheism, ritual child-murder, and incest.
3. These claims arose in part because sacred ordinances such as the Lord's supper were veiled from the unbaptized.
4. The Apologists began to use Greek methods of rhetoric and logic to support Church doctrine against the challenges of these critics.
5. Justin Martyr was one of the earliest influential Apologists. He used the style and methods of the Greek philosophers to explain the scriptures.
6. Irenaeus was the most renowned theorist among the Apologists. He studied with Polycarp as a boy, but did not write down any of his master's teachings.
7. The Apologists at the time of Irenaeus suffered from a serious lack of information about the Gospel they were defending. Tatian and Tertullian left the Church, and many heretical ideas were espoused by Origen and others.
8. There was no set canon of scripture; New Testament texts were being questioned, and spurious documents were being offered as

---

[79] Hatch, *Influence of Greek Ideas*, 347.

scripture. This made it difficult to establish a reliable canon of inspired writing.
9. Even the writings of heretics were used widely in the early Church. One example is the *Diatessaron* of Tatian.
10. The use of Greek methods of allegorical exegesis rendered the scriptures unreliable as a source of Gospel knowledge. For example, the hundreds of Old Testament references to God's body parts and His movements were interpreted as allegorical allusions.
11. The Apologists tended to make metaphysical assumptions about the figurative language used to describe the Father and His relationship to the Son in the scriptures. This led to misunderstanding because the Jews to whom these scriptures were revealed had no concept of Greek metaphysics.
12. Their opposition to the wild heresies facing the Church affected the teachings of the Apologists. For example, Irenaeus made up new doctrine about Adam and Eve and Mary, the mother of Christ as he wrote in opposition to certain Gnostic claims.
13. Another example of the errors that orthodox Christian scholars admit were made by Irenaeus is his notion that Christ was fifty years old when he was crucified, and his claim that the Apostle John taught that doctrine.
14. The Apologists tackled questions about the God of the Christians for which they were entirely unprepared.
15. Because the Jews were vigorously inflaming Roman persecution, the Apologists addressed arguments against them as well as against the Romans.
16. Greek thinking gained such a foothold in the Church by 180 A.D. that Christians who would not use Greek methods of rhetoric and analysis to defend their beliefs were ridiculed.
17. The surprising resumption of lethal persecution against the early Church by Marcus Aurelius Antoninus in 161 A.D. proved to be a significant catalyst for the theological apostasy.
18. Marcus Aurelius was a noted Stoic philosopher, and the Apologists were anxious to address him with their response to his charge that Christians were atheists.
19. The approach of the Apologists in combating the charge of atheism against the early Church was to compare the Father and the Son to the Platonist's "Supreme God" and his "*Logos.*"

20. The Stoics had no patience for Christians. The strict monotheism of Stoic philosophy was contrasted with Christian theology and became a major factor in the persecution of the early Church by Marcus Aurelius.
21. The most significant question facing the early Church was why Christians claimed to believe in "one God," the Father, but still worshiped Christ, the Son, as "God." Indeed, the hallmark of persecution by Marcus Aurelius was the question, "Who is the God of the Christians?"
22. The early Apologists made statements that offended Roman authorities, especially those who were Stoics. Most significant among those statements was the distinct separation between the Father and the Son taught by Justin Martyr.
23. Justin's teachings so offended the Romans that in approximately 163 A.D. he was one of the first to be beheaded in Marcus Aurelius' persecutions.
24. A historical review of the writings of the Apologists after 161 A.D., and second-century Christian writings before 161, confirms that the theological apostasy occurred during the reign of Marcus Aurelius.
25. The *Epistle of Barnabus,* the *Teaching of the Twelve Apostles,* the *Apology of Aristides* (Greek version), the *Epistle to Diognetus,* Polycarp's *Epistle to the Philippians,* and Justin Martyr's *First Apology,* all written before 161 A.D., taught that the Father and the Son were separate persons without including any co-substantial explanation of that doctrine and without comparing them to the Platonists' "Supreme God" or his "*Logos.*"
26. The adjective "unbegotten" was first used to describe God the Father in Justin's *First Apology.*
27. In his *Dialogue with Trypho,* written around the time Marcus Aurelius came into power, Justin described the Father as though He were Aristotle's "Unmoving Mover." This was the first attempt to Hellenize the God of the Bible. Justin offered no biblical support for his new doctrine.
28. Between 150 and 172 A.D., Tatian enthusiastically embraced the Hellenized God described by Justin in *Dialogue with Trypho.* He referred to Christ as "*Logos,*" and described His relationship to the Father exactly as the Platonists' *Logos* was described, as emanating from the Supreme God.

29. Tatian first used the term *hupostasis* to describe God. Of course, he cited no scriptural authority for his views and descriptions of God.
30. Melito of Sardis, writing between 169 and 172 A.D., was the first to introduce metaphysics into the Christian description of God. However, he never actually said that the Father and the Son were the same being ("co-substantial").
31. In 177 A.D., Athenagoras and Irenaeus openly taught that the Christian God was identical to the Platonists' god by stating that the Father and the Son were one being.
32. Irenaeus most clearly described the Father and the Son as being the same substance, but he also described them as entirely separate. He rationalized these two views using Greek metaphysics and cited figurative language in the Bible to support his idea.
33. The word "Trinity" to describe the Father, Son and Holy Ghost, was first used by Theophilus in 180 A.D. He describes the Christian God as though He were entirely singular. He describes Christ as the "mind and thought" of God the Father.
34. Minucius Felix describes God just as Philo of Alexandria did, teaching that He is entirely undescribable and incomprehensible.
35. The co-substantiality doctrine adopted by the Apologists after 161 A.D. teaches that the Father, the Son and the Holy Ghost are three separate persons, but that they are one substance (*ousia*). Thus they rationalized three "Gods," the Father, Son and Holy Ghost, into "One Principle" using the methods and beliefs of Greek philosophy.
36. Contrary to the teachings of Callistus, the Apologists insisted on the three being separate persons. This allowed them to explain the writings of Justin Martyr as though they had always been consistent with the new theory about God.
37. Justin had insisted upon an actual numerical separation of the three, the Father, Son and Holy Ghost, arguing that "that which is begotten is numerically distinct from that which begets." Therefore, the later Apologists had to add certain explanations to Justin's teachings in order to make his teachings look consistent with their new doctrine of the Trinity.
38. The writings of some early Christian writers appear to have been altered to present a united front to Rome on the new doctrine of co-substantiality devised to convince authorities that Christians were not atheists.

39. The changes in the theological teachings of the early Church brought about by the Apologists were effective in this regard: by the end of the second century, Christians were no longer charged with atheism. However, persecution continued for other reasons.
40. The deaths of the Apologists, some by martyrdom, gave their teachings increased reverence and credibility.
41. The writings of the Apologists helped to unify the doctrine of the Church and thereby spread the false concept of God they adopted to escape persecution.
42. Catholicism led to orthodoxy, the determination of "truth" by majority opinion, which forced the early Church into universal adoption of the theological errors of the Apologists. Ultimately these opinions were enforced by Constantine throughout the Church.

7

Heresies and Heretics

Many heretical movements in the early Church were motivated by an attempt to find a philosophically satisfying answer to the problem of evil. Some were the result of philosophical predispositions in some converts to Christianity. Still others were the work of scoundrels and con men. All were resisted by the early Church fathers, but in the resistance process, truths were sometimes rejected and errors adopted.

Not surprisingly, the earliest heretics were Jewish. Some of their errors are addressed in the New Testament. Some of the writings of the Apostles John and Paul, and parts of the Book of Hebrews, were specifically aimed at these heresies, and are difficult to understand without some knowledge of them. Unfortunately, it will be impossible to do more than touch briefly on their doctrines in this chapter.

The Gentile heretics imported concepts from Greek philosophy and paganism into the Gospel. These notions were very far afield from the Bible. The fact that their ideas were given enough credence to justify lengthy responses from the Apologists shows the tendency of the Church of that era to give greater credence to Hellenistic doctrines. This is further evidence of the general lack of knowledge about the Gospel in the second-century Church. These heresies are important historically, both for their impact on the men who responded to them and also for the doctrine they produced as a result.

Finally, to understand the reaction of classical theists to certain biblical ideas taught in Mormonism today, it is essential to know the concepts labeled heretical in the early Church. This chapter will provide an overview of the major heretical sects of the time along with some important smaller groups.

Heretical Jewish Sects Clung to the Law of Moses

The most notable Jewish heretics were the Ebionites, a name that refers to humble servants of Jehovah.[1] With the fulfillment of the Law of Moses, Jewish Christians were faced with a significant change in their culture. Some, especially at Antioch, claimed that circumcision was still required for salvation (Acts 15:1). The Apostles met in Jerusalem about 49 A.D., and decided that the Gentiles did not have to be circumcised. All they needed to do, in relation to the already-abrogated Law of Moses, was to abstain from "pollutions of idols," fornication, things strangled, and blood (Acts 15:20).

Unfortunately, this ruling did not resolve the contention completely. It split the group, producing two main groups of Jewish Christians who continued to cling to the Law of Moses. The first group, sometimes called the Pharisaic Ebionites, believed that the Law, though abolished by Christ's suffering, still had to be observed universally. The second held that the Law was still to be kept, but only by the Jews, not the Gentiles.[2]

The Judaizers

The second group proved to be no problem for the Church, but the first is the sect sometimes called the *Judaizers*. They were particularly strong in Galatia even before the meeting of the Twelve in 49 A.D. The *Epistle to the Galatians* was written by Paul largely to refute their activities in that branch of the early Church. This group accepted Jesus as the Messiah and the greatest of the prophets, but they denied His divinity and ignored His immaculate conception. They required that Gentiles become Jews first before they could become Christians. Not surprisingly, they rejected the Apostle Paul and his writings, and they used only the Gospel of Matthew (excluding the first part).

Cerinthus and Gnostic Ebionism

Later, Gnostic Ebionism developed from the Pharisaic Judaizers. Their teachings were refuted by Paul in Colossians 2:16-23. This group tried to make Jewish observances attractive to the Greek world by building on them a grandiose superstructure of ascetic practices justified by a strange and specious philosophy.

---

[1] Kidd, *History of the Church*, 1:95.
[2] *Ibid.*, 1:92.

Cerinthus became their chief spokesman toward the close of the first century. He was opposed by the Apostle John. Many comments in the First Epistle of John refute doctrines taught by Cerinthus.

According to Irenaeus, Cerinthus believed in one God who was supreme over all. He claimed that below the God was a Demiurge (of Platonist origin), who, though he didn't know of the Supreme God, was somehow able to create the world. Irenaeus explains Cerinthus' beliefs further as follows:

> And he added that Jesus was not born of a Virgin (for that seemed to him impossible), but was the son of Joseph and Mary, [born] like all other men, and had more than men in justice, prudence, and wisdom. And that after his Baptism there descended on him from that Royalty which is above all, Christ in the figure of a Dove, and that he then declared the unknown Father, and did mighty works, but that in the end Christ again soared back from Jesus, and that Jesus suffered and rose again, but that Christ remained impassible, inasmuch as he was a spiritual being.[3]

Thus, Cerinthus taught that Jesus and Christ were different persons, the latter being referred to by the Ebionite Gnostics as the Aeon Christus. Belief in this entity was a common thread in many Gnostic sects. John refuted this belief in 1 John 2:22 when he said, "Who is the liar but he that denied that Jesus is the Christ?" (See also 1 John 4:2-3.) John also opposed the idea that Jesus became Christ at His baptism in 1 John 5:6 when he said: "This is he that came by water and blood, *even* Jesus Christ; not by water only, but by water and blood." The words "not by water only" are a reference to Christ's baptism. The phrase "but by water and blood" indicates that Jesus was Christ not through His baptism only, as Cerinthus taught, but also by His birth into mortality ("blood").

The Essenes or Clementines

Though the Essenes were originally Jews, they later became a heretical Christian sect. Shortly before the siege of Jerusalem in 70 A.D., some Jewish Christians fled to the same district where the Essenes lived. There developed among them a strange syncretism of religious systems and beliefs. They taught that God is one, that He made all things in a certain order, first the good and then the bad. Man, they

---

[3] Irenaeus, *Against Heresies*, 1:26:1.

claimed, comes to know these things in reverse order, first the bad and then the good. Thus, Cain came before Abel, Ishmael before Isaac, Esau before Jacob, Aaron (bad because he offered sacrifice to the idol) before Moses, and John the Baptist (inferior because he was born of man) before Jesus Christ (the Son of God).

They claimed that, from the beginning of the world, there had been a double series of prophets, the good or true prophets coming from Adam, whose fall they denied, and the bad or false prophets coming from Eve. The latter prophets were the ones that first came to Man's attention. Strictly speaking, there was only one prophet in the good series. He was manifest first in Adam and finally in Jesus Christ, who, though Son of God, was not God.

This group became known as the Clementines, and their religious practice was a mixture of baptism and circumcision, daily ablutions, and vegetarianism. Early marriage was required and blood-shedding sacrifice was forbidden.[4]

Ebionites Described by Epiphanius

A similar system of Ebionites was described by Epiphanius.[5] They believed that Christ and the Devil were both the work of God, and that the Devil made this world, while Christ made the world to come. Like the Pharisaic Ebionites, they believed that Jesus was a mere man, born in the normal way, on whom Christ descended as an ethereal spirit who appeared successively in Adam, the Patriarchs and finally in Jesus. This Christ, they believed, was the Holy Ghost, he who descended on the man Jesus at his Baptism.

These Ebionites rejected the writings of Moses, especially the requirement of sacrifice and the use of flesh. They acknowledged only the Gospel of Matthew (which they called the Gospel of the Hebrews), and they rejected Paul as a deceiver. Baptism was part of their practice, and they took the Sacrament of the Lord's Supper annually, using unleavened bread and water. They also observed the Jewish Sabbath and required circumcision. In other practices, they followed the Essene Ebionites.

---

[4] Kidd, *History of the Church*, 1:100. For a more detailed look at earlier Essene communities, such as the group at Qumran, see Hugh Nibley, "More Voices from the Dust," in *Old Testament and Related Studies* (Salt Lake City: Deseret Book Co. and FARMS, 1986).

[5] Epiphanius, *Heresies*, 30.

The Elkasaites

The last group of Jewish Christian heretics to be discussed here were the Elkasaites. They claimed a revelation in 100 A.D. delivered by an angel of colossal proportions called the Son of God who came in company with a female of similar dimensions identified as the Holy Ghost. (The word for spirit in Hebrew—*ruah*—is feminine.) This revelation taught that sins, even the grossest, could be remitted by re-baptism and a confession of faith in the new revelation. Baptism was performed by immersion. They observed circumcision and the Law of Moses, and were involved in magic and astrology.

They believed that Christ had been born in the ordinary way, but that he had been incarnate before and would be incarnate again on future worlds. (This was a Pythagorean doctrine called *metempsychosis*.[6]) They rejected portions of the Old Testament and denied Paul altogether. Origen said they believed they could deny Christ with their lips, if they confessed Him in their hearts, a convenient accommodation for those threatened with martyrdom.[7]

Docetism Denied the Suffering of Christ

A specific belief that was common among many heretical sects was *docetism*, mentioned in Chapter 6. This doctrine held that Christ's suffering on the Cross was not real, but apparent only. "He suffered only in semblance" was their claim.[8] The misconceptions of the docetes are explained by Gibbon as follows:

> Educated in the school of Plato, accustomed to the sublime idea of the *Logos*, they readily conceived that the brightest Aeon or Emanation of the Deity, might assume the outward shape and visible appearance of a mortal; but they vainly pretended that the imperfections of matter are incompatible with the purity of a celestial substance. While the blood of Christ yet smoked on Mount Calvary, the Docetes invented the impious and extravagant hypotheses that, instead of issuing from the womb of the Virgin, he had descended on the banks of the Jordan in the form of perfect manhood; that he had imposed on the senses of His enemies and of His disciples, and that the ministers of Pilate had wasted their impotent rage on an airy phantom, who

---

[6] Hippolytus, *Philosophic Refutation of All Heresies*, 9:22.
[7] Kidd, *History of the Church*, 1:102-103.
[8] For information on this belief, see Ignatius, *Epistle to the Smyrnaeans*, 2.

seemed to expire on the cross, and, after three days, to rise from the dead.[9]

Thus, the docetes believed Christ was born without the participation in any way of Matter (consistent with Greek and oriental notions). All the acts and sufferings of His human life, including the crucifixion, were only apparent. Correspondingly, they denied the resurrection and Christ's ascent into Heaven recorded in the first chapter of Acts. This doctrine in various forms was a regular corollary to Gnostic faiths.

Christian Gnosticism Began in Infamy

Christian Gnosticism is said to have begun with Simon Magus, whom Irenaeus identifies as the same Simon mentioned in Acts 8:9-24. To some degree, Gnosticism was less of a philosophic quest than a longing for the mystical, fueled largely by the personalities behind the various sects: Simon Magus, Menander, Corinthus, Satornilus, Basilides, Carpocrates, Valentinus, Heracleon, Ptolemy, Marcus, and the greatest of all, Marcion, whose failure marked the end of the Gnostic movement near the close of the second century.

Simon Magus

Simon Magus believed in a Supreme God and the existence of various powers or emanations from Him, of which he declared himself to be the chief. He claimed to have appeared to the Jews as the Son, and that in Samaria he had descended as the Father. To other nations he had appeared in the past as the Holy Ghost.[10] His doctrine of redemption involved sexual association, and of course, the redeemer was not Christ, but Simon himself.

Menander

Simon's student Menander also set himself up as a rival Christ. He instituted a baptism in his own name, calling it the resurrection, and promising that it would save men from old age and death. Time soon disproved his claims.[11]

---

[9] Gibbon, *Decline and Fall of the Roman Empire*, ch. 21, quoted in Talmage, *Great Apostasy*, 111.
[10] Irenaeus, *Against Heresies*, 1:23:1.
[11] Kidd, *History of the Church*, 1:194-195.

The Nicolaitans

The next group worthy of note are the Nicolaitans. They taught a kind of compromise between Christian belief and Graeco-Roman society. Their customs involved idolatry and sensuality, justified by their belief in the evil nature of matter and the worthlessness of the body.[12]

The Ophites, the Cainites and the Sethites

Most Gnostics credited the Demiurge (from Platonism) as being the God of the Old Testament to whom they were generally hostile. Two groups, however, were formed on the grounds of glorifying God's opponents—the serpent in one case, and Cain in the other. To the Ophites (also called Naasenes or Serpentarians), the Fall was a fall upwards, from innocence to knowledge. To them, therefore, the serpent was an illuminator and liberator of Mankind.

The Cainites took Cain as their hero, seeing him as a type of virile humanity. They looked up to him as a martyr to the vindictiveness of the Demiurge, who persecuted, but could not suppress, him.[13]

A third group, the Sethites, accepted the common principles of morality and took Seth for their type of higher manhood. They imagined that he was inspired by Wisdom (often called *Sophia*), a personality ascribed to one of the Forms originally conceived by Plato. This being was seen by the heretics and Hellenized Jews of the time as the entity that speaks in Proverbs 8:12-36. According to this sect, Seth became her instrument to counteract the work of the Demiurge.[14]

Carpocrates

Carpocrates was the Gentile equivalent of Cerinthus. He was given to immorality on principal. His idea was that since the body is evil, indulging its evil tendencies was appropriate. His son, Epiphanes (not to be confused with Epiphanius), improved on his father's doctrine and advocated a Platonistic community of women and goods.[15]

The Syrian Gnostics Followed Platonistic Dualism

The groups described above were small and passing compared to the greater Gnostic schools, which included the Syrian school under

---

[12] *Ibid.*, 195.
[13] *Ibid.*, 1:196.
[14] *Ibid.*
[15] *Ibid.*, 1:197.

Satornilus, c. 120 A.D., Tatian, c. 160-180 A.D., and Bardesanes, c. 154-223 A.D.; and the Egyptian school under Basilides, Valentinus and, to a certain extent, Marcion. The Syrian system was dualistic. They drew a strong distinction between the substance (*ousia*) of God and that of Matter, i.e., created things. This led them to an austere asceticism in which they denied fleshly appetites and passions. Where Menander and Simon set themselves up as Christ, Satornilus taught about Jesus Christ.

Syrian Gnostics generally believed in a Supreme God—"one Father, unknown to all."[16] The Syrian school believed that matter was evil, and that creation, therefore, had been accomplished through secondary principals. These alternate principals were sometimes Aeons, Evil Angels or Gods, even Angels who acted to a degree as agents of the Supreme God, since a good God could not be responsible for creation using evil matter. They were also docetic.

Satornilus

As noted above, Satornilus taught that the Angels who created the earth (of which there were seven according to him), were emissaries of a rival God, and that one of the seven Angels was the God of the Jews. The Supreme God wished to do away with all these Angels, and sent Christ "to destroy the God of the Jews, and to save them that believe in Him."[17] The Old Testament was, of course, rejected, and they condemned everything connected with matter, including marriage and animal food. (In this regard see 1 Tim. 4:1-3.)

Tatian

Tatian, mentioned in Chapter 6, was born about 110 A.D. in Assyria. He became a sophist by profession, and fell in with Justin Martyr, under whose influence he was converted to Christianity in about 150 A.D. Tatian wrote his *Address to the Greeks* in about 152 A.D., in which he expressed his testimony of conversion to Christianity. He remained in Rome and was renowned as one of the leading Apologists, a teacher of some repute in the Church, until approximately 172 A.D., several years after the death of Justin Martyr. By then his theories had developed into open heresy and he moved to the East.

---

[16] Irenaeus, *Against Heresies*, 1:24:1. Irenaeus refers to Satornilus as "Saturninus."
[17] *Ibid.*, 1:24:2.

Irenaeus says that "Like the Valentinians, he made out a mythology of certain invisible aeons; like Marcion and Saturninus, he denounced marriage as corruption and fornication, but his denial of Adam's salvation he invented himself."[18]

An eclectic, Tatian borrowed from whatever school of thought seemed correct to him. His asceticism associates him with the Syrian school of Gnosticism, but he was more extreme than they. Not only did he condemn marriage and animal food, he substituted water for wine in the Sacrament of the Lord's Supper. For this he and all who engaged in this practice, were called *Hydroparastatae*. He and his followers were sometimes called Encratites, "professors of an abstinence that was truly total." [19]

Tatian's fundamental principle was a distinction between the Supreme God and the Creator. In contrast with the New Testament, he disparaged the Old Testament as the work of an inferior God, which would account for his peculiar belief about Adam's lack of salvation. He also supported the latter belief by citing Paul's statement that "In Adam all die."[20] The latter justification is typical of the level at which the later Apologists manipulated the scriptures. They were not analyzed for their true meaning but were used as a way to support pet theories.

As a docete, Tatian decided to rewrite the four Gospels, which he did in his *Diatessaron* or *Harmony of the Gospels*, from which he removed all the genealogies and all the passages that show the Lord to have been born of the seed of David after the flesh. Because of its brevity, the *Harmony* came to be commonly used by many early Church members and leaders who did not recognize what Tatian had in mind when he wrote it.[21]

Bardesanes

Bardesanes, or Bardaisân, as he was also known, is sometimes called the last of the Gnostics. He believed in one God almighty who created the worlds and the elements (fire, wind, water, light, and darkness). Darkness, he taught, was evil. It strove to ascend from its place below, in order to mix with the pure elements. These elements appealed

---

[18] Irenaeus, *Against Heresies*, 1:28:1.
[19] Kidd, *History of the Church*, 1:200.
[20] *Ibid.*
[21] *Ibid.* 1:200-201.

to God for help, and He sent Jesus Christ to their assistance. Thus the world, as Man knows it, came into being. He taught that there is evil in the world but that God allows it because of His longsuffering. At the close of the six thousand years, this world with its admixture of evil and good will end by fire, and God will create a new world from which evil will be entirely banished.

Bardesanes believed Man is controlled by the planets (astrology) in such matters as life and death, wealth and misfortune, and health and sickness, but is free to do good or evil. He also taught that Man is immortal and will be judged according to his works. He believed that Matter was co-eternal with God, and not hostile to Him. His doctrine of resurrection amounted to a denial of the resurrection of the body. Finally, he claimed that Christ had a spiritual body, as distinguished from an ordinary human body.[22]

The Egyptian Gnostics Were Monistic

The Egyptian school of the Gnostics was inspired more by Hellenistic thinking than was the Syrian school. Drawing from the philosophers a belief in only one God, who is Pure Being, or "Super-essential Essence," their problem was to connect this Being with the created universe. The oriental thinking of the Syrian school did this by supposing a duality of Gods, one good and the other evil. Hellenist thought held fast to the monotheistic idea of an only and supreme God, and that view prevailed in the Egyptian school.

Like the Platonists, the Egyptian Gnostics solved the problem of evil by inventing an elaborate system of Aeons or emanations as intermediaries between the Supreme God and the world in which Man lives. They either evolved in a series (according to Basilides, whose Aeons were celibate), or were generated in pairs (according to Valentinus) with each successive pair departing a little further from pure Spirit and approaching a little nearer to crude matter. Among the last were some capable of producing the material world.[23]

Basilides

Basilides, the first representative of the Egyptian school, and the first to pretend to a secret tradition handed down from the Apostles,

---

[22] *Ibid.*, 1:203-204.
[23] *Ibid.*, 204.

taught at Alexandria between 117 and 138 A.D. He claimed that one Aeon was the god of the Jews. This god was turbulent and ambitious, and brought his people to ruin. The supreme God intervened and sent His Mind (*Logos*), the Christ, to deliver those who believed in Him from the rulers of the world.

Christ appeared on earth, but only in semblance (docetism again). In that regard, Basilides taught that on the way to Calvary, Christ exchanged forms with Simon the Cyrenian, who was thus crucified in his stead, while Jesus, standing opposite, unseen in Simon's form, mocked those who did the deed.

Martyrdom and confession of the crucified Jesus were discouraged by his sect, it being an indication that the believer was still in bondage to the maker of the body. Later, immorality was widely practiced by this sect, as it was by Carpocrates, to show the independence of the body from the spirit. Salvation was for the soul alone. They believed there was no physical resurrection or future for the body at all.

Valentinus

Valentinus was one of the most famous of the Gnostics. He was a contemporary of Polycarp and by all accounts a very brilliant man, especially judging from the number and stature of the Apologists who arrayed themselves against him. His system of theology, like that of his fellows, drew heavily from the prevailing theology of the Platonists. He taught a three-part structure to the Universe of Being. It consisted of the Pleroma or divine (celestial) sphere, a realm beyond the Pleroma, and the world inhabited by Mankind.

The Pleroma started from a primal Being, called the Depth, from whom came pairs, or syzygies, who were male and female. From Depth and Silence came Mind and Truth; from those two came Reason and Life; then Man and Church. These formed what he called the Ogdoad. There followed a Decad and a Dodecad, making a system of thirty Aeons in all to complete the Pleroma. These comprised the totality of divine attributes.

The youngest Aeon was *Wisdom*, whom Valentinus also called Sophia, the name given by the Platonists. She wanted to comprehend the Infinite, but was stopped by Limit. While she was restored to her place in the Pleroma, her Design was cast out. To prevent further disturbances, the Father put forth another pair of Aeons, called Christ and Holy Spirit. The Aeon Christ taught that the Father is incomprehensible.

The story continues like a Greek mythology. Between the Pleroma and this earth there supposedly exists the Intermediate. There, a younger Wisdom (*Achamoth*), the personification of the banished Design, produced three grades of being: the material, which sprung from her passions: the psychic, from her conversion by the Aeon Christ; and the spiritual, from her joy at the Light. From her psychic passion sprang the Demiurge, who, at last, created the world with three classes of men: the material man (e.g., Cain), the psychic man (e.g., Abel) and the spiritual man (e.g., Seth).[24]

Christ was believed to be the author of redemption. However, this Christ was not the Aeon Christ, but the son of the Demiurge, and like him, he had a psychic and a spiritual nature. However, he had no body, or at least he had only a semblance of a body (docetism again). His relationship to Mary was that he "passed through Mary as water passes through a pipe."[25]

Valentinus' Christ could save Men, or not, only according to the class in which they belonged. If the material man predominated, no salvation was possible; if the psychic were in the forefront, the man could be saved but only by faith and works. If the spiritual man was predominant, the man was a true Gnostic, assured of salvation from the start simply by obtaining knowledge.[26] The spiritual man was considered incapable of corruption. Irenaeus said, "the most perfect among them do all forbidden things without fear . . . [and] say that 'they give to the flesh the things of the flesh and to the spirit the things of the spirit.'"[27]

Ptolemy, Heracleon and Mark

After his death, the Valentinians continued in two schools: the Oriental, represented by Theodotus, and the Italian school, headed by Ptolemy, Heracleon and Mark. Ptolemy was a contemporary of Irenaeus, and so receives considerable attention from him. He attempted to deal with some of the problems that the philosophical minds in the early Church thought they had found in the Old Testament. Some attributed the problems they saw in the Law of Moses to God the Father, and others ascribed them to the devil. Ptolemy, with the complete disregard for reality characteristic of metaphysical

---

[24] Irenaeus, *Against Heresies*, 1:1:1-3; 1:2:2, 4, 9; 1:3:1; 1:4:1; 1:4; 1:5:1, 5.
[25] *Ibid.* 1:6:1; 1:7:2, 5.
[26] *Ibid.* 1:6:1, 2.
[27] *Ibid.* 1:6:3.

Greek thinking among the Gnostics, made up his own explanation of the Old Testament in the *Epistle of Ptolemy to Flora*. He claimed that some of the Law had been revealed by God, some by Moses, some by "the elders," and so forth, the ultimate author being the Demiurge.[28]

Heracleon was one of the first Christian exegetes. He wrote a *Commentary on St. John* in which he reads into the fourth Gospel his own strange system of theology using the Greek methods of allegorical interpretation.

Mark was accounted by Irenaeus as a charlatan who dealt in magic, using his influence over women for self-indulgence.[29] His influence on the early Church was small. By the time these men were teaching, Gnosticism, as an intellectual system, had largely run its course.

Marcion

The most prominent of the Gnostics was unquestionably Marcion. His was the most morally respectable sect, and the only one of the Gnostic communities that produced martyrs. He actually established a church, and Marcionites did not disappear from the scene until as late as the fifth century. In the Syrian and Egyptian schools the heathen elements predominated, but in Marcionism, Christian elements had risen to the top.

Marcion, also a contemporary of Polycarp, was a native of Pontus and the son of the bishop of Sinope. He was a ship owner and a wealthy man. He came to Rome in 138 A.D. and fell in with the Syrian Gnostic, Cerdon. Marcion was twice excommunicated from the Church, apparently on doctrinal grounds, and ultimately applied for and was promised reconciliation, provided he would bring back with him those he had deceived. He set himself to that task, but died before he could accomplish it. He was considered a warmhearted man who needed the fellowship of the Church but disagreed with some of its teachings.

His principal problem was his criticism of the Old Testament. He was not interested in solving the problem of evil through intermediaries, and so did not invent a system of Aeons or emanations to explain how the Infinite came to produce a finite world, or the Righteous an evil one. He simply borrowed enough philosophy from the dualism of the Syrian

---

[28] See Ptolemy, *Epistle of Ptolemy to Flora* (still available today in its entirety).
[29] Irenaeus, *Against Heresies*, 1:6:2, 3.

school to support his explanation of the contrast between the Old Testament and the writings that subsequently formed the New.

Like the Syrian Gnostics, he supposed the existence of two Gods—the just God (the Demiurge), and the good God (the Supreme God). The first was the author of the Old Testament, and the second was the author of the New. He also rejected parts of the New Testament as having been corrupted because the authors were Jews. Thus, he accepted only the writings of Paul, which he manipulated to his liking, and of Luke. However, his version of the Gospel of Luke has all the passages that relate to the birth and infancy of Christ cut out (he was docetic), and he modified other passages to suit his pet theories.

Marcion was strongly anti-Jewish. He refused to accept the notion of the Law of Moses as a schoolmaster for a people being raised out of violent heathenism. He had no appreciation for this concept of development. According to him, the Supreme God had once, and only once, revealed Himself—in Jesus. Each of Marcion's two Gods supposedly had His own Christ, the Christ of the just God being yet to come as the Jewish Messiah.

As to Redemption, Marcion taught a Gospel of love only. He represented the character of the Supreme God as one of pure benevolence—entirely without justice, a characteristic reserved to his second God. Irenaeus and Tertullian easily refuted this idea, explaining that the true God must possess both the attributes of goodness and justice, or cease to be God.[30]

Marcion took much the same approach to the problem of evil as Rabbi Kushner.[31] Specifically, he expressed the problem as follows:

> If God is good, and prescient of the future, and able to avert evil, why did He allow man, that is to say His own image and likeness, nay more, His own substance, to be tricked by the devil and fall from obedience to the law into death? For if He had been good, and thereby unwilling that such an event should happen, and prescient, and thereby not ignorant that it would happen, and powerful, and thereby able to prevent its happening, it would certainly not have happened, being impossible under these three conditions of divine greatness. But since it did happen, the inference is certain that God must be believed to be neither good nor prescient nor powerful.[32]

---

[30] Irenaeus, *Against Heresies*, 3:25:2; Tertullian, *Against Marcion*, 2:11, 12.
[31] Kushner, *When Bad Things Happen to Good People*, 37.
[32] Tertullian, *Against Marcion*, 2:5.

Justin Martyr, in unison with other Apologists, responded to this argument as follows: "The nature of every created being is to be capable of vice and virtue: for no one of them would be an object of praise if it had not also the power of turning in the one direction or the other."[33]

Marcion could have answered Justin's argument by claiming that God, being all-powerful, should have been able to think of a way to accomplish the goal of praise without involving the undesirable element of vice. But that goal necessarily involves a paradox, a contradictory situation that can only be imagined through metaphysics (because of its complete disregard for reality).

Mormonism teaches that there are some things God simply will not do, even if the power to do them actually exists. One example, used by Augustine in his writings, is that God cannot lie. Likewise, He does not give Man his free agency, then eliminate the consequences of his wrongful choices. Marcion could not see this principle, nor comprehend the benefits of adversity upon Man. So he taught a gospel of universal love and forgiveness not unlike that taught in some Evangelical churches today.

Errors Made While Opposing Heretics

Occasionally, a heretic would come up with a *correct* Gospel principle, but because of the source, or because it agreed with some Greek notion that was not in favor at the time, or because the Church had taken a philosophical turn against that principle in its gradual slide toward apostasy, the idea was rejected. On the other hand, the early Church sometimes did the opposite, adopting a false principle championed by heretics.

Creation Out of Nothing

Hermogenes, who was a disciple of Marcion, taught that God created the earth out of pre-existing and eternal formless matter. For this doctrine, he was discredited by Hippolytus in his *Philosophic Refutation of All Heresies* as follows:

> A certain heretic, Hermogenes, thinking he was putting forward a very new idea, said that God made all things out of a sort of matter which was as eternal and ungenerated as himself. His reason was that

---

[33] Justin, *Second Apology*, 7.

God could not make generated things out of the non-existent, and that as God is eternally ruler and creator, matter is eternally his servant and eternally generated; . . . Hermogenes, it seems, was not aware that all this is found in the Socratic myth which Plato works out so much more fully than he does.[34]

It is clear from this quotation that, by the time Hippolytus wrote his *Refutation* in 222 A.D., the Church had either forgotten or chosen to ignore the fact that Justin Martyr taught the very same principle based on Old Testament texts. Justin had noted that the Platonists also taught it, but that had not dissuaded him from following the biblical text.

Surprisingly, another heretic, Basilides, mentioned above, is credited by Hatch as the source of the doctrine that God created the universe out of nothing.[35] Hippolytus, who wrote almost a hundred years later, details Basilides' complete theology in Book 7 of his *Refutation*. After describing Basilides' doctrine of creation out of nothing, Hippolytus says, "And these heretics bring this system to light as if it were peculiarly their own, and as if it were some novel doctrine, and some secret disclosure from the discourses of Matthias."[36]

This suggests that by 222 A.D. the Church had so long taught the *ex nihilo* doctrine that the source of it was unknown. Hippolytus' account of Basilides and that of Irenaeus are irreconcilable with each other.[37] That is in part because Basilides was the first to teach the *ex nihilo* doctrine, and Irenaeus knew that. Obviously, Hippolytus did not. This is further evidence that both the heresies and the effort to combat them brought confusion to the early Church.

A Residue of Gnosticism Remained in Orthodox Christianity

The Gnostics were the first group to put Christianity into Greek forms of philosophical treatment and analysis. As such, they were the principal object of Paul's warnings against the acceptance of Greek philosophy. Their response to Paul was typically Greek. Faith, they claimed, is a thing to be thought out, and not merely to die for or to pass on. Sadly, their position, rather than Paul's, ultimately prevailed with the

---

[34] Hippolytus, *Philosophic Refutation of All Heresies*, 8:10.
[35] Hatch, *Influence of Greek Ideas*, 195-196.
[36] Hippolytus, *Philosophic Refutation of All Heresies*, 7:8.
[37] Hatch, *Influence of Greek Ideas*, 9, n.2.

Apologists. Indeed, although Gnosticism was officially rejected by the early Church, it did much to form the Catholic Church that evolved in the third and fourth centuries.[38]

A kind of Christian *gnosis* was formulated by Clement of Alexandria in the early third century. The essential Greek element in Gnosticism is the idea that salvation is obtained through knowledge (*gnosis*). Plato taught that true knowledge is Man's end and becomes possible only when he gets away from the temporal world. According to him, the true is the good; the ultimately true is God.[39] Shades of this view, and of Gnosticism itself, are evident in the following statement by Clement of Alexandria:

> I would make bold to say that it will not just be through a wish for salvation that the true Gnostic will choose gnosis and follow it as a means to divine science. For the action of knowing through prolonged discipline becomes perpetual knowledge, and perpetual knowledge becomes by an indissoluble mingling of the very essence of the knower and remains a living substance. So if one were to propose to the Gnostic the question as to which he would choose, knowledge of God or eternal salvation, supposing these two to be separate though of course they are absolutely identical, without a moment's delay he would choose knowledge of God, judging as desirable in itself the property of ascending beyond faith through love into knowledge.[40]

Written by the monk Dionysius around 500 A.D., the following passage expresses the essence of Christian Gnosticism as it ultimately developed:

> Let us not think that the appearances of the scriptural symbols have been devised as ends in themselves. They have been set up like a screen in front of a knowledge that is ineffable and invisible to the many, thus keeping all holy things out of reach of the profane. These are disclosed only to genuine lovers of holiness who can lay aside all puerile fantasy before the sacred symbols and who have the requisite simplicity of mind and theoretic faculty to approach that simple and supernal truth residing in the symbols, a truth which surpasses nature. One must remember that there is a double heritage handed down by theologians, on the one hand the ineffable and mystical, on the other

---

[38] See Kidd, *History of the Church*, 1:225.
[39] Shiel, *Greek Thought*, 73-74.
[40] Clement, *Miscellanies* [Stromata], 4:22.

the explicit and manifest. The one is of symbols and mysteries, the other of scientific philosophy and demonstration; and both are linked together, the explicit with the mystical. The one uses persuasion and enforces by proof the truth of its statements, the other is a ritual action grounding its truth in God through initiations which admit of no technique.[41]

This is the legacy of Gnosticism in orthodox Christianity.

Monarchianism, the Foundation of Arianism

Another early sect that strongly affected the Church was Monarchianism. This sect included two groups. The *Adoptionists* viewed Christ as a unique person, divinely energized and called to be the Son of God. The Sabellians or *Modalists* taught that God is a singular being who presents himself as three persons only in relation to the world, to whom He appears in the three "modes" of the Father, the Son and the Holy Spirit. They also taught that the Son of God did not exist before His incarnation and that the Father was incarnated with and literally suffered with the Son in his passion and death. These heretics were opposed primarily by Tertullian and Hippolytus. The sect strongly influenced the Arian controversy, as will be seen in the next chapter.

Montanism Claimed Endless New Revelations

One of the most important of the heretical sects in the early Church were the Montanists, whom Tertullian, himself, joined around the turn of the second century. In some ways, this group, in its origins, might be designated as Charismatic in today's Christian nomenclature. When they first arose in Asia, they were most noted for their belief that there was no reason to think of divine revelation as limited to the Apostles. Though continuing revelation to the leader of the Church and each officer and member in respect to his or her calling is a biblical concept, the leaders of this group took it upon themselves to receive revelations of every kind and description applicable to the whole Church.

Montanus, the founder of the sect, would rise up in a sort of frenzy, or false kind of ecstasy, according to Eusebius,[42] and deliver revelations in what was described as strange utterances. This led some to take him

---

[41] Dionysius, the pseudo-Areopagite, Letter 9, quoted from Shiel, *Greek Thought*, 74-75.
[42] Eusebius, *Ecclesiastical History*, 5:16:7.

as a man possessed by an evil spirit, while others revered him as an inspired prophet.[43] He claimed that like the violin and the bow, a prophet is passive under the stroke of the Spirit. Supposedly, his utterances were in no sense his own but directly from God Himself.[44]

His raptures and claims of revelation were soon outdone by two ladies, Prisca and Maximilla, who deserted their husbands to become his disciples. About 172 A.D., they declared themselves prophetesses, and said that their mission was to inaugurate the dispensation of the Paraclete, a time of revelation through the Spirit just before the Second Coming of Christ. They settled down in a community near Phrygia, which they called the New Jerusalem, and awaited the second Advent.

Prisca apparently died during the wait. Montanus died about the same time, leaving Maximilla to carry on the leadership of the sect. This prompted Maximilla to declare, "After me, there shall be no prophetess more, but the end."[45] Unfortunately, the end did not come. Instead, the frenzied ecstasies of this group roused opposition in the local Church. They were disfellowshiped by the local bishop and appealed to Rome. The bishop there was encouraged to uphold the actions of the local authorities and so the Montanists received a deaf ear. Still, no action was taken to excommunicate them as a group.

About 25 years later, Proclus, a leader of one segment of Montanists, arrived in Rome and started to publish their doctrines again. About the same time, Praxeas, the author of Modalism and an opponent of Montanism, came to Rome and made himself popular with the Church leaders there.

Tertullian, by then a convert to Montanism, denounced Praxeas, saying that he managed to "bring off two bits of jobs for the devil in Rome: he drove out prophecy and brought in heresy; he put to flight the Paraclete and crucified the Father."[46] The reference to heresy was directed at Modalism, which was later rejected as heretical. The allusion to crucifying the Father relates to the belief of some Modalists that the Father suffered on the cross with Christ.

Though Praxeas put the bishop of Rome, Zyphyrinus, on guard against Montanism, Proclus stood his ground, and a few years later held

---

[43] *Ibid.*, 5:16:8.
[44] Kidd, *History of the Church*, 1:281.
[45] Epiphanius, *Heresies*, 48:8.
[46] Tertullian, *Against Praxeas*, 1.

a debate with the Roman presbyter, Gaïus. During that debate Praxeas noted that Philip and his daughters had lived and died in Hierapolis, the region where the Montanists had settled. Gaïus responded that the tombs of Peter and Paul were in Rome, and that these men had been greater than Philip. This frivolous debating tactic actually won the day for the Romans,[47] and Gaïus declared that the canon of the New Testament was closed. According to Eusebius, "he curbed the rashness and boldness of his opponents in setting forth new scriptures."[48]

The Defeat of Montanism Ended the Concept of Ongoing Revelation

While the reaction of the early Church to the extremes of this sect was understandable, the consequences of its rejection were extremely significant for the early Church. There was a growing tendency to limit the canon of scripture, and this approach seemed especially useful as a means to curb the extremes of the Montanist "prophets."[49] The decision is, as usual, justified by Hatch as essential to the institutional strength of the early Church.[50]

As Paul Tillich explains, the decision to exclude the Montanists resulted in four notable losses for the early Church: (1) the canon of scripture was deemed to be closed against the possibility of any new revelation; (2) the spirit of prophecy was excluded from the Church; (3) the study of end times (eschatology, e.g., the Second Coming), became less significant than it had been in the Apostolic Age; and (4) the strict discipline of the Montanists, who maintained extremely high moral standards, was discredited, giving way to a growing laxity.[51]

The End of the Battles Against Heresy and Its Effect on the Early Church

By the end of the second century the Gnostic heresies had died out, the Montanists had been defeated and problems with the Jewish heretics were largely in the past. During the third century, the Church dealt pri-

---

[47] Kidd, *History of the Church*, 1:283-284.
[48] Eusebius, *Ecclesiastical History*, 6:20:3.
[49] Kidd, *History of the Church*, 1:292-293.
[50] Hatch, *Influence of Greek Ideas*, 107.
[51] Paul Tillich, *A History of Christian Thought* (New York: Harper & Row, 1968), 41.

marily with internal schisms and the Monarchianists, the forerunners of the Arian controversy.

The second century battle against heresy left the early Church with one very significant characteristic related to the theological apostasy—the tendency to orthodoxy. Those clerics and scholars who held opinions contrary to the accepted doctrines of the Apologists were pressured in various ways to accept doctrinal unity before their influence and supposed errors could expand into conflicting heretical sects.

Views in the Alexandrian area of the Church were the last to feel this pressure.[52] Thus, Origen continued into the middle of the third century with notions that were increasingly viewed by the Roman clerics as "heretical." Some in that region taught theology that either contradicted or appeared to contradict the Trinitarian view espoused by Rome.[53] Thus the soil was prepared in Alexandria for early Christianity's next great battle over theology, the Arian controversy. Because of its significance, the history and nature of that controversy will be discussed in the next chapter.

Summary

1. A knowledge of the heresies helps in interpreting the scriptures and understanding the progress of the theological apostasy as it grew into orthodox Christian theology.
2. The Jewish heretics, or Ebionites, clung to the Law of Moses.
3. The Pharisaic Ebionites, or Judaizers, tried to get the Gentiles to live the Law of Moses even though it had been abolished by Christ's suffering. They believed the Gentiles had to become Jews before they could be Christians.
4. Gnostic Ebionites developed from the Judaizers. They tried to make Jewish observances attractive to the Gentiles.

---

[52] In this regard, see Wilfred Griggs, *Early Egyptian Christianity: From Its Origins to 451 C.E.*, Coptic Studies Series, Martin Krause, ed., no. 2 (New York: E. J. Brill, 1990).

[53] See, e.g., the dispute between Dionysius of Alexandria and Dionysius of Rome discussed in Chapter 8.

5. The Gnostic Ebionites developed the heretical teaching that the man, Jesus, was separate from the spiritual being, Christ. This doctrine was refuted in the New Testament by the Apostle John.
6. The Essenes or Clementines were a Jewish-Christian sect characterized by the belief in a double series of prophets, one set good and the other bad, who came from Adam and Eve, respectively.
7. The Ebionites generally rejected the New Testament, except for parts of Matthew, and were adamantly opposed to Paul.
8. The Elkasaites, the last group of Jewish-Christian heretics, believed that the Son of God was of colossal proportions, that the Holy Ghost was a female, and that Christ would be reincarnated repeatedly on other worlds.
9. Docetism, common to many Gnostic sects, claimed that Christ's suffering on the cross wasn't real, but was in semblance only. They denied Christ's physical resurrection and ascension into heaven.
10. Christian Gnosticism began with Simon the magician, mentioned in Acts 8, a con man claiming to have secret or mystical knowledge.
11. The Syrian Gnostics followed a dualistic theology and were highly ascetic. Generally, they believed in two different gods, one good and one evil (or at least incompetent). This helped them explain the problem of evil.
12. Satornilus, Bardesanes and Tatian were Syrian Gnostics.
13. The Egyptian Gnostics believed in one Supreme God, but drew on Platonistic ideas about intermediaries to explain the origin of evil. Many of these sects practiced gross immorality.
14. Basilides, Valentinus, Ptolemy, Heracleon and Mark were Egyptian Gnostics.
15. Marcion was the most famous Gnostic teacher. He was twice excommunicated from the Christian Church and was in the process of attempting to reconcile again when he died.
16. Borrowing ideas from the Syrian Gnostics, Marcion taught that the Old Testament had been authored by a "just God," and that the New Testament was the work of another God, whom he called the good or Supreme God, after the manner of the Platonists.
17. Marcion was strongly anti-Jewish. He taught a gospel of universal love and forgiveness and believed that the Supreme God was a being of pure benevolence, devoid of the attribute of justice.

18. The Apologists, in opposing the heretics, sometimes opposed true doctrines and adopted false doctrines. For example, they rejected the biblical teaching that God created the earth out of pre-existing, formless matter, which the Greeks and some heretics taught, and accepted the teachings of other heretics (Basilides and Tatian) that God first created all matter out of nothing.
19. Christian orthodoxy, primarily through Clement of Alexandria, adopted some Gnostic concepts. These are found in forms of mysticism that have endured from the third century.
20. The heresy of Monarchianism consisted of two sects, called the Adoptionists and the Modalists or Sabellians.
21. The Sabellians taught that the Father, the Son and the Holy Ghost were simply "modes" of appearance belonging to a singular god. The Adoptionists taught that Christ was a mere man who was adopted into the Godhead. The beliefs of the latter group are the foundation of Arianism.
22. The Montanists believed in continuing revelation, and claimed to receive it on behalf of the whole Church while in a frenzied state.
23. The rejection of Montanism ended the concept of continuing revelation in the early Church, and closed the biblical canon.

The Arian Controversy: Cementing the Theological Apostasy

The theological history of the early Church was strongly influenced by the Roman persecutions that continued from the end of the second century until 313 A.D. As noted in Chapter 6, persecution resulted in veneration of the men who were martyred, and with that reverence came acceptance of their teachings. Other factors also figured in the wide acceptance of the new theology espoused by the Apologists. Though non-biblical and misguided, the doctrine of co-substantiality was ingenious in many ways.

For one thing, it satisfied the early Church's craving for philosophical respectability. By the end of the second century, the public perception of Christianity had changed markedly from the disgusting rumors that characterized the beginning of that century. In fact, Christianity had achieved almost too much respectability. Roman persecution in the third century was motivated more by fear of the Church than by opposition to its doctrines.

Secondly, by adopting Greek philosophy into Christianity, the Apologists turned Christianity itself into a philosophy. Many brilliant minds were drawn to this new religion, not the least of whom was Tertullian,[1]

---

[1] No less of an authority than Berkhof has claimed that Tertullian was the first to use the term "Trinity" in his writings. See Louis Berkhof, *The History of Christian Doctrines* (Grand Rapids: Baker House, 1937) reprinted in 1992, 63. That is not this author's observation. The first use of the word "Trinity" in any early Church writings of which this author has become aware is found in *To Autolycus,* written in 180 A.D. by Theophilus of Antioch, as mentioned in Chapter 6. That was five years before Tertullian even became a Christian. Notably, Roberts and Donaldson agree. See *Ante-Nicene Fathers*, 2:101., fn. 2.

who joined the Church in 185 A.D. These men were instrumental in formulating doctrinal statements ("creeds") that appealed to the Hellenized masses. They also formulated a systematized theology, which, although it was based on a false premise, has maintained a strong appeal to the philosophical mind for nearly two millennia.

The last great threat to this doctrine and the growing accord that characterized the third century was the Arian controversy. That controversy had its roots in the fundamental question of the age, the question that had been erroneously answered by the Apologists in their responses to Marcus Aurelius' charge of atheism. From the Romans that question was, "Who is the God of the Christians?" From a biblical perspective, the issue was, **Why does the New Testament identify three "Gods," the Father (John 17:3), the Son (John 1:1, 14) and the Holy Ghost (Acts 5:3-4), while it retains Old Testament references to "one God" (Mark 12:29; 1 Cor. 8:4; Eph. 4:6)?** This enigma will occasionally be referred to in this chapter as the Nicene Question, since it was at the heart of what that Council eventually considered.

Those involved in the Arian controversy never actually reexamined the erroneous intrusion of metaphysics into Christianity in their efforts to answer the Nicene Question. Arianism accepted the God defined by the Apologists, at least as far as their description related to the person of the Father. What they questioned fell into the area of "Christology," the study of Christ and His relationship to the Father. The debate began early in the third century against the backdrop of Roman persecution, and continued to rage through most of the fourth century.

How Roman Persecution Was Triggered

The nature of the Roman persecution that was directed against Christians in the third century had a profound effect on both the Church and, ultimately, on the entire Gentile world. Like the persecutions in early LDS history, most were inspired by mob fury. Sometimes, however, personal revenge was involved and sometimes professional rivalry was a factor. The martyrs of Lyons and Vienne were the victims of accusations from heathen servants who feared torture.[2]

Nevertheless, following Trajan's instructions to Pliny dating from 112 A.D., Rome did not specifically seek out Christians during the

---

[2] Kidd, *History of the Church*, 1:252.

second century. Most of the actual instances of persecution were connected with great pagan festivals, or an Emperor's birthday, or some gladiatorial show that engendered mob fury. Being a highly civilized people, however, the calls of the mob were always carried out with at least a show of legality.

Roman Trials Preceded the Condemnation of Christians

Two levels of trial were normally involved as a prelude to the actual murder of Christians. This format was much the same as it is in the English and American criminal justice systems of today. There was a preliminary hearing before a local magistrate, followed by a trial either before the Proconsul or, in Rome, before the Prefect of that city.

The procedure followed a regular course. First were questions about the person's identity, followed by the incriminating question, "Are you a Christian?" This question was routinely answered zealously in the affirmative. Sometimes, as in Marcus Aurelius' persecutions, other incriminating questions were asked. "Who is the god of the Christians?" was a common question during his reign.

Third, the judge would ask if the person would agree to do sacrifice to the gods. This demand was commonly refused. Fourth, the magistrates and judges, being generally humane, would attempt to persuade the martyrs to reconsider, and sometimes gave them time to think over their decision. A delay of thirty days was common for this purpose.

Appeals for reconsideration routinely fell on deaf ears. Many were zealous for the opportunity to be martyred, and turned the occasion into the ancient equivalent of a media event on behalf of the Church. For example, Polycarp was offered the chance to "repent and say, 'Away with the Atheists,'" a reference to the Christians who were about to be executed. In response, he turned to the pagan crowd that had gathered in the stadium to witness his execution and, waving his hand at *them*, said, "Away with the Atheists."[3]

Martyrdom was considered the ultimate opportunity to bear testimony to the Gentiles, and those who were its victims took every occasion to use their own deaths as a witness to God and to the world. As a result, judges would frequently order torture as an alternative to the

---

[3] Eusebius, *History of the Church*, 4:15:19.

more extreme penalty of death. The object was to break down the Christian's resistance to persuasion. In most cases, however, the effect of this alternative was to stiffen the Christian's resistance all the more.

The seventh stage was formal sentencing to death. This was followed by the eighth and final stage, execution of the sentence by decapitation, or fire, or by wild beasts.

Christian Reactions Bewildered Roman Authorities

The Roman governors found the reaction of Christians to this process baffling. One man, Arrius Antoninus, Proconsul of Asia during the reign of Marcus Aurelius and his son, found himself suddenly confronted by all the Christians in his territory. They presented themselves as a body before his judgment seat requesting martyrdom pursuant to law. He ordered a few to be led away to execution, and said to the others, "Wretched men! If ye wish to die, there are precipices and halters!"[4]

Kidd gives the flavor of this phenomenon in the following language:

> To the heathen onlooker, it was teaching; to the authorities, mere obstinacy; while their sufferings were to the catechumen "a baptism of blood," with effects as efficacious as the Sacrament of Baptism for which they were preparing; to the Church, at once seed, since the bystanders—Lucius, Agathonice, and many more—declared their sympathy, but also the door by which, through sheer admiration for these "noble athletes" of the arena, practices, which afterwards became superstitions, obtained entrance.[5]

The latter effect on the Church is of particular note. As mentioned earlier, it was natural for the members of the Church to treasure the memories and the remains of those who so nobly gave their lives for the Faith. Latter-day Saints may imagine the feelings of orthodox Christians about these men by considering their own feelings about Joseph Smith and his brother Hyrum.

But venerating the writings and opinions of the early Christian martyrs presented a serious problem for the Church. Unfortunately, false theology, as well as the good in Christ's teachings, was perpetuated, in

---
[4] Tertullian, *To Scapula*, 5.
[5] Kidd, *History of the Church*, 1:254-255.

part, because of this veneration. It reached an almost superstitious level throughout the third century. Many classical theists retain the same reverential attitude toward the early Church fathers to this day, making it more difficult for them to acknowledge the errors these great men made.

Roman Persecution After Marcus Aurelius

Despite the Apologists' efforts to combat the charge of atheism, persecution under Marcus Aurelius continued throughout his reign, which ended in 180 A.D., and into that of his son, Commodus. In approximately 185 A.D., however, Marcia, a highly respected concubine of Commodus, convinced him to stop the persecution. The early Church, however, enjoyed only a brief respite.

It should come as no surprise to Latter-day Saints that persecution, especially the kind that provides a public forum for the martyr's death, actually stimulated the growth of the early Church. Combined with the new intellectual respectability provided by the Apologists, the situation presented a new and different threat for Rome. Persecution led to zeal and zeal to conversions, and early in the third century, this formula led to alarm.

In 202 A.D., the Emperor, Septimius Severus, put out an edict forbidding people to "become Christians."[6] Unlike all the persecutions since Trajan, this edict required that converts actually be sought out. This was a new situation for the early Church, and it raised a new question: Was it legitimate to flee martyrdom? The Montanists, under Tertullian, like the critics of Joseph Smith when he tried to flee the mob that ultimately murdered him, said, "No," but the Church held that it was permissible. The Catechetical School of Alexandria dispersed without even awaiting that instruction.

The persecution of Severus was most severe in Egypt, where many male and female converts were beheaded or burned to death, including Leonides, the father of Origen, and several of Origen's pupils. Origen was spared only because his mother hid his clothes so he could not go to the tribunal to request martyrdom. The persecution died down under Caracalla (211-217 A.D.), the son of Severus, who was confronted with more pressing political problems.

---

[6] *Ibid.*, 1:347.

Cementing the Theological Apostasy

In approximately 210 A.D., there followed a lengthy peace for the Church. The Roman empire was beginning to disintegrate, hedged by enemies from within and without. The Church had grown beyond the empire, giving it some additional resources and the impression of greater influence. Tertullian claimed that, "parts of Britain inaccessible to the Romans are subject to Christ."[7] Origen garnered some powerful benefactors, and the Church was even granted a few favors by Emperor Alexander Severus (222-235 A.D.).

Persecution was again reinstated for a brief period under Maximin the Thracian (235-238 A.D.), but his persecution was aimed specifically at bishops. Hippolytus was exiled to Sardinia where he died, and both Pontianus, bishop of Rome 230-235 A.D., and his successor, Anteros, 236 A.D., were martyred by this Emperor.

Maximin's successor, Gordian III, stopped the persecution in 238 A.D. Eusebius claims that he became a Christian and was made to do penance for the murder of his predecessor.[8] Whether or not that is true, he was concerned with defense of the empire and let the Church remain at peace. In fact, his Empress, Octacilia Severa, became one of Origen's correspondents. It was at this time that Latin started to take precedence over Greek in the Church at Rome.

The Persecution by Decius

In 248 A.D., the millennium of Rome, patriots of the state began to murmur against the long-standing toleration of Christians. In 249, Decius rose to power. His was a time of social degeneracy, which he believed was the result of decades of religious liberty. He restored the office of Censor and conferred it on Valerian, who later succeeded him both as emperor and as persecutor.

From 249 to 251 the Roman state conducted an official persecution that was both universal and systematic. All were brought to a pagan temple, where they were required to make sacrifice to the gods, renounce Christ, and partake in the sacrificial meal. They received a certificate, or *libellus*, from the magistrate if they would do this.

Some Christians purchased a *libellus* without actually performing the required rituals, but the rest were tried, imprisoned and tortured in an effort to obtain not martyrs but apostates. The idea was to discredit

---

[7] Gwatkin, *Early Church History*, 1:173.
[8] Eusebius, *History of the Church*, 6:34.

and weaken the Church, whose growing organization the Roman emperors feared. Those who would not apostatize were either executed or exiled and their property confiscated.

Peace had weakened the Church, and so there were some, including several bishops, who rushed to do sacrifice and obtain their *libellus*. Many others, however, refused and were tortured or put to death, including Origen, who was tortured during this persecution and eventually died of his injuries in 254 A.D.

Records of this persecution indicate that by this time the term "Catholic" had taken on the meaning not only of "universal" but "orthodox" as opposed to "heretical."[9]

The title "Confessor" came into existence at this time. Confessors were members who had confessed to being Christians during the trials, but, for various reasons, were allowed to live. For example, at Alexandria, a young man of only fifteen, named Dioscorus, was dismissed from the tribunal by the magistrate in sheer admiration for his courage.[10] These men later became highly respected in the Church.

This round of persecution subsided in 251 as Decius changed his attention from helpless Christians to invading Goths. It ended in November of that year, when he fell in battle.

A Controversy Arises Over Treatment of the "Lapsed"

At the end of Decius' reign those who had obtained a *libellus*, referred to as the "lapsed" by the rest of the Church, tried to return to fellowship. This raised questions about re-baptism, and the issue of rigor or laxity on this point began to divide and weaken the Church. The Council of Carthage met in April and June of 251 to resolve these issues, and policies were adopted under which the "lapsed" could be readmitted to the Church.[11]

A group led by Novatian disagreed with the policies thus established, and a schism developed which remained strong in Asia Minor, and later played a part in the Arian controversy. This was the first time a group had broken off on other than doctrinal grounds, and it required the Church to deal with the difference between a schism and heresy. Cyprian, then bishop of Carthage, recognizing the importance of unity

---

[9] Kidd, *History of the Church*, 1:434-435.
[10] Eusebius, *History of the Church*, 6:41:19-20.
[11] Kidd, *History of the Church*, 1:451-452.

in the Church, argued that schism was worse than heresy, and that to separate from your bishop was to separate from Christ.[12]

In 252 A.D. the plague broke out in Africa and Rome. As many as five thousand a day died in Rome, and the population of Alexandria was cut in half over a twenty-year period. The pagans ascribed this plague to the Christians, and so persecution was revived under Gallus, who succeeded Decius from 251 to 253 A.D. As Tertullian put it, "If the Tiber rises as high as the city walls, if the Nile does not send its waters up over the fields, if the heavens give no rain, if there is an earthquake, if there is famine or pestilence, straightway the cry is, 'Away with the Christians to the lion!'"[13]

In response to this renewed persecution, the Church loosened its restrictions on the "lapsed" in order to present a united front in the face of renewed persecution. This only exacerbated the controversy over re-baptism for these people and for converts from heretical sects like the Marcionites.

The Baptism of Heretics Is Accepted by the Early Church

The issue that arose was whether a baptism administered by heretics was valid. Cyprian, with most bishops in Africa and Asia Minor, argued that it was not, that only those who belong to the Church can admit others to it. Stephen, then bishop of Rome, however, opposed him. He ordered that converts from schism or heresy were not to be re-baptized.

The controversy continued for decades in the Church, but eventually, Stephen's position won out. In 314 A.D., the Council of Arles decided that if a convert from schism or heresy had been baptized "in the name of the Father, the Son, and the Holy Ghost," he need merely receive the laying on of hands to receive the Holy Ghost and not be re-baptized.

The eastern churches rejected this policy, arguing that baptism in the right form but without the right "intent," i.e., without "sound faith," was not baptism. Thus, Athanasius later argued that baptisms by the Arians were invalid.[14]

---

[12] Cyprian, *On the Unity of the Church*, in *Ante-Nicene Father*, 5:4421, *et seq.*
[13] Tertullian, *Apology*, 40.
[14] Kidd, *History of the Church*, 1:472.

Roman Persecution Continues

Valerian, who had been Censor under Decius, took the throne in 253 A.D. During the first half of his reign (which lasted through 260 A.D.) he favored the Church, though persecution continued in the Empire to a limited extent. Eventually, however, his minister, Macrianus, talked him into initiating a persecution against the Christians aimed at its leadership and property. That commenced in 257 A.D. when Valerian ordered imprisonment or banishment of bishops and forbade Christian assemblies. This was an attempt to crush the Church without bloodshed and it had little effect. So, the following year, he issued a new edict requiring punishment, including, especially, confiscation of Church property.

Many were martyred in Rome under Valerian, including Lawrence, who was roasted alive on a gridiron. In Africa, Cyprian was beheaded by Galerius Maximus at Carthage. This persecution was not as great in the East, however.[15] There, only those who actually sought martyrdom were executed.

The persecution ended with the imprisonment in 260 A.D. of Valerian, whose son issued an edict of toleration in 261. For over forty years (261-303 A.D.) the Church had peace, and during that time, it grew in power, numbers and territory.

The Final Battle, Diocletian's Persecution

The final persecution of the early Church was directed by Diocletian, who ruled as Emperor from 283 until 305 A.D. when he abdicated the throne as part of a prearranged reorganization of the Empire. Thereafter, he continued to direct the persecution, but not from the Emperor's seat.

Diocletian's persecution against the Church was largely unexpected. His wife, Prisca, and his daughter, Valeria, were both Christians, as were his chief chamberlains, Dorotheus, Gorgonius, and Peter. Historians suspect the influence of Galerius in Diocletian's support of this persecution.

Signs of unrest could be seen as early as 295 A.D. when two Christian members of the Roman Legion, Maximilian and Marcellus, were put to death under Maximian for what was essentially insubordina-

---

[15] *Ibid.*, 1:477-478.

tion.[16] Shortly afterwards, Galerius persuaded Diocletian to "purify" the army by ordering that all soldiers should be required to offer sacrifice to the Roman gods. As a result, two more soldiers, Nicander and Marcian, and a veteran, Julius, were executed at Dorostorum.[17]

In the winter of 302-303 A.D., Galerius conferred with Diocletian at his new headquarters in Nicomedia. On February 23, 303 A.D., the cathedral in Nicomedia was burned to the ground and the next day the first of five edicts was issued that began the final reign of terror against the Church. It forbade worship services, commanded churches to be leveled to the ground, required the scriptures to be surrendered and burned, and deprived Christians in official positions of both their rank and Roman citizenship. Those of Caesar's household were also deprived of their freedom.

The purpose of this persecution was to destroy the Church's property and the foundation of its faith, the written scriptures, without creating the fanaticism that accompanied martyrdom. In the Church, it resulted in a new offense, that of *traditor*. That term was applied to those who surrendered their scriptures to the agents of Diocletian.

Despite Diocletian's plan, bloodshed was inevitable. The first edict was torn down by a Church member in Nicomedia, and he was burned to death for high treason. After two fires "mysteriously" broke out in the Emperor's palace during Galerius' stay, Diocletian forced his wife and daughter to renounce Christianity and had his Christian chamberlains put to death. He also issued a second edict, requiring the imprisonment of the clergy. They were not to be put to death, however. Diocletian wanted hostages, not martyrs.

These two edicts were put into effect diversely in different parts of the Roman Empire, but the net result was the destruction of churches, scriptures, and the deaths of many notable Church leaders. A third edict, late in 303, extended amnesty to clerics who would sacrifice to the Roman gods. Torture was once again employed as a supposed act of mercy to persuade the imprisoned clergy to take advantage of this offer of leniency.

On December 18, 303, Diocletian suffered a mental collapse and left Rome for nearly a year. Maximian, who had put the Christian soldiers to death in 295, issued a fourth edict under his and Diocletian's

---

[16] *Ibid.*, 1:515.
[17] *Ibid.*

names that made the persecution general. It abandoned Diocletian's original efforts to avoid bloodshed, and required the Church members to sacrifice to the Roman gods or be punished by death.

This edict unleashed the zeal of the martyrs once again. So Maximian and Galerius, who had things their way with Diocletian indisposed, sought revenge through a punishment worse to the Church than death, by assaulting Christian virginity.

In 305 A.D., as noted above, Diocletian (along with Maximian) abdicated the throne as part of a reorganization of the Roman Empire. At this time, monuments were raised to Diocletian "for having extinguished the name of Christians who brought the Republic to ruin," and "for having everywhere abolished the superstition of Christ; for having extended the worship of the gods."[18]

These proved to be a gross exaggeration of his effectiveness in suppressing Christianity. The ultimate result of his persecution is best described in the facetious tone of Friedrich Engels, who said "it was so effective that seventeen years later the army consisted overwhelmingly of Christians, and the succeeding autocrat of the whole Roman empire, Constantine, called the Great by the priests, proclaimed Christianity as the State religion!"[19]

After 305 A.D., Galerius ruled over Thrace and Asia while his nephew Maximin ruled Syria and Egypt. Together, they issued a fifth edict requiring all Christians, even infants, to sacrifice, and all the meat in the markets was sprinkled with water that had been consecrated to pagan gods, making it inedible to the zealous Christians.[20] Under Galerius and Maximin, a reign of terror followed in the East from 305 to 311 in which many perished.

In 311, Galerius died of venereal disease. On his death bed, he issued a grudging edict of toleration, saying that Christians may exist again and may again set up their meetings.[21] After his death, however,

---

[18] Milner, *Church History,* Cent. IV, ch 1, p. 38.

[19] Friedrich Engels, *Introduction to Karl Marx, The Class Struggles in France, 1848-50* (London, 1895, trans. Lawrence. Reprint: London, 1934).

[20] According to Gwatkin, this edict required that Christians should have their left foot disabled and their right eye cut out and its socket seared. Then they were to be sent to slavery in the mines where further cruelty could be imposed on them without attracting too much sympathy. See Gwatkin, *Early Church History,* 2:345.

[21] Galerius said: "We never quarreled with the Christians for worshiping their own god, but for not worshiping our gods also: . . . But we forgot one thing. In compelling the Christians to worship our gods we made it impossible for them to worship their

Maximin, who succeeded to the rule of Asia, instituted a theological persecution of the Church in which he tried to revive paganism while putting to death the chief bishops and theologians still left in the Church. He raked up the old charges against the early Church and some despicable rumors about Christ and included them in textbooks that he distributed to schools for use by the youth of the Empire.

In this final phase of the Diocletian persecution, Lucian of Antioch, the teacher of Arius, was martyred. This lent greater prestige to his name and teachings, and increased respect in the Church for his pupils.

The Rise of Constantine and the Edict of Milan

In 312 A.D., there were two Emperors in the West, Constantine in Britain and Gaul, and Maxentius in Italy, Spain and Africa, and two in the East, Maximin, who had succeeded to Asia, and Licinius, who held Illyricum and Thrace. Maxentius had never been recognized by the others who ruled under Diocletian's reorganized Empire, and he was considered a tyrant by his own people. Constantine therefore invaded Italy from the North and defeated Maxentius in the famous battle of October 27, 312 A.D. in which Constantine is said to have seen the fiery cross and the words "*Hoc vince.*"[22]

He there discovered that Maxentius had been in league with Maximin, so he joined Licinius in Milan with the intent of overturning Christian persecution and bringing the reign of Maximin to an end. Maximin attempted to obtain Christian support by issuing an edict that suspended the persecution in the East and imputed "all the severities which the Christians suffered to the judges and governors who had misunderstood his intentions."[23] This lie did him no good. Licinius pursued him to Tarsus, where he died of *delirium tremens* in August, 313. About the same time Diocletian died at his palace at Salona. Thus ended the last official Christian persecution.

---

own god; and this was not our intention. . . . He is also a god who has lately shown a good deal of power [Galerius himself having been struck with venereal disease], so that he may be able to help us now in our extremity, if we set right the wrong we are doing him. We still regret the self-willed and undutiful action of the Christians; but even so, we are satisfied that it is better to let them worship their god in their own way than to continue doing what prevents him from being worshiped at all; and for this our clemency we hope they will be duly grateful to us." Gwatkin, *Early Church History*, 2:347-348.

[22] Gwatkin, *Early Church History*, 2:355.
[23] Eusebius, *History of the Church*, 9:10:6.

In March 313, Constantine and Licinius issued the Edict of Milan, which contains the first announcement in the history of the Gentile world recognizing religious liberty as a human right. Among other things, it declared:

> We judge it . . . consonant to right reason that no man should be denied leave of attaching himself to the rites of the Christians or to whatever other religion his mind directs him. . . . Accordingly, . . . the open and free exercise of their respective religions is granted to all others, as well as to the Christians; for it befits the well-ordered state and the tranquillity of our times that each individual be allowed, according to his own choice, to worship the Divinity.[24]

This policy was an enormous change from the historical one in which a man's religion was considered an interest of the State. Though it required centuries before it became a regular practice of government, this Edict was one of the most notable positive consequences of Christian persecution in the Gentile world. In addition to this significant declaration, the Edict required reparation to the Church for the property taken during the persecutions of the past. Property confiscated was to be returned, and in cases where return of property would damage an innocent holder-in-due-course, the state promised to make reparations to the injured party.

The Untimely Rise of the Arian Controversy

Into the new and unique environment of Christian supremacy exploded the festering controversy known as Arianism, the most divisive of the early "heresies." Arianism was named after Arius, a deacon and later a presbyter (member of the council of elders) of the Church in Alexandria early in the fourth century. Arius was schooled in the scriptures by Lucian of Antioch, who, in turn, had learned from Paul of Samosata, a bishop of Antioch who was excommunicated for his doctrines in 269 A.D. Before this controversy arose under the name of Arius, it seethed throughout the third century as Monarchianism.

Monarchianism the Great Heresy of the Third Century

Noted briefly in the last chapter, Monarchianism was a reaction to Gnosticism's polytheistic and dualistic doctrines. It asserted a firm

---
[24] Kidd, *History of the Church*, 1:529-530.

monotheism, and attempted to provide a rational answer to the Nicene Question. The doctrine of the Trinity was openly irrational. Outside of importing metaphysical notions into the equation, it did nothing to explain why the Three are One. It spoke of the Three being "co-substantial" but did nothing to explain what that meant in real terms. Indeed, its proponents often denied that any rational explanation was possible. It was pure metaphysics, consistent with its origin in Platonistic philosophy.

While the Monarchianists attempted to meet the challenge of providing a rational answer to the Nicene Question, they could arrive at only two rational explanations, neither of which included the biblical truth. This was because they failed to reject the metaphysical philosophy that had become the foundation of orthodox Christian theology under the influence of the Apologists.

Their alternatives were these: Either Christ was a totally separate individual from the Father and therefore not divine, or He was divine and therefore not a totally separate individual from the Father. According to their belief in these two alternatives, the Monarchists divided into the two groups mentioned in Chapter 7. The Adoptionists believed that Christ became divine by adoption into the Godhead, and the Modalists regarded Him as nothing more than a mode of the Father's existence. They were the forerunners of Arianism.

Adoptionist theology was first championed by Theodotus the Elder in the late second century. He taught the heretical notion that Jesus was an ordinary man who lived an extraordinarily religious life, so that, at his baptism in the Jordan, the Father sent down the Christ, His *Logos*, who descended upon Jesus in the form of a dove (see Chapter 7). Some of his followers believed that this investiture made Him God then, while others maintained that He became God after the resurrection.[25]

The Modalist theology was first championed by Praxeas, who taught that the Son is simply a mode or aspect of the Father.[26] Thus, according to Praxeas, it was, in some sense, God the Father who suffered on the cross. This is the doctrine Callistus espoused, as noted in Chapter 6. It contradicted the orthodox idea that the Son had been the Son of God through all eternity, and denied any reality to the doctrine of mediation between God and Man through the Son. Although it

---

[25] Hippolytus, *Philosophic Refutation of All Heresies*, 7:23; cf., 10:19.
[26] Tertullian, *Against Praxeas*, 1.

found favor with one Roman bishop for a time, this version of Modalism was opposed by Tertullian and did not gain much acceptance in the early Church.

Modalism Under the Hand of Sabellius

Modalism was modified slightly and became far more popular under the hand of Sabellius early in the third century (approximately 214-222 A.D.). He taught that God was one substance but three activities, each equal to the other. That is, God was a Monad or solitary unity who manifested himself in three *successive* aspects—as the Father in creation and the giving of the Law, as the Son in respect to redemption, and as the Holy Spirit in respect to sanctification and living the life of grace. Thus, the Father did not suffer on the cross, because, by then, he had ceased to be the Father and had become the Son.

This doctrine meant that when the Father became the Son, at His birth, He passed over entirely into the material world and thereby ceased to be transcendent. That aspect of Sabellius' doctrine conflicted with orthodox theology, which by then had fully adopted the Greek idea that God existed outside the real world of Matter. Origen was then teaching that God was pure mind or thought, transcendent above all bodily forms, even the spirit.[27] Therefore, Sabellianism was identified as heretical. (By then, "heretical" had come to mean "non-orthodox" more than "non-biblical.")

Sabellius described the progression of God between modes as one of "expansion" or "extension." The three successive phases of the divine life he referred to by the Greek word, *homoousios*, meaning same substance, or same person, in the sense of a single actor who plays one part in a play, then lays that part aside to play another.

The use of this word at first caused confusion in the early Church, especially between Latin writers in Rome and Greek writers, especially in Alexandria. The issue related to the use of *ousia* and *hypostasis* as substitutes for *homoousios*. Greek writers regarded *ousia* as a reference to substance (Latin: *substantia*) in the sense of that which exists only in the realm of thought, e.g., the one God. *Hypostasis* was used by them to refer to *ousia* that has an objective existence in the sensory world, the individual person, e.g., the persons of the Father or the Son or the Holy

---

[27] Origen, *De Principiis*, 1:1:6.

Ghost. This helped them to express the inconceivable idea of three persons in one substance which the Apologists had devised. (To the Greek mind, if it could be expressed, it could be true.)

To Latin writers, the two words were essentially the same, both translated "*substantia*" in Latin. Eventually, to separate the concepts, *ousia* retained the Latin translation "*substantia*," and a new Latin word was selected as a translation for *hypostasis*. That word was "*persona*," which meant "a character in a play," or a "person" in the legal sense, e.g., a party to a contract. This allowed the Latin writers to express the same false, metaphysical doctrine as the Greek writers were expressing without contradicting each other's terminology. Before that accommodation, however, a revealing controversy arose out of an effort to combat Sabellianism without using the proper words.

The Conflict Between Dionysius of Rome and Dionysius of Alexandria

After his death, Sabellius' brand of Modalism became very popular in Libya where he had lived. Dionysius, the bishop of Alexandria, had direct responsibility for that area, and in 257 A.D. he felt it necessary to intervene in order to correct the local bishops. His opponents complained to Rome, the bishop then being a man who was also named Dionysius. They alleged that Dionysius of Alexandria was in error on five points of doctrine. These were as follows: (1) he had separated the Father from the Son; (2) he had denied the eternity of the Son and by consequence the eternal paternity of the Father; (3) he had named the Father without the Son, and the Son without the Father; (4) he had virtually rejected the Greek term *homoousios* (meaning "of one substance [or essence] with") to describe the Son in relation to the Father; and (5) he had spoken of the Son as a creature of the Father, and had used misleading illustrations of their relationship.[28]

These five complaints are mentioned here as proof of the extent to which the apostasy had progressed by this time. The fact that Dionysius of Alexandria would be called to task because, for example, he failed to use a completely non-biblical term (*homoousios*) to describe the relationship between the Father and the Son, is a testimony to the overriding influence of Greek philosophy on the Church by this time.

---

[28] Kidd, *History of the Church*, 1:487-488.

More interesting for its relation to the Arian controversy and the development of Trinitarian doctrine is the reaction of Dionysius of Rome to these accusations, and the subsequent response of Dionysius of Alexandria. Dionysius of Rome expressed his concern about the way in which his namesake attacked Sabellianism. He accused the Alexandrian teachers of being "virtually tritheists," for, in answering Sabellius, who "blasphemously says that the Son is the Father and the Father is the Son," they "divide the sacred Monad into three subsistences foreign to each other and utterly separate." Further, he accused the Alexandrians of denying the eternity of the Word, saying "He came to be Son, and so once He was not." (To refute this doctrine, Dionysius of Rome noted that the scriptures speak of Christ as "begotten," but not as having "come into being.") Finally, he complained of any attempt to find a logical harmony between the Triad and the Monarchy.[29]

Dionysius of Alexandria replied by responding directly to the five charges stated above.[30] He denied the first charge, claiming that one cannot mention the Father without implying the Son, nor the Holy Spirit without involving "His Source" (the Father) and "His Channel" (the Son). This response also dealt with the third accusation. He denied the second charge, using the Alexandrian analogy, taken directly from the Greek philosophers, of a light and its ray. If the sun in the heavens were eternal, he said, daylight would also be eternal.

Typical of the Greek influence at the time, it was not as important to understand the idea in terms of reality as it was to express it using the proper metaphor. Thus Dionysius of Alexandria missed the fact that this analogy is completely inapplicable to the Father and the Son because it separates an attribute of the sun (light) from its source (the sun). As will be seen below, Paul of Samosata did not miss this distinction and carried the analogy to its logical and equally false conclusion, viewing the *Logos* as nothing more than a divine attribute of the Father.

As to the fourth accusation, Dionysius was frank enough to state that he did not find the term (*homoousios*) in the scriptures, and therefore had not used it. However, he claimed to have used analogies that teach the same relationship, e.g., that of parent and child who are "of one kin." This was not enough for the Church at that time, though

---

[29] Quotations are from C. L. Feltoe, *The Letters of Dionysius of Alexandria* (Cambridge, 1904), cited in Kidd, *History of the Church*, 1:490-491.

[30] Dionysius, *Fragments*, 4, from *Ante-Nicene Fathers*, 6:92-93.

Athanasius later argued that saying the Son is the "offspring" of the Father is the same as saying that They are "co-essential."[31]

The position of most orthodox theologians is that "such figures [a parent and child] reach only to the generic, and not to the essential oneness of the Godhead."[32] What these theologians fail to recognize is that the generic figure given by Dionysius of Alexandria is the only biblical one, while the effort to find an "essential" oneness is strictly a Greek exercise.

Subordination of the Son to the Father

Dionysius' response to the fifth charge deals with the subordination of the Son to the Father. At that time, the principle of *Principatus Patris* required that in thinking of the Godhead one must always begin with the Father. The Son and the Holy Spirit, though equal to the Father, were viewed as somehow being derived from and, to that extent, dependent upon the Father. This principle is seen by classical theists as the one that prevents Trinitarianism from turning into tritheism. The doctrine of subordination will be examined further in Chapter 17.

The Alexandrians (and later the Arians) were prone to think of subordination in terms of time or rank, and this the early Church rejected. Consistent with the Apologists' explanation of Justin Martyr's teachings about the separateness of the Father and the Son, the Father was not to be seen as coming first or being of a higher rank than the Son. Dionysius of Alexandria denied holding any such views, but some analogies he used to explain the relationship between the Father and the Son suggested a view that was unacceptable to the Church at that time, namely that Christ was "created" by the Father rather than being merely "begotten."[33] These ideas were later used to support Arianism in Alexandria, and are part of the reason it arose from that locale.

Paul of Samosata, The Forerunner of Arius

The next stone in the foundation of the Arian controversy was laid by Paul of Samosata. He was an Adoptionist. What Sabellius was to Modalism, Paul was to Adoptionism. He insisted on the unity of God, and that God is one Person. Like all the Greek-oriented theologians of

---

[31] Athanasius, *On the Councils of Ariminum and Seleucia*, 42.
[32] Kidd, *History of the Church*, 1:492.
[33] *Ibid.*, 1:492-494.

the time, he believed God had a Word (*logos*) and a Wisdom (commonly seen as the Holy Ghost). Where he differed with the current opinions of orthodoxy was that, although he taught that the Word was begotten of God from all eternity, he claimed that this *Logos* was impersonal, an attribute only, like human speech or reason or the light of the sun. In other words, he took Justin Martyr's analogy literally.

According to Paul of Samosata, the attribute of God known as the *Logos* had acted upon Moses and the prophets and at length came to dwell in Jesus Christ. Jesus was supposedly a mere man, though born of a virgin and "inspired from above." He was "united" with the Word in the same way as the spirit might come into and abide in a temple. To Paul of Samosata, Jesus was not personally God, nor did the Word have a personality. It was simply a divine attribute imparted to Jesus "by education and association," dwelling in him "not essentially [i.e., not as an aspect of His basic nature] but as a quality."[34]

Thanks to this "indwelling," supposedly, Jesus was called Christ. He attained to moral perfection, and redeemed Man making his union with God indissolvable. For the sufferings he endured, he received "the Name that is above every name" (Phil. 2:9) and is so divine that Men may speak of Him as "God born of a virgin, and God manifest at Nazareth." However, Paul "did not acknowledge the divinity of Christ in any sense that would permit worship to be rendered to him."[35]

Paul of Samosata taught that Jesus had a pre-existence. Arius went further, teaching that Jesus had a pre-existence as the firstborn and highest of the creatures. However, neither man taught that Christ's pre-existence was eternal or that He was in any way on a par with the Father.

This was the basic Adoptionist view and it became the characteristic tenet of Arianism, namely, that Jesus was an ordinary mortal man who became God. "He was by advance made God, from being made by nature a mere man."[36] He was not God "by nature," as orthodoxy demanded, but became God "by virtue." This notion allowed Paul of Samosata to maintain the idea of a transcendent God, who merely invested a man, Jesus of Nazareth, with His Word, a divine attribute. Thus, he taught that Christ was a created being. For all this, he was excommunicated in 269 A.D.

---

[34] Kidd, *History of the Church*, 1:500-501.
[35] *Ibid.*, 1:501-502.
[36] *Ibid.*, 1:502.

Lucian Takes the Next Step Toward Arianism

Lucian of Antioch, whose martyrdom was noted above, was a student of Paul of Samosata and the teacher of Arius. Unlike Paul, Lucian held that the *logos* was personal and did become man in Christ. He said, "God sent into this world His Wisdom clothed in flesh."[37] But Lucian still taught that this *logos* was a second essence, created by God before He created the world. Thus, Christ was not "perfect man," because the personal element within Him was a divine essence; yet He was not "perfect God," because His divine essence had been created.[38] These concepts found their way into Arius' teachings around the turn of the fourth century.

The Tenets of Arianism

Arius (256-336 A.D.) was a presbyter in Alexandria at the dawn of the fourth century. He was highly regarded by his bishop, Alexander, as a man of unimpeachable lifestyle. This, and his education at the hands of a noted martyr, made his opinions more difficult to assail or dismiss. Further, he did not present his doctrine as a schism, but as the answer to a problem that required the Church's attention—a problem that began with Monarchianism and culminated in the excommunication of Paul of Samosata followed by the martyrdom and resulting veneration of his student, Lucian of Antioch. This was a problem that would have been raised by someone else if not by Arius.

In 319 A.D., Arius began to teach that Christ "had come into being out of non-existence," that "once He was not," that "as possessing freewill He was originally capable of vice no less than of virtue," and that "He was created and made."[39] The Arian syllogism (all who would present doctrines to the Church by that time were well trained in Aristotelian syllogistic logic) ran as follows:

> What is true of human fatherhood is true of the relation between the Father and the Son;
> But the father's priority of existence is true of human fatherhood;
> Therefore it is true in regard to the Father and the Son;[40]

---

[37] Eusebius, *History of the Church*, 9:6.
[38] *Encyclopaedia Britannica*, 1960 ed., s.v. "Arius."
[39] Sozomen, *History of the Church*, 1:14:3.
[40] Socrates, *History of the Church*, 1:5:2.

In other words, "once there was no Son," that is, at some very remote time, He was "created" by the Father.[41] This may sound like Mormon doctrine, but it lacks certain crucial understandings taught in Mormon theology that make it inconsistent with the scriptures and hence contradictory to Mormonism, as will be seen below.

The Controversy Begins With the Excommunication of Arius

The position of orthodoxy on the relationship between the Father and the Son was well entrenched by this time. There had been no changes in that position since its appearance at the hands of the Apologists in the late second century. As noted in Chapter 6, it was that the Father and the Son are co-substantial (having the same substance or essence) and co-eternal (both in their persons and in their relationship as father and son) while at the same time they remain separate persons. This false precept was incompatible with the false teachings of Arius.

Accordingly, in 320 A.D., Alexander took action to correct Arius, first by private interview, then by discussion at a conference of local clergy. These efforts, a second conference, and a letter (addressed to Arius and his supporters among the clergy) were all to no effect. Alexander therefore summoned a synod of the bishops of Egypt and Libya in 321.

At this synod, Arius and his supporters admitted to such teachings as "God was not always Father," "the Son was a creature and a work" and "foreign from the essence of the Father," and "being something made and created, His nature is subject to [moral] change."[42] Upon making these professions, Arius and his followers were excommunicated.

Differences Between Arianism and Mormonism

The tenets of Arius are repeated, almost word for word, in certain charges made by classical theists against Mormonism. That is because Christian orthodoxy tends to view LDS theology as a re-run of Arianism. As noted above, however, there are major distinctions between Arianism and Mormonism.

---

[41] Kidd, *History of the Church*, 2:15.
[42] Socrates, *History of the Church*, 1:6:9, 11 and 12.

Mormonism would agree with Arius that "what is true of human fatherhood is [in many ways, at least] true of the relation between the Father and the Son." However, the true nature of human fatherhood in light of the pre-mortal existence of human spirits, was never correctly contemplated by Arius. Mormonism declares that the birth process in human beings does no more than create a mortal body in which a pre-existent spirit body dwells. This is the same for all Men. When the physical body of Christ was formed, with Mary as the mother of His body and God the Father as His "natural" father, it was invested with His pre-existent spirit (Phil. 2:7). During His pre-mortal existence, His spirit had been known as Jehovah, the very God of the Old Testament.

If the same principle holds true with respect to the relationship between the Father of spirits (Heb. 12:9) and His spirit offspring, then spirit "creation" involves nothing more than the formation of a spirit body in which a pre-existing, eternal personality or "intelligence" (Pearl of Great Price, Abraham 3:22) dwells. (It is also possible that the spirit body is, itself, an organized form of this "intelligence.") "Intelligences" are eternal and uncreated according to Mormon theology (D&C 93:29), meaning that Christ (with all Men) is, in fact, co-eternal with God as a pre-existing intelligence, no matter what form of body was created for Him during the progress of His eternal existence.

Thus, Mormonism does not believe that Christ came into being "out of non-existence," or that "once He was not." They reject the Arian idea that there was ever a time when Christ did not exist. He existed as an intelligence, an individual personality, before becoming the firstborn spirit child of God (Col. 1:15), and eventually became the Father's "only begotten" in the flesh.

That Christ was, at one time "created" by the Father is also denied by Mormonism if the term "created" is used in the sense it was by the Arians. Mormons believe that Christ was "begotten" as a spirit being by His Heavenly Father (and Heavenly Mother) in the same sense that He was subsequently "begotten" as a mortal man by Mary, His mortal mother, and God the Father, His mortal father.

"Created" does not really communicate the Mormon understanding of this process, especially to orthodox Christians. The term "begat" best expresses the process that creates the relationship of a child to its parents both in terms of human fatherhood and the fatherhood of spirits.

Obviously, there are concepts in this aspect of LDS theology that differ from classical theism as well as Arianism. But, when it comes to the bottom line, Mormon Christology agrees on more points with orthodoxy than it does with Arianism. In Mormonism, the Son is of the same "substance" as the Father in the sense that a child is of the same "substance" as its parents. This is precisely the biblical analogy that Dionysius of Alexandria used to describe the relationship between the Father and the Son. Mormons also believe that the Father and the Son are co-eternal, though not in their relationship as Father and Son. That relationship was initiated as "the beginning of the creation of God" (Rev. 3:14). This concept will be discussed further in Part 3.

Mormonism would also disagree with Arius' conclusion that "being something made and created," Christ's nature is "subject to [moral] change." Mormons teach that Christ is the same yesterday, today and forever (Heb. 13:8). However, a complete explanation of this aspect of Mormon theology, the issue of immutability, must also await a chapter in Part 3.

The only point on which it is fair to say that Mormonism agrees with Arius is in the understanding that Christ is a brother to Man (John 20:17), though on that point too, the agreement is not complete. Arius taught that Christ was a "creature," a man who became God. Thus, Arius lowered Christ to the level of a humanity who, according to his beliefs, were created out of nothing and so were intrinsically inferior to God.

Mormonism disagrees with that teaching. Its theology takes exactly the opposite approach, raising humanity to the level of Christ, at least in respect to Man's potential (Rom. 8:17). It teaches that, like Christ, all Men are uncreated in their essential personalities. They contain within them an eternal element that makes them, like Christ, co-eternal with and the spirit offspring of God, destined (*conditionally*) to become like Him (1 John 3:2-3). That Christ is the first (Col. 1:15) and by far the greatest (Heb. 1:8-9) of God's spirit children is acknowledged in Mormon theology, which also acknowledges Christ's deity and equality with His Father. Arius used the term "creatures" to describe the relationship between God and Man, including Christ. Mormons use the term "spirit children" to describe that relationship.

The True Nature of the Arian Controversy

What the early Church did was to adopt a Platonistic view of God and Christ. The question Arianism presented was whether Christ was to be viewed within the Platonistic context as (1) the Reason (*Logos*) of

God, a personification of His thoughts, or (2) more like the Demiurgus, a created being who acted as God's servant. From the moment the early Church began to adopt Greek theology, a contest between these views of God, as presented by the Greek philosophers, was inevitable. That is the true nature of the contest held in 325 A.D. at Nicaea.

This was not, as some have supposed, a controversy between the true God of the Bible and the Greek God envisioned by the Apologists. The biblical God was never in the running. The entire context of the Arian conflict was non-biblical. There was no triumph for truth possible by 325 A.D. The truth about God had been lost long before Arius, and he only divined a small portion of it from his studies. What the Church needed was to break from all philosophy and seek biblical truth, but that was not possible in the fourth century. By then, Greek philosophy had so infused Christianity that it had become, in effect, a branch of Hellenistic thought.

How the Controversy Came to Nicaea

At first, many championed Arius' views, especially other students of Lucian. His doctrine threatened to split the Church in two. Constantine was having problems with Licinius, who had become hostile to Christianity after the Edict of Milan in 313 A.D. They were engaged in what amounted to a civil war, and the last thing Constantine needed was the support of a divided Church. Accordingly, in 325 A.D. he summoned an Ecumenical Council to meet at Nicaea. This was truly a first for the early Church. Synods had commonly been called to solve problems in local areas of the Church, but this was the first assembly of Church leaders from throughout the known world for the purpose of establishing doctrine.

The question presented differed from the issue identified above as the Nicene Question. It was this: Were the Father and the Son of the same substance (*homoousios*), consistent with the views of Greek philosophy adopted by the Apologists, or were they of an entirely different (*avomoios*) or merely similar (*homoousia*) substance, consistent with the various theories of Arianism? Was Christ an inferior "created" being like the Platonist demigod or the Gnostic Aeons, or was he some kind of eternal emanation of the Father? These were the only choices available to solve the basic problem, namely the Nicene Question as it was presented at the beginning of this chapter.

The Nicene Council decided against Arius' flawed view, and chose the equally false view popular among the Trinitarian majority. The Platonistic doctrine of the Apologists was upheld. The Son, the Council decided, is *homoousios*, or "of the same substance," as the Father, and the Arians were banished. Thus did the early Church render God utterly incomprehensible.

The introduction of this word is often attributed to Constantine, but although he suggested its use to break the stalemate that had developed during the Council, he was not a theologian, and cannot be identified as the real source of the doctrine. The word had been used commonly throughout the Church before the Council, and Constantine was prompted in its use by his religious advisor, Bishop Hosius.[43]

One criticism of the Nicene formula at the time relates to its use of a word (*homoousious*) which appears nowhere in the Bible.[44] The answer to that objection was that this word was the best way to express the view of God commonly held then. But it was a Greek word that described a Greek concept. That it was not the original understanding of Christianity had long been forgotten by 325 A.D.

Arianism After Nicaea

The Nicene Council did not spell the end of Arianism. For a time, there was a backlash, and the Arians won favor in the Church in spite of the Nicene Council. During this period, Athanasius, the chief proponent of the Council's decision, was banished. But that did not last for long. In response to the Council's decision, the sect divided into various groups, depending on how closely they clung to Arius' original position, and this weakened the movement.

There arose radical Arianism, which claimed that the Son was completely dissimilar to the Father, semi-Arianism, which taught that the Son was similar yet distinct from the Father, and, at the furthest extreme of semi-Arianism, the *Homoousians*. They used the catchword "likeness of nature" from *homoousia* to preserve some notion of separateness in the nature of the Father and the Son, while essentially adopting the Nicene formula.

---

[43] Kidd, *History of the Church*, 2:30.
[44] *Ibid.*, 2:32-33.

As fate would have it, Arius died suddenly in 336 A.D., and in the years that followed, the groups spawned by his controversy drew closer to the Nicene view. The Council of Constantinople in 381 A.D. easily asserted that the Nicene formula was the only orthodox view, and the final language of the creed was prepared by Athanasius.

Systematizing the Theological Apostasy

By the end of the fourth century the theological apostasy was complete. It remained only for minds like Augustine to arrange the officially sanctioned philosophical opinions about God into an organized system. That systematic theology is now called "classical theism." It encompasses all "orthodox" Christian teachings about God, and is embraced by the majority of Protestants and Catholics alike. It is that system that is called into question by Mormonism.

Having demonstrated that changes in the Christian concept of God occurred during the second century A.D., it remains only to show that these changes were not, as classical theists claim, improvements or clarifications of biblical doctrine. A careful review of the attributes of God espoused by Christian orthodoxy after the second century, and the dissimilarity of those attributes to the teachings of the Bible regarding God's nature and characteristics, follows in Part 3.

Summary

1. The Arian controversy arose over the questions: Who is Christ? and What is His relationship to the Father?
2. Roman persecution of Christians during the third and fourth centuries had a profound effect on the Church and the world.
3. Most acts of persecution against Christians were triggered by mob fury, but actual killings were usually carried out through trials.
4. Many Church members were zealous for martyrdom and used the occasion to obtain sympathy for the Church. This was often effective, leading the Romans to try other alternatives.
5. The Romans were perplexed at the refusal of the Christians to take advantage of the leniency provided by torture and renounce Christianity.
6. Beginning in the third century, Roman persecution was motivated more by fear of the Church's growing power. From 202 to 210 A.D.,

Septimius Severus ordered Christian converts sought out for prosecution.
7. Persecution broke out briefly in 235 A.D. under Maximin the Thracian, resulting in the death of Hippolytus.
8. Decius persecuted the Church between 249 and 251. During his persecution, in order to avoid death, Christians had to obtain a libellus from the magistrate saying that they had sacrificed to idols.
9. Decius' persecution resulted in the death of Origen in 254 A.D.
10. Those who confessed their Christianity but were spared by the Roman tribunals were called "Confessors" and were highly respected in the Church.
11. After Decius' persecution the "lapsed" (those who had obtained a libellus, either through cowardice or bribery) tried to return to the Church. This resulted in a schism over readmittance and "re-baptism," including the re-baptism of those converted from heresy.
12. It was decided in 314 A.D. not to require re-baptism of the lapsed or of converts from heretical groups, provided they had been baptized according to an accepted formula.
13. Between 257 and 261 A.D., Valerian persecuted the Church in an effort to destroy it without creating martyrs. Still, many were tortured and killed, including Cyprian.
14. The final persecution was incited by Galerius and carried out by Diocletian.
15. During Diocletian's persecution five escalating edicts were issued, aimed at systematically destroying the Church and its scriptures and confiscating its property.
16. Lucian, the teacher of Arius, was martyred during Diocletian's persecution. This lent greater prestige to his name and credibility to his students.
17. Constantine came to the Church's rescue, and, in 313 A.D., he issued the Edict of Milan, the first official declaration by a government recognizing religious freedom.
18. Against the backdrop of Roman persecution, Monarchianism became the leading heresy of the third century. It was the beginning of Arianism.
19. Monarchianism tried to find a rational explanation for the Old Testament's reference to one God (the "Monarchy," or "Monad") and the New Testament's mention of three (the "Triad" or "Trinity").

20. Monarchianists reasoned that either Christ was a totally separate person from the Father and therefore not divine (the "Adoptionist" view), or He was divine and therefore not totally separate from the Father (the "Modalist" view).
21. The Modalists, led by Sabellius, taught that one God manifested Himself in three separate "modes," while the Adoptionists, led by Paul of Samosata (excommunicated in 269 A.D.), taught that Jesus was a mere man who had been adopted into the Godhead.
22. Dionysius of Alexandria disciplined Sabellius, but was criticized for his approach. He taught that the Father and the Son were the same "substance" or "essence" in the sense that a child is of the same "substance" or "essence" as its parents.
23. The bishop of Rome accused Dionysius of Alexandria of being a tritheist, and insisted on a more "essential" oneness between the Father and the Son.
24. Principatus Patris was the principle that recognized the subordination of the Son to the Father. Some Alexandrians viewed this principle as an indication that the Son was inferior to the Father in time or rank.
25. Paul of Samosata taught that Jesus was a man who became "united" with God's "Word" (*Logos*), which he believed to be an impersonal attribute of God. Lucian, a student of Paul of Samosata, taught that the Word (*Logos*) was a person who was created by God before He created the world and later became Christ.
26. To the Church at that time, being created meant there was no existence prior to the point of creation, and that the created being was inferior to the Creator. If He was created, that meant Christ was not "co-eternal" or "co-substantial" with the Father.
27. Arius taught that Christ was created out of nothing by the Father and was intrinsically inferior to the Father.
28. Arius was excommunicated in 321 A.D. for teaching that Christ was "a creature," "foreign from the essence of the Father," and "subject to moral change."
29. Mormonism differs from Arianism because of its understanding of "intelligence," the pre-existing and eternal bases for personality and self-consciousness, which are born first as sprits and then as physical beings. Mormons believe Christ was "begotten" by the Father, but not "created out of non-existence" as Arius taught.

30. The Arians taught that Christ was fundamentally different from the Father. Mormonism teaches that they are alike because they are parent and child.
31. Arianism lowers Christ to the level of something inferior: a being who is *not* eternal; while Mormonism elevates Men by recognizing that they *are* eternal.
32. The Arian controversy did not offer a choice between the true God of the Bible and the God of Greek philosophy. It pitted one erroneous philosophical view of God against another.
33. Selecting one view over the other at the Council of Nicaea simply made the doctrine of the Godhead more incomprehensible and sealed the theological apostasy.
34. At first, Arianism found favor in the Church despite the Nicene Council, but the movement split into factions and ultimately lost ground to the Nicene formula.
35. The theological apostasy was systematized by the writers of the fourth and fifth century and has come to be known in the modern era as "classical theism."

Part III

The Influence of Greek Philosophy On Classical Theism Today: What Are the Attributes of God?

Edwin Hatch

We have been able to see, not only that the several elements of what is distinctive in the Nicene theology were gradually formed, but also that the whole temper and frame of mind which led to the formation of those elements were extraneous to the first form of Christianity, and were added to it by the operation of causes which can be traced.

Influence of Greek Ideas Upon the Christian Church, p. 332.

Understanding the Attributes of God

More than eighteen centuries have passed since the true understanding of God held by the early Christian Church was corrupted. Principles of Greek philosophy have so infiltrated the teachings of orthodox Christianity that by now they are viewed, not as an element foreign to the Gospel, but as the foundation itself. As a result, any attempt to teach a completely biblical concept of God is considered heretical by adherents to classical theism.

The effort to correct the errors of the past eighteen hundred years is brimming with roadblocks. These barriers to understanding must be addressed before any attempt can be made to compare God's attributes as taught in the Bible with those taught by classical theism.

The Importation of Greek *A Priori* Assumptions Into Christianity

In *Meno* and *Phaedo* Plato expressed a belief that the learning of fundamental truths (e.g., the principles of geometry) is nothing more than the recollection of knowledge obtained in a prior existence. Though of much later origin, the term *"a priori"* perfectly describes this kind of knowledge. Literally, the term means, "from the earlier." It refers to intuitively perceived truths that all rational Men are expected to accept without proof.

When prominent Greek scholars, like the early Apologists, became Christians, they naturally brought with them the *a priori* assumptions common to Hellenism. For example, the idea of a God who, among other attributes, possesses a body of flesh and bones and exists within the aegis of the real universe is one that directly contradicts what they considered *a priori* knowledge. Since the Apologists had little or no oral tradition to direct them, they misinterpreted many scriptural references that teach the truth about God, doing so on the basis of their *a priori* assumptions. The Bible taught many truths about God that they could not even think of accepting in a literal sense. Allegorical interpretation of the scriptures was common among the Greeks, so it was easy for them to justify interpretations that were more comfortable for them. It was natural for them to import into Christianity the fundamental assumptions of Greek philosophy that corrupted early Christian theology. Rather than the teachings of the Bible, those ancient Greek assumptions remain at the foundation of classical theism to this day.

Because of their fundamental belief in a metaphysical universe, the Apologists did not see themselves as limited to a rational explanation of God. In any scientific or mathematical analysis, if the researcher arrives at a contradictory conclusion, he or she realizes that an error has been made, either in the computation or in the assumptions on which it is based. When the Apologists arrived at contradictory conclusions, such as the belief that God is both three persons and one at the same time, they did not admit that anything was wrong with either their assumptions or their analysis. Instead, they cloaked their mistakes in the term "paradox," and turned them into points of faith.

The Apostles and other early Church leaders knew that the metaphysical reasoning common to Greek philosophy was the essence of "fables" (2 Tim. 4:1-4), but they were murdered in the Roman persecutions of Nero, Domitian and Trajan. The deaths of these key leaders made it easier for false teachers to spread Greek doctrines. With their Hellenized background, it was difficult for Gentile Christians to distinguish between what was true and what was false in the doctrines of the Apologists (Eph. 4:11-14). The proliferation and popularity of heretical sects in the early Church is evidence of the confusion that prevailed in the second century.

Greek thinkers were drawn to Christianity in large numbers, and Hellenistic philosophizing was natural for them. Given the popularity of Greek scholarship, it was difficult for anyone to argue against the *a priori* assumptions of Hellenism without looking foolish. As a result, the profound and fundamental errors introduced into the Church during the second century came not so much by the preaching of heretics as through the adoption of *a priori* assumptions common among the Hellenized nations.

The Danger of Using *A Priori* Assumptions to Learn About God

The idea that Men can make accurate *a priori* assumptions about God is essential to the belief of the Greek philosophers who believed that they could learn the truth about God by simply thinking. In order for a man's thoughts to generate truth about God, it must be presumed that *a priori* knowledge of Him is innate in Men, independent of any particular experience. Such knowledge would have to be obvious and without a possibility of question. Augustine regarded this knowledge as existing in the mind of God, who from time to time gave intellectual illumination to Men.[1] However, there is no scriptural authority for that notion.

Some might argue that Man's conscience, referred to in John 1:9; D&C 93:2; and 84:46, gives him innate knowledge of God, but that is not what the scriptures say about it. The function of conscience is explained by Paul in Romans 2:14-15. It is not to teach Men theology, but to assist them in discerning right from wrong. The ability to tell good from evil is what all Men have been given through their conscience, not an innate knowledge of God's true attributes.

Joseph Smith correctly taught that "without the revelations which he has given us, no man by searching could find out God."[2] He also warned, "we never can comprehend the things of God and of heaven, but by revelation. We may spiritualize and express opinions to all eternity; but that is no authority."[3] Those who seek the truth about God, therefore, must focus on the facts revealed in scripture and forsake *a priori* assumptions regarding His attributes that contradict the plain language of the Bible.

Unbiblical Assumptions About God Must Be Rejected

It has been the author's consistent experience that, whenever a classical proof about the attributes of God conflicts with Mormon theology,

---

[1] *Encyclopaedia Britannica*, 1960 ed., s.v. "A Priori and A Posteriori."
[2] *Lectures on Faith*, N. B. Lundwall, compiler (Salt Lake City: Bookcraft, n.d.), Lecture Third, 7.
[3] *Teachings of the Prophet Joseph Smith*, 292.

the basic premise of that proof is an *a priori* assumption that has no biblical support. Honest scholars who have given such proofs invariably recognize that fact. Some counter by saying that they are sure there is a biblical basis for the assumption, though they cannot cite one. Others recognize that these assumptions come from the theological teachings of the early Church fathers. Few, however, are aware that their assumptions originated in Greek philosophy rather than the Bible.

It was not always easy for the Apologists to see how their Greek *a priori* assumptions dictated an interpretation that conflicted with the literal language of the Bible. An example of this situation is found in Justin's rejection of passages that say God "came to" or "departed from" a place.[4] While his position is, for the most part, correct—Christ, as a pre-mortal spirit named Jehovah, was the person acting on behalf of the Godhead throughout most of the old Testament—his explanation for that fact was based on his assumption, as a Greek philosopher, that God is metaphysically transcendent.[5] He gives no biblical support for that assumption. It just seemed self-evident to him based on his background.

Why have classical theists allowed these *a priori* assumptions, rather than the Bible, to dictate their doctrine? In part, it is because assumptions that are thought to be *a priori* tend not to be questioned, especially when they are reinforced by religious fervor. To paraphrase the fictitious mathematician, Finagle, "in any erroneous proof it is the assumption believed to be the most accurate, beyond any reasonable possibility of doubt, that is the mistake." That is especially true of the assumptions that support classical theism.

Examples of False *A Priori* Assumptions in Aristotelian Physics

One of the best reasons for rejecting classical doctrines about God is that, over the centuries since the days of the Apologists, Greek *a priori* assumptions have consistently proven false and unreliable. Such assumptions were so fundamental at the time of Christ that it took great creative minds centuries to identify the errors in them. In the meantime, scientific progress was at a standstill. The great minds that tackled the field of theology during those same centuries were, unfortunately, less

---

[4] Justin, *Dialogue With Trypho*, 127.
[5] *Ibid.*

successful than the pioneers of science during the Renaissance. To this day they remain at a standstill.

Pure *a priori* assumptions are supposed to be intrinsically perceived and have nothing to do with experience, but in truth they are frequently based on inaccurate empirical observations. Not conscious to the misguided individual who relies on them, there are often elements of experience that seem to support the assumptions being made.

While the Greeks were astute observers for their time, they were unable to imagine the many influences that were invisible to their eyes. Their limitations greatly affected their *a priori* assumptions and often restricted their ability to understand natural as well as cosmological and theological truths. Not infrequently they reached what to them seemed completely logical conclusions that, in fact, were entirely false. This was simply because they could not observe, and so could not grasp, the minute complexities of the real universe. Also, being rationalists, they refused to seek guidance from God.

For example, though it was not a proven fact to Aristotle, it came to be viewed (especially in the Peripatetic schools) as *a priori* knowledge that a body would not remain in motion unless it was acted upon by a force. In reality, nearly the opposite is true. Unless acted upon by a force, a body will not *stop* moving. (Of course it is also true that, if a body is at rest, it will not *start* moving without the application of a force.) However, to anyone living at the time of Christ the Aristotelian principle seemed self-evident, *a priori*.

But this assumption was not the result of *a priori* insight at all. It came from the everyday experience of the common people. Observe a wagon being drawn by a horse. If the horse stops pulling, the wagon stops moving. That was a fact that required no proof to the ancient Greeks. The concept of friction escaped from them entirely. That is because it worked at microscopic levels and only became obvious when technologically superior wheels were developed.

A second example from Aristotelian physics is found in the effect of gravity on falling objects. Modern physicists know that (discounting some very minute variations) gravity works to accelerate all objects at the same rate. A feather will fall as fast as a rock (in a vacuum, of course). To the ancient Greek observer, however, it was *a priori* knowledge that the heavier an object was, the faster it fell. Greek rocks always fell faster than Greek feathers, and so another completely false, but supposedly *a priori* law of physics was born.

While Aristotle has taken the rap for these errors, his principles were offered tentatively, not as assumptions but as theorems subject to more careful observation. It is likely that, if his work had gone on in the same manner as he started it, a truer knowledge of the laws of physics would have been developed much earlier in Man's history. Unfortunately, his notes were lost for two hundred years following his death and his conclusions were remembered with such reverence by his pupils that they became as though written in stone rather than as Aristotle intended them—merely as steps in a progressive journey toward discovery.

Respect for Aristotle, as well as the technological limitations of the early Greeks in observing the universe around them, led to a culture in which *a priori* assumptions were made that certainly would not be made in today's technological environment.

Recognition of the errors inherent in Greek *a priori* assumptions changed the face of science during the Renaissance. Classical theists, however, still trudge in the footsteps of their ancient Greek predecessors, never reexamining the basis for the premises they assume as support for their conclusions about the attributes of God. It will be necessary for theologians to make some of the same advances that scientists have made in the last two thousand years in order for them to leave erroneous Greek thinking behind and accept the pure and plain testimony of the Bible about God.

False *A Priori* Assumptions About Metaphysics

The most critical *a priori* assumption made in classical theism is that there is, in fact, a metaphysical realm in which God dwells, transcending the known space-time continuum. Many errors made by the Apologists are the result of reasoning from that assumption, which is based entirely on the Greek idea that reality is not real. That idea has largely been rejected by modern scientists and by many philosophers as well.

There are good reasons for their disbelief. Most significant among those reasons is the fact that the scientific thinking that laid the foundation for metaphysics has long since been discredited. Parmenides' idea that there cannot be change in the universe because it is composed of a single substance has long been disproven. Modern science provides no support whatever for the metaphysical notion of a timeless eternity outside the real universe.

There is certainly a spiritual realm, as yet largely unexplored by scientists. The spiritual realm, however, is also real, part of the real universe and subject to the laws of God which scientists call "natural." Insight into that realm is just now starting to receive scientific attention through the study of near-death experiences. As more becomes known about it, the idea that it constitutes a metaphysical state of existence will undoubtedly be debunked, as have all previous metaphysical theories.

From a biblical standpoint, theologians fail to recognize another crucial point regarding their acceptance of this ancient Greek doctrine. Metaphysics assumes a state of the universe that has not been confirmed by Christ or through any prophet or apostle. The basic concepts of metaphysics appear nowhere in the Bible. Although the Hellenized nations of the Gentile world at the time of Christ assumed the reality of the metaphysical universe, the Jews, to whom the scriptures were revealed, did not.[6]

Those who accept the importation of metaphysics into Christianity believe that its concepts are compatible with the Bible and provide insight into the true nature of God and the spiritual realm spoken of in holy writ. But there is no biblical reason for classical theism to accept the idea that God exists in the world of thought, as a reality that exists outside space and time. Scripture must be interpreted from the perspective of the people to whom it is revealed.

The Greek concept of the Pleroma, though it may appear similar to Hebrew teaching about Sheol, assumes very different conditions and a completely different relationship to the physical world. In the Greek's metaphysical universe, natural law did not prevail. The Greeks called the realm of God reality and the physical world an illusion. The Bible makes no such distinction between the physical and spiritual realms. It simply treats one as visible to the human eye and the other as invisible (Col. 1:1 6).

From a philosophical standpoint, the idea that Man lives in an illusory world is illogical. Anyone who has had a bad day will readily observe that, if the universe were a figment of *their* imagination, things

---

[6] Philo of Alexandria may have assumed the truth of metaphysics, but he claimed no revelations from the God he described in his Hellenized distortion of Judaism.

would be very different. The self-consciousness of each individual makes it impossible to conclude that the universe is a figment of any one person's imagination, even God's. This leads all individuals to the conclusion that either *they* are the center and cause of the universe, or the universe is, in fact, real. No one would take seriously the philosophy student who claims, "I am a figment of your imagination."

Reality has proven itself reliable and consistent, while the Greek tendency to question it is now supported by nothing but paranoia. Paraphrasing the author's philosophy professor at UCLA: "Reality may not be real, but it *always* seems *exactly* as if it were." The assumption that it is not, that there is a realm where the laws of the known universe (laws authored and sustained by God Himself) are suspended so that three persons can be one person, and so that time can be looked upon from a vantage point outside it, are not biblical. One must assume that they are false in order to understand the biblical God.

Classical Theism Recognizes Some of Its Own Assumptions

Some careful Christian theorists have recognized the problem inherent in adopting Greek assumptions. Professor Hatch, the great defender of Greek influence on Christianity, candidly makes the following admission that relates to the *a priori* assumption noted above:

> Whether we do or do not accept the conclusions in which the greater part of the Christian world ultimately acquiesced, we must at least recognize that they rest upon large assumptions. Three may be indicated which are all due to the influence of Greek philosophy.
>
> (1) *It is assumed that metaphysical distinctions are important.*
>
> I am far from saying that they are not: but it is not less important to recognize that much of what we believe rests upon this assumption that they are. There is otherwise no justification whatever for drawing men's thoughts away from the positive knowledge which we may gain both of ourselves and of the world around us, to contemplate, even at far distance, the conception of Essence.
>
> (2) *The second is the assumption that these metaphysical distinctions which we make in our minds correspond to realities in the world around us, or in God who is beyond the world and within it.*
>
> Again, I am far from saying that they do not; but it is at least important for us to recognize the fact that, in speaking of the essence of either

the world or God, we are assuming the existence of something corresponding to our conception of essence in the one or the other.

(3) *The third assumption is that the idea of perfection which we transfer from ourselves to God, really corresponds to the nature of His being.*

It is assumed that rest is better than motion, that passionlessness is better than feeling, that changelessness is better than change. We know these things of ourselves: we cannot know them of one who is unlike ourselves, who has no body that can be tired, who has no imperfection that can miss its aim, with whom unhindered movement may conceivably be perfect life.

I have spoken of these assumptions because, although it would be difficult to overestimate the importance of the conceptions by which Greek thought lifted men from the conception of God as a Being with human form and human passions, to the lofty height on which they can feel around them an awful and infinite Presence, *the time may have come when—in the face of the large knowledge of His ways which has come to us through both thought and research—we may be destined to transcend the assumptions of Greek speculation by new assumptions which will lead us at once to a diviner knowledge and the sense of a diviner life.*

As Professor Hatch feared, subsequent "thought and research" has proven that all three of the assumptions he mentions must be found not merely false but unbiblical, unworthy to have been accepted in the first place. Greek philosophy has truly taken Men from the biblical understanding of "God as a Being with human form and human passions," to philosophically lofty heights "on which they can feel around them an awful and infinite Presence." But this has not been progress. Greek philosophy has diverted Man from a true understanding of God as the Father of all Men to the belief in an incomprehensible and foreign presence, the "awful and infinite Presence" invented by the Greek philosophers. In order to regain a biblical perspective of God, it is critical to recognize and reevaluate these assumptions based on the scriptures *alone*.

Dogmatism

The word "dogma" comes from a Greek phrase that means, "It seems to me." It was, in its original sense, a personal conviction. At first,

Understanding the Attributes of God

it came to identify an affirmation made by a philosopher that is accepted as true by those who are his followers. *In the early Church, however, it was applied to doctrines that were the result of group efforts to reach an understanding of complex theological problems.* The idea of inspiration or revealed knowledge was never a part of its meaning.

Though modern usage has changed that meaning to some degree, the term "dogma" still implies a certain degree of speculation, whether true or false, about scriptural fact, as opposed to a pure statement *of* scriptural fact.[7] This is not to say that dogma is evil, not by any means. As Professor Hatch put it, "It would be a cold world in which no sun shone until the inhabitants thereof had arrived at a true chemical analysis of sunlight."[8]

Unfortunately, however, the tendency toward transforming speculation into dogma became dangerous in the early Church. Beginning in the third century, most of the churches insisted not only on uniform belief in fundamental facts about Christianity, but also in a *"uniformity of speculations in regard to those facts."*[9] *"The holding of approved opinions was elevated to a position at first co-ordinate with, and at last superior to, trust in God and the effort to live a holy life."*[10]

In many ways, dogma became as great a barrier to truth in the early Church as *a priori* assumptions. The Gospel was transformed and systematized by a tendency toward dogmatism that characterized the third and fourth centuries. This was done contrary to the Apostle Paul's warning in 1 Timothy 6:20, where he instructed Timothy to avoid "profane and vain babblings, and oppositions of science falsely so called." "Science falsely so called" is a reference to early Christian Gnosticism, but "profane and vain babblings" refers to speculation. The Church did not follow this instruction and, as Professor Hatch explains, *"Under the touch of Greek philosophy, knowledge had become speculation:* whatever obligation attached to faith in its original sense was conceived to attach to it in its new sense: *the new form of knowledge was held to be not less necessary than the old."*[11]

---

[7] Hatch, *Influence of Greek Ideas*, 137-138
[8] *Ibid.*, 333.
[9] *Ibid.*, 136
[10] *Ibid.*, 137.
[11] *Ibid.*

Protestants think their position on *sola Scriptura* has allowed them to escape dogma in the form of false traditions, leaving it behind in the Roman Church, but they have, in fact, retained the most crucial errors, the very foundations of early dogmatism. The opinions of Irenaeus, and other early Church fathers are treated with the same respect as the inspired writers of the New Testament, sometimes with even greater reverence. The dogmatism that resulted from that acceptance cannot be allowed to replace the truths of the Bible. What is said *in* the Bible must be the standard, not what the early Church fathers said *about* the Bible.

The Danger of Relying on Greek Terminology

Another intellectual barrier that has proven misleading to classical theologians is found in the use of labels placed on ideas by the early Apologists and others who were trying to appeal to a Greek audience. *When adopting the terminology of Greek philosophy, one tends to enter unwittingly into the realm of metaphysics it assumes. Great care must be taken to avoid confusing an attribute of God with the Greek label used to identify it.*

In the third and fourth centuries, the early Church suffered greatly from this problem. They associated specific terminology with doctrines that had become binding on the Church through dogmatism. The failure to use that terminology, rather than expressing the meaning intended by the terminology, was often seen as grounds for an accusation of heresy.

For example, terms such as *homoousios* caused great misunderstanding and contention in the third-century Church because they were understood differently in different parts of the world. Witness for example the exchange between Dionysius of Rome and Dionysius of Alexandria in the latter half of the third century (see Chapter 8). Dionysius of Alexandria was placed in jeopardy of being excommunicated as a heretic because he failed to use the word "*homoousios*" in his rejection of the Sabellians.

To avoid such confusion and error, one must always remember that Greek labels, especially those that appear nowhere, or are used differently, in the Bible, are distinct from the attributes they identify. Words like "monotheism" and "polytheism" are good examples. They are used nowhere in the Bible, yet Mormonism, whose doctrines are sometimes falsely identified as polytheistic rather than monotheistic (see Chapter

17) has been rejected by adherents to classical theism as a non-biblical cult even though its teachings are exclusively biblical.[12] Even terms like "omniscient," "omnipotent" and "omnipresent," must be identified for the Greek designations they are. Otherwise, it is difficult to avoid a theological dissertation that is actually describing a label rather than a true biblical attribute of God.

Like the headings in a legal contract, the Greek labels for doctrines need to be ignored in favor of the actual language they are intended to summarize. Any words with roots in Greek philosophy, rather than Hebrew or New Testament Greek, can be especially misleading and should be treated with suspicion until they are understood in a true biblical context. Certainly, no conclusions should be drawn about God's attributes based on the Greek labels used to describe them.

The Attributes of God

In the chapters that follow, the attributes of God named by Dr. Frank Beckwith in his article cited in Chapter 1 will be discussed and analyzed. They have been slightly rearranged and the concept of transcendence so fundamental to classical theology, has been included. The chapters compare each attribute as described in classical theism with the LDS and the Greek philosophical views. Classical references that discuss God's attributes often list additional attributes and characteristics of God, but these are the major themes and the points on which Mormonism is most often called to task by classical theists.

A Note About the History of Theology After the Fourth Century

Reviewing the extensive history of philosophical thought, and the many alternative theologies that shaped classical theism after the fourth century, is a study that will not be possible in these chapters. The purpose of this book is to identify biblical truth and separate it from the Greek ideas that lie at the foundation of mainstream orthodox Christianity.

Because of this narrow focus, some may be tempted to criticize the discussion here as naive or uninformed. That is far from the case. The fact is that current theology is so thoroughly grounded in philosophy

---

[12] See, Richard Hopkins, *Biblical Mormonism: Responding to Evangelical Criticism of LDS Theology* (Bountiful: Horizon Publishers, 1994).

that much of it has lost all relevance to biblical truth. It attempts primarily to justify or resolve the conflicts that have arisen over the centuries because Christianity accepted false doctrines about God in the second century. Delving into that kind of analysis is foreign to the aims of this book. That is why it is not considered here.

Many modern Evangelical scholars have departed from this trend and are trying to emphasize a more biblical approach. Their works will be more frequently cited in the discussions that follow simply because they evidence a greater respect for biblical truth. They too have failed to reject the philosophical foundations of their theology, however. As a result, they remain steeped in Greek philosophy. But it is hoped that this review will help some of these scholars to see that Mormons do, in fact, understand theology—biblical theology—and that the teachings of classical theism differ in important ways from real biblical theology.

If a theological tenet is not biblical, it is irrelevant that it is supported by the teachings of other theologians, whether Calvin or Barth, Augustine or Berkhoff, Athenagoras or Kierkegaard. Hence, a study of historical theology, while it would be educational, is beside the point of this book. The discussion here will, instead, focus on the Bible and how its teachings were lost in some measure to modern Christianity through the introduction of Greek philosophy. Accordingly, the author will decline the temptation to joust with the great thinkers of classical theism. That is no reason to assume that he, along with many other Mormons, are unaware of their views.

Summary

1. Significant barriers to understanding make it difficult to communicate the truths in the Bible to those steeped in Christian orthodoxy.
2. One barrier is the adoption of *a priori* assumptions made by the Greek philosophers of Christ's time.
3. The adoption of Greek *a priori* assumptions by Christian theologians was the natural result of the education and influence of Hellenism on the Apologists.
4. Assumptions about God common to the Hellenistic thinkers in the second century remain at the foundation of classical theism today.

5. Though the Hellenistic assumptions adopted in the second century seemed to be *a priori*, they were actually based on observations made with the naked eye and the limited technology of the ancient Greeks.
6. Contrary to the basic premise of Greek philosophy, Men cannot be trusted to arrive at true information about God by simply thinking.
7. Men need to rely strictly on His revelation of Himself in order to understand God.
8. Based on the Greek *a priori* assumption that metaphysics expresses the state of reality in the universe, classical theists have embraced paradoxes—contradictory theological conclusions such as the doctrine of co-substantiality—and made them tenets of faith.
9. The assumption that Matter is evil and the body is incapable of perfection is the basis for orthodox rejection of the biblical concept that God has a physical body.
10. Modern scientists have long since discarded Aristotelian thinking in order to arrive at scientific truth. Modern theologians should do the same. They should re-examine the Greek assumptions of Christian orthodoxy, especially those based on metaphysical distinctions.
11. Dogma is the expression of personal convictions *about* scriptural fact rather than the exposition *of* scriptural fact.
12. Dogmatism in the early Church turned speculation into binding tenets of faith and established another barrier to understanding the truths taught in the Bible.
13. Greek terms used to identify the attributes of God can also present a barrier to understanding. The labels used to describe God should not be confused with the actual attributes they identify.
14. No conclusions about God or His attributes should be derived from the Greek labels used to describe Him. Rather, conclusions about God should be drawn exclusively from the Bible.
15. The attributes of God will be studied under eight categories in the chapters that follow.
16. The focus of this book is biblical theology and the elements of Greek philosophy that lie at the foundation of classical theism. The refusal of this book to address all the philosophies of classical and other theologians since the fourth century does not mean Mormons are unaware of their thinking.

The Personal God

Classical theism declares that God is personal. According to Dr. Beckwith, God is "a perfect person" having the attributes of "self-consciousness, the ability to reason, know, love, communicate, and so forth."[1] He cites Genesis 17:11, Exodus 3:14, and Jeremiah 29:11 for these truths. This description lists purely mental attributes. That they are among the attributes of the biblical God, Mormons would heartily agree. There can be no argument that the Bible describes God in these terms. But the Greek philosophers described their God in the same terms.[2]

Personality as an attribute of God is seen by classical theists largely as a distinction between a God who has a center of consciousness and a being whose consciousness is diffuse throughout the universe.[3] Lack of a localized center of consciousness is the characteristic of God that most typifies pantheism, a system of belief that sees God as present in everything. Often this is understood in the sense that God actually *is* everything.[4] Yet the classical description of God given above hardly separates Him from a god that is pantheistic. Does the classical view of God really identify Him as a person, or does classical theism's doctrine of co-substantiality turn the Christian God into a pantheistic deity?

Greek Philosophy and Christianity Merged

As indicated in Part 1, Greek philosophy prepared the Hellenized masses for many of the truths of Christianity. The down side of that preparation was the tendency of the educated classes to impose con-

---

[1] Beckwith, "Philosophical Problems," 2.
[2] Hatch, *Influence of Greek Ideas*, 209; Nash, *Christianity and the Hellenistic World*, 73.
[3] Millard Erickson, *Christian Theology*, 1 vol. ed. (Grand Rapids: Baker Book House, 1992), 268-269.
[4] Nash, *Christianity & the Hellenistic World,* 69.

cepts familiar to them on Christian doctrines that were seen as similar to the ideas of the Greek philosophers. As Hatch expressed it:

> On its ethical side [Christianity] had, as we have seen, large elements in common with reformed Stoicism; on its theological side it moved in harmony with the new movements of Platonism. And those movements reacted upon it. They gave a philosophical form to the simpler Jewish faith, and especially to those elements of it in which the teaching of St. Paul had already given a foothold for speculation. The earlier conceptions remained; but blending readily with the philosophical conceptions that were akin to them, they were expanded into large theories in which metaphysics and dialectics had an ample field.[5]

Hatch's view of the resulting syncretism of Christianity and Greek philosophy represents the view of most classical theists. Unfortunately, many of the "earlier conceptions" did not "remain." Christianity, as it came from the mouth of Christ, was not a "simpler Jewish faith," and rather than "blending" it was actually changed by the influence of "the philosophical conceptions that were akin to them." That classical theists justify the resulting mix is the essence of their apostasy. That Hatch acknowledges it is at least candid.

The Philosophers' View of God as a Person

In Greek philosophy, Stoicism was originally pantheistic, but by the time of Christ, Stoic philosophers had given God a personality, thereby joining the Platonists in declaring that God is a person, i.e., a being or entity, not just an impersonal force.[6] The Platonists made a dualistic distinction between the world of sense and the world of thought. To them, God belonged to the world of thought only. He was viewed as Mind, beyond the world of sense and matter.[7] He was said to-be "unborn, undying, uncontained."[8]

Unfortunately, a transcendent God such as the Greeks contemplated was effectively incapable of contact with the sensory world of Matter. The stronger their belief in His transcendence, the greater was their need to devise some form of intermediary link between God in the world of thought and Man in the world of sense.[9] Popular mythology included the belief in "*daemons*," spirits inferior to the gods but superior to men.

---

[5] Hatch, *Influence of Greek Ideas*, 238.
[6] Nash, *Christianity and the Hellenistic World*, 69, 73.
[7] Hatch, *Influence of Greek Ideas*, 240-241.
[8] *Ibid.*, 244.
[9] *Ibid.*, 245.

They were credited with creating everything but the human soul.[10] This philosophical concept was found in Plato's Forms (*ideai*) and the Stoic's Reasons (*logoi*).[11] They believed these were outflows from and reflections of God's nature.[12] Philo connected the Greek concept of *daemons* with the Old Testament's teachings about angels.[13]

All these ideas tended to fuse into one concept of an intermediary between the world of thought, where God lived, and the sensory world where Men dwell. That intermediary was most commonly spoken of in the singular, the *Logos*.[14]

The *Logos* was seen as the reflection of the Supreme Being, like a messenger sent to reveal Him to Men and Men to Him.[15] In the Greek belief system, He was also a kind of go-between, not only revealing God to Man, but pleading the cause of Man to God.[16]

Two ideas about his nature were popular in Hellenistic thought at the time of Christ. One idea was that the *Logos* evolved from God. He was seen as being projected by God as a man's shadow or ghost, and was sometimes conceived of as being thrown off by his body. God was seen as the substance of which the Logos was the insubstantial form, almost like a reflection in a mirror.[17] The second idea was that the *Logos* was the "first-begotten" of God.[18] God was seen as Father, and Wisdom as Mother.[19]

Each of these conceptions progressed from the idea that Reason, as the intermediary projection of God's mind, had made the sensory world, to the idea that the Reason of God had in some way detached itself from God to work as a subordinate, but self-acting power.[20] None of these ideas ever considered the *Logos* as truly separate from God. Rather, the *Logos* was imagined as part of God, a totally foreign and incomprehensible being.[21] Given the metaphysical nature of this God, the concept of His personality was very nebulous and flexible.

---

[10] *Ibid.*, 246.
[11] *Ibid.*
[12] *Ibid.*, 246-247.
[13] *Ibid.*, 247.
[14] *Ibid.*
[15] *Ibid.*, 245-247.
[16] *Ibid.*, 248.
[17] *Ibid.*, 249.
[18] *Ibid.*, 250.
[19] *Ibid.*
[20] *Ibid.*
[21] *Ibid.*, 255-256.

The Classical Attempt to Define the Personal God: The Trinity

Hatch admits that "all the conceptions which we have seen to exist in the sphere of philosophy were reproduced in the sphere of Christianity."[22] Many of these conceptions were expressed in the various Gnostic schools described in Chapter 7, but they were by no means restricted to the heretics. Though the Apologists resisted Gnostic excesses, the mainstream of Greek reasoning that ran through Gnostic philosophy was often assumed as a given by the early Church fathers.

The Greek idea of God's transcendent incomprehensibility, to be discussed more fully in Chapter 11, was associated with God the Father as early as Justin Martyr's *Dialogue With Trypho*.[23] As that concept developed, it became generally believed that only Man's intelligence was made in God's image.[24] Despite this affinity with God, however, Men were thought to be incapable of even a basic understanding of Him. Their knowledge was explained as being like the vision of a spark compared with the splendor of the sun.[25] In reality there was a much greater difference between the God revealed to Men in the scriptures and the God envisioned by the philosophers.

Various theories arose as to how this incomprehensible God had revealed Himself to Man. The heretical doctrines of Valentinus and other Gnostics on this subject were refuted, but the direction of their thinking was not rejected so much as the specifics of their theology. The dominant ideas being accepted by the early Christian Church were directly in line with both Greek philosophy and Greek religion on these points.[26]

Thus, just as the Greeks saw their *Logos* as the means by which God came in contact with matter and created the world, so the idea arose that the mind of Man could only know the mind of God by receiving a particle of the divine *Logos*.[27] The difference between the knowledge other men had received about God, and the inspiration received through Christ's revelation of Him was seen as the difference

---

[22] *Ibid.*, 250
[23] Justin, *Dialogue with Trypho*, 127
[24] *Ibid.*, 256
[25] *Ibid.*
[26] *Ibid.*, 258.
[27] *Ibid.*, 261.

between receiving only "a seed of the *Logos*," and receiving the "whole *Logos*."[28]

The Apostle John's reference in his gospel (John 1:1-3, 14) to Christ as the "Word," translated from the same Greek word (*logos*), was greatly misunderstood in the late second century. Irenaeus used that word for the Son in describing His relationship to the Father in terms that were almost identical to those used by the Greek philosophers to describe the relationship between their *Logos* and Supreme God.[29] While Christ clearly taught that He was the revelation of the Father (Matt. 11:27; John 14:7-9), the nature of that doctrine was changed by these comparisons from a literal concept appropriate to Hebrew thinking into a metaphysical concept consistent with Greek beliefs. This transition led the Apologists to adopt other ideas about the *Logos* from Greek philosophy, including the Greek terms *ousia* and *homoousios*,[30] which aided in their development of the doctrine of co-substantiality.

The problem Christian orthodoxy has today in describing God as a "person" stems from that development—the acceptance of the metaphysical doctrine of co-substantiality.[31] Three "persons" are identified using the title "God" in the New Testament, yet the Three are declared to be "one God." If co-substantiality is accepted as the explanation of that seeming dichotomy, what does that do to the personality of God? The development of the terminology used by the early Church to express the concept of co-substantiality sheds some light on that issue.

The doctrine of co-substantiality was defined in Chapter 6, which also demonstrated the gradual appearance of that doctrine in the writings of the second-century Apologists between 161 and 180 A.D. The Greek Apologists (those who wrote in Greek) used the word *ousia* and its derivative terms to express that idea (that the Father and the Son are separate but of the same substance or *ousia*). Those words were satisfactory at first, but their Latin equivalents did not express exactly the same ideas. Nor were the Greek words understood the same way by all Greeks.[32]

---

[28] Justin, *Second Apology*, 8; Hatch, *Influence of Greek Ideas*, 261-262.
[29] See Irenaeus, *Against Heresies*, 4:6:3, 5, 6.
[30] Hatch, *Influence of Greek Ideas*, 274.
[31] *Ibid.*, 252-253.
[32] *Ibid.*, see discussion from 269-279.

At first, the Latin word *substantia* was used to express the way in which the three persons of the Trinity were supposedly united. The difficulty was to find a word that expressed the way in which they were separate. No Greek word had been found that was fully satisfactory for that purpose.[33] The Latin word that was employed, and which became the basis for the Catholic doctrine, was *persona*. This word was most likely developed by Tertullian, the greatest of the early Latin Apologists (those who wrote in Latin). He was a lawyer, and the common use of this word was in the legal sense of an entity that could be a party to a contract.[34] Thus, it became common to say that the Trinity consisted of three persons (*personas*) in one substance (*substantia*).

The idea of God being analogous to a legal entity lay at the heart of Christian theology during the third and fourth centuries. It made the doctrine of co-substantiality more palatable to those in the Church who were seeking to digest and understand it, but it was a very different concept from that which defines the personal God of the Bible.

In modern times, the concept of personality has been more fully examined. Both scientists and philosophers recognize that the idea of a personal being, as opposed to a legal entity, involves a distinct *center of consciousness* that has a specific location in time and space. This understanding of personality simply does not fit into the makeup of a being like that imagined in the Trinity of classical theism.

The modern understanding of personality has required classical theists to concoct a unique definition of the term "personal" as it applies to God. This definition highlights the errors of the untenable doctrine known as co-substantiality. Classical theists must teach that God is personal, for it is taught both in the Bible and in the Greek philosophical systems. But with the greater understanding of the term "personal" that has come from modern study, they turn around, practically in the same breath, and take that attribute away.

The Modern Expression of an Unsolvable Enigma: The Trinity As Three Separate Persons, But One Individual

Classical theists today play a theological word game in which they separate the idea of "personality" from the concept of "individuality." They claim that God is three "persons" but only one "individual." How

---
[33] *Ibid.*, 275-277.
[34] *Ibid.*, 277.

this can be true has never been rationally explained, nor indeed can it be. Most have admitted that it is not rational, taking refuge in the claim that God is incomprehensible. With that defense, they are not limited by common sense, as scientists would be, nor by the fact that their doctrine is stated nowhere in scripture, as theologians should be.

The idea of a "person" who cannot be described as an "individual," a separate "center of consciousness," is not merely incomprehensible, it is a contradiction in terms—a logical impossibility. It is the essence of what is wrong with the concept of the Trinity.

God has identified Man as having been made in His image (Gen. 1:26-27). Each man or woman has his or her own center of consciousness. If Man is in the image of God, one should expect God's personal nature to be like that of Man, His offspring.

According to classical theism, however, the term "personal" means something very different in God than it does in Man. Donald Bloesch in his *Essentials of Evangelical Theology* explains the reason for that conclusion in the following statement:

> Barth rightly recognizes that the modern concept of personality includes the attributes of self-consciousness and this, therefore, creates problems for the doctrine of the Trinity. To hold that there are three distinct centers of consciousness, three self-conscious personal beings, comes close to tritheism.[35]

Note that Bloesch and Barth are drawn to this conclusion not by the need to be rational, nor by the desire to be biblical. The concept is based on a desire to avoid the Greek label, "tritheism," a word that appears nowhere in the Bible.

Bloesch cites no scriptural support for the idea that the three separate members of the Godhead are not individually self-conscious. Neither does *The Concise Evangelical Dictionary of Theology*, edited by Walter Elwell, which expresses the classical theory as follows:

> While the term "person" in relation to the Trinity does not signify the limited individuality of human persons, it does affirm the I-thou of personal relationship, particularly of love, within the triune Godhead.[36]

---

[35] Donald Bloesch, *Essentials of Evangelical Theology: Volume 1, God, Authority, and Salvation* (San Francisco: Harper & Row, 1978), 35, fn.

[36] Walter Elwell, ed. *The Concise Evangelical Dictionary of Theology*, abridged by Peter Toon (Grand Rapids: Baker Book House, 1991), s.v. "God, Doctrine of: The Trinity."

This sentence will require some explanation. It gives lip service to the fact that each member of the Godhead uses the first person singular ("I-thou") to communicate with Man. But the nature of such communication is in direct conflict with their theory of personality in the Trinity. To resolve that conflict, classical theists claim that God uses the first person singular differently than do Men. When a specific person of the Trinity speaks, they say, the individuality implied in His use of the first person singular does not exist because, among the three, there is only one center of consciousness.

To make this shortage appear as though it were a sign of God's superiority, Elwell has done a subtle turnaround. That which is missing in the persons of the Trinity is identified as a *"limitation"* in Man. Without reason, logic or proof, he states that the "individuality of human persons" is "limited." No support for such a "limitation" is found in scripture, however, nor is there any discussion of this limitation in the writings of the early Church fathers.

The Separateness of the Persons in the Trinity

The Greek philosophers saw God and His *Logos* as separate only in a metaphysical sense.[37] Thought, they argued, could never truly be separated from the Mind of its origin. As noted in Chapter 6, this idea was adopted theologically by Irenaeus, and expressed apologetically by Athenagoras. These men adopted their model of the Father and the Son directly from the Greek notion. This was a point the Apologists painstakingly noted in their letters to Marcus Aurelius, complaining about the law that forbad them from worshiping a God whom they claimed was just like the God whom the Greek philosophers were allowed to worship freely. As Hatch put it, "The dominant Theistic philosophy of Greece became the dominant philosophy of Christianity. It prevailed in form as well as in substance."[38]

The Greeks had glossed over the issue of personality in their personalization of such attributes as Wisdom and Design. They thought of these fictitious entities vaguely as separate persons, but did not analyze that thinking in terms of a Being like the Trinity. Likewise, the Gnostics did not think about their Aeons having separate centers of consciousness. Instead, they imagined these Aeons as imperfect creations of the Supreme Being.[39]

---

[37] Hatch, *Influence of Greek Ideas*, 200.
[38] *Ibid.*, 207-208.
[39] *Ibid.*, 217.

But the Trinity postulated three uncreated *Gods*. The effort to make this concept fit into the ancient Greek mold was focused on the doctrine of the *Logos*, who was seen as more closely associated with the Supreme Being than any Aeon. But the issue of the *Logos* having a center of consciousness separate from the Supreme Being was never directly addressed by the Apologists any more than it was by the Greeks.

A real person can say, "Here I am" (Isa. 58:9; cf., Deut. 5:31; Acts 10:33), or "I come unto thee" (Exod. 19.9; cf., Exod. 33:5; Josh. 5:13-15; Zech. 2:10; Rev. 22:20) and his center of consciousness will come to or be at the spot designated. A different person will have a center of consciousness that is located elsewhere. There is no biblical reason to think that the Father, the Son or the Holy Ghost function any differently, and that was the position of Justin Martyr.

Justin and the Separateness of the Father and the Son

As noted in Chapter 6, Justin Martyr was careful to separate the persons of the Father and the Son in his *First Apology*.[40] In *Dialogue With Trypho*, he attributed all divine activity in the Old Testament to Christ.[41] He based this conclusion on his mistaken notion that the Father was Aristotle's Unmoving Mover, but he clearly attributed a separate personality to Christ. Indeed, he taught that Christ and the Father were *numerically* separate personalities.

He described Christ as a separate and subordinate power to the Father, as follows: "And the first power after God the Father and Lord of all is the Word, who is also the Son."[42] In his *Dialogue with Trypho*, Justin specifically calls Christ "another God and Lord subject to the Maker of all things."[43] Likewise, he states, "There is, and is spoken of, another God and Lord beneath the Maker of the universe."[44] He writes:

> And now I shall again recite the words which I have spoken in proof of this point. When Scripture says, "The Lord rained fire from the Lord out of heaven" [Gen. 19:24], the prophetic word indicates that there were two in number: One upon the earth, who, it says, descended

---

[40] Justin, *First Apology*, 36-38.
[41] Justin, *Dialogue With Trypho*, 127.
[42] Justin, *First Apology*, 32.
[43] Justin, *Dialogue with Trypho*, 56.
[44] *Ibid*.

to behold the cry of Sodom; Another in heaven, who also is Lord of the Lord on earth, as He is Father and God; the cause of His power and of His being Lord and God. . . . You perceive, my hearers, if you bestow attention, that the Scripture has declared that this Offspring was begotten by the Father before all things created; and that that which is begotten is numerically distinct from that which begets anyone will admit.[45]

Anticipating efforts by other Christian writers of his time to fuse the Father and the Son into a numerically singular being, Justin warned as follows:

I know that some wish to anticipate these remarks and to say that the power sent from the Father of all . . . is indivisible and inseparable from the Father, just as they say that the light of the sun on earth is indivisible and inseparable from the sun in the heavens; as when it sinks, the light sinks along with it; so the Father, when He chooses, say they, causes His power to spring forth, and when He chooses, He makes it return to Himself. . . . And that this power which the prophetic word calls God [referring to Christ], as has been also amply demonstrated, and Angel, is not numbered as different in name only like the light of the sun, but is indeed something numerically distinct, I have discussed briefly in what has gone before.[46]

It is obvious from this language that the development of the co-substantiality doctrine was a process arising out of disagreements among the Christian leaders of the time. Here, Justin appears to be contradicting the notions of other Apologists (most likely Tatian). The idea that the Son is the Mind or Thought of the Father was intended to combine the Two numerically into one God. That effort was an attempt to explain biblical references to God's oneness in a literal manner, through use of the metaphysical term *ousia*. That belief Justin saw as contrary to his own views.

As noted in Chapter 6, Justin's writings do not teach co-substantiality. Instead, he appears to have interpreted the oneness of God in a figurative manner. In *Dialogue With Trypho*, he wrote:

I will endeavour to persuade you, that He who is said to have appeared to Abraham, and to Jacob, and to Moses, and who is called God, is distinct from Him who made all things,—numerically, I mean,

---
[45] *Ibid.*, 129.
[46] *Ibid.*, 128.

not distinct in will. For I affirm that He has never at any time done anything which He who made the world—above whom there is no other God—has not wished Him both to do and to engage Himself with.

Thus, Justin affirms a *figurative* unity of "will" between the Father and the Son, whom he declares to be absolutely, and numerically, distinct individuals. This teaching characterized the writing of all the earliest church writers.[47]

Metaphysics, the Cradle of the Trinity

The classical idea of co-substantiality or "consubstantiality" as it is sometimes called in early Christian literature, is now expressed as follows: "The sense of consubstantiality is that the essential being of the Son is neither different in kind nor numerically other than the substance of the Father, but the very same."[48] This statement is in direct conflict with Justin's specific teachings about the numeric separateness of the Father and the Son, as stated above. The oneness yet separateness of the members of the Godhead can be resolved on a fully satisfying biblical basis, as will be explained in Chapter 17. However, Justin's writings on the subject, while biblical, did not resolve the issue to the satisfaction of his colleagues, and vice versa.

The resolution chosen by the later Apologists was not biblical, but metaphysical. Rather than accept the separateness of the Father, Son and Holy Ghost as literal, and their unity as figurative, as Justin did, the later Apologists insisted that *both* doctrines were to be interpreted literally. Such a resolution would never have been conceived if the Apologists had not been oriented to a metaphysical universe and under the thumb of a Stoic Emperor.

From that orientation was born the irrational theory of the Trinity. On the one hand, the Apologists taught that the persons of the Father, the Son and the Holy Ghost were essentially and numerically the same. On the other hand, they acknowledged and taught *with equal force* that they were *numerically separate and distinct*. (Book Four of Irenaeus' *Against Heresies* opines to that effect at length.)

---

[47] Gregory A. Boyd, *Oneness Pentacostals & The Trinity* (Grand Rapids: Baker Book House 1992), 159. He admits "They [the earliest Church Fathers] at times erred (by later Nicene Standards) in emphasizing the distinctness of the Father, Son, and Spirit too much!"

[48] Miley, *Systematic Theology*, 1:239.

Metaphysics allowed the Apologists the illusion of rational thought in the formulation of this doctrine. They could ignore the numerical distinction of the Godhead by envisioning it as His condition in the *Pleroma*, and they could imagine the three to be separate in respect to their appearance in the sensory world. In a real universe this is a true paradox, unresolvable and logically irrational. The only theological explanation given by classical theism for this paradox is that God, being transcendent, is incomprehensible. That response, however, does not address the real issue: Is the Trinity a logical contradiction, a true impossibility? How can three *numerically* distinct persons be a *numerically* singular individual?

Over the centuries since this paradox was first accepted at Nicaea, answers given by theologians to that question have been many and varied. Some liberal theologians have rejected the entire rationale of the Trinity as flawed beyond redemption, but, in so doing, have thrown the baby out with the bath water. Along with the Trinity, they reject the divinity of Christ, thereby advocating greater error than their predecessors.[49] The truth can be found in the Protestant cry of *sola Scriptura*, but only if it is applied strictly—by rejecting the traditions of the second-century Church fathers and those who followed their lead.

What Does the Bible Say About "Co-substantiality"?

It is well known that the term "co-substantial," or *homoousios*, appears nowhere in the Bible. As noted in Chapter 8, that was one of the criticisms leveled against the Nicene Creed at the time of its adoption. Even the root word *ousia*, which lies at the base of the Nicene formula, appears only twice in the New Testament, both times in Luke 15 (verses 12 and 13) during the Parable of the Prodigal Son. It is used only to refer to the property that the Prodigal Son took with him and wasted in the far country.

The metaphysical idea of substance (*ousia*) developed by the Greek philosophers and the Apologists is taught nowhere in the Bible. To the extent the Bible teaches anything akin to co-substantiality, it is limited to the way in which the term was used by Dionysius of Alexandria—the Father and the Son have the same substance in the sense that a par-

---

[49] See, e.g., Robert Morey, *Battle of the Gods: The Gathering Storm in Modern Evangelicalism* (Southbridge: Crown Publications, 1989), 62-67.

ent and child have the same substance. There can be no rational argument that the doctrine of co-substantiality comes from the Bible.

Why, then, do classical theists cling so tenaciously to this Trinitarian dogma? What is it about this logically irrational and unbiblical doctrine that accounts for its continuation over the centuries? The answer lies in the complex interrelationship of Greek doctrines that lies at the heart of co-substantiality, as devised by the Apologists. One of the most important aspects of that doctrine is that it resolves what, for the Apologists, was a particularly thorny problem—the origin of Christ. Where did a second personal deity come from? For Greek thinkers, this was a major issue.

Justin Martyr's Teachings About the Genesis of Christ

Consistent with the Bible, Justin Martyr taught that Christ was the "first-born" of God (Col. 1:15), the "first offspring of God," the "first force after the Father of all and the Lord God."[50] Commenting on Revelation 3:14, Justin wrote as follows in *Dialogue With Trypho:*

> [A]s the beginning, before all created things, God begat from Himself a kind of rational Force, which is called by the Holy Spirit sometimes 'the Glory of the Lord,' sometimes 'Son,' sometimes 'Wisdom,' sometimes 'Angel,' sometimes 'God,' sometimes 'Lord and *Logos*,' sometimes he speaks of himself as 'Captain of the Lord's host:' for he has all these appellations, both from his ministering to the Father's purpose and from his having been begotten by the Father's pleasure.[51]

As noted above, he also said, "there is, and is spoken of, another God and Lord beneath the Maker of the universe."[52]

This is the earliest reliable discussion of the origin of Christ by an Apologist. It is very different from the notions that prevailed only a decade or two later. While it does not teach the co-substantiality theory promulgated by the later Apologists, its description of Christ as "a rational Force" was not entirely inconsistent with that idea, and Justin's belief that the Father was, in essence, Aristotle's Unmoving Mover was equally unbiblical and erroneous. In fact, as will be seen below, Justin's writings were sufficiently ambiguous on this subject

---

[50] Justin, *Dialog with Trypho*, 61.
[51] *Ibid.*
[52] *Ibid.*, 56.

that it was possible for the later Apologists to use them in developing their theory of co-substantiality without labeling Justin a heretic.

Christ, the "Beginning of the Creation of God"

Revelation 3:14 is a very significant passage, and Justin's remarks above are revealing enough to interject a comment on that verse alone. It introduces Christ's message to the branch of the Church then organized in Laodicea. In the NASB, it reads, "And to the angel of the church in Laodicea write: The Amen, the faithful and true Witness, *the Beginning of the creation of God*, says this:"

The side notes of the NASB state that the word "Beginning" in this passage should be understood to mean the "origin or source." Some translations even render the phrase, "*head* of the creation of God."[53] These interpretive slants are not the sense in which Justin used the term "firstborn." In his comments on Christ's origin as the Father's "firstborn," he was true to the original Greek.

The Greek word is *arché*, and of the 56 times it is used in the New Testament, it is 40 times translated "beginning." Unless the context suggests otherwise, "beginning," is the preferred translation, and it is properly so translated in both the KJV and the NASB (despite the side note from the editors of the latter version). In fact, concerning the use of *arché* in Revelations 3:14, Bauer admits that, linguistically, the meaning could be translated "first created."[54] This is exactly the way Justin appears to have understood the term. It was, therefore, essential for the later Apologists to address Justin's writing and the issue of Christ's origin.

Rejection of Pre-Mortal Birth As the Means for the Genesis of Christ

After Justin, the reasoning of the Apologists on the origin of Christ was largely a process of elimination. First, they were impelled by their Hellenistic background to explain the relationship between the "Father" and His "Son" without ever suggesting that They actually were father

---

[53] Jay P. Green, Sr., *A Literal Translation of the Bible*, in *The Interlinear Bible*, ed. Jay P. Green Sr., 2nd ed. (Unknown. Hendrickson Publishers, 1986).
[54] Walter Bauer, *A Greek-English Lexicon of the New Testament and other Early Christian Literature*, William F. Arndt and F. Wilbur Gingrich, trans. 2nd ed. (Chicago: University of Chicago Press, 1979), s.v. ἀρχή.

and son. At the time of Christ, the pagan belief in gods who bore offspring and behaved much like human beings had long been rejected by the Greek philosophers largely on moral grounds.[55] But paganism was the most popular religion of the masses well into the fourth century, and many Gnostic tales of creation were reminiscent of this popular culture (see Chapter 7). The philosophical distaste for such pagan doctrines was repeatedly expressed in the writings of the Apologists.[56]

From very early in the effort to express Christian doctrine in Greek terms, the idea that Christ was actually born to the Father was rejected. Indeed, it was never given any serious consideration at all. The Hellenized leanings of the Apologists on this subject were strong enough that they even ignored the testimony of the Bible in its much-repeated description of the Son's relationship to the Father using the word "begotten" (Ps. 2:7; John 1:14, 18; 3:16, 18; Acts 13:33; Heb. 1:5; 5:5; 11:17; 1 John 4:9; 5:1). This they did despite the fact that, in both Greek and Hebrew, that word has the principal connotation of creation by physical birth. By introducing a mockery of the truth into paganism, Satan was able to keep the early Church from even looking at the biblical truth about the origin of Christ.

Rejection of Pre-Mortal Creation as the Means for the Genesis of Christ

As noted in Part 1, the Greeks had long struggled with the problem of evil—reconciling the existence of a perfect God with an imperfect world. The prevailing explanation was that God created the world through intermediaries who were imperfect because they were created beings. Their imperfections were thought to account for the imperfect world in which Men now live.[57] Therefore, if a thing were created, according to the Greeks, it was inferior, flawed by nature, incomparable to the "uncreated" or "unbegotten" God. This notion was amplified in Gnosticism and in later Christianity by the notion that created things were made out of *nothing*.

Justin, though he cited Revelation 3:14, refrained from using the word "created" in his writings about Christ's origin. He said that the Father *"begat* [Christ] *from Himself."* As will be seen below, his use of

---

[55] Hatch, *Influence of Greek Ideas*, 57-59.
[56] See, for example, Athenagoras, *A Plea for the Christians*, 21.
[57] Hatch, *Influence of Greek Ideas*, 217.

the word "begat" was probably not meant to convey the idea that Christ had actually been born of the Father. He was clear in teaching that Christ came *from the Father*, but his explanation of Christ's actual origin was ambiguous.

The later Apologists were much less ambiguous about their belief in the inferiority of "created" things. They took a step closer to Greek philosophy and away from the Bible in expressing their position as follows:

> For, a thing is either uncreated and eternal, or created and perishable. Nor do I think one thing and the philosophers another. . . . Plato teaches that that which always is, the intelligible, is unoriginated, but that which is not, the sensible, is originated, beginning to be and ceasing to exist.[58]

Note that Athenagoras here cites Plato as agreeing with this reasoning, but, contrary to the pattern established in Justin's writings, he gives no scriptural support for the concept. Nevertheless, that did not prevent the Apologists from rejecting the idea that the origin of Christ involved any form of "creation."

The Idea of "Emanation" and the Rejection of "Division" as the Means for the Genesis of Christ

The emerging view of the Apologists was that in some way the *Logos* had come forth from God.[59] In an attempt to clarify his position on the issue, Justin expressed a view of Christ's genesis that ultimately became the ruling analogy of classical theology on the subject.[60] He was simply trying to explain that the Father had not been split into two Gods as a consequence of His "begetting" the Son, but the analogy he used was given a Stoic interpretation by his successors.

The care with which Justin addresses his concern suggests that it may have been a point raised by early critics of Christianity. It may have been voiced by Trypho, the critic Justin addressed in *Dialogue With Trypho* where the doctrine was first introduced, though the text does not say so. In any case, Justin expressed the following view regarding Christ's genesis:

---

[58] Athenagoras, *A Plea for the Christians*, 19.
[59] Hatch, *Influence of Greek Ideas*, 264.
[60] *Ibid.*, 263-267.

[A]nd since He was begotten of the Father by an act of will; just as we see happening among ourselves; for when we give out some word, we beget the word; yet not by abscission, so as to lessen the word which remains in us, when we give it out: and just as we see also happening in the case of a fire, which is not lessened when it has kindled another, but remains the same; and that which has been kindled by it likewise appears to exist by itself, not diminishing that from which it was kindled.[61]

Justin's reasoning on this point was later emphasized in the following language:

I asserted that this power was begotten from the Father, by His power and will, *but not by abscission, as if the essence of the Father were divided; as all other things partitioned and divided are not the same after as before they were divided:* and, for the sake of example, I took the case of fires kindled from a fire, which we see to be distinct from it, and yet that from which many can be kindled is by no means made less, but remains the same.[62]

In these passages, Justin never asserts that Christ was "begotten" in any literal sense of that word. Likewise, his flame allegory imparts no clear impression of the means by which Christ actually came into being. However, it is consistent with the Stoic notion of emanation by which the *logoi* were thought to have been generated,[63] and that consistency was used by the later Apologists to rationalize Justin's teachings into the prevailing notion of Christ's pre-mortal genesis.

It is unlikely Justin fully agreed with Tatian, his pupil, on the doctrine of Christ's origin. Tatian was far more metaphysical than Justin, and not long after the death of the latter he developed into a full-fledged heretic. His view of Justin's doctrine, however, is much closer to the writings of the later Apologists, and indicates how they received and interpreted Justin's teaching. The doctrine of Christ's origin is explained by Tatian as follows:

God was in the beginning; but the beginning, we have been taught, is the power of the *Logos*. For the Lord of the universe, who is Himself the necessary ground of all being, inasmuch as no creature was yet

---

[61] Justin, *Dialogue With Trypho*, 61.
[62] *Ibid.*, 128.
[63] Hatch, *Influence of Greek Ideas*, 263-265.

in existence, was alone; but inasmuch as He was all power, Himself the necessary ground of things visible and invisible, with Him were all things; *with Him, by Logos-power, the Logos Himself also, who was in Him, subsists.* And *by His simple will the Logos springs forth;* and the *Logos,* not coming forth in vain, becomes *the first-begotten work* of the Father. *Him (the Logos) we know to be the beginning of the world.* But He came into being by participation, not by abscission; for what is cut off is separated from the original substance, but that which comes by participation, making its choice of function, does not render him deficient from whom it is taken. For just as from one torch many fires are lighted, but the light of the first torch is not lessened by the kindling of many torches, so the *Logos,* coming forth from the *Logos-power* of the Father, has not divested of the *Logos-power* Him who begat Him. I myself, for instance, talk, and you hear; yet certainly, I who converse do not become destitute of speech by the transmission of speech, but by the utterance of my voice I endeavor to reduce to order the unarranged matter in your minds. And as the *Logos,* begotten in the beginning, begat in turn our world, having first created for Himself the necessary matter, so also I, in imitation of the *Logos,* being begotten again [a reference to his conversion to Christianity], and having become possessed of the truth, am trying to reduce to order the confused matter which is kindred with myself.[64]

Tatian's concept of the *"Logos-power"* in this passage is without repetition in any other Apologist's writings. What he meant by that term is unclear. Yet these comments were given enough credence that they were used as a way to rationalize Justin's teachings, making them appear consistent, to a degree, with the doctrines of the later Apologists.[65] (They also form the basis of the *ex nihilo* doctrine of creation in Christianity, as will be seen in Chapter 12.)

Of course, the problem Justin addressed should not have come up in the first place. The birth of a son does not diminish his father, nor are God's creations so inferior as the Greeks supposed. But anything involving birth or creation was anathema to the Apologists. Indeed, whenever they wrote of Christ's origin the Apologists carefully avoided the word "created" in favor of the word "generated." Even Dionysius of Alexandria only saw Christ's generation as *analogous* to birth, and for that doctrine he was called on the carpet.

---

[64] Tatian, *Address to the Greeks,* 5.
[65] Hatch, *Influence of Greek Ideas,* 266.

The issue of Christ's "generation" by some means that did not cause division of the Father only became a concern because the Apologists had rejected birth and creation as the means for His origin. The Bible says nothing about this concern, but implies Christ's *creation* in Revelation 3:14. This shows how far afield from the Bible the thinking of the later Apologists went in their analysis of this subject.

What's Wrong With Being Created by God?

To understand just how speculative the Apologists became on the issue of Christ's origin, and how their departure from scripture on this point led them into even greater error in postulating the co-substantiality doctrine of the Trinity, a note about the Bible's teachings in regard to creation will be helpful.

In Genesis, the Bible speaks of "creatures" being subordinate to Man (Gen. 1:26, 28), and in Job, God notes the obvious superiority of God over Man, whom He created (Job 4:17-19; 33:12). But nowhere does the Bible imply a metaphysical distinction between "created beings" and their Creator like that expressed by Plato. Nowhere does it suggest the inferiority of created things assumed by the Apologists and described by Athenagoras above.

The fact is that the God of the Bible is a much better Creator than the God of Greek philosophy. When He finished the earth and all that He created in it, He pronounced it "very good" (Gen. 1:31; see also 1 Tim. 4:4). For God, a perfect being, that statement can only be taken as an indication that His creation was perfect.

That conclusion is supported by the fact that, when He made Adam and Eve, they were immortal (cf., Gen. 2:17; 3:3). Even after they were poisoned by partaking of the forbidden fruit of the tree of knowledge of good and evil, it took them nearly a thousand years to die (Gen. 5:5). The perfection of God's creation was declared by the Preacher as follows: "I know that everything God does will remain forever; there is nothing to add to it and there is nothing to take from it, for God has so worked that men should be in awe before Him" (Eccl. 3:14, NASB, literal translation).

What God made was perfect, not inferior, and it was meant to last forever. It was the Fall of Man—the result of Man's voluntary disobedience—that resulted in the imperfections seen in the world today. Eventually, the earth will be purified by fire (2 Pet. 3:7, 10-12), and

The Personal God

renewed (Isa. 65:17; 2 Pet. 3:13; Rev 21:1) to remain forever as the abode of the righteous (Isa. 66:22), a redeemed and perfect creation of God. The Greek doctrine of inferior creation is an insult to the power of the biblical God.

The words "uncreate," "uncreated," and "unbegotten," and the orthodox concepts behind these terms appear nowhere in the Bible. They are all misguided Greek efforts to explain the presence of evil in a world created by a perfect God. Nothing in the Bible even suggests that Christ was "generated."

The biblical testimony is that Christ was the "firstborn" (Micah 6:7; Zech. 12:10; Rom. 8:29; Col. 1:15, 18; Heb. 11:28, 12:23). This word is translated from Greek (and equivalent Hebrew) that means "born first." He was the "only begotten" (see, e.g., John 3:16), a term translated from the Greek word "*monogenes*," which means "only child," referring to His flesh. Being born a child of God is nothing to be disparaged. It does not include any implication of inferiority. Just as an earthly son may attain equality with his father, so Christ as a literal child of God was never barred from achieving equality with Him by the fact that, in the sense of actual reproductive birth, He was created by God.

The Orthodox Answer to the Genesis of Christ

Undaunted by the fact that their reasoning had strayed so far from the Bible, the Apologists ultimately arrived at a position on Christ's "genesis" that was consistent with their Greek views. In deriving that position, they actively imported Greek notions about the *Logos* into the biblical understanding of God.[66]

The main problem presented to the Apologists at the time was the one that was causing all the persecution by Marcus Aurelius. It was the apparent inconsistency between the separateness of the Father and the Son taught by Justin and the belief of the Greek philosophers in the unity of their God. The Greeks had maintained the oneness of God against ideas like those displayed in the Syrian school of Gnosticism, which taught that the problem of evil could be explained by two Gods in conflict with each other. They decided that the *Logos*, who reflected God and revealed Him to Man, must also be God in some sense.[67]

---

[66] Hatch, *Influence of Greek Ideas*, 263-268.
[67] *Ibid.*, 265.

In this regard, Justin's ideas were at first thought to be ditheistic. They were transformed by two distinctions, both of which Hatch identifies as coming from external philosophy—one from Stoicism, and the other from NeoPlatonism.[68] The first was the distinction noted above, namely that the generation of Christ had taken place within the Father, not by division. The Greek *Logos* was seen as an "emanation" from the Supreme Being, not really a separate person, but the embodiment of the reason, mind, will or "word" of God. This was the view adopted by the Apologists in regard to Christ's origin from the Father.

The first description of the Father as inclusive of the Son, consistent with this view, was given by Athenagoras, who wrote as follows: "God is Himself all things to Himself, unapproachable light, a perfect universe, spirit, force, *logos*."[69] This description is highly monistic. It does not distinguish in any way between the Father and the Son. It describes God in the metaphysical terms of Greek philosophy both as "Himself," the Father, and as the Father's thought, the *"logos."*

Origen later cemented this doctrine by teaching that the nature of the *Logos* came out of God's essence. He asserted that the Savior is God, not by partaking, but by essence, begotten of the very essence of the Father. Thus, Christ was no longer seen as having been literally born or otherwise created by the Father. He was *an "emanation," an outflow as of light from light.*[70]

These Greek concepts allowed the Apologists to explain the origin of Christ without admitting that He was born of the Father ("begotten"), that He was created by Him, or that His creation diminished the Father in any way. The idea was comfortable to the Apologists because it was familiar Platonistic doctrine, even though it had no support in scripture.

The Timing of Christ's Genesis

Justin also made the important distinction about the timing of Christ's genesis that was interpreted by the later Apologists in a manner consistent with Neoplatonism.[71] In addressing Revelation 3:14, he interpreted the phrase, "beginning of the creation of God," as an indication that Christ's genesis preceded God's acts of creation. He said, *"Before all created things*, God begat from Himself a kind of rational Force."

---

[68] *Ibid.*, 266.
[69] Athenagoras, *A Plea for the Christians*, 16.
[70] Hatch, *Influence of Greek Ideas*, 268.
[71] *Ibid.*, 266-267.

The later Apologists claimed that the generation of the *Logos* occurred before the creation of time itself. The idea that God created time when He created the heavens and the earth will be discussed in Chapter 12. That Christ was generated before the creation of time has continued as a classical doctrine to the present. Thus, Miley's *Systematic Theology* explains, "*His* [Christ's] *existence is not by creation, but by generation, and before all created existences.... The Son is born or begotten of God before creation and time.*" [72]

This doctrine made it entirely unnecessary to decide the precise means of Christ's generation. If it occurred before the supposed creation of time, the whole notion of His origin could be more easily confined to the metaphysical and moved backward into the oblivion of timeless eternity. *If time did not exist at His genesis, one could say that Christ was never actually generated at all, that He always existed as the "Son" while the Father always existed as His "Father."* Under Origen, that, in fact, became the orthodox view.[73]

The Biblical View of the Genesis of Christ

The idea that the Thought emanating from the Mind of a Being could be a separate person from that Being occurs only in the realm of Greek metaphysics, not in the Bible. As noted from the start of this chapter, even modern classical theists are stymied in their efforts to explain how the personal nature of God fits into biblical doctrine. Their solution is found nowhere in the Old or New Testament. Even the ruling analogy for Christ's generation, that of the flame that lights another spark producing a flame of identical substance, appears nowhere in the Bible. Nothing in scripture even hints at a relationship between the Father and the Son known as co-substantiality.

In the Bible, the relationship between the Father and the Son is consistently treated as one of parent to child. Christ refers to God specifically as "my Father" (not just "Father" or "the Father") *51 times* in the New Testament. The only passage that claims to tell the "generation" of Christ is Matthew 1:1, which goes on to give His physical genealogy from David.

---

[72] John Miley, *Systematic Theology* (Peabody: Hendrickson Publishers, 1893, reprinted 1989), 1:237.
[73] Origen, *De Principiis*, 1:2:2-3. Hatch admits that it is uncertain Justin taught this concept. Hatch, *Influence of Greek Ideas*, 267, fn. 4.

The True Origin of Christ

It is clear from the biblical account that Christ pre-existed His incarnation in the flesh (cf., John 8:56-58; Phil. 2:5-9). Consistent with this account, Mormonism teaches that although Christ received incarnation first as a spirit, and second as a physical human being, He pre-existed both of these stages as an eternal being or "intelligence" (D&C 93:29-30; Abraham 3:21-22).

Thus, in a way that he never expected, Origen was right. In His basic personality, at least, Christ was never actually "originated" at all. However, he did not become the Son of God until He was born as a spirit, the first of Father's spirit children (Col. 1:15). Later, when He was born as a man, He became the "only begotten" of the Father (John 1:14) referring to His position as the only son of God the Father *in the flesh*. To the extent Christ underwent any kind of "generation," it was through birth, a form of creation that *embodies* a pre-existing and eternal personality.

It is not surprising, therefore, that the Bible contains no information about Christ's original "genesis." The Apologists were looking for something that could not be found, and instead of seeking guidance from God on the issue, as Joseph Smith later did, they engaged in "rational" speculation. Because of their background, their speculations tended to paraphrase Greek philosophy. In the centuries that followed, these speculations became dogma, and that dogma came to be regarded as binding doctrine.

God's True Nature as an Individual

If one dispenses with the Greek influence imported by the Apologists into Christian theology, the doctrine of God's individuality becomes clear. Since Man was made in God's image and likeness (Gen. 1:26-27), there can be no misunderstanding about God's personality. His attributes include the individuality common to Men. The Bible assumes the idea of separate identities for the Father, the Son and the Holy Ghost. To claim that these three are "persons" but deny that they are also "individuals" is an irrational concept that appears nowhere in the Bible and should be rejected.

The understanding that each member of the Godhead is a separate individual is reaffirmed in holy writ every time one of them uses the personal pronoun, "I" (cp., Matt. 3:16-17 and John 17:5). The personal nature of Jehovah, the pre-mortal Christ (John 8:58),[74] as a separate individual was declared unequivocally when He told Moses that His name is "*I* AM" (Exod. 3:14). The Father did likewise when He spoke from heaven at Christ's baptism using the same personal pronoun: "This is my beloved Son, in whom *I* am well pleased" (Matt. 3:17).

Was the Godhead Different in the Old Testament?

Is it possible that the Three only appeared as separate persons in the New Testament? Some claim that references such as Exodus 3:14, prove the literal unity of the triune god since only one person is referred to as "God" there and in the Old Testament generally. This argument is contrary, not only to the Bible, but also to the careful reasoning of Justin Martyr in chapter 56 of his *Dialogue With Trypho*. There he proves to the Jews, using the Old Testament, that two separate persons were referred to as God from the very beginning of Moses' writings.

It is a firm tenet of Trinitarianism that the Three persons of the Trinity have always been distinctly separate (as well as literally united). Thus, Trinitarian doctrine teaches that the Father, the Son and the Holy Ghost were three separate persons in the Old Testament, though they were not clearly revealed as such to Israel.[75] Thus, Old Testament references to the oneness of God do not prove the metaphysical doctrine of co-substantiality. They are part of the theological problem the Apologists tried to resolve using that strange notion derived from Greek philosophy.

Does the Bible teach that the three persons referred to as one God are one individual, a singular center of consciousness, as taught in Trinitarianism, or three separate centers of consciousness, as taught in Mormonism? Extensive efforts have been made over the centuries to find biblical support for the Trinitarian concept, but to no avail. Rather, the opposite is the case: there are hundreds of Bible passages that unequivocally show God the Father, God the Son, and God the Holy Ghost as three completely distinct individuals. Only through strained

---

[74] For a thoroughly documented presentation of the extensive evidence showing that Jesus Christ was Jehovah of the old Testament, written by an evangelical author, see Ron Rhodes, *Christ Before the Manger* (Grand Rapids: Baker Book House, 1992).
[75] Erickson, *Christian Theology*, 328-329.

metaphysical reasoning, foreign to the Jewish scriptures, could anyone imagine a different interpretation of those passages.

Biblical Evidence for Three Separate Centers of Consciousness

The only verse in the Bible that sounds remotely Trinitarian, 1 John 5:7, has been rejected by Bible scholars as a later addition to the text.[76] However, certain passages in the Bible directly contradict the Trinitarian notion of the Godhead's singular individuality. Many passages in the Gospel of John (5:19, 8:28 and others) explain that the Son imitated the Father, doing exactly what the Father must have done at some point in the infinite past. The Father showed the Son and the Son acted according to the Father's will and example. The Savior's explanation of this principle is very revealing in its information about the Father and the Son as separate centers of consciousness. John 5:19-21, and 30 explain as follows:

> Then answered Jesus and said unto them, Verily, verily, I say unto you, The Son can do nothing of himself, but what he seeth the Father do: for what things soever he doeth, these also doeth the Son likewise.
>
> For the Father loveth the Son, and sheweth him all things that himself doeth: and he will shew him greater works than these, that ye may marvel.
>
> For as the Father raiseth up the dead, and quickeneth them; even so the Son quickeneth whom he will.
>
> ***
>
> I can of mine own self do nothing: as I hear, I judge: and my judgement is just; because I seek not mine own will, but the will of the Father which hath sent me.

It is clear from this passage that Christ has His "own *self*," His "own *will*," and that His will is separate from the "will" of His Father. Christ's prayer in Gethsemane further demonstrates that point (see Matt. 26:42; Mark 14:36; Luke 22:42—"not my will, but thine, be done"). Christ's statement that He seeks only the will of the Father and "can do nothing of himself," only what the Father has shown Him, is an expression of the perfect voluntary submission of His will to the will of the Father. That submission would have been meaningless if Christ did not have a center of consciousness separate from the

---
[76] *Ibid.*, 327.

Father. A person who has voluntarily submitted his will to the will of another remains a separate individual, necessarily distinct from the person to whom he submits. If the Father and the Son did not have separate centers of consciousness, Christ would have been submitting his will to *Himself*. Such an act would be a nullity.

Separateness of will is the essence of individuality and self-consciousness. The will is precisely what makes one individual exist as a separate source of wants, feelings and needs, acting differently than other individuals. Without a separate will, one cannot be personal. With it, one cannot share a center of consciousness with anyone else. That does not mean two separate individuals cannot voluntarily agree, uniting their wills in the sense Justin saw the Father and the Son doing. But if the Father and the Son were the same individual, they would have the same will. Since they do not, as the passages cited above clearly indicate, it cannot be denied on any biblical basis that they are separate *individuals*.

Separate Knowledge Dictates Separate Centers of Consciousness

If Christ were the embodiment of the Father's thoughts, as the Apologists taught, He would always have known what the Father knows, for His knowledge would be that of the Father. Irenaeus made this very point when he argued against a heretical notion—Cerinthus' idea of a Demiurge who had created the world without knowing about the Supreme God. Irenaeus argued that it was impossible for "Reason" (the Platonistic notion of the Demiurge) to be unaware of the "Mind" (i.e., the Supreme God) from whence it emanates.[77]

While it is true that the Son knows the will of the Father, the scriptures clearly indicate that such knowledge was imparted to Him (John 8:28, "I speak these things as the Father taught Me"—NASB). That is not consistent with Irenaeus' reasoning cited above. The Greek Demiurge he discussed automatically knew the mind of the Supreme God, being his *Logos*. If the Father and the Son were, in fact, related as Mind is to Thought, as Irenaeus taught (see Chapter 6), it would be equally necessary to say that Christ was automatically aware of the Father's thoughts. It would have been entirely unnecessary for the Father to "*sheweth* him [the Son] all things that himself [the Father] doeth" (John

---

[77] Irenaeus, *Against Heresies*, 2:28:4-5.

5:20). The Son, if He were the very Thought of the Father, would know all that the Father did without the necessity of being shown. But according to the Bible, He did not (see, especially Matt. 24:36; Mark 13:32).

This point, along with the New Testament's other clear indications that Christ was a separate individual, present great difficulties for classical theists.[78] Regarding Mark 13:32 ("But of that day or hour no one knows, not even the angels in heaven, nor the Son, but the Father alone"—NASB), Professor Erickson opines, "Perhaps we could say that he [Christ] had such knowledge as was necessary for him to accomplish his mission; in other matters he was as ignorant as we are."[79] John 8:28, cited above, is not so easily explained. It is in the past tense, and there is no account in the New Testament of the Father teaching Christ these things during His incarnation.

Few classical theists even attempt to explain what Christ's individuality during His incarnation means in terms of the Trinity. If Christ knew less because He was incarnate, why, if the doctrine of co-substantiality were true, would the Father know more? If Christ was taught by His Father *before* His incarnation, as indicated by John 5:20, how could they have been co-substantial then? If the two were *ever* separate centers of consciousness, the doctrine of co-substantiality is negated.

Biblical teachings about the personalities of the Father and the Son are irrefutably *inconsistent* with the very foundation of Trinitarian doctrine. The separate will of Christ and the fact that He learned from the Father and was fully portrayed in the New Testament as an independent personality completely contradicts the doctrine of co-substantiality.

Conclusion

With a metaphysical model for God, classical theists are forced to deny the individuality of the Father, the Son and the Holy Ghost, even while they are declaring the personal nature of God. The doctrine of co-substantiality teaches that there is only one center of consciousness among the three members of the Godhead. This is not an interpretation of the oneness of God taught in the Bible. In fact, *it is not an interpretation of the Bible at all*. It is an idea adopted at a time of great peril for the Church by men trained in Greek philosophy who were trying to

---

[78] Erickson, *Christian Theology*, 723-724.
[79] *Ibid.*, 710.

resolve biblical teachings about the Godhead in a way that satisfy the Greek minds who then controlled Rome.

Since one of God's attributes is that He is personal, it follows that each person in the Godhead is an individual. That is a biblical doctrine and should not be rejected on the basis of ancient Greek assumptions and preferences. Nor should it be rejected because it makes Christianity look "tritheist." That the members of the Godhead are "one" is explained by the Bible itself in a completely rational way, as will be seen in Chapter 17. The Father, the Son, and the Holy Ghost are not just separate "persons," as classical theists have attempted to define that word, but entirely separate "individuals," separate centers of consciousness.

Summary

1. Classical theists admit that God is personal, but do not acknowledge that the Father, the Son and the Holy Ghost have separate centers of consciousness. This leaves them with a problem in defining the personality of God so that He differs from pantheistic deities.
2. Classical notions of God are a mix of Greek philosophy and "the simpler Jewish faith" that was early Christianity.
3. The Greek philosophers believed God was personal and transcendent. He therefore needed intermediaries between Himself and the sensory world. In Greek thought, the intermediary at the time of Christ was the *Logos*, who acted as a reflection of God in the metaphysical universe to Man in the sensory universe, and vice versa.
4. The Apologists saw Christ in the light of this Greek *Logos*, and translated Greek ideas about the relationship of their Supreme God and his *Logos* into Christianity through their doctrine of co-substantiality.
5. The current theory by which classical theism explains the personal nature of God is that God is three "persons" but only one "individual." This is the modern doctrine of the Trinity.
6. Classical theism gives no scriptural justification for this irrational doctrine. It is explainable only by resorting to metaphysics and the claim that God is incomprehensible.
7. The Trinity postulates three *Gods* who are *one individual*. The modern understanding of personality makes this theory even more difficult to explain or justify.

8. Justin Martyr taught the absolute numerical separateness of the Father and the Son, and warned against efforts among the Apologists of his day to unite them numerically.
9. Justin treated the unity of the Father and Son as figurative. The later Apologists invented the paradoxical doctrine of the Trinity by claiming that Their unity and Their separateness were *both* to be taken literally.
10. The Bible does not support the doctrine of co-substantiality.
11. If they denied the metaphysical concept of the Trinity, classical theists would be faced with the dilemma of explaining where Christ came from.
12. Justin taught that Christ was the firstborn of the Father, but he described Christ as "a rational force" and the Father as Aristotle's Unmoving Mover.
13. Christ was truly the beginning of the Creation of God in the sense that He was the first created, the Father's first-born Son.
14. Classical theism could not accept the concept that Christ is the *actual son* of God the Father because of the distaste Greek philosophers had for the pagan notion of humanistic gods.
15. The philosophical schools at the time of Christ blamed the existence of an evil world on the imperfections of God's intermediaries, who were assumed to be inferior because they were "created." The idea of Christ being "created" (out of *nothing*) by the Father, therefore, was also unacceptable to the Apologists. Rather, they spoke of Christ as having been "generated."
16. The Apologists (and later classical theists) used the Apostle John's reference to Christ as the Word (*Logos*) as an excuse to import Greek philosophical views into Christology (the study of Christ).
17. The Apologists explained Christ's existence as an "emanation" of the Father so as not to imply that He resulted from God splitting in two. The ruling analogies spoke of a torch lighting other torches without diminishing its own light, or a word being spoken without actually departing from the mind of the speaker.
18. There is nothing in God's creations that can be disparaged as the Greeks were wont to do. His creations are perfect and their fall, which was due to Man's disobedience, will be redeemed. What God creates is perfect, not inferior.

19. The later Apologists rationalized Justin's writings so they could teach that the *Logos* was an emanation of the Father and, hence, in some sense God.
20. The later Apologists decided that Christ had eternally been the Son, the *Logos* or "Thought" of God, making it unnecessary for them to explain how He came to be.
21. There is nothing in the Bible that supports the idea that Christ is an emanation of the Father. The idea that Mind and its "Thought" could ever be treated as separate "persons," the way the Father and the Son are in the Bible, is a purely non-biblical fabrication of Greek metaphysics.
22. The Bible nowhere infers any other process for the "generation" of Christ than birth. The birth (or "creation") of Christ, however, did not produce a Son inferior to His Father.
23. The Bible does not distinguish between the personal nature of God and the concept of individuality. God is always identified as an individual.
24. Even Trinitarian doctrine demands that God was "three separate persons" in the Old Testament as well as in the New Testament. Hence, when God speaks in the first person in the Old Testament, it is one of the separate persons of the Godhead speaking, usually Christ.
25. The New Testament teaches that Christ has His own will, which he voluntarily submits to the will of the Father.
26. To have one's own will clearly indicates individuality. The Bible never suggests that the Father, the Son and the Holy Ghost are anything but separate *individuals*.
27. If Christ and the Father were related as thought is to mind, the thought would never be without the knowledge of the mind. Yet the Bible teaches that the Father showed things to Christ, and knows things He does not (or did not) know.
28. Science, common sense and the Bible all reject the notions of metaphysics that lie at the heart of the Trinitarian explanation of God's personal nature.

The Corporeal God

There is no valid reason to restrict the similarity between God and Man to strictly mental and emotional attributes. Genesis 1:26-27 speaks of God making Man in His own "image" and "likeness." This implies the likeness of a father to his children. Indeed, the very same language is used in Genesis 5:3 (NASB) to describe the relationship between Adam and his son, Seth ("he became the father of a son in his own likeness, according to his image"). The Hebrew word translated "likeness" comes from the word for "shadow," and is sometimes translated "idol." The implication is of an exact *physical* replica.

Since the child—Man—is corporeal, it follows that the father—God—also has a body of flesh and bones. That doctrine, however, has been vehemently denied by Christian orthodoxy since the mid-second century. The reasons for its denial are intimately connected with the idea of God's transcendency. Therefore, these two concepts will be considered here together.

False Assumptions About Corporeality

The assumption that God is incorporeal is founded, in part, on the Greek and oriental attitude toward matter and the physical world. Greek antipathy to the material universe has led to the assumption that a physical body must always be subject to limitations that are incompatible with Deity. Without even attempting to reason out the attributes one could expect in a God who is as real as the worlds He has created, classical theists always assume that a being who possesses, among other attributes, a physical body, must be as limited as mortal Men.

That assumption, like other false *a priori* assumptions, is not really intuitive. It is based on misleading observations. Old age, disease, birth defects and other infirmities were axiomatic in the ancient world. This made it appear that the human body was an undesirable evil, something to be escaped in a perfect eternity. Such a body, the Greeks assumed, could never be associated with so perfect a being as God.

They had no idea of the resurrection or its salutary changes because they had never observed such an occurrence nor allowed their imagination to run in that direction. They rejected any possibility that God had a body because, unlike the Apostles, they never stood in the presence of the Risen Savior. The reality of the resurrection must be acknowledged for what it truly means. The assumption that corporeality limits Deity is in direct conflict with the physical resurrection of Christ.

"Face to Face" With the Biblical God

The Bible contains many eyewitness accounts testifying to the corporeal appearance of God. Which member of the Godhead appeared is irrelevant. The characteristics described are those of deity, whether in physical or spirit form. Mormons believe that the spirit body looks just like the physical body (Ether 3:6-17).

Two of the most noteworthy accounts showing the corporeal nature of God are in the Old Testament. They are the appearance of God to Moses on Mount Sinai (Deut. 5:4, see also Deut. 34:10), and at the tabernacle (Exod. 33:7-11). On these two occasions, God spoke to Moses "face to face." Of His meetings with Moses at the tabernacle, the Bible says, "the Lord used to speak to Moses face to face, just as a man speaks to his friend" (NASB).

God also appeared to Moses, Aaron, Nadab, Abihu, and seventy of the elders of Israel (Exodus 24:9-11). The record indicates that all of them saw God. He was corporeal, in the sense that He had a body (either a spirit body or a physical body) in the form of a man. That is apparent from the specific mention of His hands and feet. In Genesis 32:30 (NASB), Jacob proclaimed that he saw God "face to face, yet my life has been preserved." Stephen the Martyr, in Acts 7:55-56 (NASB), declared that he saw the "glory of God" and Jesus standing "at the *right hand* " of the Father.

God refers to His own body parts in several Old Testament passages. For example, in a discussion with Moses about seeing Him in "glory," God is quoted as follows:

> And he said, Thou canst not see my *face:* for there shall no man see me, and live.
>
> And the Lord said, Behold, there is a place by me, and thou shalt stand upon a rock:

> And it shall come to pass, while my glory passeth by, that I will put thee in a clift of the rock, and will cover thee with my *hand* while I pass by:
>
> And I will take away mine *hand*, and thou shalt see my *back parts:* but my *face* shall not be seen. (Exod. 33:20-23.)

The context of this passage distinguishes it from the references above, and shows that it was only in His "glory" that Moses was not allowed to see God's face. In Numbers 12:8, He praises Moses, saying that He will speak with him "mouth to mouth." The implication is clear. In order to speak "mouth to mouth" or "face to face" with someone, *both* parties to the conversation must have a face and a mouth.

In Ezekiel 20:33-36 God promises that He will gather Israel back in the last days to "the wilderness of the people," and there "will I plead with you *face to face*." In John 5:37, Christ told the Pharisees about His Father, saying that they "have neither heard his voice at any time, nor seen his *shape*." "Shape" is translated from the Greek word for external or outward appearance. The rebuke would have been meaningless if the Father had no outward appearance that the Pharisees could have seen.

Most telling of all are the repeated references in the New Testament to the fact that Christ, as a resurrected being, is a mirror image of His Father. In 2 Corinthians 4:4, Paul refers to Christ as "the image of God." Colossians 1:15 states that He is "the image of the invisible God." The author of Hebrews 1:3 was even more specific, calling Christ the "express image" of the Father's "person." These passages show conclusively that the Father's image or appearance is identical to that which the Apostles saw when they looked at Christ.

New Testament writers never questioned Christ's identity as a man. The docetes, of course, had a problem with that idea, but their conclusions were not biblical and were correctly rejected by both the Apostle John and the Apologists as heretical. When Christ appeared to His Apostles in the upper room after His resurrection, He went to great lengths to demonstrate that He had a physical body (Luke 24:36-43). When He ascended into Heaven after spending forty days with His disciples, the description indicates that He went up bodily and will return in the same form (Acts 1:9-11). James explains that the body without the spirit is dead (James 2:26), and Paul states unequivocally that, having died once, Christ will never die again (Rom. 6:9). These passages can have no other meaning than that Christ's spirit and body are eternally and inseparably united in His corporeal, resurrected form.

Christ taught his Apostles in John 14:7, "If ye had known me, ye should have known my Father also: and from henceforth ye know him *and have seen him.*" This and other passages teach that Men are required to learn about the Father from the Son. Given the unequivocally physical nature of Christ's body, both in the flesh, when He made the above statement, and after His resurrection, these passages allow of no other conclusion than that the Father has a resurrected physical body like His Son. A major part of Christ's mission was to reveal the Father to Man (Matt. 11:27, Luke 10:22). The fact that Christ, Himself, is corporeal, gives absolute certainty to the conclusion that the same is true of His Father.

"Theophanies" and "Anthropomorphisms" in Bible Passages

Despite the biblical teachings cited above, classical theologians maintain that references in the Bible to God's body, other than the incarnation of Christ, are "theophanies." This Greek-rooted word "refers to the temporal and spatial manifestation of God in some tangible form."[1] The implication of this definition is that such appearances are not accurate representations of God, but are intended to give Man something familiar to look at so he will not be frightened. The idea that God actually has such a form, however, is referred to by modern theologians as "anthropomorphism." That term is defined as "the attribution of human form, or the character or qualities of humanity, to objects believed to be above humanity in the scale of being, and in particular to God or the gods."[2]

Of course, neither the words "theophany" nor "anthropomorphism," nor the concepts they express, appear anywhere in the Bible. One would expect the Lord to be honest in His dealings with Man. If He appeared to Men in human form, but was not Himself human, one would expect that, at some point, He would reveal that fact. Yet there is no indication in scripture that God is something other than what He has appeared to be during His many visits to Men. Because they do not express any biblical truth, these words should not be used in Mormon theology.

Does the Bible Say That God Has Wings?

Classical theists try to justify their belief in God's incorporeality on the basis of certain passages in the Bible. A careful analysis of

---

[1] Van Harvey, *A Handbook of Theological Terms* (New York: Collier Books, 1964), s.v "Theophany."
[2] *Encyclopaedia Britannica*, 1960 ed., s.v. "Anthropomorphism."

those passages shows that, like the heretics before them, they have taken the passages out of context.

One argument critics attempt to use against the corporeality of God is to point out the passages in the Bible that speak of God as though He had wings. They are found in Psalms 17:8, 36:7, 57:1, 61:4, 63:7, and 91:4, and in Ruth 2:12 and Malachi 4:2. These passages are cited to support their claim that all the eyewitness accounts of God's appearances to Man in human form should be interpreted figuratively. The argument is that, if eyewitness accounts of God's physical appearance are to be interpreted literally, then passages that describe Him as having wings must also be interpreted literally. Since the accounts of God's "wings" are obviously figurative, they argue, the references to His physical body must be figurative also.

That argument has no hermeneutic validity. The passages about God's wings are almost entirely contained in the Book of Psalms, the ancient hymnal of Israel. Psalms is a book of Hebrew poetry, inspired poetry of course, but poetry nonetheless, and poetic language is normally interpreted more figuratively than the language of eyewitness accounts.

In any case, all doubt about the proper interpretation of the passages describing God as having wings was put to rest by the Lord Himself in Matthew 23:37 (see also Luke 13:34). There He said, "O Jerusalem, Jerusalem, thou that killest the prophets, and stonest them which are sent unto thee, how often would I have gathered thy children together, *even as* a hen gathereth her chickens *under her wings*, and ye would not." The words "even as" clearly indicate that the reference to "wings" is merely a simile. In some passages, such references are phrased metaphorically, but in each instance, the language is clearly figurative.

No similar language suggests that the Bible's eyewitness accounts of God's physical appearance should be interpreted figuratively. Some claim that God's first appearance to Moses provides an argument for anthropomorphism. In that regard, they imagine that God appeared as a burning bush to Moses. But the passage states, "the angel of the Lord appeared to him *in* a blazing fire *from the midst of a bush*" (Exod. 3:2, NASB). The bush was not burning. It was the "angel of the Lord," a phrase commonly used in the Old Testament to refer to Jehovah, the pre-mortal Christ, who appeared "in a blazing fire" in the midst of the bush. He did not appear *as* a blazing fire or *as* a burning bush.

Occasionally, figurative language is used in the eyewitness account of an appearance by God, but such language is always associated with words that set the specific description apart as figurative. For example, the eyewitness accounts of Christ's baptism consistently describe the Holy Ghost descending *"like* a dove." See Matthew 3:16, Mark 1:10, Luke 3:22 and John 1:32 (KJV). (The translation is *"as* a dove" in Matthew 3:16 and John 1:32 according to the NASB, but the difference in no way affects the meaning.) This wording compares the events that actually occurred (the Holy Ghost's descent) to an image that helps describe those events ("like a dove").

Notably, the Holy Ghost is a spirit. He is the only member of the Godhead whose name implies His physical nature. There is no rational explanation for that special designation other than as a means for pointing out a distinction between His physiological nature and that of the other two members of the Godhead. The fact that He is designated as the Holy Ghost or Holy Spirit indicates the contrast between His status as a spirit only, and the nature of the other two members of the Godhead, as spirits that are now permanently tabernacled in physical bodies.

Is God Only a Spirit?

The passage that is perhaps most commonly cited by classical theists to assert that God has *only* a spirit body is John 4:24, which states, "God is spirit" (NASB). Quoting only that much of the passage, they claim that it teaches "God cannot have a body because He is infinite spirit."[3] Of course, that is not what the passage says. It does not say God is *"only* spirit," or "infinite spirit," only that He "is spirit" ("a spirit" in the KJV).

The biggest problem with this passage being used to support the claim that God is only a spirit is that its use for that purpose implies Men must also be restricted to spirit form in order to worship Him. After declaring that God is spirit, the verse goes on to say, "and they that worship him must worship him *in spirit* and in truth." "They that worship him" are Men. The passage requires Men to worship God *"in spirit"* as well as "in truth." If the first half of John 4:24 were interpreted to say that God is *only* a spirit, the second half would have to be understood in

---

[3] Morey, *Battle of the Gods,* 189.

the same sense, indicating that Men can worship God *only* in spirit. To obey that command, a man would have to kill himself in order to worship God. Since that is untenable, the premise that God is *only* a spirit must be false. God has a spiritual nature and Men, who also have a spiritual nature, must emphasize that nature in worshiping Him.

Dr. Robert Morey, a modern Evangelical theologian, attempts to use this passage as a demonstration of God's supposed incorporeality in his book, *Battle of the Gods*, which is aimed at refuting some false notions about God that Evangelicals recognize in modern liberal theologies. He argues that a "spirit" by definition does not have a physical body, citing Luke 24:39.[4] What he fails to note is that the converse is not true. A living physical body most definitely *does* have a spirit. In fact, it is physically dead without one (James 2:26). A spirit alone does not have a physical body. But if God has a physical body, He also has a spirit. Therefore, even though God is corporeal, it is appropriate to say that God "is spirit," for spirit is the central part of His nature as a corporeal being.

It would not be appropriate, however, to say that He is "*only* a spirit." In Luke 24:39 Christ clearly had a spirit and a physical body composed of "flesh and bone." His spirit had just been recombined with His perfected and glorified physical body in the resurrection, a point that He took great pains to demonstrate (Luke 24:41-43). He was not, however, "a spirit" in the sense of being only a spirit. The reference to "a spirit" in that passage, therefore, was meant to identify spirits that are absent from a physical body. That is not the distinction made in John 4:24.

John 4:24 assumes that mortal Men are also "spirit." Their bodies are the tabernacles of their spirits (Job 32:8; Zech. 12:1), and they can worship God "in spirit" while they are yet in their physical bodies, just as God can have a physical body and still be "spirit." Indeed, when Men "join" themselves to God, they are spoken of as "one spirit with Him" (1 Cor. 6:17, NASB). This does not mean that they lose their physical bodies when they worship God. God can be "spirit" and be joined, in a figurative sense, with Men who truly worship Him (1 Cor. 6:17 and Phil. 3:3). Both He and the Men who so worship Him will still have their physical bodies.

---

[4] *Ibid.*

John 4:24 is no more a statement that God has no physical body than it is a statement that Men have no physical bodies. It is about worshiping God and cannot be used to support the notion that God is incorporeal. It tells Men that they must seek spirituality and truth to worship God, for He is a spiritual being.

God's Resurrected Body is Different From That of Mortal Men

The fact that God has a physical body should not be understood the way the ancient Greeks viewed such a prospect. On this point there is a totally illogical dichotomy in classical theology. With respect to the Father being corporeal, comments such as the following are commonly made: "One consequence of God's spirituality is that he does not have the limitations involved with a physical body."[5]

Their view changes dramatically, however, when they consider Christ's incarnation and physical resurrection. In the resurrection, Christ received what classical theists recognize as a "spiritual body" (*soma pneumatikon*). According to Elwell, the "spiritual body" is,

> [t]he resurrected spiritual body in contrast to the physical body (*soma psychikon*), which is subject to sin and death (1 Cor. 15:44). Paul's teaching, like that of Jesus, (1) stands in contrast to the denial of the afterlife by the Sadducees (cf. Matt. 22:23-33; Acts 23:6-8), and (2) contrasts with the Greek notion of the bare immortality of the soul, separated from the tomb of the body. On analogy of God's revelation in nature, where the sown seed dies and rises to something that bears identity with the seed but is immeasurably different, Paul describes the resurrection of the dead. For Paul, again as with Jesus in his resurrected state, the person is conceived as a gestalt unity of body-spirit, not as a soul separated from the body. The whole person is lifted to a new level of existence, from the fallen and death-prone body-soul of Adam to the imperishable body-spirit of life in Christ (1 Cor. 15:35-50). Jesus in his resurrection appearances embodies the new imperishable existence, and though not of flesh and blood of the old order, nor limited by physical parameters of that order (John 20:19-20), nevertheless has identifiable characteristics of flesh and bones, hands, and side, and can partake of food (Luke 24:36-43). This mysterious and "logically odd" language of the apostolic witness is not contradictory

---

[5] Erickson, *Christian Theology*, 267.

but complementary, as Jesus, John, Luke, Paul, and the other NT witnesses convey the divinely revealed fact that the new existence is like, yet different from, the old, an analogy of the identity and difference between the seed and the full grain. *Soma pneumatikon* is Paul's way of saying that the believer's personal identity as a body-spirit unity will be raised to a new life like that of Christ himself.[6]

Perhaps Mormon theologians should also explain the glorified resurrected body of Christ as "a gestalt unity of body-spirit." Perhaps if they used such obtuse philosophical language to express these simple biblical truths, classical theists would get the point. If classical theists understand that Christ has both a human and a divine nature (cp., spiritual nature),[7] all they need to do is apply that understanding to the Father.

The Father's physical, or human, nature does not diminish in any way His spiritual nature. His resurrected, celestial body, like Christ's, is different from a mortal body in ways Men do not yet understand, as Elwell capably explained in the quotation above. In 1 Corinthians 15:44, Paul describes the celestial body that rises from the dead in the physical resurrection as a "spiritual body," implying an inseparable combination of spirit and physical natures. While it will be physical (Job 19:25-27), it will also be *spiritual* and "bear the image of the heavenly" (1 Cor. 15:49, NASB). It will be imperishable and composed of "flesh and bones" (Luke 24:36-43), unlike the mortal body, which is composed of "flesh and blood" (1 Cor. 15:50, NASB).

A "spiritual body" is a perfect, incorruptible joining of the spiritual and physical elements now found imperfectly in corruptible Man. Clearly, if the resurrected bodies Men will obtain in the resurrection "bear the image of the heavenly" (1 Cor. 15:49, NASB), and if the resurrection is physical, as Luke 24:36-43 proves, the "image of the heavenly" must include a physical element. Clearly, the heavenly image is corporeal as much as it is spiritual.

Classical theists have visualized the true nature of such a body for Christ, but when the term "corporeal" is applied to the Father, they invariably link it with Man's corruptible body. That is not Mormon

---

[6] Walter Elwell, *Evangelical Dictionary of Theology*, (Grand Rapids: Baker Book House, 1984), s.v. "Spiritual Body."

[7] Elwell, *Evangelical Dictionary of Theology*, "The Nature of the Incarnation," s.v. Incarnation.

theology. Mormons believe both Christ and the Father have a body like that described by Paul in First Corinthians. The failure of classical theists to comprehend this point of similarity between the Father and the Son prevents orthodox theologians from envisioning the true capabilities of God as a corporeal being. The body God the Father possesses is such that it does not limit Him, any more than the same kind of body limits Christ. It enhances the Father's capabilities and glory in ways that will be discussed in the chapters that follow.

To speak of God as spiritual is consistent with such a body. To speak of Him as physical and corporeal is equally so. Indeed, to speak of God as *infinite* is not inconsistent with the corporeality of His perfect resurrected "spiritual body." Otherwise, Christ can no longer be spoken of as infinite. Biblical doctrine has no dichotomies in its views of Christ and the Father. They are both infinite, divine beings with glorified, resurrected bodies of flesh and bones combined with spirit. If it helps classical theists to call such a body a "spiritual body," as Paul did, that is entirely consistent with Mormon theology on this point.

Numbers 23:19 As Proof That God Is Corporeal

Frequently cited by classical theists in their attempt to prove that God is an incorporeal spirit, Numbers 23:19 actually means quite the opposite. In the NASB, this passage reads, in pertinent part, as follows: "God is not a man, that He should lie, Nor a son of man, that He should repent." Ignoring the context, this English translation appears on its face to give some credence to the classical argument. But examination of the original Hebrew reveals a very different meaning.

The first word translated "man" in this verse comes from the Hebrew word, *ish*, which is a *comparative* form of the word "man." This word is used to compare one type of man with another, not to contrast men with other species of beings. It is used, for example, to refer to a man as opposed to a woman, a husband as opposed to a wife, a younger man as opposed to an older man.[8]

Women, wives and older men are all beings of the same species. The Hebrew word "*ish*" assumes that characteristic as the point of similarity on which it is used to make comparisons. Those comparisons are

---

[8] *Gesenius' Hebrew and Chaldee Lexicon*, Samuel Tregelles, trans. (Grand Rapids: Baker Books, 1979), s.v. "איש."

made only on the basis of gender, marital status, age, etc., not on the basis of species. In this passage, the attribute being compared through use of the word *ish* is the trait of *honesty,* not manhood. The verse compares God as a man who does not lie with mortal men who do. The passage always assumes that God is a man.

The words translated "a son of man" in the next portion of the verse are taken from the Hebrew, *ben adam*, a phrase used to refer specifically to a mortal man, literally a descendant of Adam.[9] The contrast is not between God and Man, for that would have required use of the Hebrew word *adam* alone. The contrast is between God, an *immortal* Man who is morally perfect, and *mortal* Men who are morally imperfect and in need of repentance. Again the assumption is that God is a man.

The language of this verse in the original Hebrew was obviously chosen with great care to avoid any suggestion that God is a different species or has a different nature than Man. Unfortunately, that care did not survive translation into English. Numbers 23:19 proclaims that God does *not* differ from Man in nature, substance or essence. Rather, it teaches that mortal Men are imperfect, while God is a perfect Man.

The Invisible God

Classical theists often argue that references to God as "invisible" (e.g., Col. 1:15) demonstrate that He is incorporeal. But the Bible does not give that sense to the term "invisible." The meaning is *"unseen,"* not *"unseeable."* God the Father does not make Himself visible to Man, except on very rare and special occasions such as the martyrdom of Stephen (Acts 7:55-56). Men are not privileged to see Him unless they become like His Son (John 6:46). If Men will know the Father, they must first learn of the Son (John 8:19). Thus, He is called "invisible," in contrast to His Son, who appeared to all Men during His earthly incarnation.

Of the contrary opinion, Robert Morey, like other classical theists, claims that God is called "invisible" because "there is nothing physical to see."[10] If that were so, there would have been nothing for Christ to see either. Yet, John 6:46 is clear in saying that Christ has seen the Father. Nor do the scriptures leave the ability to see the Father exclusively with Christ. If it is truly impossible for other Men to see God

---

[9] *Ibid.*, s.v. "בְּאָרָם."
[10] Morey, *Battle of the Gods*, 189.

because He is invisible by nature, then Matthew 5:8 ("blessed are the pure in heart for they shall see God") would be an empty and deceptive promise.

So perfectly is Christ in the image of His Father that to see the Savior is said to be the same as seeing the Father (John 14:7-9). If God were truly invisible by nature, then to see Christ in physical form, as Philip did in John 14, would most certainly not be the same as seeing the Father. Christ was not invisible to Philip, nor would the Father have been invisible to him if He had been present as Christ was.

Classical theists sometimes argue that John 14:10-11 supports a metaphysical joining of the Father and the Son consistent with their view that God is incorporeal and transcendent. The NASB translates these verses as follows:

> Do you not believe that I am in the Father, and the Father is in Me? The words that I say to you I do not speak on My own initiative, but the Father abiding in Me does His works.
>
> Believe Me that I am in the Father and the Father in Me; otherwise believe on account of the works themselves.

That this is figurative, rather than metaphysical, language is apparent from a number of clues. The first is that Christ was a Jew in Israel talking to other Jews in Israel. The Jews of that region were not Hellenized and eschewed metaphysical thinking and language as something associated with the Gentiles. Note also that Christ speaks of His "own initiative" in verse 10, implying again that He has His own will and is, therefore, a separate individual, as demonstrated in Chapter 10.

Lastly, note the clue in verse 12 (NASB), which reads: "Truly, truly, I say to you he who believes in Me, the works that I do shall he do also; and greater works than these shall he do; because *I go to the Father.*" This passage clearly indicates that the Father is in another physical location, to which Christ will go. Therefore, the statement that the Father is "in" Christ and that Christ is "in the Father," couched in the present tense, was purely figurative. It was certainly not literal in any metaphysical sense. The language was used to emphasize the agency relationship that exists between the Father and the Son and the voluntary submission of Christ's will to that of His Father (see Chapter 17).

There is no passage in the Bible that contradicts the eyewitness accounts describing God as corporeal. Consistent with Genesis 1:26-27, both God and Man have a dual nature, they have a spirit housed in a physical body. Thus, they have both a spiritual and a physical nature. Man's body is fallen, mortal and imperfect. God's body, like that of the resurrected Savior, is eternal and perfect. Man enjoys the promise, however, that, in time, he can receive a body similar to Christ's.

Greek Origins of Incorporeality as a Supposed Attribute of God

If classical theists can understand the concept of Christ having a "spiritual body" after His resurrection, why do they refuse to grasp the concept as it applies to God the Father? It is because of their background in Greek philosophy. Classical theists seem unaware, however, that their preference for interpreting passages about God's body as "anthropomorphisms" comes, not from the Bible, but from second-century Greek thinking. Take, for example, the following by Millard Erickson, a research professor of theology at Southwestern Baptist Theological Seminary:

> There are, of course, numerous passages which suggest that God has physical features such as hands or feet. How are we to regard these references? It seems most helpful to treat them as anthropomorphisms, attempts to express the truth about God through human analogies. There also are cases where God appeared in physical form, particularly in the Old Testament. These should be understood as theophanies, or temporary manifestations of God. It seems best to take the clear statements about the spirituality and invisibility of God at face value and interpret the anthropomorphisms and theophanies in the light of them. Indeed, Jesus himself clearly indicated that a spirit does not have flesh and bones (Luke 24:39).[11]

This paragraph contains no rational argument for the interpretation chosen. If, in fact, the truth about Him is that He is *not* human, why would God choose to "express the truth" about Himself "through human analogies? Why do classical theists assume God's appearances to Men are "temporary" revelations of His nature? Nothing in the Bible supports such assumptions. Why interpret the many hundreds of physical references figuratively, rather than seeking to understand less than a dozen references to Gods' spiritual nature in a way that is consistent with the biblical testimony of His corporeality?

---

[11] Erickson, *Christian Theology*, 268.

The Classical Doctrine of a Transcendent God Is Based on Greek Metaphysics

The view of God as incorporeal that became part of early Christian theology was derived from a larger concept—the transcendency of God. That concept affects every aspect of orthodox Christianity's views about God's nature and attributes. The idea that God is transcendent assumes the reality and truth of the Greek metaphysical view of the universe. It postulates that God exists in the "*Pleroma*" outside the real universe, that is, outside space and time. In this view, God was not even a spirit, let alone corporeal.

There was some controversy among the Greek philosophers as to how far above the real universe the *Pleroma* is, and this area of disagreement carried over into classical theism. Orthodoxy accepts the Greek idea that God exists outside space, but there is some question about His existence in time. As Dr. Beckwith explains, "Although all orthodox Christians agree that God is *eternally* God, they dispute whether He exists *in* time (i.e., the temporal eternity view) or *out of* time (i.e., the timeless eternity view)."[12] Dr. Morey is not so equivocal on this issue. He claims "Christians have always believed that time and space are attributes of created things, not of the Creator."[13]

The latter statement is demonstrably incorrect. No view of God as transcendent, and as the creator of space and time, can be found in the New Testament. Nor can such views be found in the writings of the Apostolic Fathers or the Apologists earlier than the latter half of the second century A.D. (There is the possible exception of Aristides, if the Syriac version of his *Apology* is to be believed, but that version is dubious at best, as explained in Chapter 6.)

The idea that time and space are only attributes of created things and not of God appears nowhere in the writings of the Old Testament either. Of course, that fact did not deter men like Philo of Alexandria from interpreting its passages to that effect using Greek allegorical techniques.[14] Like Philo, classical theists assert that God exists somewhere outside everything Man perceives as reality, and so is necessarily incorporeal. That belief is clearly and entirely based on Greek metaphysics.

---

[12] Beckwith, "Philosophical Problems," 14.

[13] Morey, *Battle of the Gods,* 189.

[14] Hatch, *Influence of Greek Ideas,* 244-245.

The Greek Notion of a Transcendent, Incorporeal God

The entire idea of a transcendent God was rooted in Parmenides' metaphysics. These concepts were further developed by Plato, and fully realized in Platonistic dualism.[15] Plato believed that only God really exists, eternal, now and everywhere, a continuous unity, a perfect sphere that fills all space, undying and immovable.[16] Opposite Him were the objects of sense, the phenomenal world. Plato claimed that this world is not real, but only seems to exist.[17] He believed man's knowledge of it is mere illusion, not the truth. In contrast to this world of sense objects, God belongs to the world of thought, to which He can retire, as though He were leaving time and space and stepping back from the material universe.[18] All created things, according to Plato, belong to the world of sense.

Thus, in the theology of the Greek philosophers, God was transcendent, pure thought, beyond the world of sense and matter.[19] "God therefore is Mind, a form separate from all matter, that is to say, out of contact with it, and not involved with anything that is capable of being acted on."[20] This concept is the essence of dualism that characterized the Platonistic and other Greek schools.[21]

The situation seemed simple enough to the early Greeks. Matter is entirely different from thought. Thought, if it can be imagined as a "thing" the way the Greek philosophers did, has no apparent existence in the material world. The philosophers, whose emphasis was entirely on thought, chose to believe that thought—their favorite activity—was, in fact, the only reality and refused to trust the testimony of their feeble, unaided senses.

Plutarch, the famous Greek biographer of ancient philosophers who lived between 46 and 120 A.D. (yet never commented on Christianity), expressed the transcendency of God in precisely the terms championed by classical theists:

---

[15] *Ibid.*, 239-245 (See Chapter 2).
[16] *Ibid.*, 240.
[17] *Ibid.*
[18] See Plato, *Republic*, 509.
[19] Hatch, *Influence of Greek Ideas*, 241.
[20] Plutarch, *Doctrines of the Philosophers* 1:7.
[21] Hatch, *Influence of Greek Ideas*, 241.

What, then, is that which really exists? It is the Eternal, the Uncreated, the Undying, to whom time brings no change ... God is: and that not in time but in eternity, motionless, timeless, changeless eternity, that has no before or after: and being One, He fills eternity with one Now, and so really "is," not "has been" or "will be," without beginning and without ceasing.[22]

The "eternity" Plutarch described above is none other than the *Pleroma*, which became the heaven of classical theism. This is the definition of "eternity" that classical theists embrace, but it is not a biblical notion in any sense, and there is no place in it for Men. Of course, the Bible uses the term "eternity," but the idea that it is a place outside space and time is Greek alone.

Maximus of Tyre, a professor at Plato's Academy in Athens, expressed God's transcendency as follows: "God, the Father and Fashioner of all things that are, He who is older than the sun, older than the sky, greater than time and lapse of time and the whole stream of nature."[23] He also taught:

> [W]e cannot apprehend His essence ... the Deity Himself is unseen by the sight, unspoken by the voice, untouched by fleshly touch, unheard by the hearing, seen only—through its likeness to Him, and heard only—through its kinship with Him, by the noblest and purest and clearest-sighted and swiftest and oldest element of the soul.[24]

No similar statements are made in the Bible. Can there be any doubt about the origin of classical theology on this subject?

Consonant with the idea of transcendency was the idea that God is incorporeal. The Greek philosophers taught that God was the Absolute Unity, the ultimate generalization of all things, expressed as the ultimate abstraction of number by Pythagoras. According to them, God was not "limited" by passion, parts or bodily form. "All of Him is sight, all of Him is understanding, all of Him is hearing," they taught.[25] As noted above, the philosophers taught "God therefore is Mind, a form separate from all matter."[26] This is far from Christ's statement that "a spirit hath not flesh and bones *as you see me have*" (Lk. 24:39). Christ is saying

---

[22] Plutarch, *de Ei ap. Delph.* 18.
[23] Maximus of Tyre, *Diss.* 8, 9.
[24] *Ibid.*
[25] Hatch, *Influence of Greek Ideas*, 240.
[26] Plutarch, *Doctrine of the Philosophers*, 1:7.

that a spirit's composition is not the same as resurrected flesh and bone, as He then had. This remark notes only that a spirit is not composed of solid matter as perceived by human touch. It does not attribute to spirit the insubstantiality of mere thought.

Transcendence and Incorporeality in Hellenized Judaism

As noted above, the idea of a transcendent God found its way into Hellenized Judaism through Philo of Alexandria long before it was adopted by the Apologists. Though beautifully phrased in the Greek style of his time, Philo's statements are entirely unsupported by any of the scriptures to which he occasionally makes reference.

According to Philo, God "is not in space but beyond it; for He contains it. He is not in time, for He is the Father of the universe, which is itself the father of time, since from its movement time proceeds."[27] Philo died in 50 A.D. while most, if not all the original Apostles yet lived. Yet none of their statements confirm his views. If Philo's teachings about God were inspired, why don't they appear in any Apostolic writings? Why was it that more than a hundred years passed before Philo's views on God were adopted by Christian writers? There is but one valid explanation. They were heretical when Philo taught them, and they were a sign of apostasy when the early Church later adopted them.

With the idea of a transcendent God, the concept of incorporeality was first applied to the God of the Bible, not in the early Church, but in Hellenized Judaism by Philo of Alexandria. Some time before 50 A.D., he wrote the following about God's nature: "He is 'without body, parts or passions;' without feet, for whither should He walk who fills all things: without hands, for from whom should He receive anything who possesses all things: without eyes, for how should He need eyes who made the light."[28]

This language has great poetic beauty, but there is no biblical nor logical foundation to the ideas expressed. Why should God's creation of light imply that He has no eyes to see it with? The whole idea is illogical. Philo quotes no passages of scripture in support of his notions, for there are none. His ideas are borrowed entirely from Greek philosophy,

---

[27] Philo, *De post. Cain* 5:1:228-229.
[28] Philo, *Quod deus immut.* 12:1:28.

the source later used by the Apologists to arrive at the same false conclusions. There was no inspired basis for adopting any of his notions.

Earliest Christian Views on the Transcendency and Corporeality of God

Professor Hatch admits that the early Christians had no idea of the transcendent God described by the philosophers:

> From the earliest Christian teaching, indeed, the conception of the transcendence of God is absent. God is near to men and speaks to them: He is angry with them and punishes them: He is merciful to them and pardons them. He does all this through His angels and prophets, and last of all through His Son. But he needs such mediators rather because a heavenly Being is invisible than because He is transcendent. The conception which underlies the earliest expression of the belief of a Christian community is the simple conception of children: . . .
>
> In the original sphere of Christianity there does not appear to have been any great advance upon these simple conceptions. The doctrine upon which stress was laid was, that God is, that He is one, that He is almighty and everlasting, that He made the world, that His mercy is over all His works. There was no taste for metaphysical discussion: there was possibly no appreciation of metaphysical conceptions.[29]

Thus, Hatch describes the biblical theology that prevailed in the early Church under the direction of the Apostles as the "simple conception of children." That view reflects the thinking of the later, apostate Church, looking as it did upon the original, uncorrupted truths of the Bible as childish compared with the supposedly brilliant mental gymnastics in which the Apologists and other early Church fathers saw themselves indulging. By adopting this viewpoint, classical theists actually heap esteem upon the very thing about which Paul warned the early Church—the influence of Greek philosophy. They actually do regard the Apologists in some ways as superior to the inspired Christian writers of the first century.

The truth is that the thinking of the Apologists was the thinking of Men. In contrast, the inspired writers revealed to Men the thinking of God. The ideas based on Greek philosophy adopted by the Apologists,

---

[29] Hatch, *Influence of Greek Ideas*, 251-252.

rather than being an improvement on early Christianity, were the very false doctrines against which the early Church was warned. It is reprehensible egotism to suppose that the ideas of the Apologists were *advancements* on the fundamentals established by Christ and His Apostles, as though the truths of the Bible needed a little improvement at the hands of Greek intellectuals.

Early Christian Belief in a Corporeal God

The early Church believed in a corporeal God. That is what the Bible taught, and it appears from criticism leveled at Christians well into the second century that most of them still maintained that belief. Celsus, the famous anti-Christian writer of the late second century, wrote:

> Again they will ask, "How can we know God, unless by the perception of the senses? For how otherwise than through the senses are we able to gain any knowledge?" This is not the language of a man; it comes not from the soul, but from the flesh. Let them hearken to us, if such a spiritless and carnal race are able to do so: if, instead of exercising the senses, you look upwards with the soul; if, turning away the eye of the body, you open the eye of the mind, thus and thus only will you be able to see God.[30]

It goes without saying that Men should "look upwards with the soul," as Celsus suggests. But this distinctly Greek invitation, which proved so irresistible to the Apologists, suggests a contrast between the God of earlier Christianity and the God Celsus believed in. Celsus' criticism contrasts the transcendent and incorporeal God of Greek theology apprehensible only by thought, with the Christian God. The god of the philosophers, whom Celsus espoused and the Apologists described, was invisible by His nature. The Christians, however, obviously expected to perceive Him with their physical senses. The implication is that Christians once believed their God was corporeal, that He could be apprehended by the senses.

The Apologists Imported the God of Greek Philosophy Into Christianity

As seen in Chapter 6, Celsus' criticism helped to impel the Apologists toward a Greek interpretation of the descriptions of God contained

---
[30] Origen, *Against Celsus* 7:36.

in the Bible. The Greek view of God was generally absent from the earliest Christian writings, and totally missing from the New Testament. Yet, by the end of the second century, the Apologists were describing a God who would have been entirely satisfactory to Celsus. As shown in Chapter 6, even Justin Martyr, who understood the distinct personalities of the Father and the Son,[31] had drifted towards apostasy enough that he protested against a literal interpretation of the Old Testament descriptions of God the Father as follows:

> You are not to think that the unbegotten God "came down" from anywhere or "went up." For the unutterable Father and Lord of all things neither comes to any place nor walks nor sleeps nor rises, but abides in His own place wherever that place may be, seeing keenly and hearing keenly, not with eyes or ears, but with His unspeakable power, so that He sees all things and knows all things, nor is any one of us hid from Him: nor does He move, He who is uncontained by space and by the whole world, seeing that He was before the world was born.[32]

Justin, like the other Apologists, rationalized the plain meaning of the Bible's language to fit the demands of Greek philosophy. He even ignored Revelation 9:20, which contrasts God's ability to walk with the immobility of idols, and deferred to a description of the Father that matches Aristotle's "Unmoving Mover" more than it does any description of God contained in the Bible. His insistence that God has no sensory organs directly contradicts the clear statements of the Bible (Deut. 4:27-28; Rev. 9:20). If not the beginning of classical attempts to rationalize these passages, his was the first to appear in early Christian writing.

As noted previously, the change in the Christian understanding of God occurred from approximately 161 to 177 A.D., when the Apologists were anxiously dealing with the resurgence of lethal persecution from Rome. The motivation that led them in this direction can be seen in the frustrated statements of Athenagoras as follows:

> All the philosophers agree, even without their intending it, when they investigate the first principles of the universe, that God is one. We Christians also affirm that the unified order of the cosmos comes from one God. Why then are they allowed to say and write what they please

---

[31] Justin, *First Apology* 63.
[32] Justin, *Dialogue with Trypho* 127.

about the divine, whereas there is a law forbidding us to do so, even though we can advance cogent proofs and reasons for our conviction about the unity of God?[33]

As the Apologists incorporated Greek philosophy and metaphysics in their "cogent proofs" regarding "the unity of God," they imported the Greek ideas of transcendence and incorporeality into Christianity. Thus, Athenagoras' language included the following adjectives to describe Deity: "unbegotten, eternal, unseen, impassible, incomprehensible and uncontained." Except for the descriptions "eternal" and "unseen," these words appear nowhere in the Bible. Further, the context of passages containing those two words does not include the Greek conceptions of them.

The Bible describes Christ as the only *begotten* of the Father (see, e.g., John 1:14), while the term, "*un*begotten," appears nowhere in the scriptures. The word from which "only begotten" is translated is *monogenes*, which literally means "only child." Christ was "begotten" of the Father and is the revelation of God to Man (John 14:7). His is the only example in the Bible of the genesis and progression of one who holds the title "God." Objective, unbiased logic would, therefore, suggest that any other person holding that title, e.g., the Father, must have progressed in a similar way. Since Christ was "begotten," why should the Father be called "*un*begotten?"

But the logic of the Apologists was not objective. It was engulfed by preexisting bias. The Apologists were strongly influenced by their Greek training and background. The Greek notion of a transcendent God was ubiquitous among the Hellenized population of the world. By the middle of the second century the only people who had rejected metaphysics were the Jews, formerly of Palestine, and they were widely scattered. The Church was fully in the hands of the Gentiles. It was easier for scholarly Church leaders of that era to interpret the Bible in light of what was familiar to them. The idea of a transcendent, and so incorporeal God, was all their intellectual predispositions would allow. The transcendent, incorporeal God came from them. It was a Greek fabrication, not a biblical one.

---

[33] Athenagoras, *A Plea for the Christians* 7.

Not All the Apologists Agreed That God Was Incorporeal

Not all the Apologists were swept away by the tide of Greek thinking on this subject. Tertullian reasoned that God must be material. Sadly, he did not join the Church until approximately 185 A.D., many years after the Apologists had developed their concept of a co-substantial, metaphysical, transcendent, and hence incorporeal, God. By the time he joined, the Greek notion of God's transcendent incorporeality was well entrenched in the early Church.

Nevertheless, Tertullian argued against the idea of incorporeality as follows: "How could one who is empty have made things that are solid, and one who is void have made things that are full, and one who is incorporeal have made things that have body?"[34] This wise reasoning came too late. The early Church rejected the God who created and inhabits the material universe, and who is Himself a real being. Tertullian's idea was rejected as heretical.

What Does the Bible Teach About the Transcendency of God?

The Bible is not silent on the fundamental issue of God's relationship to Man and the universe. Romans 11:36 (NASB) says that "from Him and through Him and to Him are all things"; 2 Corinthians 4:6 (NASB) teaches that God is the one "who has shone in our hearts to give the light of the knowledge of the glory of God in the face of Christ"; and Acts 17:28 (KJV) states that "in Him we live and move and have our being." These statements were easily interpreted by those with a Greek education as metaphysical references, but they have a very different meaning when viewed from the Hebrew perspective that rejected metaphysics. They actually place God at the heart of the universe and its operations, not *outside* it in some lofty Pleroma.

Uniquely Mormon scriptures provide further insight into the relationship between God and the space-time universe, consistent with the biblical verses cited above. For example, D&C 88:13 explains that "the light of Christ" is "the light which is in all things, which giveth life to all things, which is the law by which all things are governed, even the power of God who sitteth upon his throne, who is in the bosom of eternity, who is in the midst of all things."

---

[34] Tertullian, *Against Praxeas,* 1:3.

This verse is consistent with biblical teachings about the relationship between God and reality. It places God at the absolute core of the real universe. The basic building blocks from which God created the heavens and the earth and all things that inhabit them were brought into their present state by and through Him.[35]

These passages describe a "hands-on" God, not one who is transcendent or aloof, existing above or outside the real universe, but one who is immanent and involved. The God of the Bible, unlike the God of the philosophers, obviously has no reluctance about contacting Matter.

Classical Attempts to Defend the Transcendence of God From the Bible

Biblical passages that teach the closeness of God to Man have not gone unnoticed by classical theists. They refer to the principle taught in these passages as *"immanence."*[36] While acknowledging the doctrine of God's nearness to His creations, however, classical theism has continued to insist on His transcendence, despite the fact that the two doctrines are fundamentally in conflict with each other. Professor Erickson goes so far as to defend the doctrine of God's transcendence from the Bible as follows:

> A number of Scripture passages affirm the concept of divine transcendence. It is a particular theme of the Book of Isaiah. In 55:8-9 we read that God's thoughts transcend man's: "For my thoughts are not your thoughts, neither are your ways my ways, says the Lord. For as the heavens are higher than the earth, so are my ways higher than your ways and my thoughts than your thoughts." In 6:1-5 the Lord is depicted as "sitting upon a throne, high and lifted up." The seraphim call out, "Holy, holy, holy is the Lord of Hosts," an indication of his transcendence, and add, "The whole earth is full of his glory," a reference to his immanence. Isaiah responds with an expression of his own uncleanness. Thus, God's transcendence over us must be seen not only in terms of his greatness, his power and knowledge, but also in terms of his goodness, his holiness and purity. Isaiah 57:15 also expresses

---

[35] How the power of God functions to achieve this effect on the universe is a subject which cannot be fully covered in this volume. For a clear understanding of the principles involved, see Mark Smith, *The Power of God* (Bountiful: Horizon Publishers, 1997).

[36] See, e.g., Harvey, *A Handbook of Theological Terms*, s.v. "Immanence."

both the transcendence and immanence of God: "For thus says the high and lofty One who inhabits eternity, whose name is Holy: 'I dwell in the high and holy place, and also with him who is of a contrite and humble spirit, to revive the spirit of the humble, and to revive the heart of the contrite.'"

We read of God's transcendence in other books of the Bible as well. Psalm 113:5-6 says, "Who is like the Lord our God, who is seated on high, who looks far down upon the heavens and the earth?" He is described as "enthroned in the heavens" in Psalm 123:1. In John 8:23, Jesus draws a contrast between himself and his hearers: "You are from below, I am from above; you are of this world, I am not of this world."[37]

It is a testimony to the continuing and profound influence of Greek philosophy on classical theism today that the biblical references cited by Professor Erickson above are interpreted as though heaven was entirely outside space and time like the ancient Greek *Pleroma* instead of merely a long distance away. The Bible never implies that "eternity," the high and holy place of God's dwelling, where He lives with the righteous, is outside the real space-time universe. It is never identified as the realm of thought envisioned by the Greek philosophers. Of course, as to God's attributes, there is no argument that He is far above fallen Men, but that, again, does not place Him outside time and space.

If the passages cited by Professor Erickson had been written by Plato, Athanagoras, Plutarch, or another Greek contemporary of the Old or New Testament writers, his interpretation of them might be justified, but the Hebrews were entirely without the metaphysical orientation of the Greeks. References by them to God's thoughts being higher than Man's were intended to show that Man is ignorant when compared with God. References to God's holiness reflect the contrast between His perfection and Man's fallen state of sin. References to His location simply indicate a vast physical and spiritual separation. They cannot be seen as making God transcendent in the classical sense. That was never a Hebrew notion, only a Greek one.[38]

Incorporeality, an Idolatrous Doctrine

Professor Erickson, in arguing for an incorporeal God, makes another amazingly inaccurate claim:

---

[37] Erickson, *Christian Theology*, 312-313.
[38] Hatch, *Influence of Greek Ideas*, 238, *et seq.*

274 How Greek Philosophy Corrupted the Christian Concept of God

In biblical times, the doctrine of God's spirituality was a counter to the practice of idolatry and of nature worship. God, being spirit, could not be represented by any physical object or likeness. That he is not restricted by geographical location also countered the idea that God could be contained and controlled.[39]

This reasoning, in many ways, is exactly the opposite of the truth. The idea that God is incorporeal is the very essence of idolatry, which is possibly the reason that the pagans learned to tolerate the theology of the Greek philosophers but vehemently resisted Christianity in its original form. Idol worshippers know that what they make is wood or stone—materials graven by Man. But they believe God, as a personal force or power, invests Himself in the images they make, thereby transforming those images into appropriate objects of worship.[40]

Mormon theology teaches that, at all times mentioned in the Bible, God the Father had a physical body. However, before His incarnation in the meridian of time, Christ was a spirit. He did not have a physical body until He was born into this world and obtained one. The God of Abraham, Isaac and Jacob, often designated "Jehovah," whom the Bible declares to be the very same person incarnated as Jesus the Christ (John 8:56-58), was a spirit before that event.

His spiritual nature was part of the problem Israel had with idol worship. Being drawn to the idea was easy for them, because, knowing that the God of their fathers was a spirit, they could imagine that He might invest Himself in the images they made.

The Old Testament never counters idolatry by saying that God is a spirit. Nor does it counter such beliefs by teaching that representing an incorporeal God by any physical object or likeness is impossible. Rather, God contrasted Himself with idols in a way that is directly opposite to Professor Erickson's arguments.

The Real God Contrasted With Idols

The gods of idol worshippers see, and hear and smell in exactly the same way the God of classical theism does—without benefit of sensory organs. Their gods are specifically pointed out as the opposite of the true

---

[39] Erickson, *Christian Theology*, 268.
[40] *Encyclopaedia Britannica*, 1960 ed., s.v. "Idolatry."

God in this very respect. Deuteronomy 4:27-28 (NASB) states that the Lord was going to scatter Israel among the nations where they "will serve gods, the work of man's hands, wood and stone, *which neither see nor hear nor eat nor smell.*"

It is no mistake that the true God contrasts Himself with idols on His possession of the senses of sight, hearing, taste and smell. Acts 17:29 states, "Forasmuch then as we are the offspring of God, we ought not to think that the Godhead [NASB: "the Divine Nature"] is like unto gold, or silver, or stone, graven by art and man's device."

If not "graven by art and man's device," what did Paul intend that Men should think the Divine Nature was like? His reference in the same passage to Man as the offspring of God is the plain answer to that question. The idea that God exercises the senses of sight, hearing, taste and smell without benefit of sensory apparatus, as classical theism teaches, defeats the very point of Paul's message. The true God of the Bible is not like the god of the idol worshippers or the god of Greek philosophy, He is like Man, who is His "offspring."

The Book of Revelation goes even further. Professor Erickson claims that God's nature as a spirit counters the idea that He could be restricted geographically, or contained or controlled, like an idol. God's own argument against idols on this specific issue shows a very different contrast.

Revelation 9:20 (NASB) states, "And the rest of the men which were not killed by these plagues yet repented not of the works of their hands, that they should not worship devils, and idols of gold, and silver, and brass, and stone, and of wood: *which neither can see, nor hear, nor walk.*" God here compares Himself with idols by pointing out that *they* have no sensory organs and cannot move on their own. Clearly, His point is that He can and does! God not only has sensory organs with which to see and hear, but feet and legs with which to walk and move. Thus, God Himself sees His corporeality as an empowerment, a point of His superiority over idols, not as a limitation.

Conclusion

The earliest Christian writers, the writers of the New Testament, expressed no notion of God being above and outside the material universe. There is nothing in the scriptures that even remotely implies, let alone states, that God exists outside time and space. The idea of God's transcendency is a notion born purely of Greek philosophy, and should be rejected in favor of the biblical God—the real God who lives in the real universe.

God has always been described in the Bible as having the form of Man. Christ had a body of flesh and bones. Accordingly, so does His Father. This is the biblical truth, whether or not it comports with the notions of infinity that were conceived by the ancient Greeks. It may be difficult for classical theists to accept this, but as the attributes of God unfold in the chapters that follow, it will at least become easier to comprehend.

Summary

1. The Bible is filled with references to God's corporeality. Some are eyewitness reports, others mention His bodily parts, and still others explain that Christ and the Father look exactly alike.
2. Classical theists dismiss biblical references to God's corporeality as "theophanies," and assert that attributing to God actual corporeality is "anthropomorphism."
3. Sometimes classical theists argue that references to God's corporeality in the Bible are no more to be believed than references to His "wings." References to wings in the Bible, however, are clearly similes or metaphors.
4. One argument against God's corporeality is based on John 4:24, which says that "God is spirit." This reference does no more than emphasize one aspect of God's person. He is spirit, but so is Man. Likewise, He is corporeal as Man is corporeal.
5. God's body differs from that of mortal Men. The Father's body is resurrected in glory, like that of Christ. Paul called it a "spiritual body."
6. Numbers 23:19 is often quoted in an effort to prove that God is not corporeal, yet the original Hebrew demonstrates that the passage contrasts God as a physically and morally perfect man with mortal and imperfect Men.
7. Classical theists often argue that the Father is spoken of as the "invisible" God because He is incorporeal and cannot be seen. In fact, however, Christ and others have seen Him. He is called

invisible in the Bible because the privilege of seeing Him is not granted to Men unless they become like Christ.
8. Classical theists sometimes argue that figurative language about God in the New Testament should be interpreted metaphysically. In fact, however, metaphysics is entirely absent from the Bible. Metaphysics makes assumptions that have never been confirmed by science or any inspired revelation.
9. The idea of an incorporeal God comes from the writings of the Greek philosophers. The idea was infused into Judaism by Philo of Alexandria.
10. The corporeality of God is taught in the Bible, and appears to have been the understanding of Christians until sometime around 150 A.D.
11. The Apologists imported the idea of an incorporeal and transcendent God into Christianity. Nothing in Christian writing before Justin Martyr's *Dialogue with Trypho* (159-165 A.D.) contains that doctrine.
12. Tertullian, for one, argued that God must be corporeal.
13. The doctrine of the incorporeality of God is at the foundation of idol worship and is a pagan doctrine. In the Bible, God is contrasted with idols and false gods on the basis of His corporeality and possession of physical senses.
14. A physical body is a powerful, eternal tool of unlimited value, and God the Father possesses such a body just as Christ does. A physical body was only viewed as a limitation by the Greeks and, with them, the Apologists who did not understand its nature.

God, The Creator

The Bible informs Man about His Creator, God the Father, acting with and through His Son, Jesus Christ and the Holy Ghost, who unitedly formed "the heavens and the earth" (John 1:1-3, Heb. 1:2). According to the inspired words of the prophets, "God," translated from *elohim*, the *plural* form of the Hebrew word for "god," created the reality Men see as "the heavens and the earth" (Gen. 1:1), the "worlds" (Heb. 1:2; 11:3), and *"all things . . . that are in heaven, and that are in earth"* (Col. 1:16; Rev. 4:11).

That is the testimony of the Bible. It tells what "things" God created and what materials He used to make them. Classical theism differs with this testimony markedly. Though classical theists assume that their differences with the sacred record are well founded, it will be shown in this chapter that they are the result of heretical speculation, arising from purely Greek sources.

The Classical Doctrine of Creation

The classical doctrine of creation is expressed by Dr. Beckwith as follows, "All reality has come into existence and continues to exist because of Him."[1] Other classical theists make the same claim, namely that "The entirety of reality has come into being through his act."[2] According to them, God is the only ultimate reality, and everything that is not God was created by Him. This aspect of God's creation—the creation of *reality* itself—is not biblical, but comes to Christianity from various Greek sources.

---

[1] Beckwith, "Philosophical Problems." 2.
[2] Erickson, *Christian Theology*, 370-371.

The orthodox view is much more than a claim that God created the contents of the real space-time universe. Classical doctrine claims that God created *time* and *space*, in addition to everything Men perceive as reality. They divide the act of creation into (1) "immediate or direct creation," and (2) "mediate or derivative creation, God's subsequent work of developing and fashioning what he had originally brought into existence."[3] All this, they claim, God created out of nothing, or, as Professor Erickson expresses it, "without the use of pre-existing materials."[4]

What "Things" Did God Create?

As to "all things," the Bible is clear that God is the creator of them (Neh. 9:6; Prov. 16:4; Isa. 66:1-2; Jer. 14:22; John 1:3; Acts 7:50; 14:15; 17:24; Eph. 3:9; Col. 1:16-17; Rev. 4:11). The question, however, is what the inspired writers meant when they used the phrase "all things" in these passages. To answer that question, one must first recognize that in both New Testament Greek and Old Testament Hebrew, the word "things" does not actually appear in the text. The word is "all . . . ," which in the Greek comes from the root word "*pas.*" What things the word "all . . ." is intended to encompass generally appears from the context of the passage in which it is used.

Sometimes, the form of *pas* used can imply a very broad and general scope of "things." In those instances, what the reader may see as included in the term "all" will depend largely on his assumptions about the universe around him. Here is where caution must be exercised—the reader must employ the same assumptions as the inspired writer. The early Church fathers generally did not make this distinction, and employed their Greek assumptions about the universe to interpret these crucial Hebrew passages. The result was a metaphysical slant on creation that could never have been intended by the Hebrew writers to whom these passages were revealed.

No Biblical Support for the Idea that God Created Reality

Robert Morey is one of the few classical theists who has tried to present biblical evidence of the doctrine that God created time and space. His points, of course, are not supported by actual language in the scriptures. But he claims that the concept can be derived from biblical

---
[3] *Ibid.*, 367-368.
[4] *Ibid.*, 370.

passages using what he considers good logic. Unfortunately, his logic is based entirely on his *a priori* assumptions, which he, along with all classical theists, adopted wholesale from the Greek philosophers just as the second-century Church fathers did.

For example, after demonstrating that the scriptures testify that God is infinite (a proposition that can be proven more easily from the Book of Mormon than from the Bible), Dr. Morey argues that "God can be 'infinite' only as long as He exists prior to, independent of, and apart from the world He made out of nothing."[5] The reasoning here is that, since the world God created had a beginning in time and God's infinite existence extends before that beginning, He must have existed before time.

Dr. Morey's assumption in arriving at this conclusion is that time began with the beginning of God's creation of this world. That was Augustine's position,[6] but it was a parochial assumption at best. Because the Bible tells the Men who inhabit this planet only about the creation of the world on which *they* live does not mean that creation, nor the universe, nor space nor time began with the events described in that account.

As noted in Chapter 3, Origen thought this world had a beginning in time preceded by an infinite cycle of previous worlds all created by the eternal God, each with its own beginning and end. His idea was highly reminiscent of reincarnation and, to that extent, was heretical (Heb. 9:27). But it does recognize some truth. The Bible does not support the assumption that time began with the creation of this world.

All Dr. Morey's reasoning proves is that God existed before the creation of this earth, a proposition with which no Mormon would argue. Indeed, Christ acquired Wisdom before He engaged in the creation of the earth (Prov. 8:22), and the "sons of God" shouted for joy when its foundations were laid (Job 38:7). Thus, not only God, but His spirit children, of whom Christ was the first, existed with God before the creation of this earth (Eph 1:5).

There is no logical basis for the argument that the infinite nature of God requires His existence before time and space, or that He must be independent of and apart from time and the worlds He has created. These are purely Greek assumptions based upon a metaphysical view

---

[5] Morey, *Battle of the Gods*, 196.
[6] Harvey, *Handbook of Theological Terms*, s.v. "Creation," 63-64.

of the universe that is grossly inaccurate by modern standards. An entirely different view arises from assuming the eternal existence of *both* God and reality. The latter view is consistent with the Bible, science and reason. The word "beginning" is used in reference to many different events in the Bible, but the beginning of time and space is not among them.

"All Things" Does *Not* Include Space and Time

The Greek idea of a God who created and exists outside time and space cannot be supported by Colossians 1:16-17, as Dr. Morey attempts in his thesis. That passage is quoted by him as follows:

> For by Him all things were created, both in the heavens and on earth, visible and invisible, whether thrones or dominions or rulers or authorities—all things have been created through Him and for Him. And He is before all things, and in Him all things hold together.

In this passage, the word translated "all things" is *panta*. It is fairly general in scope, but the "things" encompassed by it are specifically stated in the passage itself. Under such circumstances, the "things" referred to are limited to the things specified. In this instance, those "things" include everything that is in the heavens and on the earth, whether it can be seen or is too small for the naked eye to detect, including Man and his various governments. Although this is a broadly inclusive description, it does not mention time and space. There is no evidence that the Jews of Palestine ever taught that God created time and space. Hence, it is unlikely that a Hebrew writer would have intended to include them by using the word "*panta*" without specifically mentioning them.

Space and Time Are Not "Things"

Again, there is no evidence that the Jews of Palestine even viewed time and space as subjects of creation. Dr. Morey does even more than that.[7] The ancient Greeks personalized attributes such as Love, Wisdom, Good, etc. Dr. Morey treats the dimension of time as though it were just such a personality. Referring to Kronos, the Greek god of time, Dr. Morey concludes, "for time to exist alongside of God means that it too

---

[7] Morey, *Battle of the Gods*, 207.

must be 'divine' in that it is self-existent and not dependent on anything outside of itself including God."[8]

This argument is pure Greek philosophy and assumes a definition of deity for which there is no biblical support. It is not only unbiblical, however, it has no foundation in reality. Time is merely a dimension, a measurement, like height or width. Measurements cannot rationally be described as "self-existent" or "divine."

Likewise, space can hardly be described as a "thing." Strictly speaking, it is, with time, a coordinate system based on distance—height, depth and width, nothing more than empty measurement. In a sense, it is exactly the opposite of a "thing." It is whatever is left over in the *absence* of "all things." (Thus, it would be easy to create space "out of nothing," not that God would bother with so meaningless a gesture.)

A Theological Argument Against the Creation of Time and Space

A purely theological argument against the idea that God created space is somewhat more complex, but no less valid. Without space it would be impossible to describe God as omnipresent. Classical theists teach that God has never changed in His attributes. Yet He could not have possessed the attribute of omnipresence if there were no space in which He could be present. Ergo, He never created space. Rather, it has always existed, as a mathematical concept at least. Physically, space is where God and His handiwork exist. Wherever and whenever God existed, there would have to have been space, or He would not have been a creative being.

Likewise, it would be impossible for the scriptures to say that God is *eternal* without the use of time as a measurement for that eternity. The testimony of the Bible that He is eternal (Deut. 33:27; 1 Tim. 1:17), means that God is *not* outside time. Rather, the fact that He is designated as "eternal" indicates that His existence has been measured by the passage of time for an infinite duration.

God Is Not Confined, or Limited by Space or Time

In a further effort to prove from the Bible the proposition that God created space and time, Dr. Morey notes that God is "self-existent" because He "has life in Himself " (John 5:26). That proposition is, of

---

[8] *Ibid.*, 206.

course, clear throughout the scriptures. However, he goes on to argue that, if God were "in" time, He would be dependent on time for His existence, and so, would not be "self-existent."[9]

How any self-existent being, such as God, whose eternal life is *measured* by time, could be seen as *dependent* upon a form of measurement because He is "in" it, Dr. Morey does not explain. Dr. Morey does not even explain what he has in mind when he speaks of God being "in" time. Subjectively, the phrase would mean that a person's actions are perceived as occurring in some chronological order. Objectively, there are numerous factors affecting the measurement of that time and its duration relative to different observers in the universe. But those issues are irrelevant to any idea of "dependence" on time. No element of dependence is implied by the act of measuring a course of events.

If God did not pay any attention to the order in which His actions occurred or did not know how to count time, one might say He was not "in" time, subjectively speaking, but then He would hardly be a God worthy of worship. The fact that God has life in Himself, while, as Dr. Morey painstakingly points out, lifeless pagan idols do not, has no rational relationship to God's existence "in" time.

Of course, time, as a dimension, is inextricably connected with spatial dimensions in the space-time universe. According to the Theory of Relativity, space-time is closely related to and affected by mass.[10] The full extent of that relationship, however, especially in extreme cases, is not clearly understood by scientists today. A whole new set of rules may come into play when the mass of objects approaches either infinity or zero.

If God had no mass, as classical theists claim, it would be difficult to draw any conclusions about His perception of time. But even if God had no mass, as might be the case for unembodied spirits, He would still be "in" time. If He were active in any way, time would be measurable subjectively as a chronology of His actions. Thus, His existence alone, attended by His eternal activity, would create time. Thus, if God exists, so must time; otherwise, He is not an active God.

---

[9] *Ibid.*, 185.
[10] *Encyclopaedia Britannica*, 1960 ed., s.v. "Space-Time."

Being "In" Time Does Not Give God a Beginning or an End

Dr. Morey argues that God is outside time because He is eternal. He reasons that, "if God were 'in' time like the pagan deities, then He would have a 'beginning' and an 'end.'" This reasoning demonstrates Morey's confused thinking about the concept of time and infinity. There is no reason that being "in" time would require God to have a beginning or an end. In fact, the opposite is true. Only if nothing exists, including God, could one argue that there is no subjectively or objectively measurable time. Thus, only if God were *not* "in" time at some point in the past could He be said to have had a beginning. As long as He has existed, His activities were a subjective measurement of time. To say that there was a beginning of time, is to say that there was a beginning of God. The Bible describes God as eternal, without beginning or end, and the only way for that to be true is if He has *always* existed "in" time.

"Eternity" Is Not the Pleroma

Likewise, there is no merit in the next argument made by Dr. Morey based on Isaiah 57:15. That passage reads: "For thus saith the high and lofty One that *inhabiteth eternity*, whose name is Holy." Dr. Morey claims that the fact God inhabits eternity means that He exists outside time. This argument assumes the very thing it is offered to prove, namely that the term "eternity" refers to a place outside time, the equivalent of the Greek *Pleroma*.

Isaiah was a Hebrew prophet, not a Greek philosopher, and he wrote long before Plato. Thinking that his words would carry Plato's connotations is unreasonable, especially if the balance of the verse is included in the analysis. The passage goes on to say that God dwells in His "high and holy place, with him also that is of a contrite and humble spirit." If Dr. Morey's reasoning were correct, all who have a contrite and humble spirit would also live with God in the *Pleroma*, outside time and space. Classical theism rejects any notion that Men can be transcendent with God.[11] Hence, Dr. Morey's reasoning is self-contradictory.

Straining the Scriptures Provides No Biblical Support

Dr. Morey further cites Isaiah 43:13 in the effort to prove his point. In the NASB (literal translation), that passage reads as follows: "Even

---

[11] See, e.g., Erickson, *Christian Theology*, 1231.

from the day I am He; And there is none who can deliver out of my hand; I act and who can reverse it?" Dr. Morey points out that "from the day" is interpreted in the Septuagint and the Latin Vulgate to mean "before the first day." That translation is consistent with other teachings in the Bible that show God existed before this earth saw its "first day."

However, Dr. Morey goes on to assert that this phrase actually means "before time itself began."[12] That is a stretch the language will not bear. The "first day" is described in Genesis 1, and there is nothing in that chapter, or any other passage of scripture, that says time began with Genesis 1:1.

Being "In" Time Does Not Make God Dependent on Time or Space

The last scriptural argument Dr. Morey mounts is based on Acts 17:24-25. In that passage, Paul explains to the Greeks, consistent with John 5:26, that God does not need anything, "since He Himself gives to all life and breath and all things."[13] From this truth, Dr. Morey argues that God does not need time and space. Rather, time and space are dependent on Him.

This argument is based on the view that reality is a figment of God's imagination. In a real universe, a person is "dependent" on space only if he wishes to build something and there is no space available for him to do so. God has all the limitless space of an infinite universe[14] in which to create heavens and worlds, and there is no one to foreclose Him from using any portion of it. Hence, He is not "dependent" on space in any rational sense.

Dependency on time would only occur if God had a limited period in which to accomplish something. But He is eternal and has perfect foresight with which to plan His actions so as to avoid time management problems. Hence, He is not dependent on time either. God does not have to exist outside time and space in order to avoid

---

[12] Morey, *Battle of the Gods*, 205-206.
[13] *Ibid.*, 187.
[14] Some scientists postulate that the universe is finite, but only in the context of the matter that comprises the universe. There is astronomical evidence, first presented by E. Hubble, that the galaxies and nebulae most distant from earth are receding from it most rapidly. There is no evidence, however, that they are receding into oblivion or coming back upon the earth in some cyclical fashion (as would be the case if the universe were finite and closed). Every indication so far has been that the space available for the expansion of the universe is infinite.

being dependent on either! The idea that, if God were "in" space and time, He would somehow depend on the space-time continuum, or be confined by it is neither a rational nor a biblical notion.

Philosophical Problems With the Creation of Time and Space

The mistaken idea that God created space and time in a dimensional sense presents some serious philosophical problems classical theists have not addressed. The Apologists may have missed these points, but classical theists have simply chosen to ignore them, though they have been raised by other philosophers over the centuries. If God created time, what did He do before its creation? If He created space, where did He do it? Where did He find room for it all? To say that there was plenty of room available for God to create space is to imply that space already existed.

God either did something or He did nothing before He supposedly created time and space. If He did nothing, He could not be described as eternal. If He did something, it can hardly be said that He did it outside some dimensional context defined by space and time. If God did *anything* before He created the earth, He did it in some order, thus creating a subjective chronology of events that was objectively observable by at least one person, namely God Himself. Any objectively discernable chronology of events implies the existence of time as a dimension.

Likewise, if God did anything before He created space, His actions must have taken place in some context, some*where*. That context is what the word "space" defines. If God existed at all before He created space, He must have existed somewhere. The Greeks, who invented the concept, even had a name for the place—the *Pleroma*, a realm of thought. But thoughts, contrary to the notions of Greek metaphysics, do not have an external existence, and even if they did, their existence would necessarily be defined in terms of space and time. To claim that God exists outside any dimensional context definable by space and time is to claim that He does not exist at all. Given the notions of classical theology on this subject, it is no wonder philosophers like Nietzsche, who rejected Greek thinking, declared that God is dead.

Vacuum and Quantum Theory

The foregoing discussion is not intended to address the issue of quantum theory regarding the nature of vacuum. According to modern quantum theory, that which appears empty to Man is actually filled with structure. In certain ways, a detailed description of that structure is equivalent to defining all the physical processes that can take place within it.[15] It is likely that God created this structure and sustains it. He certainly uses it (D&C 88:37, "there is no space in which there is no kingdom; and there is no kingdom in which there is no space"). This may be the way by which God is "the law by which all things are governed." But that issue relates to the creation of *laws*, not the creation of space apart from quantum structure. There is nothing in the Bible about the creation of space and time or "all reality."

Nor does the quantum structure of vacuum vindicate the theories of classical theists. If God created the fabric of space-time, the only rational conclusion is that He did so to His satisfaction and for His personal occupancy and use. There is no reason to think that He would dwell outside a space-time continuum He created, and there is absolutely no indication in the Bible that He does.

Irenaeus Missed an Important Argument

It is interesting that Irenaeus did not detect the fallacies inherent in the notion that God exists in a realm outside the space-time continuum. He argued against the Gnostic idea of a realm beyond the *Pleroma* using logic that also proves there can be no realm that is not defined in some way by the dimensions of space and time.

Irenaeus' simple argument was as follows: "If there is anything beyond the *Pleroma*, there will be a *Pleroma* within this very *Pleroma*, which they declare to be outside of the *Pleroma*, and the *Pleroma* will be contained by that which is beyond."[16]

The same argument can be applied to the idea that God exists in some transcendent location outside time and space. If there were a place beyond time and space, there would necessarily be both time and space in that continuum or God could not be said to exist there at all. Both the real space-time universe and the alleged transcendent location of God must necessarily be defined in terms of space and time. To use Irenaeus' own words and reasoning, both the real universe and that "which they declare to be outside" it is "contained by" it, i.e., defined in terms of space and time. There is no reason to suppose that God would decline

---

[15] *Encyclopaedia Britannica*, 1960 ed., s.v. "Space-Time, Recent Developments."
[16] Irenaeus, *Against Heresies*, 2:1:3.

to live in a space-time continuum He created, rather than the space-time continuum postulated by classical theists.

Biblical Creation of the Heavens and the Earth

The true account of God's creation of this planet was provided by Moses in Genesis 1 and 2. That record recites an orderly, step-by-step process involving specifically identified materials. These are not the actions of a being who shapes reality by His imaginings. It describes a God who acts within the laws He Himself sustains.

In Genesis 1:2, Moses says, "the earth was formless and void [empty], and darkness was over the surface of the deep [the ocean]; and the Spirit of God was moving [moving gently] over the surface of the waters" (NASB, alternate translation in brackets). This passage describes the material God started with when He began to create the Earth as it now exists.

From this verse, it appears the great mass of the earth, consisting largely of water, was already present when the creation account began. It is clear, therefore, that the story of creation given by Moses is not that of the Earth's original creation. It certainly does not involve the idea of bringing space and time into existence. The story in Genesis is one of renovation of pre-existing materials to prepare the earth for Man. The classical idea that there was an original creation of space and time out of nothing is, therefore, extra-biblical speculation.

Renovation of the Earth Appears in the Original Hebrew

That creation of this earth involved the renovation of an existing planet is apparent from a review of the original Hebrew text of Genesis 1:2. The word translated "formless" (NASB) or "without form" (KJV), is *tohu*, which means "a ruin," or "that which is wasted, laid waste."[17] The original Hebrew of the phrase translated "darkness was upon the face of the deep" (KJV) implies that the surface of the ocean was completely hidden from the sun. Thus, the verse could be rendered: "the earth had been ruined and was empty (i.e., lifeless), and sunlight could not penetrate to the surface of the ocean." The last phrase, "and the Spirit of God was moving over the surface of the

---

[17] *Gesenius' Hebrew-Chaldee Lexicon*, s.v. תהו

waters," merely indicates that God, through His Spirit examined these conditions preparatory to beginning His work of reclamation.

Scientists who claim that dinosaurs were wiped off the face of the earth when the sea was partially vaporized by a great asteroid hitting the earth millions of years ago may find some vindication of their theory in this description, but that is not the point here. What appears is that this planet has had a longer history than that given in the Old Testament, and the creation account clearly describes work done on pre-existing materials. No other information about the creation of the heavens and the earth is given in the Bible.

What Is Included in "The Heavens and the Earth?"

Professor Erickson claims "the expression 'the heavens and the earth' is not intended to designate those items alone. It is an idiom referring to everything that is. It is an affirmation that the whole universe came into being through this act of God."[18] No biblical or other authority is given for this assertion, and no rational basis for it appears in Genesis 1:1-3. The phrase does not read as though it had been used idiomatically, nor does Professor Erickson offer any credible support for his claim.

Idiomatic usage can be difficult to determine since idioms often change with time. For example, words used idiomatically by the Jews of Christ's era may not have had the same meaning fifteen hundred years earlier when Moses used them. Unless an idiomatic usage is apparent from the context or other clear evidence, it is better hermeneutics to let the words speak for themselves. Thus, the claim that the Bible describes the creation of the whole universe is not consistent with its plain language.

God's Additional Creations Told in Modern Revelation

Information of any kind about God's creations other than this earth was re-revealed in modern times through the Prophet Joseph Smith. Moses 1:31-35 removes some of the mystery involved in this aspect of the Genesis account:

> And behold, the glory of the Lord was upon Moses, so that Moses stood in the presence of God, and talked with him face to face. And the

---

[18] Erickson, *Christian Theology*, 371.

Lord God said unto Moses: For mine own purpose have I made these things. Here is wisdom and it remaineth in me.

And by the word of my power, have I created them, which is mine Only Begotten Son, who is full of grace and truth.

And worlds without number have I created; and I also created them for mine own purpose; and by the Son I created them, which is mine Only Begotten.

And the first man of all men have I called Adam, which is many.

But only an account of this earth, and the inhabitants thereof, give I unto you. For behold, there are many worlds that have passed away by the word of my power. And there are many that now stand, and innumerable are they unto man; but all things are numbered unto me, for they are mine and I know them.

This is the fullest understanding of "all things" given in inspired writ. Men have only been given an account of their own world. The heavens include innumerable other creations of God, but time and space are never mentioned as being among them.

Ineffective Efforts to Support the *Ex Nihilo* Doctrine From the Bible

No passage in the Bible contradicts Moses' account. None says that God made the universe, the heavens, this earth, time or space, out of nothing (*ex nihilo*). Classical theists, though they preach the *ex nihilo* doctrine,[19] supply no direct biblical support for it, and most of them admit that the doctrine "is not explicitly taught in the Bible."[20]

Professor Erickson claims those passages in the New Testament that refer to the beginning of the world or the beginning of creation (Matt. 13:35; 19:4,8; 24:21; 25:34; Mark 10:6; 13:19; Luke 11:50; John 8:44; 17:24; Rom. 1:20; Eph. 1:4; 2 Thess. 2:13; Heb. 1:10; 4:3; 9:26; 1 Pet. 1:20; 2 Pet. 3:4; 1 John 1:1; 2:13-14; 3:8; Rev. 3:14; 13:8; 17:8) "show that creation involves the beginning of the existence of the world, so that there is no pre-existent matter."[21]

That is far too great a leap to be sustained by the words "beginning" or "foundation" used in these passages, especially in light of Genesis 1:2.

---

[19] E.g., Morey, *Battle of the Gods,* 155-156; Erickson, *Christian Theology,* 367-370.

[20] Van Harvey, *A Handbook of Theological Terms,* s.v. "Creation."

[21] Werner Foerster, *Theological Dictionary of the New Testament,* Gerhard Kittel and Gerhard Friedrich, ed., Geoffrey Bromiley, trans., 10 vols. (Grand Rapids: Eerdmans, 1964-1976), 3:1029.

God, the Creator

The beginning of the existence of the world does not imply the beginning of the existence of matter. There is no logical relationship between the two. The Book of Job speaks of the morning stars singing together and the sons of God shouting for joy when the "cornerstone" was laid for the "foundations of the earth" (Job 38:4-7). This passage gives the impression that the universe, at the time of the earth's beginning, was widely inhabited with a variety of life and matter. The *ex nihilo* doctrine was not taught by the Jews to whom these passages were revealed, nor is there any language in these passages that would support Professor Erickson's proposition. The plain truth is that the Bible does not teach creation *ex nihilo*.

In fact, quite the opposite is implied by the very word Moses used to describe the creation process. The word "created" in Genesis 1:1 is taken from the Hebrew word *bara*. Four meanings of this word are given by Gesenius: (1) to cut, to carve out, or to form by cutting; (2) to create or produce; (3) to beget; and (4) to eat, to feed, or to fatten.[22] Even classical theists have had to admit that creation out of nothing is not consistent with any of these meanings, including "create or produce."[23]

The same word (*bara*) is used to describe God's creation of Man in Genesis 1:27. Later, in Genesis 2:7, Moses states that man was "formed ... of the dust of the ground." The word "formed" in this verse is, again, translated from the Hebrew word, *bara*. Clearly, the use of that word was never intended to imply creation out of nothing. God specifically states the substance out of which Man was created, namely "dust" (Gen. 2:7). Likewise, in Genesis 1:2 he identified the material from which this world was made, a lifeless and ruined planet. Anything more than this is pure speculation, and must be identified as such.

Passages Used to Support *Ex Nihilo* Creation Actually Refute Metaphysics

Some comments in the New Testament are mistakenly seen by classical theists as expressions of support for the idea of *ex nihilo* creation. Romans 4:17 and Hebrews 11:3 are the passages most commonly used for that purpose.[24] In so doing, classical theists misinterpret these passages. That is not surprising. They are quite difficult to translate. They

---

[22] *Gesenius' Hebrew-Chaldee Lexicon*, s.v. בָּרָא.
[23] Erickson, *Christian Theology*, 368.
[24] *Ibid.*, 369.

are practically unintelligible except in the original Greek, and then only if the reader has a clear understanding of the people to whom they were addressed and the culture that prevailed at the time.

Romans 4:17 and "Being"

Romans 4:17 in the KJV reads in pertinent part as follows: "God, who quickeneth the dead, and calleth those things which be not as though they were." The NASB attempts the following translation of this text: "God, who gives life to the dead and calls into being that which does not exist." In the footnotes to the NASB, it is noted that the literal translation of the last phrase reads as follows: "calls the things which do not exist as existing." This passage is the source of orthodox claims that God "spoke" the worlds into existence.[25] The claim is stated thus by Dr. Morey: "We read that God calls things into being by his word."[26] The assumption is that this means God created them out of nothing by simply forming the words that commanded it to be so.

That is not a reasonable interpretation of these passages, even using the translations given above. If God "spoke" everything into existence in the sense of creating it out of nothing, why didn't He simply make it appear in its final form with His first words. Why does Moses describe six scientifically logical stages, or "days," of creation? If God had created everything out of nothing, there would be no reason for Him to employ such a step-by-step approach. This seems especially true if God also created space and time as part of the bargain. He would not have had to engage in any "mediate or derivative creation"[27] such as that described by Moses in Genesis 1 and 2.

Even the translations of Romans 4:17 given above do not teach creation *ex nihilo*. The language of this verse, as it is translated in most Bibles, would best be interpreted as a statement that God gave instructions to others, e.g., Christ, to carry out the work of creation He had planned. That plan clearly involved the use of pre-existing materials (Gen. 1:2).

Unfortunately, none of the translations given above is precisely literal. That is because an exact translation appears, at first, to be unintelligible. The translators have attempted to render the passage so that it

---
[25] Morey, *Battle of the Gods*, 155.
[26] *Ibid*.
[27] Erickson, *Christian Theology*, 367-368.

makes some sense in English, and have assumed that the passage is talking about the method of God's creation. But the literal wording of the Greek text does not address the issue of creation at all. The word-for-word translation is, "God, the (one) making live the dead, and calling the things not being as being."[28]

What does this mean? To understand this expression, one must remember that Paul's letter was addressed to the Romans, a highly Hellenized society in his time. It must also be noted that the word "being" was a term of art in Greek philosophy. It had a specific meaning in Greek metaphysics. "Being" was the word the Platonists used to describe that portion of the metaphysical universe they considered the only true reality, the *Pleroma* where God dwells. Everything else was "not being" or "becoming." That which was "not being" comprised the sensory universe perceived by Men as reality, but believed by the Greek philosophers to be an illusion.

This passage, which discusses Abraham, the father of the Jews, is actually giving the Lord's view of metaphysics. What the literal wording would say to a Hellenized audience is that God declares "the things not being," i.e., the sensory universe that the Greeks thought of as an illusion, as "being," i.e., the universe they believed to be reality. The Hellenized Romans of the time were being told that the God of Abraham, who raises the dead, declares that the sensory universe *is reality*.

Hebrews 11:3 and "Phenomenon"

Hebrews 11:3 in the NASB confirms this biblical message. It reads: "By faith we understand that the ages were planned by the word [command] of God so that what is seen was not made out of things which are visible" (alternate translation in brackets[29]). Like Romans 4:17, even this translation does not teach creation out of nothing. It could be seen as a confirmation of modern scientific views that visible matter is composed of particles too small to be seen by the naked eye. But the translation given above fails to reflect the true import of the original Greek.

The Book of Hebrews is believed by scholars to have been written by someone very familiar with Hellenized Judaism as taught by Philo of Alexandria. The Hebrews to whom this letter was addressed may have been those of that city. There are many internal indications that the

---

[28] *The Interlinear Bible*, Jay Green, trans..
[29] Alternate translation from Bauer, *Greek-English Lexicon*, s.v. ῥῆμα.

book was written, in part, as a refutation of the false notions then rampant among the Jews at that location.[30] This verse should be interpreted in that context.

The English text says that "what is seen" was not made out of things "which are visible." The Greek words translated "what is seen" are *ta blepomena*. These words relate to activity of the human eye. They describe the operations of that sensory organ in the sensible world, the world Men perceive with their sense of sight.

The phrase, "which are visible," comes from the Greek word *phainomenōn*, the very word Plato used to indicate his view that this world is mere appearance, a phenomenon, an apparition. That word is negated in this verse, meaning that the passage is denying the phenomenal nature of "what is seen," i.e., the sensible world.

Thus, the verse teaches that the world of the senses, the real world in which Men live, the world they see with their eyes, is *not* "phenomenon," i.e., illusion. It is not made out of the imaginings of Men, as Parmenides claimed, nor from the imaginings of God, as the Platonists taught. This passage could be rendered, "By faith we understand that the worlds were prepared by the command of God so that what Men see with their eyes is not an illusion." This declaration is a direct refutation of the Greek concept of metaphysics, and appears to have conveyed that understanding to the Hellenized Jews of Alexandria.

Ginomai Does Not Teach Creation Out of Nothing

Some classical theists point to the Greek word *ginomai*, a form of which appears in Hebrews 11:3, as a supposed "proof" that the heavens and the earth were made out of nothing. *Ginomai* is occasionally translated "made," as in Hebrews 11:3. The basic meaning is "come into being," but it is translated quite broadly in the New Testament. Bauer lists four ways the word is used alone as a verb: (1) to be born or begotten; (2) to be made or created; (3) to happen, or take place; and (4) of persons and things that change their nature, to indicate their entering a new condition, i.e., to become something new.[31] The last meaning is especially appropriate in light of Genesis 1:2, but in each case, the meaning is contrary to the notions of classical theism.

---

[30] See Nash, *Christianity and the Hellenistic World*, 89-112.
[31] Bauer, *Greek-English Lexicon*, s.v. γίνομαι.

Development of the *Ex Nihilo* Doctrine in the Early Church

The idea that God created the heavens and the earth out of nothing is unique in that it is a development within Christianity after it became, in essence, a branch of Greek philosophy. The early Greeks and the most notable of the early Apologists, Justin Martyr, taught that God made the earth out of pre-existing matter. The error into which the later Apologists fell with this doctrine is demonstrated by the fact noted in Chapter 7 that it was first promulgated by a Gnostic heretic.

The earliest reference to the idea of creation *ex nihilo* in post-New Testament Christian writing is thought to be the verse in Hermas' *Shepherd* noted in Chapter 5.[32] Irenaeus cited the Shepherd for what he thought was scriptural proof of his position on creation *ex nihilo*.[33] The verse he quotes, however, states "First of all believe that there is one God, who has established all things, and completed them, and having caused that *from what had no being*, all things should come into existence;" (emphasis added).

Irenaeus' interpretation of the phrase "from what had no being" is a reflection of his own bias. It was out of *matter* having "no being" that the Platonists believed the sensory universe was made. While many viewed it as unorganized chaos or chaotic matter, which, under the direction of God, was "becoming," the unrefined matter out of which they believed God made the universe was generally considered an illusion. It had "no being."

The Apologists believed in the metaphysical universe and also assumed that it was an illusion. An illusion, no matter what it is made of is, basically, nothing. It was that step the Apologists took in declaring that God had made the world out of nothing. Thus, the entire concept was based on the Greek view of the universe. Even Hermas' reference appears to reflect the early Greek view of creation out of some kind of unreal, pre-existing matter—something that had "no being." How they made this significant philosophical step is necessary to an understanding of the origins of classical theism today.

Justin Martyr lived much closer in time to Hermas than did Irenaeus. In fact, they were contemporaries in Rome. Justin was undoubtedly familiar with the *Shepherd*, yet he did not take from it the doctrine

---
[32] Hermas, *The Shepherd*, Book 2, Commandment 1.
[33] Irenaeus, *Against Heresies*, 4:20:2.

of creation *ex nihilo*. He believed that the universe was the result of God's action on pre-existing matter. In his writings, that matter appears to have been more substantial than the Greeks or the later Apologists imagined it. His language implies that this was the unified teaching of the Church at that time. Specifically, he wrote:

> And that you may learn that it was from our teachers—we mean the account given through the prophets—that Plato borrowed his statement that *God, having altered matter which was shapeless*, made the world, hear the very words spoken through Moses, who, as above shown, was the first prophet, and of greater antiquity than the Greek writers; and through whom the Spirit of prophecy, signifying how and from what materials God at first formed the world, spake thus: "In the beginning God created the heaven and the earth. And the earth was invisible and unfurnished, and darkness was upon the face of the deep; and the Spirit of God moved over the waters. And God said, Let there be light; and it was so." So that both Plato and they who agree with him, and we ourselves, have learned, and you also can be convinced, that by the word of God *the whole world was made out of the substance spoken of before by Moses*.[34]

Justin's position on this doctrine, however, did not satisfy Irenaeus. The later Apologists were developing a doctrine centered around a transcendent God and based on the metaphysical foundations of Greek philosophy. Hence, they were obsessed with the same questions that had occupied the Greek philosophers. What was the ultimate relation of Matter to God? How did God come into contact with it so as to shape it?[35] These questions assumed ideas about God that differed from biblical teaching, so the answers given by the later Apologists were often vastly different from the answers given in the Bible.

The dualistic view of the universe, common in Platonism at that time, was that Matter and God coexisted as separate things, or substances.[36] There was also an idea that beneath the outward appearance of existing matter was a more basic structure that gave things a certain unity.[37] Democritus taught that all existing things were formed out of atoms.[38] This understanding of the universe is close to

---

[34] Justin, *First Apology*, 59.
[35] Hatch, *Influence of Greek Thought*, 194.
[36] Ibid., 174-175, 177-178.
[37] Ibid., 194-195.
[38] *Encyclopaedia Britannica* (1960 ed.), s.v. "Democritus."

God, the Creator

the modern scientific view of atomic theory, though some much deeper substrata of particles have since been discovered as the most fundamental building blocks of the universe. Other philosophers had differing theories.[39]

At the time of Christ, beliefs about the substructure of matter varied from the position that it was composed of gross and tangible material, e.g., earth, wind, fire and water, to the position of the Apologists, that it was made of empty and formless nothingness.[40] Matter was sometimes conceived as a mass of atoms that would not coalesce according to any principle of order or arrangement without the actions of the Creator, who was seen as a kind of Major General changing a rabble into an organized army.[41] At other times, the matter of which the universe was composed was seen as a vast shapeless but plastic mass, to which the Creator gave form.[42]

It was Basilides, the leader of one of the major branches of Christian Gnosticism in the early second century, who first postulated that God's creation was "out of that which was not."[43] His idea was that creation was like the development of a seed. God made the original seed out of nothing ("immediate creation"). It was the ultimate *summum genus*, the broadest classification of *ousia*, inclusive of all classes of created things. According to Basilides, the "seed" was then developed into the universe and its contents ("mediate or derivative creation").[44] This idea was not unlike Anaxagoras' theory of creation described in Chapter 2.

Basilides taught that the process by which all things came into existence as they now appear was an almost infinite breakdown of the *summum genus* into subordinate groups. The result was an array of things descending from the highest of all abstractions, the Absolute Being and the Absolute Unity, who is God, to the visible objects of sense.[45]

This idea was impressed upon Christianity by Tatian before his defection to the Gnostics. He wrote:

---

[39] Hatch, *Influence of Greek Ideas*, 190-196.
[40] *Ibid.*, 195.
[41] Plutarch, *de anim, procreat.*, 5:3.
[42] Justin, *First Apology*, 10.
[43] Hatch, *Influence of Greek Ideas*, 195.
[44] *Ibid.*, 195-196.
[45] *Ibid.*

> The Lord of the universe being Himself the substance of the whole, not yet having brought any creature into being, was alone: and since all power over both visible and invisible things was with Him, He Himself by the power of His word gave substance to all things with Himself.[46]

Thus, Tatian departed from the teachings of his mentor, Justin, in his speculation on the creation of the matter out of which God ultimately formed the heavens and the earth. He decided that God had made the universe out of . . . Himself! Later, that view was slightly modified by Hippolytus, as will be indicated below.

Professor Hatch acknowledges and rationalizes this philosophical development as follows:

> It had probably been for a long time the unreasoned belief of Hebrew monotheism: the development of the Platonic conception within the Christian sphere gave it a philosophical form: and early in the third century it had become the prevailing theory of the Christian Church. God had created matter. He was not merely the Architect of the universe, but its Source.[47]

Hatch gives the apostate notions of this new theology an appealing sound, but seekers after biblical truth must keep in mind that there is no basis for his statements in the Bible. Nor is there any basis to surmise that this doctrine was ever the "unreasoned belief of Hebrew monotheism." There is no evidence for that assumption in the Old Testament. Indeed, the notion presents serious philosophical problems of its own.

The idea of God making matter directly out of His own *ousia* was Stoic in nature.[48] The early Church tended toward Platonistic dualism.[49] They did not accept the idea that God, whom the philosophers and the Apologists believed to be transcendent, above matter, created it from Himself. The Platonistic idea also involved the *Logos*, an intermediary, who was seen as the active energy of God moving in accord with His thoughts so that it was conceived as being the cause of creation.[50] It is not surprising, therefore, that this explanation was subsequently adopted by the early Church as a refinement of Tatian's teachings.

---

[46] Tatian, *Speech to the Greeks*, 5.
[47] Hatch, *Influence of Greek Ideas*, 197.
[48] *Ibid.*, 175-177.
[49] *Ibid.*, 194-196.
[50] *Ibid.*, 180-181.

The one recognized Christian intermediary, identified by John as the true *Logos*, was Christ. So, Hippolytus took the *ex nihilo* theory to its final stage, responding to the problem of a transcendent and perfect God creating a material and imperfect universe by using the very reasoning the Greek philosophers had employed. According to him, God first made His *Logos* or Reason *out of Himself*, then Reason produced the material universe out of nothing. His view was expressed as follows:

> He was one, alone by Himself, and by His will He made the things that are, that before were not, except so far as they existed in His foreknowledge.... This supreme and only God begets Reason first, having formed the thought of him, not reason as a spoken word, but as an internal mental process of the universe. Him alone did He beget from existing things: for the Father himself constituted existence, and from it came that which was begotten. The cause of the things that came into being was the Reason, bearing in himself the active will of Him who begat him, and not being without knowledge of the Father's thought.... so that when the Father bade the world come into being, the Reason brought each thing to perfection one by one, thus pleasing God.[51]

Though the scriptures teach that Christ acted under the direction of the Father in creating the heavens and the earth, the rest of Hippolytus' statement has no biblical support whatever. It is practically a carbon copy of the Greek notions, theories and philosophies of the time. He does not follow the story of Creation, but gives a slightly Christianized version of the explanation taught for centuries by the Greek philosophers.

Conclusion

What the Apologists and the Greek philosophers were seeking was more information about the Creation than they could ascertain from the Bible, even more information than they had the technological ability to comprehend. Rather than accept what they had been given in the Bible at face value or seek further revelation, as Joseph Smith did, they satisfied their thirst for knowledge by drinking from the cup of Greek metaphysics. The result, not surprisingly, was error.

Their first error was the idea that God created reality—not just the real universe, but reality itself, including space and time. Compounding

---

[51] Hippolytus, *The Refutation of All Heresies*, 10:28-29.

this error, they reasoned that God created all reality *ex nihilo*, out of nothing. These ideas are not biblical, yet they have been perpetuated for centuries in classical theism. As demonstrated above, their conception is exclusively Greek.

Summary

1. Classical theism teaches that God created not only "the heavens and the earth" but "all reality," including *space* and *time*.
2. Classical theism asserts the doctrine that God created all things out of nothing.
3. The Bible teaches that God created "all things" (Col. 1:16-17, and others), but it is important to maintain a Hebrew perspective when deciding what "all things" includes.
4. Efforts to find biblical support for the idea that God created space and time have been scanty. In making such efforts, classical theists have made assumptions founded in Greek philosophy on which to ground their interpretations. One such assumption is that time did not begin until the creation of this earth.
5. God existed before this earth was created, but nothing in the Bible says that time did not also exist then.
6. "All things" in Colossians 1:16-17 comes from a Greek word that includes only the things being discussed in the context of the passage in which the word appears. Space and time are not mentioned in the context of that passage.
7. Time is merely a dimension, and space is the *absence* of everything. Apart from the quantum structure of the universe, space and time are not "things" as that word is used in Colossians 1:16-17.
8. Without space, there would be no context in which to describe God as "omnipresent." If there were no space before the creation of this earth, God would not have been omnipresent.
9. The fact that God "has life in Himself" (John 5:26)—that is, He is "self-existent"—does not mean that He exists outside space and time. Space and time are not confinements to the Creator.
10. Seeing time in the ancient Greek context of beginnings and endings, classical theists claim that if God were "in" time, He would have a beginning. The Bible, however, describes God as eternal, which

God, the Creator

would require His existence during all time. In the absence of time, God would not be eternal.
11. Classical theists view "eternity" as the Greek "*Pleroma.*" Thus, when Isaiah 57:15 says that God "inhabiteth eternity," they claim it proves their point about God's metaphysical transcendence above time and space. However, to make that connection requires a *Greek* view of the universe. Isaiah was a *Hebrew* prophet, to whom the notions of metaphysics were unknown.
12. Isaiah 57:15 states that those with a contrite and humble spirit will live in "eternity" with God. If "eternity" were the Greek "*Pleroma,*" as classical theists claim, it would mean that the contrite and humble are going to live in the same transcendent state as God. That is contrary to orthodox Christian doctrine. Hence, the classical belief that "eternity" is outside the real space-time universe contradicts other teachings of classical theism.
13. Contrary to some classical arguments, Isaiah 43:13 does not say that God existed before time, only that He existed before the first day of this earth's existence.
14. The fact that God is not in need of anything (Acts 17:24-25) does not mean He exists outside space and time. He is not dependent on space or time, because He has all that He needs.
15. If God created time, what did He do before its creation? Any series of actions on His part would result in a chronology, and hence a subjective timetable.
16. If God created space, in what context did He act before its creation?
17. To claim that God lives outside space and time is to claim that He does not exist.
18. If God exists and acts, there is space and time where He is. If He lives outside space and time, there must be space and time in that realm also.
19. The biblical account of creation implies a God who acts within the laws He Himself has established.
20. Genesis 1:2 contradicts the notion that God created the earth out of nothing.
21. Genesis 1:2 suggests that the Spirit of God found the earth "wasted," or ruined, and lifeless, with its atmosphere contaminated, and renovated it for man.

22. "The heavens and the earth" is not an idiom that includes all reality. Genesis 1:1-3 clearly indicate the context of the phrase.
23. Modern revelation specifically states that God gave Moses an account of this earth and its inhabitants only.
24. Nothing in any biblical reference to the beginning of the world or to God's creation implies the absence of matter prior to the earth's creation.
25. The Bible does not teach the doctrine that the earth or the heavens were created out of nothing (*ex nihilo*).
26. The Hebrew word for created, "*bara*," clearly implies formation out of pre-existent matter.
27. Romans 4:17 does not teach that God "called" the universe into existence out of nothing. It explains that God has declared the sensory universe, which the Greeks thought was unreal or "not being," to be true reality, what the Greeks called "being."
28. Hebrews 11:3 has also been misinterpreted in regard to the *ex nihilo* doctrine. It, too, contradicts the Greek belief in metaphysics. It teaches that what Man perceives with his senses is not an illusion.
29. Contrary to the efforts of some classical theists to twist the scriptures, the word "*ginomai*" does not mean "come into being out of nothing." Rather, it refers to something entering into a new condition, i.e., becoming something new.
30. The idea of creation out of nothing contradicts not only the Bible, but early Christian writings through the time of Justin Martyr.
31. The early Apologists gradually developed the *ex nihilo* doctrine by working from their foundation in Greek philosophy, which saw the sensory universe as an illusion. An illusion is basically nothing. It has "no being."
32. The *Shepherd* of Hermas said that God created all things out of that which had "no being." This writing suggests the direction taken by later Apologists, many of whom regarded the *Shepherd* as scripture.
33. The step from "no being" to "nothing" was first taken by Basilides, a Gnostic heretic, who postulated that God made His creation "out of that which was not."
34. Tatian taught that God created all things out of "Himself." That doctrine was later modified, as expressed by Hippolytus, to the teach-

ing that He made the *Logos* out of "Himself" and the universe out of nothing.
35. Hatch regarded the development in Christian/Greek philosophy of the *ex nihilo* doctrine as a positive development. God, as he put it, was not only the "Architect" of the universe, He created it all out of nothing. Like other classical theists, he was not concerned that this doctrine has no biblical basis.

The Omnipotent God

Classical theism, the Bible, and Mormonism all teach that omnipotence is an attribute of Deity. But what is omnipotence? The word does not occur in the Bible, so how is this attribute to be understood in scripture? Is it a real attribute of a real deity, or can it only be possessed by a Being who has the nature ascribed to Him by classical theists? What powers does this attribute include? Can God make a rock so large He cannot lift it? These are a few of the questions that intrigued the early Church fathers and classical theologians over the centuries.

How Powerful Is Omnipotence?

Dr. Beckwith states the doctrinal position of orthodox Christianity, as follows: "God can do anything that is (1) logically possible (see below), and (2) consistent with being a personal, incorporeal, omniscient, omnipresent, immutable, wholly perfect, and necessary Creator."[1]

Of course, Mormons disagree with some aspects of Beckwith's assertion, but insofar as it describes God's omnipotence, it is a reasonably accurate expression of Mormon doctrine. In fact, it is reminiscent of a passage in the Book of Mormon that states, "the Lord God hath power to do all things which are according to his word" (Alma 7:8).

The "(see below)" in Dr. Beckwith's statement refers to the following explanation that is not only illuminating but problematical for classical theists: "God can only do what is logically possible . . . God cannot do or create what is logically *im*possible."[2]

---

[1] Beckwith, "Philosophical Problems," 2.
[2] *Ibid*.

THE OMNIPOTENT GOD 305

The Bible never actually makes that broad of a statement. Numbers 23:19 says that God does not lie, and both Titus 1:2 and Hebrews 6:18 teach that He *"cannot* lie," that such an act would be *"impossible"* for Him. It would appear therefore that there are certain things He cannot do, but it is not because He lacks the power to do them. It is because they are inconsistent with His nature and position as God.

That He *does not* do anything logically impossible is apparent from an examination of His works, but that He *cannot* do something logically impossible is a concept first expressed by Augustine. Dr. Beckwith quotes him, as follows: "Neither do we lessen [God's] power when we say He cannot die or be deceived. This is the kind of inability which, if removed, would make God less powerful than He is. . . . It is precisely because He is omnipotent that for Him some things are impossible."[3]

In Matthew 19:24, Christ said, "It is easier for a camel to go through the eye of a needle, than for a rich man to enter the kingdom of God." The Greek word for "needle" that Christ used in this statement was *raphis*, which refers to a sewing needle. To fit a camel through the eye of a sewing needle certainly seems an impossible task, though perhaps not a logically impossible one.[4] Christ's disciples were astonished at His statement, and questioned it (Matt. 19:25). In verse 26, Christ explains that "With men this is impossible, but with God *all things are possible*."

That the phrase "all things are possible" was meant to be limited in its scope is made clear in the Joseph Smith Version (JSV) of that passage. There, the pertinent portion of Matthew 19:26 is rendered as follows: "With men this is impossible, but if they will forsake all things for my sake, with God whatsoever things I speak are possible." The implication is that God can do all that He *says* He will do.

A similar statement is made by the angel who came to Mary before the conception of Christ. Mary questioned the possibility of a virgin conceiving the Son of God (Luke 1:34), and the angel explained how the feat would be accomplished without the loss of her virginity (Luke 1:35). Then, as if anticipating Mary's disbelief, the angel mentioned her

---

[3] Augustine, *City of God*, 5:10.
[4] It is often noted that a small gate through the city wall in Jerusalem was called "the Eye of the Needle." Those who used this gate had to completely unload their camels in order to get them through on their knees. Although this is a wonderful analogy, there is nothing in the biblical record that indicates it was specifically what Christ had in mind when He taught this doctrine.

cousin Elizabeth's recent conception and stated (Luke 1:37, NASB): "For nothing will be impossible with God."

The NASB notes the literal translation of this passage as "For not any word will be impossible with God." The import of that language is exactly the same as that of the JSV in Matthew 19:26. The point of both verses is that whatever God says He will do, He can do, no matter how impossible the task may seem to Men. Nowhere in scripture does God say He will do something that is logically impossible. Therefore, Augustine's point may be well taken even though it is not a strictly biblical expression.

In fact, the truth of Augustine's reasoning can be seen in the circumstances that followed Christ's prayer in Gethsemane the night before He was crucified. Mark 14:36 (NASB) records His words as follows: "Abba! Father! All things are possible for Thee; remove this cup from Me; yet not what I will, but what Thou wilt." Subsequent events demonstrated that, although "all things are possible" for God, the course of the atonement, as prophesied by God from the beginning, was not modified despite Christ's touching request. All things may be possible for God, but not all things are expedient to Him (1 Cor. 6:12; 10:23).

Problems with the Classical View

Consistent with the reasoning of Thomas Aquinas,[5] Dr. Beckwith analyzes the words of the angel to Mary in Luke 1:37 quoted above. He states that the angel "is not talking about internally contradictory or contrary 'entities,' since such 'things' are not really things at all. They are merely words strung together that appear to be saying something when in fact they are saying nothing. Hence, *everything* is possible for God, but the logically impossible is *not* truly a *thing*."[6]

While Mormons would generally agree with this statement, it presents a serious philosophical problem for classical theists. As noted in Chapter 10, classical theism asserts that God is three numerically separate persons who are numerically only one individual. That is clearly a paradox, a logical impossibility. Does that mean the Trinity is "not truly a thing," as Dr. Beckwith's reasoning suggests? If a logical impossibility is not a "thing," if it is something that cannot exist at all,

---

[5] Thomas Aquinas, *Summa Theologica*, 1:25:3.
[6] Beckwith, "Philosophical Problems," page 3.

as Dr. Beckwith has so insightfully declared, then it follows that the Triune God of orthodox Christianity cannot exist.

This argument is not presented either facetiously or disrespectfully. Classical theists simply need to apply the same good logic and reasoning to their position on the triune nature of God as they do to other aspects of their beliefs. If they would do so, the fallacies in their theology could be stripped away.

Omnipotence and Corporeality

The biggest obstacle to understanding biblical teachings about the omnipotence of God is the refusal of classical theists to accept the idea that the "anthropomorphic" God described in the Bible could possess this attribute. They assume, from nothing more than *a priori* reasoning, that a God who is corporeal, as the Bible describes Christ and the Father, is "finite," and therefore "limited," incapable of infinite power, i.e., omnipotence.

This assumption is based on ancient Greek notions and reflects the limited understanding of the universe, and the laws by which it is governed, possessed by the philosophers of that day. As previously noted, the early Greek philosophers believed God exists outside the real universe, above space and time. In their limited view, He was pure Mind or Being and could not be better described to Men because He was incomprehensible.

The Greeks were prone to establish hierarchies as a means of increasing their understanding. The technique was part of their orderly approach to gaining knowledge. To the Greek mind, Matter, being farthest from their idea of God, has always been lowest in the hierarchy of materials, with pure Mind or Spirit at the highest end. That the Spirit is manifest as fire (Judges 15:14; Acts 2:1-4) suggests a relationship between spirit and light or pure energy. In the Platonistic hierarchy, therefore, pure energy would have been at the highest end of the material spectrum, with mass, the gross characteristic of material, at the lowest end.[7]

This assumed hierarchy of materials, a fundamental precept of Greek philosophy, is at the heart of many assumptions about God made by the Apologists and by classical theists today.[8] To orthodox

---
[7] Hatch, *Influence of Greek Ideas*, 176-177, 196.
[8] *Ibid.*, 195-197.

theologians, being the greatest and most powerful Being in the universe means God is farthest from gross, imperfect, undesirable Matter, and closest to pure spirit or energy.[9] This is an important factor in the reasoning of classical theists against the corporeality of God and His omnipotence.

Einstein and the Power of Corporeality

The entire Greek concept was turned upside down in 1905 when a physicist from the University of Zurich named Albert Einstein derived a simple equation that demonstrates conclusively the equivalence of matter and energy. What was philosophically important about that discovery was not its consistency with Stoic monism, but the ratio of that equivalence.

The formula is $e=mc^2$. It states that, if m units of mass could be made to disappear, the units of energy that would be liberated would be m times the speed of light *squared*! In actual numbers, using the speed of light in a vacuum (2.99793×10^{10} centimeters per second), this means that it would require nearly 900 quintillion (900,000,000,000,000,000,000) units of energy to be equivalent to just *one* unit of mass!

The theological implications of that ratio have never been considered by classical theists. What it means is that the ancient Greeks had their hierarchy of materials in an order exactly the opposite of what exists in the real universe. A being composed of Matter contains, by nature, 900 quintillion times more energy (i.e., power) than would a being composed of pure energy.

Thus, the hierarchy of materials conceived by the ancient Greeks, when viewed from the perspective of energy or omnipotence, is exactly the opposite of that which exists in the universe God created. In His universe, Matter is at the high end of the scale. A material, corporeal being represents, by nature, a much greater concentration of energy than an immaterial, incorporeal being. In fact, Einstein's simple formula suggests that a corporeal God would represent, by nature, a concentration of energy approximately 900 quintillion times greater than an incorporeal God.

Classical theists might argue that concentration of energy in a corporeal God is irrelevant to any theological discussion of His omnipotence. But, if God is real, and the Bible treats Him as though He were,

---
[9] *Ibid.*, 184-185.

His omnipotence would require the ability to exercise real power, and real power requires energy.

They may also argue that, since their idea of an incorporeal God is one who fills the universe, there is no need for God to be corporeal—infinite size being a more than adequate compensation for lack of energy density. Rational consideration of that argument leads, however, to the conclusion that an incorporeal entity who is attenuated throughout the universe would simply be weaker everywhere than a corporeal being who could instantaneously travel to any spot in the universe He chose.

Under any logical scenario, the nature of matter, as demonstrated by Einstein, will always make corporeality a better medium in which to exercise omnipotence than any medium that is incorporeal. This is especially so in light of the fact that the ratio of corporeality to incorporeality could be as much as 900 quintillion to one. The point is that it is entirely logical and consistent to teach that the corporeal God described in the Bible is omnipotent.

Mormonism Teaches that God Is Omnipotent

The understanding that God has all power is expressed not only in the Bible, but in many uniquely Mormon scriptures. For example, in the Book of Mormon, Mosiah 4:9 and Alma 26:35 each state that God has "all power." The Doctrine and Covenants teaches that "he [God] is possessor of all things; for all things are subject unto him, both in heaven and on the earth, the life and the light, the Spirit and the power, sent forth by the will of the Father through Jesus Christ, his Son" (D&C 50:27).

This passage teaches that God remains, not only omnipotent, but the *most* powerful, the One to whom all other powers, principalities, thrones and administrations are subject. The fact that God is corporeal, that He has what Paul called a "spiritual body," is both biblically and scientifically consistent with that view.

Classical theists must avoid the assumption that corporeality limits God. That is a Greek notion that should be rejected along with Aristotelian physics. Einsteinian physics is consistent with the Bible's teachings that an all-powerful being is corporeal.

Summary

1. Mormon doctrine teaches that God is all-powerful ("Almighty").
2. "Almighty," from a scriptural perspective, means God has "power to do all things according to his word." Whatever God says He can or will do, He has the power to do it.
3. Classical theists believe that God can do only what is logically possible. Doing that which is logically impossible is not a real power. While that is inconsistent with aspects of their own theology, it is a fair statement of biblical teaching.
4. Classical theists are reluctant to accept the idea of corporeality as consistent with omnipotence. To them corporeality is "finite" and therefore "limited." This notion is not based on any biblical doctrine, but on the hierarchy of substance established by the Greek philosophers.
5. In the Greek hierarchy, Mind was at the top of power and perfection, and Matter was at the bottom.
6. The Greek hierarchy was shown to be exactly the opposite of reality by Einstein's Theory of Relativity which equated energy vastly disproportionate to mass.
7. In the real universe, matter is highly concentrated energy. That suggests that a corporeal being will, by nature, have 900 quintillion times as much energy ("power") as an incorporeal being.
8. In light of the ratio implied in $e=mc^2$, a large incorporeal being, even one of infinite dimension, would simply be weaker everywhere than a corporeal being who can be at any spot He chooses.
9. The belief of Mormon theology that God is corporeal is more consistent with omnipotence than the Greek notion that He is incorporeal.

14

The Omniscient God

Classical Theism's Position on God's Omniscience

Classical theists believe that "God is all-knowing, and His all-knowingness encompasses the *past, present*, and *future*"[1] (emphasis in original). This statement sounds perfectly biblical, but because classical theists accept the metaphysical idea of God's transcendency, they have an entirely non-biblical view of *how* God knows the past, present and future. Since Mormons reject the metaphysical view of the universe, classical theists accuse them of not believing in God's omniscience at all. Without the doctrine of transcendency, they cannot understand how God could know everything.

Another reason for the orthodox rejection of Mormon theology on God's omniscience is the LDS belief in God's corporeality. Because of the limitations they see in fallen Man based on Greek philosophical beliefs, classical theists claim that this aspect of Mormon theology denies the very possibility of God's omniscience altogether. These allegations, like their claim that a corporeal God cannot be omnipotent, reflect a naive view of the universe based on a lack of scientific understanding and a refusal to accept the Bible's teachings at face value.

Can God Know the Future?

While some Evangelical theologians disagree with the assertion that God knows the future as well as the past and present, orthodox Christianity holds strictly to the view stated above by Dr. Beckwith.[2]

---

[1] Beckwith, "Philosophical Problems," 3.
[2] *Ibid.*

Classical theists have recently been contending with process theologians who follow the thinking of Alfred North Whitehead. He rejected the idea that "being," the *ousia* of the Greek *Pleroma*, is the only true reality. He did not, however, divorce himself entirely from Greek philosophy, but maintained that process or "becoming" is true reality. By so doing, he takes a position similar to that of Heraclitus. Not surprisingly, these modern anti-metaphysical thinkers have made no improvement on the philosophies of the Greeks. That is in part because they continue to seek the truth about God by merely thinking, without seeking the benefit of guiding revelation from God.

Process theologians shortsightedly argue that it is impossible in principle to know the future, so it does not detract from God's perfection for Him not to know the future. For this heresy, Dr. Morey has correctly taken process theology to task in his book, *Battle of the Gods*, where he employs numerous biblical passages to prove the foreknowledge of God. (See, e.g., Isaiah 41:21-23, 25-26; 44:6, 7, 26, 28; 45:11, 21; 46:9-11; Acts 2:23; 15:18; Romans 8:29, 30; 11:2; Ephesians 1:5,11; Galatians 3:8; 1 Peter 1:2.)

Unfortunately, although the Bible speaks of God's foreknowledge, significant disagreements between the Bible and the classical view of God's omniscience remain. The classical view is expressed by Miley as follows:

> Omniscience must be God's perfect conception of himself, and of all things and events, without respect to the time of their existence or occurrence. Any limitation in any particular must be a limitation in the divine knowledge.
>
> Omniscience must be an immediate and eternal knowing. The knowledge which is not immediate and eternal must be an acquisition. For the acquisition there must be time and a mental process. Such knowledge must be limited. An acquired omniscience is not a thinkable possibility. The ideas are too alien for any scientific association in rational thought. Hence we must either admit an immediate and eternal knowing in God or deny his omniscience. These alternatives are complete and absolute.
>
> Omniscience, in the truest, deepest sense of the term, must be prescient of all futuritions, whatever their nature or causality. Future free volitions must be included with events which shall arise from necessary causes. Only with such prescience can there be a true

omniscience. Such a divine omniscience is the common Christian faith.[3]

This reasoning shows how classical theism has become more impressed with the Greek label used to describe this attribute of God than with the biblical teaching itself. Combined with their metaphysical viewpoint, this misguided focus has caused classical theists to err in their understanding of how God knows the past, present and future.

The idea that God could acquire omniscience is rejected despite the fact that the Bible says Christ *acquired* wisdom before the earth was created (Prov. 8:22). (This passage will be discussed in Chapter 16.) Yet classical theists recognize that "Jesus has this attribute of deity also, for Peter says, 'Lord, you know all things; you know that I love you' (John 21:17)."[4] If Christ acquired wisdom and He knows all things, acquisition of omniscience must be possible (see Part 4).

The other point of disagreement between classical theism and biblical theology revolves around the basic Greek assumption that God cannot be corporeal without being limited in some fashion. That view leads to the false notion that if God were corporeal, it would limit His ability to understand, making Him incapable of omniscience. This, too, is contradicted by the Bible's clear testimony that Christ is corporeal and omniscient. Men are to learn of the Father through the Son. It follows that the Father must have obtained omniscience in the same way Christ did, and must possess it despite being corporeal.

Mormon Theology On God's Omniscience

This does not mean God is *currently* learning new things about the universe or the future, or is otherwise in the process of becoming omniscient. As noted above, classical theists have routinely accused Mormons of rejecting the idea of God's omniscience on this very basis. Dr. Beckwith claims that Mormons believe God "does not know the future."[5] Instead, he says, Mormons believe God progresses

---

[3] Miley, *Systematic Theology*, 1:180.
[4] Elwell, *Evangelical Dictionary of Theology*, 454.
[5] For this proposition, Dr. Beckwith has cited Blake Ostler, "The Mormon Concept of God," *Dialogue: A Journal of Mormon Thought* 7 (Summer 1984): 76-78. If Ostler has not been misquoted, the fact he has misconstrued Mormon doctrine on this point is irrelevant. Mormon doctrine is not found in the writings of philosophers, but in the scriptures and the teachings of the prophets released to the Church in official doctrinal statements.

in knowledge as the future unfolds.[6] This is basically the view of process theology, mentioned above, and is an entirely incorrect statement of Latter-day Saint belief. Mormons teach that God, like Christ, once made such progress, but that He is now and has been, from before the beginning of creation, omniscient of all things, whether past, present or future.

Because Mormons believe God has a physical body, it has been easy for classical theists to believe that Mormon doctrine denies God any certain knowledge of the future. It is understandable that they take this position, given their own understanding, derived from Greek rationalism, of how God knows all things. But that fundamental misconception is not Mormon doctrine.

Mormon scriptures, which include the Bible, do not suggest any progression in the Father's omniscience, except by analogy to Christ's progression (see John 5:19), and His progression is specifically said to have predated the creation of the earth (Prov. 8:22-23). (See also Luke 2:52, which indicates some progression in knowledge by Christ during His mortal life here on earth.)

There is no record of any progression in knowledge by the Father in any scriptural record Mormons possess. Rather, the LDS position is succinctly stated in the Book of Mormon, 2 Nephi 9:20, which says: "For he knoweth all things, and there is not anything save he knows it." That statement covers omniscience completely, and applies with equal force to all members of the Godhead. Philosophers of any religion who rationalize that view, claiming that the future is not a "thing" which can be known, are worthy of the question God directed at Job (Job 38:2 NASB): "Who is this that darkens counsel by words without knowledge?"

The Book of Mormon repeatedly refers to God's "foreknowledge of all things" (e.g., Alma 13:3, 7), and denounces those who teach that no one can know the future or anything else they cannot see (e.g., Alma 30:13-15). The Doctrine and Covenants makes the doctrinal point crystal clear in Section 93, which defines truth as "knowledge of things as they are, and as they were, *and as they are to come*" (verse 24). Verse 26 states that Christ "received a fulness of truth, yea, even of *all truth*" (emphasis added). "All truth," under the definition just given in verse 24

---

[6] Beckwith, "Philosophical Problems," 6.

of that passage, definitely includes knowledge of the future: "knowledge of things . . . as they are to come."

The point could not be made more clearly. God is a God of truth (Deut. 32:4), the truth is in Him (Book of Mormon, 2 Nephi 1:26, 2:10), and He is full of truth (D&C 84:102). Claiming that God does not have that portion of the truth defined as "knowledge of things . . . as they are to come" (i.e., knowledge of the future) directly contradicts these passages, and hence is *not* Mormonism.[7]

Classical Theism's Idea of How God Knows the Future

Orthodox Christian theologians reject the understanding that the corporeal God described in the Bible knows all of the past and present, let alone the future. That is because the real God lives in the real universe, while the God they have adopted from Greek philosophy exists outside the real universe, outside of space and, specifically, outside of *time*. From that vantage point they believe He can look forward or backward in time at will, and thus, *literally*, see "the end from the beginning" (Isa. 46:10).[8]

This view follows directly from the position of orthodox theology that the universe is, in essence, a figment of God's imagination. For classical theists, God's knowledge of the future is related to their belief that He imagined all reality into existence.

In an effort to communicate this concept, classical theists will sometimes compare God to a person who sits on a steeple while he watches a parade:

> He sees all parts of the parade at the different points on the route rather than only what is going past him at the moment. He is aware of what is passing each point of the route. So God also is aware of what is happening, has happened, and will happen at each point in time. Yet at any given point within time, he is also conscious of the distinction between what is now occurring, what has been, and what will be.[9]

---

[7] Supposedly, Ostler claims that Brigham Young, Wilford Woodruff, Lorenzo Snow and B. H. Roberts all held views consistent with the idea that God's omniscience does not include the future (Ostler, "Mormon Concept of God," 76-78). However, there are no official, or canonical statements or declarations by these men to that effect, and their statements could easily be misconstrued if they were taken out of chronological context.

[8] Morey, *Battle of the Gods*, 238.

[9] Erickson, *Christian Theology*, 275.

This analogy is typical of many devised by the ancient Greeks. It has no relationship to reality. Rather, it is intended to make an irrational concept feel comfortable to those who have accepted it. Sitting on top of a steeple, one would see three-dimensional objects all at a single moment in time. The dimension of time does not enter the equation or the analogy in any rational way. Nor is it possible to translate this analogy into any scientifically accurate view of time. The idea of God sitting up in a Greek *Pleroma* watching actual events that have not yet occurred parade past Him in the future is a figment of Greek metaphysical imagination. It is not taught in the Bible, nor in science, and is not true.

There is the possibility, that God could see holographic records of the past and, in the same format, precise representations of projected future events. It is surprising how classical theists will deny God the power to accomplish such things, when even Man has been able to achieve a rudimentary level of such technology. The technology necessary to produce a precise view of the future must surely be known to God. The fact that the ancient Greeks never imagined the possibility is no reason to bar the implications of technology from theological consideration.

How Does God Really Know the Future?

There is no reason to believe that, in a real universe, there is any way to view events as they occur when they have not, as yet, transpired. Though some scientists may disagree, time does not appear to be the kind of continuum that extends beyond current existence. By viewing the light traveling away from past events, it is theoretically possible to see things that occurred in the past, even in one's *own* past.[10] But the ability to see the future literally appears to be a logical impossibility. As

---

[10] One could see his own past if he were traveling in a spaceship near a black hole at a speed close to the speed of light. For reasons derived from Einstein's Theory of Relativity, the speed of light across a black hole is slower than the speed the spaceship can attain if it skirts around the edge of the black hole. When the spaceship gets to the opposite side, it will arrive before its image from the other side can get there, allowing the occupants to look back across the black hole and see themselves before they made the trip. But obviously, the ship cannot travel to the new position on the opposite side of the black hole unless it leaves its earlier position. Hence, it is never possible, even theoretically, to look across a black hole and see into the future. One can only see into the past.

noted in Chapter 13, there is no reason to believe God does anything that is logically impossible.

How then does the real God of the Bible know the future? Speculation on the possibility of time travel is not necessary to answer that question. One need merely read God's own explanation of His omniscience regarding the future in the verses relied on by Dr. Morey. In Isaiah 46:10-11 (NASB) God describes Himself and His powers, as follows:

> Declaring the end from the beginning
> And from ancient times things which have not been done,
> Saying, "My purpose will be established,
> And I will accomplish all My good pleasure;"
> Calling a bird of prey from the east,
> The man of My purpose from a far country.
> Truly I have spoken; truly I will bring it to pass.
> I have planned it, surely I will do it.

Notice that the passage does not say God *sees* "the end from the beginning," as classical theists claim. He "*declares* the end from the beginning." Of course, as a practical matter, His foreknowledge and foreordination or predestination of His purposes may be spoken of as a kind of "foreseeing," as it is in Galatians 3:8. That verse says that the *scriptures* contain its foresight. God knows the future not because He has observed it from some vantage point beyond time, but because He has "*declared*" it and has "*planned*" it," and He has the power to carry out His plans ("surely, I will *do* it").

Other scriptures agree with this understanding of how God knows the future. Lamentations 3:37 (NASB) indicates that God knows the future because He has declared what it will be. It asks, "Who is there who speaks and it comes to pass, Unless the Lord has commanded it?" Likewise, in Mark 13:31, Christ said, "Heaven and earth will pass away, but My words will not pass away." (See also, Matt. 24:35, and Luke 1:20.) In the Book of Mormon, God says "I will fulfil all that which I have caused to be spoken by the mouth of my holy prophets" (3 Nephi 1:13). The Doctrine and Covenants states that "as the words have gone forth out of my mouth even so shall they be fulfilled" (D&C 29:30). And the Pearl of Great Price, Moses 4:30, agrees as follows: "For as I, the Lord God, liveth, even so my words cannot return void, for as they go forth out of my mouth they must be fulfilled."

Thus, both the Bible and uniquely Mormon scriptures teach that God's perfect knowledge of the future is derived from His perfect knowledge of all things past and present, coupled with perfect wisdom and complete power over all things. God has existed for all eternity. His knowledge of the past is both infinite and the result of direct experience. His knowledge of the present follows from His ability at all times to be in communication with every portion of the universe simultaneously. Knowing everything about the past and the present, knowing all the laws that govern the universe and how to apply them properly, and having all power to accomplish His purposes, God can determine with perfect accuracy everything that will happen in the future, just as if it were before His eyes at the present moment.

This is a rational conclusion based on a real universe, a real God and real laws established by Him. It is entirely consistent with God's corporeal nature and with modern scientific theory. God has a perfect knowledge of the genetic code of every living thing, and knows, from all eternity, the personalities of every sentient being in the universe, so that their volitional acts can be anticipated with the highest degree of precision in any given situation. He knows the movements and influence of every quark, every atom, and every molecule in the universe, and can control those movements, if necessary. He can call on both Men and beasts to help bring to pass His will. To such a Being the future cannot be a mystery. Such knowledge would make all future contingencies as plain as a television drama. God's omnipotent power will fulfill all His purposes. There can be no doubt that every detail of the future is under His exacting influence and within His perfect knowledge, without His ever having to interfere with the free agency of any individual.

Truly, the Doctrine and Covenants (38:1-2) declares:

> Thus saith the Lord your God, even Jesus Christ, the Great I AM, Alpha and Omega, the beginning and the end, the same which looked upon the wide expanse of eternity, and all the seraphic hosts of heaven, before the world was made;
>
> The same which knoweth all things, for all things are present before mine eyes.

Greek Barriers to Understanding the Omniscience of a Corporeal God

The knowledge God has of the universe has been hard for mortal Men to grasp. Modern scientists are just beginning to gain an inkling of what is possible for *Man* to learn. It is no wonder that the ancient Greeks struggled with the idea of a corporeal God knowing the future. But their problem was not just that they believed such a God would be limited like themselves. A bigger problem for those influenced by Greek philosophy was the Platonistic notion that the only things of which it is possible to have real knowledge are those that exist outside the bodily realm, in the *Pleroma*, the World of the Forms. Plato could not imagine God having a body because, in his mind, God would have been consigned, with Man, to the lesser realm where nothing is real and nothing can actually be known.[11]

The influence of this belief remains with classical theism today. For example, Dr. Beckwith contrasts "knowledge" with "opinion or highly probable guesses," in the following statement: "Isaiah quotes God as saying that *knowledge (not opinion or highly probable guesses)* of the future is essential for deity (Isa. 41:21-24)."[12] The assumption that lies behind the parenthetical phrase in this sentence is the same as that of the Greek philosophers. If God were corporeal, they suppose, He would suffer from the same limitations relating to knowledge that the ancient Greeks imagined. Based on this philosophical orientation, they imagine that a corporeal God would only be able to formulate opinions or highly probable guesses about the future. Besides its basis in metaphysics, this view fails to take into account the power of God to assure that His word is fulfilled. Whichever contingency He has planned and decreed to be the future will, in fact, be brought to pass.

The ancient Greeks were intelligent and highly analytical, but they were technologically incapable of observing the universe with the degree of accuracy and detail necessary for even a moderately satisfying knowledge of the laws of nature, let alone the course of future events. They had no understanding of microbiology, DNA, brain chemistry, neurology, electromagnetic fields or the expansive power of com-

---

[11] Plato, *Parmenides,* 134.
[12] Beckwith, "Philosophical Problems," 3.

puters. Further, they did not even suspect their ignorance of these things, let alone the vast body of knowledge Man has yet to discover.

For people of such high intelligence, this inability was often frustrating. It led Parmenides to invent a universe of the mind. The metaphysical world he created was easier to deal with because it did not require that Men understand the complexities of the real world. The realm of Logic was something the Greeks could develop without technology. They simply failed to realize that, as with all logical analysis, the results are only as good as the assumptions on which they are based. Without a greater knowledge of the basic laws of physics, chemistry, mathematics and other hard sciences, their logical conclusions were flawed. They had no concept of what could be accomplished by someone who is the author of natural law, has a complete and perfect memory of the past, complete knowledge of the present, and the power to do all things. Without that vision they could never have understood God's real omniscience of the future.

Modern Advances in Knowledge Support the Corporeality of God

In these, the last days, Man has progressed dramatically in knowledge about the universe. Man has made enough progress that, if he will look in the right direction, he can see much of God's extraordinary creation through the haze and fog of what is still a limited perception. For example, a review of the questions God asked in the 38th chapter of the Book of Job reveals several queries to which modern scientists now have some answers.

In verse 16 of that chapter, the Lord asked, "Hast thou entered into the springs of the sea? Or hast thou walked in the search of the depth?" In 1960, the bathyscaph *Trieste* settled to the bottom of the Challenger Depth, the deepest spot in the ocean, and just recently Men have discovered hot springs at great ocean depths (3000 to 4000 feet) that spew forth bacteria critical to the ocean's food chain. In verse 17, He asked, "Have the gates of death been opened unto thee? Or hast thou seen the doors of the shadow of death?" The recently developed ability of medicine to revive some who have died has, through near-death experiences, literally, opened "the gates of death" to Men. In verse 18, the question is, "Hast thou perceived the breadth of the earth? Declare if thou knowest it all." Geographic surveys of the entire earth's surface are another fairly recent accomplishment of Man.

The way some questions were asked of Job, it is as though God knew when He posed them that mankind would someday unravel the answers. They read almost like a list of suggested areas of inquiry. See, e.g., Job 38:34, "Canst thou lift up thy voice to the clouds, that abundance of waters may cover thee?" Those who engage in the modern art of cloud seeding might soon be able to answer this question in the affirmative. Verse 35 reads, "Canst thou send lightnings, that they may go, and say unto thee, Here we are?" Could this be hinting at the relatively recent harnessing of electrical power and the development of telecommunications? If Men are capable of gaining wisdom regarding these matters, there is no reason to suppose that a corporeal God would be limited in His understanding of them.

Power of the Human Brain

The progress and ability of God's children suggest the capabilities of their corporeal Father. Yet classical theists, carrying the baggage of their ancient Greek counterparts, assume that God would be limited if He had a corporeal brain like that of Man. Only recently have the true capabilities of that extraordinary organ been realized. Dr. Gary Lynch of UC Irvine's Center for the Neurobiology of Learning and Memory has found that "the brain's memory storage capacity is effectively unlimited."[13] Thus, a corporeal brain is *not* a limitation, as classical theists have mistakenly claimed. In fact, it is exactly the infinite tool a real omniscient Being would be expected to possess.

In a normal human brain approximately ninety percent of the neurons are inhibitor neurons. Their job is to reduce neural activity so that the brain does not overload itself. It is sometimes said, therefore, that Man only uses one-tenth of his brain's full capacity. But if a higher brain function were possible for Men so that no inhibitor neurons were necessary, the effective increase in capacity and function could prove to be exponential.

Why should not God have a brain as wonderful as the one He made for Man? It is reasonable to assume that God's resurrected brain, though similar to that of mortal Men, is capable of functioning on a much

---

[13] Reported by Steve Emmons in "The Mystery of Memory," *Los Angeles Times*, Tuesday, January 11, 1994, Section E.

higher level, one that requires no inhibitor neurons, that uses a slightly different chemistry to increase the speed of synaptic connections between neurons. These and other improvements would make God's brain vastly superior to that of mortal Men.

God, as a glorified corporeal Man, clearly has unlimited capacity for knowledge, in part, because He has a corporeal brain. His body is the tool by which His omniscience becomes a reality. It is not a limitation but the means that assures the end.

Summary

1. Classical theists believe God is all-knowing ("omniscient") and that He knows the past, present and future.
2. According to classical theism, God knows the future because He transcends time. Since Mormons teach that God is real and corporeal, classical theists refuse to acknowledge that Mormons believe God knows the future.
3. Some liberal theologies reject the transcendency of God and teach that He does not know the future.
4. Classical theology teaches that God knows all things without learning them.
5. The Bible teaches that Christ *acquired* knowledge before He helped to create the earth (Prov. 8:22). The Bible also teaches that Christ was corporeal. Yet He was omniscient (John 21:17).
6. Mormon scriptures, including the Bible, are emphatic in teaching that God knows the future.
7. Classical theism teaches that God is able to observe actual future events from His vantage point in the "*Pleroma*," outside time. That is, He *sees* the end from the beginning. This view follows from their belief that, in essence, the universe is a figment of God's imagination.
8. The Bible explains how God really knows the future. It does *not* say He *sees* the end from the beginning; rather, it says He *declares* the end from the beginning (Isa. 46:10-11 NASB). He has a perfect and complete knowledge of the past and present; and He plans perfectly for the future, then brings His plans to pass. With His complete knowledge of the past and present, His wisdom and His power,

The Omniscient God

every aspect of the future is as plain to Him as if it were present before His eyes (D&C 38:1-2).
9. Classical reticence about God's corporeality stems from ancient Greek ideas about Man's ability to learn. They failed to grasp Man's true capabilities, and hence reasoned that God could not be corporeal or He would be limited like the Men they knew. Since even the brightest Greek philosophers did not understand much about the laws of nature, they had no idea of how to map the course of future events.
10. Modern science has advanced considerably since the Greek philosophers. It is starting to crack the mysteries of God's natural law, and can even answer some of the questions God asked Job (Job 38). As knowledge increases, it becomes increasingly clear that God can know the future through a perfect knowledge of the past and present and a complete knowledge of the laws that govern the universe.
11. The human brain has been found to be "effectively unlimited." As a corporeal resurrected being, God's brain is of similar design, but superior to Man's. If Man's brain is "effectively unlimited," God can clearly be both corporeal and omniscient.

15

The Omnipresent God

One of the most significant factors in classical theism's insistence upon an incorporeal God is their inability to conceive of a corporeal Deity who can be described as omnipresent. The idea of a God who "fills" the universe has been easier for philosophers to accept if they believe Him to be pure thought, immaterial, ethereal and undefined by space or time. But, if a *personal* being can fill the universe in any sense of that term, the additional fact of corporeality presents no logical impediment to omnipresence.

The complexity of this attribute, when applied to a real space-time universe, presented a barrier to the Greek mind that proved insurmountable in the early Church. To this day, even those classical theists who recognize the difference between the pantheistic notion of omnipresence and the kind of omnipresence that characterizes a personal God typically assume that corporeality would be an impediment to omnipresence. Fortunately, current advancements in technology should awaken even the most metaphysical thinker to the truths taught in the Bible. Until they are thus awakened, however, omnipresence will remain for classical theists one of the most problematic attributes of God.

Understanding Omnipresence

Both classical theism and Mormonism reject the pagan notion that God is everything (pantheism).[1] God is not everything, and everything is not God. What, then, does the Bible mean when it says that God is "in" everything (1 Cor. 15:28; Eph. 4:6), or that He "fills" the heavens and the earth (Jer. 23:24)? Does omnipresence mean that God occupies

---

[1] Elwell, *Evangelical Dictionary of Theology*, s.v. "Pantheism."

every point in the universe simultaneously? If so, that is equivalent to pantheism. Does He infuse all things with His spirit? That comes very close to the theology of idol worship. In exactly what sense is God omnipresent according to the Bible?

The question takes on greater significance in light of the personal nature of God. While Mormons teach that the Godhead includes three separate centers of consciousness, even one center of consciousness must be centered at a specific location. If instead it is diffuse throughout the universe, the notion of personality is converted into pantheism. Being a personal God means that He is cognizable as a person in a specific space at a specific time. How then can He hear the prayers of all men offered simultaneously throughout the world? That is one of the many aspects of the classical dilemma.

Classical Theism's Notions of God's Omnipresence

Dr. Beckwith, without any citation to biblical authority, explains the orthodox view as follows: "Since God is not limited by a spatio-temporal body, knows everything immediately without benefit of sensory organs, and sustains the existence of all that exists, it follows that He is *in some sense* present everywhere."[2] What is especially significant about this statement is Dr. Beckwith's recognition that there are some ways in which God is not present everywhere. He is present everywhere only "in some sense."

Dr. Morey is less circumspect. He expresses the idea of omnipresence in reasoned philosophical language, but provides no key to understanding the concept. He says,

God is everywhere present in the totality of His person....

The historic Christian view is that the God of Scripture is omnipresent in the sense that He is infinite in His presence, i.e., His existence has no limits. There is no "cutting off point" for God where we can say that He begins or ends. God does not end on the boundaries of the finite universe we live in. He is greater than the universe. It is a mere speck of dust to the Almighty.[3]

Dr. Morey doesn't explain what he means by the phrase, "He is infinite in His presence, i.e., His existence has no limits." He assumes that

---
[2] Beckwith, "Philosophical Problems," 3-4.
[3] Morey, *Battle of the Gods*, 225-226.

the universe is "finite," that it is like a "speck of dust" to God, but he doesn't indicate the relationship between this supposedly tiny universe and the infinite "presence" he describes or the infinite universe scientists generally propose. Is God's presence extant everywhere in the tiny universe Morey imagines, or is it somewhere outside, too large to fit in the dimensions of a finite universe?

The usual explanation of God's omnipresence by classical theists relies entirely on the assumed existence of the metaphysical universe invented by Greek philosophy and the concept of God's transcendence over *space* and time. Professor Erickson expresses the classical view as follows:

> God is not subject to limitations of space. By this we do not mean merely the limitation of being in a particular place—if an object is in one place it cannot be in another. Rather, it is improper to think of God as present in space at all. All finite objects have a location. They are somewhere. This necessarily prevents their being somewhere else. The greatness of finite objects is measured by how much space they occupy. With God, however, the question of whereness or location is not applicable. God is the one who brought space (and time) into being. He was before there was space. He cannot be localized at a particular point. There can be no plotting of his location on a set of coordinates. This seems to be a function of his immateriality or spirituality. There is no physical body to be located at a particular place. Consider here Paul's statement that God does not dwell in man-made shrines, because he is the Lord of heaven and earth; he made the world and everything in it (Acts 17:24-25).
>
> Another aspect of God's infinity in terms of space is that there is no place where he cannot be found. We are here facing the tension between the immanence of God (he is everywhere) and the transcendence (he is not any*where*). The point here is that nowhere within the creation is God inaccessible.[4]

This idea of omnipresence can only be justified on the basis of the Greek notion that this universe is not real. It has already been demonstrated that the Bible contradicts that notion (Rom. 4:17; Heb. 11:3). Thus, the classical concept of God's omnipresence has been completely undermined. There is not the slightest indication in the Bible that He exists in any transcendent state.

---

[4] Erickson, *Christian Theology*, 273.

But even if God were located in a metaphysical universe, that would not explain how His center of consciousness could be present simultaneously in every location in the universe. The notion entirely contradicts the personal nature of God and biblical references to His "presence."

God Has a Specific Location in Space and Time

The Bible is filled with accounts of appearances by one or another member of the Godhead. In every instance, they specify a space-time location for God's "presence." It is indisputable that deity has been localized in space and time on each occasion of such an appearance. For example, in Exodus 3:2 (NASB, lit. trans.) "the angel of the Lord appeared to [Moses] in a blazing fire from the midst of the bush." As previously noted, the term "angel of the Lord" is a common Old Testament reference to the pre-mortal Christ. The following are accounts of appearances in the Old Testament by Christ under the name "angel of the Lord": Gen. 16:9, 13; 22:11; 48:16; Ex. 3:2-6 (compare Rev. 22:8-9); Ex. 14:19; 23:20-23; Num. 22:22; Judges 2:1, 4; 6:11; 13:3, 18 (compare Isa. 9:6); 2 Kings 19:35; Isa. 63:9; Zech. 1:12; 12:8. In each instance, the spatio-temporal location of Christ is identified in the passage even though He was, at the time, only a spirit being.

Exodus 19:18-20 describes Jehovah *coming down* on the top of Mount Sinai. See also Deut. 5:4. Isaiah 64:3 (NASB) states that Jehovah *came down* ("from heaven," according to Isa. 64:1), and the mountains quaked at His presence (see also Nah. 1:5). Note that the mountains did not quake until His actual arrival, suggesting a difference between His presence on the mountain and His physical absence from it before and after His arrival at that space-time location.

The Lord was personally with Israel in the wilderness (Exod. 13:21), and Ezekiel 20:34-36 indicates He will be with them again, "face to face," when, in the last days, He brings them out of the places to which they have been scattered. Acts 3:19-21 refers to "times of refreshing" that will "come *from* the *presence* of the Lord," which suggests a temporal location from which the refreshing will come. Gospel accounts of Christ's baptism specify space-time locations for each of the three separate members of the Godhead (see, e.g., Matt. 3:16-17). Stephen's vision of the Father and the Son, while he was "full of the Holy Ghost," indicates that he saw the glory of the Father, and Jesus standing to the right of Him, as he "looked *up* steadfastly *into heaven*" (Acts 7:55).

The only reasonable conclusion that can be drawn from all these passages is that the "presence" of God, whether the Father, the Son or the Holy Ghost, can always be identified in real space-time. Consistent with modern analysis of the characteristics of personality, God's center of consciousness is localized in space and time. This is as true for the one center of consciousness that classical theists acknowledge as it is for the three centers of consciousness Mormons recognize.

The Personal God and the Dilemma of Omnipresence

Classical theists, therefore, face the same problem they see in LDS theology. If God's center of consciousness is present simultaneously everywhere in the universe, the Christian understanding of God is converted into pantheism. But if God's center of consciousness is localized in space-time, how can He be omnipresent? A careful consideration of the problems associated with this issue has been made by some classical theists. In his *Systematic Theology*, Miley addressed the problem as follows:

> Thus, if we think of God as essentially present in all worlds we tend to think of his essence as a magnitude reaching all in a mode of extension, and as filling all the interspaces. The notion is utterly inconsistent with pure spirituality of being. If, however, we still assert the essential ubiquity of God, but hold our thought rigidly to the notion of pure spiritual being, we must at once be conscious of an utter incapacity to form any conception of the manner in which he is thus omnipresent.[5]

Thus, as it affects the discussion of God's omnipresence, it doesn't really matter whether one believes that God is only a spirit, or that He has a "spiritual body" like that of Christ. The same problem must be addressed in either case—the localized nature of a personal center of consciousness militates against any notion that God is present everywhere simultaneously.

In the case of Christ, the issue is even more obviously problematical. He is acknowledged by classical theists to possess a resurrected "spiritual body"—He clearly has a physical aspect to His nature.[6] Yet

---

[5] Miley, *Systematic Theology*, 1:218.
[6] Elwell, *Evangelical Dictionary of Theology*, s.v. "spiritual body."

classical theists note that He is omnipresent. In that regard, Professor Erickson states: "In giving the Great Commission, he commanded his disciples to go as witnesses everywhere, even to the end of the earth, and he would be with them to the end of the age (Matt. 28:19-20; Acts 1:8). Thus, he in effect indicated that he is not limited either by space or by time."[7]

Classical Reactions to the Dilemma of Omnipresence

Dr. Morey attempts no explanation of God's omnipresence as he addresses that issue. Instead, he asserts that the classical understanding of this attribute is basically irrational. Like Dionysius of Rome in the third century, he eschews the idea of seeking a rational explanation at all:

> Once God's nature is determined solely on the basis of what is "coherent" or "rational," then God's omnipresence must go the way of all the other 'omni' attributes of God. After all, who can give a "coherent" explanation of "how" and "in what way" God can be everywhere without somehow becoming everything? Do God and the world occupy the same space and time? Then how do they differ?
>
> Or, again, if God is finite and is "in" time like man, then the fastest He can go is the speed of light. Thus, to go from one end of the universe to the other means that God cannot be everywhere at the same time....
>
> The rationale of prayer is based on the omnipresence of God. We can pray anywhere because God is everywhere....
>
> If God is not omnipresent, then He can hear our prayers only if He happens to be near us at that moment. Maybe we'll get "lucky" and choose the right moment when God is passing by. We shudder to think of all the consequences of denying the omnipresence of God.[8]

This view expresses the kind of technological shortsightedness that was typical of the ancient Greeks. Of course, it does not help Morey that he must contend with detractors like the process theologians. Their position on this point is noted by Morey as follows: "Thus, Whitehead and his disciples claimed that God must struggle to overcome gravity and inertia."[9]

---

[7] Erickson, *Christian Theology*, 273.
[8] Morey, *Battle of the Gods*, 225-226.
[9] *Ibid.*, 225.

This is simply the other side of the same technological shortsightedness Morey displays. In process theology, God is seen as extant in the real universe, but He is assumed to have the same level of competence as Man. Morey also assumes, wrongly, that if God lived in the real universe, He would be as limited as Man is now. That conclusion is exemplified by his concern that, if God were a real being in a real universe, He could only hear Man's prayers if He were passing by them at the right time. Therefore, he concludes that God must not live in the real universe. Both conclusions are wrong because they have both made the same false assumption.

Miley comments on this perspective as follows:

> The necessity of an essential ubiquity to these attributes can be asserted only on the assumption that God can have knowledge and exert energy only where he is locally present. If this be true, then personality in God must itself be so broadened in extension as to be omnipresent. Nothing could be more inconceivable or more contradictory to the nature of personality.[10]

Thus, Miley correctly reasons that if God must be nearby to hear Man's prayers, He would have to be locally present at an infinite number of places simultaneously to hear them all. This would make Him omnipresent in the sense Dr. Morey contemplates, but that idea contradicts any notion of a personal center of consciousness, and so must be rejected as unbiblical. Morey doesn't seem to care about the problem, however. He, with many other classical theists, is satisfied to leave God's omnipresence a paradoxical mystery.

Is God's Omnipresence an Irrational Paradox?

The Hebrew prophets accepted the statements given them about God's attributes on faith. The Greek thinkers, however, ridiculed those who exercised blind belief.[11] Like Dr. Morey above, they could not simply leave philosophical questions unanswered without some kind of speculation on the subject. Though he claims that "many questions must be submissively left in the hands of God,"[12] there is hardly an issue Irenaeus leaves untouched in his speculations. Origen left none to the

---

[10] *Ibid.*, 219.
[11] Origen, *Against Celsus*, 3:44.
[12] Irenaeus, *Against Heresies*, 2:28.

imagination. What Irenaeus really meant was that the paradoxical results of his erroneous reasoning should be left for God to unravel, rather than being questioned by Men.

The speculation of the Apologists was grounded in the limited scientific awareness of their day. It became rigid dogma by the fourth century, and left modern classical theists with a tendency to think in terms grounded on the same primitive level of scientific knowledge that prevailed at that time. As the views of process theology show, some theologians today struggle with the concern that a real God might not be able to travel faster than the speed of light. To assume that He cannot, however, is to be as scientifically naive as the ancient Greeks.

In this enlightened age, it should have occurred to theologians that, since God is the author of all the laws of the universe, He might just have included a few ways to get around some of the apparent limitations in the galaxy, like the speed of light. The fact that Men have not yet discovered how to do that, and cannot explain how a real God could accomplish the feat, does not mean that they must either limit God's travels to the speed of light, or jump on the metaphysical bandwagon with Parmenides.

Mormons Believe God's Omnipresence is Rational

Mormons also believe and teach that God, a resurrected being, is omnipresent "in some sense," as Dr. Beckwith put it. Joseph Smith taught: "We here observe that God is the only supreme governor and independent being in whom all fullness and perfection dwell; who is omnipotent, *omnipresent* and omniscient; . . ."[13] Mormonism firmly asserts that God the Father, a real corporeal being, possessing a "spiritual body," is omnipresent, though not in any pantheistic sense.[14]

The Risen Lord is as clear an argument in favor of Mormon theology on this point as anyone can cite. It is the incarnation of the Son of God that must be considered in order to understand any of the attributes of God (John 14:9). If the incarnation of the Son of God did not eliminate the omnipresence of Christ, remembering that His incarnation was *permanent* (Acts 1:11; Rom. 6:9), it is clear that being a real, corporeal,

---

[13] N. B. Lundwall, compiler, *Lectures on Faith* (Salt Lake City: Bookcraft, n.d.), Lecture Second, 2.
[14] See, for instance, Bruce R. McConkie, *Mormon Doctrine* (Salt Lake City: Bookcraft, 1966) 2d ed., s.v. "omnipresence."

resurrected human being does not prevent God from being omnipresent. If the Son lived as a real, rational being in this, the real universe, His attributes, though they may seem incomprehensible to Men, are real and rational. How then does LDS theology provide an understanding of the attribute of omnipresence that is not pantheistic?

Biblical Omnipresence

The Bible never uses the word "omnipresent," or any word like it, to describe God. Instead, it portrays Him in a way that makes the use of that word appropriate to summarize one of His abilities. Therefore, the word cannot be used as a guide to define this attribute of God. Rather, the teachings of the Bible must be used to define it.[15]

What does the Bible say about God's omnipresence? The passages that describe this attribute include: 1 Kings 8:27; 2 Chronicles 2:6; Psalm 139, especially verses 7-10; Isaiah 40 (though not specifically in any single verse); Jeremiah 23:24; Acts 17:24-28; Ephesians 1:22-23; 4:9-10; and Colossians 1:17. In uniquely Mormon scriptures, the following verses can also be cited as descriptive examples: 2 Nephi 18:8; D&C 88:11-12; and 109:74. Reviewing some of these passages will put this attribute into the correct biblical perspective.

Where Is God? Not in Temples Made With Hands?

One misconception about God's omnipresence was expressed by Professor Erickson above. He said:

> This [omnipresence] seems to be a function of his immateriality or spirituality.[16] There is no physical body to be located at a particular place.[17] Consider here Paul's statement that God does not dwell in man-made shrines, because he is the Lord of heaven and earth; he made the world and everything in it (Acts 17:24-25).[18]

---

[15] Miley, *Systematic Theology*, 1:219-220.

[16] There is a distinction between these terms that is missed by many classical theists today. Some in the early Church considered the spirit to be a kind of material, as does Mormonism today. See e.g., Origen, *De Principiis*, 1:1 in which Origen disputes the view that God is a spirit in any material sense, as others in the Church were teaching. He claimed that God is pure Mind.

[17] Erickson misses Miley's point that God's personal nature is the real problem. His center of consciousness must be "located at a particular place," as the Bible passages previously cited clearly indicate. Otherwise, Christianity becomes pantheistic.

[18] Erickson, *Christian Theology*, 273.

The latter passage is frequently misunderstood by classical theists, who fail to account for the many passages that speak of God coming to His holy temple, as will be shown below.

Another oft misunderstood passage comes from the prayer dedicating the Temple of Solomon—1 Kings 8:27. It is often cited by classical theists to support the argument Professor Erickson makes above. It states: "But will God indeed dwell on the earth? behold, the heaven and heaven of heavens cannot contain thee; how much less this house that I have builded?" (See 2 Chron. 2:6 to the same effect.)

This statement seems at first glance to suggest that God is of immense size. Such a characteristic may be consistent with the classical idea of God's omnipresence, but size, no matter how great, would not actually help Him to be omnipresent in any sense taught in the Bible. Nevertheless, the passage has been a source of confusion for some theologians and should be examined more closely.

The word "contain" in this passage is misinterpreted if it is taken to mean that God is so immense He would not fit within the Temple of Solomon. That is the sense in which it is understood by many classical theists. They feel bolstered in that conclusion by passages such as Acts 17:24 (NASB), which say that God "does not dwell in temples made with hands," and they assume that the Temple of Solomon comes within that definition.

To understand the meaning of these passages, one must keep in mind the many passages that positively state God *can and does* abide in His temple. In biblical times, "His temple" was the Temple of Solomon (see, e.g., 2 Sam. 22:7; Psalm 11:14; 18:6; and Hab. 2:20). During His sojourn on earth, Christ visited the temple often and jealously guarded the sacredness of that edifice (Matt. 21:12). In the last days, Malachi states that Christ will "suddenly come to his temple" (Mal. 3:1). According to the dedicatory prayer (1 Kings 8:13), Solomon built that temple as "a place for [God's] dwelling forever."

Thus, the word "contain," as it is used in 1 Kings 8:27, cannot be taken to mean that the Temple was a building into which God could not fit. Rather, that language in the dedicatory prayer can be understood as a way to show respect for God, to acknowledge that He is far greater than Man so that anything Men make as a dwelling place for God would be grossly inferior to His dwelling place in heaven. It has no reference to God's size.

Unworthy Temples

Paul's statement to the Greeks that God does not dwell in "temples made with hands," appearing as it does in Acts 17:24 at the beginning of his sermon on Mars' Hill, presents a related but contrasting concept. Mars' Hill is thought to be the Areopagus, a hill in the center of Athens lying in the western shadow of the Acropolis.[19] Standing on it, Paul would have been surrounded by the pagan temples of the Greeks. His remark, therefore, should be recognized as a direct reference to the temples of the heathen made under human direction and for human purposes ("with hands"). Such temples are not made under God's direction or to worship Him, as was the Temple of Solomon. (Cf., 2 Cor. 6:16.)

In each instance where the word "temples" (plural) is used in the Bible, it is a reference to heathen, pagan or otherwise false houses of worship (Hos. 8:11-14; Joel 3:4-6; Acts 17:24). The reference is always derogatory indicating that God does not dwell in such "temples" (Acts 7:48). The singular word, "temple," on the other hand, is usually spoken of reverently as the House of God or the temple of the Lord. There are only three instances in the Bible where "temple" is used otherwise, and in each case the context clearly indicates the special usage (1 Chron. 10:10, Acts 19:27, 1 Cor. 8:10).

Classical theists acknowledge that the Bible also refers to Man's body as the temple of God (1 Cor. 3:16-17; 6:19), and states that the Spirit of God may dwell there. But, contrary to the claims of classical theists, not one passage in the Bible contrasts the "temple" of Man's body with the temple of the Lord in a way that implies God dwells in Men but not in that temple.

Obviously, Men are much smaller than the temple of the Lord or the temples of the heathen, and both they and the temples in question are clearly part of the real universe. Therefore, Bible references to the fact that God does not dwell in "temples made with hands" have nothing to do with God being transcendent, or too large. The reason He does not dwell in such temples made with hands is that they are unworthy of His presence.

Unworthiness is also a reason for God's refusal to dwell with certain Men. In Stephen's speech to the Sanhedrin in Acts 7:49-53 (NASB), he quotes part of Isaiah 66:1-2 as follows:

---

[19] *Encyclopaedia Britannica*, 1960 ed., s.v. "Athens" and "Areopagus."

> Heaven is My throne,
> And earth is the footstool of My feet;
> What kind of house will you build for Me? says the Lord;
> Or what place is there for My repose?
> Was it not My hand which made all these things?

He then condemns the Jewish leaders for not keeping the law (Acts 7:50-53). His condemnation clarifies the difference between a temple in which God dwells and "temples made with hands," in which He does not. The clarification is found in the distinction between Men (and temples) that obey God's will and are fit for the Spirit of the Lord, and temples (and Men) that do not and so are not fit.

Heathen temples are unworthy of God's presence. So is the body of a man who disobeys God's commandments. Thus, Stephen likened the Jewish leaders to unworthy "temples," the same as those condemned in the portion of Isaiah 66 he quoted to them. Because of their unworthiness, Stephen did not quote the balance of Isaiah 66:2 (NASB), which says, "But to this one I will look, To him who is humble and contrite of spirit, and who trembles at My word." Such a man is a "temple" in which the Spirit of God may dwell, just as He dwelt in the temple built under His command and dedicated to Him by Solomon.

The phrase "temples made with hands" is an idiom referring to unworthy temples (and Men). It is not intended to suggest, as some classical theists assert, that God is so large He would not fit in such a temple, or that He is unable to do so because of any supposed "immateriality or spirituality." [20]

Omnipresence As a Consequence of Omniscience

Psalm 139:7-10 provides some direct information about the attribute of God known as omnipresence. It states:

> Whither shall I go from thy spirit? or whither shall I flee from thy presence?
>
> If I ascend up into heaven, thou art there: if I make my bed in hell, behold, thou art there.
>
> If I take the wings of the morning, and dwell in the uttermost parts of the sea;
>
> Even there shall thy hand lead me, and thy right hand shall hold me.

---

[20] Erickson, *Christian Theology*, 273.

In this passage the Psalmist asks where he could flee to escape God's "presence." The Hebrew word translated "presence" is the word for "face," or "front." Note also the references in this passage to God's "hand." The question posed by the Psalmist assumes the existence of a Being who actually has a face and hands and thus a specific location in space and time. Though the passage is figurative in the sense of the Psalmist actually being in the physical presence of God, there is no valid reason to conclude that it is also figurative about God having a presence to which the Psalmist could be proximate.

The passage also implies that God is omniscient of the present. He always knows where the Psalmist is. It is in the latter context that the scriptures most often describe God's omnipresence. From this, it is possible to observe that omnipresence is better explained in terms of knowledge and communication theory than physics. This point has not gone unnoticed by some classical theists. Dr. Beckwith recognized that one of the principal aspects of this attribute is the fact that God "knows everything immediately." [21]

The relationship between God's omniscience and His omnipresence is especially apparent in Jeremiah 23:23-24, which reads as follows in the NASB (see also Eph. 4:10):

> "Am I a God who is near," declares the Lord, "And not a God far off?
> "Can a man hide himself in hiding places, So I do not see him?" declares the Lord. "Do I not fill the heavens and the earth?" declares the Lord.

In what sense does God declare here that He "fill[s] the heavens and the earth?" The answer is found in His statement that no man can hide from Him. The word translated "fill" in this verse comes from a somewhat rare usage of the Hebrew word for full. It is used in Isaiah 6:1 (NASB) to explain a vision in which Isaiah saw the "train" of the Lord's robe "*filling* the temple." The phrase is figurative in its usage in both passages. It does not mean that God "is greater than the universe," as Dr. Morey argues.[22] (The Bible nowhere states that God "fills" anything more than "the heavens and the earth.") The point of the passage

---

[21] Beckwith, "Philosophical Problems," 3-4.
[22] Morey, *Battle of the Gods*, 226.

is simply that there is no place in the universe Man can go where God "[does] not see him."

Immanence and Transcendence

There is no indication in the foregoing passage or any other verse in the Bible that God's ability to see every spot in the universe is metaphysical, a function of His supposed transcendence. As previously demonstrated, the Bible actually denies the existence of the metaphysical universe (Rom. 4:17; Heb. 11:3). Consistent with that position, verse 23 of Jeremiah 23 asks rhetorically, "Am I a God who is near? . . . And not a God far off?" This statement is in direct opposition to the idea of God being transcendent—above and outside the real universe. (See also Acts 17:27, "though He is not far from each one of us.")

While classical theists acknowledge God's closeness to Men, a characteristic they refer to as His *immanence*,[23] they fail to note that the scriptures never speak of His being transcendent. Immanence is the characteristic classical theists see as the essence of omnipresence.[24] It is, therefore, in conflict with the idea of God being transcendent in the metaphysical sense. Nevertheless, classical theists insist that both characteristics are true of God, just as they do with the doctrine of co-substantiality.[25]

God's Ability to Travel As an Aspect of Omnipresence

Greater insight into the omnipresence of God can be found in Ephesians 4:9-10 (NASB), which states:

> Now this *expression*, "He ascended," what does it mean except that He also had descended into the lower parts of the earth?
> He who descended is Himself also He who ascended far above all the heavens, that He might fill all things.

The Greek word translated "He might fill" is *plērosē*, which is rarely used in a physical sense. In Acts 5:28 it is used in the phrase "you have filled Jerusalem with your teaching." In Philippians 4:19, Paul uses the term to say that God "will supply [i.e., fill] all your need." In the passage quoted above, therefore, it refers to the concept of Christ visiting all cosmic realms, earth, Hades (or Sheol) and the heavens. It

---

[23] See, e.g., Elwell, *Evangelical Dictionary of Theology*, 458-459.
[24] Erickson, *Christian Theology*, 302.
[25] *Ibid.*, 301, *et seq.*

shows that Christ and His Father, likewise, fill the universe in the sense that they have visited, and have the power to revisit, all of it.

This is the aspect of God's omnipresence that has to do with His ability to travel. He is capable of reaching any spot in the universe at will. The claim of some theologians that He cannot do so at speeds greater than the speed of light assumes that God has a level of scientific knowledge no greater than Man's. Such travel is not logically impossible. The fact that it would appear to violate a law of science only reflects the level of Man's scientific knowledge. Just a few years ago, Man's science was at a level that led many to believe it was impossible to break the sound barrier.

God's Nearness As an Aspect of Omnipresence

Passages like Ephesians 1:22-23 and Colossians 3:11, which refer to Christ as "all in all" or "all, and in all," are especially helpful in understanding God's omnipresence. The same message is given in uniquely Mormon scripture (D&C 63:59-60). The biblical passages are most likely contracted versions of the statement in Ephesians 4:6: "One God and Father of all, who is above all, and through all, and in you all." This passage is clearer in the Greek than in English, and presents four characteristics of God. The issue of God's oneness will be dealt with in Chapter 17, but the word translated "God" here is the Greek *Theos*, a term best applied to the Godhead.

First, God (*Theos*) is "Father of all." The indication here is that the Godhead created all things, whether as the Father (natural or adoptive) of spirits (Heb. 12:9; Ether 3:14), or the one who conceived the plan of creation, or the one who executed it (1 Cor. 8:6). The word "all" in this phrase is translated from the Greek, *panton*, which includes all things referred to in the context of the phrase in which it is used. In this case, it is used in connection with the Father, and hence defines the scope of "all" for the balance of the verse as that which the Father created. This appears from the context of the whole passage as well.

Second, God is "over all [*panton*]," indicating explicitly that the authority of the Godhead extends over all creation.

Third, God is "through all [*panton*]." The word "through" (*dia*) is used in this context to refer to time. Hence the phrase means that God has always existed.

Fourth, God is "in all." In contrast to the three previous uses of that word, "all" in this phrase is translated from the Greek, *pasin*. It is plural and has no object. Used in this manner, it is not restricted like the other phrases, but refers to "all things" in the most widely inclusive sense. The word "in" here is from the Greek preposition *en*. Paul, like John, used that word to designate a close personal relationship, a nearness, as of someone close by.[26]

Thus, the phrase "in all," as used in these passages, means that God is close to, or very near, everything in the universe. It is a specific reference to the Godly attribute called omnipresence. The expression is consistent with Paul's statement in Acts 17:27 ("he be not far from every one of us"). This is one sense in which the Bible teaches God's omnipresence. The implication is of God's nearness. This nearness should not be thought of in terms of distance, but in the sense of time. The man who lives in East Los Angeles but claims he lives only 15 minutes from the beach, can do so only because he drives very fast. Likewise, the implication of this nearness is that God can be at any spot in the universe in an instant, no matter what the actual distance.

This understanding of God's nearness does not require an attenuated physical presence throughout the universe. As Miley correctly reasoned, the idea of God's personality being extended throughout the universe is entirely incompatible with the notion of His being a person. However, there is one other element involved in God's omnipresence.

Communication As an Aspect of Omnipresence

The *last* element of God's omnipresence is expressed in the dedicatory prayer of Solomon on the Temple in 1 Kings 8 (NASB), which has already been mentioned above. In verses 32, 34, 36 and 45 of that chapter Solomon asks God to "hear Thou *in heaven* . . . ," followed by a description of various appeals by His people who go to the temple. In verses 39, 43 and 49, the request is even more specific: "hear Thou *in heaven Thy dwelling place* . . . ," is the request there.

These passages indicate that there is a place located away from Earth, "in heaven," where God dwells. It is the implicit understanding of Solomon, who is giving the dedicatory prayer, that God can hear Israel from that distant location. Unlike Dr. Morey, Solomon did not believe that God was either a metaphysical paradox or a being so powerless that he would have to be right next to the temple in order to hear the various prayers of its attendees. He had faith that God could

---

[26] Bauer, *Greek-English Lexicon*, s.v. ἐν.

hear the prayers of his people in His dwelling place even when He was "in heaven," a great distance away. How could the God of Solomon hear prayers offered in a temple here on earth if He were in His dwelling place in heaven? Solomon may not have known the details of the answer, but he accepted the fact.

To those who live in this age of technology and communication, the answer should be elementary. Yet classical theists like Dr. Morey, quoted previously, claim that God's presence as a "rational" and "coherent" being in the real space-time universe would mean that He could only hear Man's prayers while standing nearby. This assumes that a corporeal God capable of creating the natural universe is still a limited and ignorant being, lacking even the technological abilities of modern Man. That view is a mockery of the true God to whom Men should ascribe a vastly superior communications network than their own.

Ancient Greek philosophers can be excused for assuming such limitations in a corporeal being whose location can be fixed in real space-time, but there is no excuse for such ignorance today. God is not less technologically advanced than Man! One can safely assume that He has a perfect telecommunication system by which everything is known to Him without the necessity of His being physically present at every point in the universe in order to see or hear it.

Though he was more ancient than the philosophers, Solomon had no trouble understanding that God had such a telecommunication system. It is important, too, to note that Solomon was not a philosopher. He did not teach metaphysics. His understanding of God's telecommunication system must be recognized as one grounded in reality, not in the metaphysical concepts of the Greeks. Thus, God is everywhere in part because He is in communication with everything, everywhere.

A Modern Analogy to Biblical Omnipresence

God's omnipresence based on the various aspects discussed above can be understood today through an analogy that was not technologically available to the ancient Greeks. That analogy is as follows: Suppose that a large complex of apartment buildings are protected by a security guard. The guard has security equipment set up in each building, with cameras and microphones throughout the complex, so that the guard, who observes from a remote location, can keep all the sites he is protecting under surveillance at the same time. The buildings are close enough to allow immediate access by the guard (or his agents) to any spot in the complex where there may be trouble. Under such a security system, one could say that the guard is effectively omnipresent.

A similar arrangement, though infinitely more efficient and effective, may be seen in God's omnipresence. If God is aware of and has the power to achieve immediate physical closeness with anyone or anything in the universe, it does not matter where His presence is physically located at any one time, He is always close to everyone and everything in the universe.

God also works in great measure through agents and messengers, the physical presence of whom is treated in the Bible as equivalent to the presence of God (e.g., Rev. 19:9-10). This is another way in which God's reach is extended throughout the real universe. Omnipresence may thus be seen, not as much as an attribute of God, as a natural result of His omniscience of the present, coupled with His omnipotence in respect to travel.

Miley comes to essentially the same conclusion as follows:

> The Scriptures repeat the sublime utterances of the divine ubiquity. These utterances are the expression of a personal ubiquity through the perfection of knowledge and the plenitude of power. "Whither shall I go from they Spirit? Or whither shall I flee from thy presence?" These words are the center of a long passage which expresses the omnipresence of God in terms of the deepest intensity. In these terms we find the reality and the absoluteness of this omnipresence in the omniscience of God and the omnipotence of his will.[27]

As demonstrated in the last two chapters, omniscience and omnipotence are attributes that can be possessed by a real, corporeal being, not just a being who "is not limited by a spatio-temporal body."[28] Ephesians 1:22-23; 4:9-10, and Colossians 3:11 all describe Christ's omnipresence *after* His resurrection, when He was distinctly and permanently corporeal (Luke 24:36-43; Rom. 6:9). If Christ is omnipresent, omnipresence is clearly an attribute that may be possessed by a corporeal being.

---

[27] Miley, *Systematic Theology*, 1:219-220.
[28] Beckwith, "Philosophical Problems," 3.

Some Insights on the Nature of God's Telecommunication System

The scriptures imply that God's telecommunication system is facilitated by His "spirit" (see, e.g., Acts 2:4). Doctrine and Covenants Section 88 has direct bearing on this point. It describes God's system as follows:

> And the light which shineth, which giveth you light, through him who enlighteneth your eyes, which is the same light that quickeneth your understandings;
>
> Which light proceedeth forth from the presence of God to fill the immensity of space—
>
> The light which is in all things, which giveth life to all things, which is the law by which all things are governed, even the power of God who sitteth upon his throne, who is in the bosom of eternity, who is in the midst of all things.

The "light" described in this passage, the power of God that fills "the immensity of space," may be the means by which God communicates with everything that occupies that "immensity." Men can tap into that communication system by worshiping God "in spirit and in truth" (John 4:24). This is generally called "prayer." The technology is obviously beyond anything comprehensible by Man at this time, but that it is real and allows communication with God in the real universe cannot reasonably be denied.

Conclusion

God does not need to be incorporeal and transcendent, outside space and time, to be omnipresent in the way the Bible describes Him. The ancient Greeks had no clue about the possibilities of telecommunications, and so they made up the only reasonable explanation they could imagine for God's omnipresence—a metaphysical one.

But metaphysics is not contained, or even intimated, in the Bible. The biblical God is real, and He uses real means to fill the universe with His presence. Now that Man has learned something of the possibilities of telecommunications, classical theists can give up their pantheistic tendencies and cease to cling to ancient Greek notions about a metaphysical, incorporeal God adopted by Men whose thoughts were limited by the technology that prevailed in the second century A.D. Instead, they can accept the teachings of the Bible as they were originally delivered. The real, corporeal God of the Bible can be, and indeed, is omnipresent.

Summary

1. The personal nature of God is an even greater obstacle to the classical idea of God's omnipotence than His corporeality.
2. God is not pantheistic. If then He is not everything, the problem for classical theism is to explain how He can be everywhere, as they conceive Him to be, and still remain a personal being.
3. Classical theists have decided that God is omnipresent only "in some sense," and that His omniscience is somehow related to his omnipresence. However, they view the idea of His being incorporeal as a factor to His omnipresence.
4. Some classical theists make no attempt to explain God's omnipresence rationally. They see metaphysics, and the idea of God being transcendent over space as holding some incomprehensible answer to the puzzle of a personal center of consciousness being anywhere in the real universe. This kind of thinking depends entirely on the Greek notion that this universe is not real and contradicts biblical references to God's "presence."
5. References to the "presence" of God in the Bible clearly indicate that His center of consciousness, His person, always has a physical location in space and time.
6. Classical theists recognize the dilemma of understanding God's omnipresence (sometimes referred to as His "ubiquity") in light of His personal nature. This is especially true when they contemplate the omnipresence of the risen Savior.
7. Some classical theists openly declare that God's omnipresence is not rational, and that if it were, God would be as limited as they imagine Man to be.
8. The failure of classical theists to find a rational explanation of God's omnipresence is the result of their reliance on ancient Greek thinking, which was scientifically limited.

9. In light of today's technological advances, it is not so hard to understand how God could rationally be omnipresent in the biblical sense.
10. One misconception classical theists have about God is that he does not reside in temples because He has no physical body or is too large.
11. The Bible teaches that God can and does "abide" in His temple. It is unworthy temples ("made with hands") that He will not visit. This includes Men who defile the temple of their bodies.
12. God is aided in His omnipresence by His knowledge of everything that happens in the universe. He "fills" the heavens and the earth in the figurative sense that He can see everything that occurs in the universe.
13. God is immanent, not transcendent. That is, He always remains in close contact with Man. He is also able to be present at any spot in the universe whenever He desires. Thus, God is near everything in the universe.
14. Solomon recognized that God is able to hear the prayers His children offer in His temple while He is in heaven, His dwelling place. This requires a telecommunication system. God is in communication with all parts of the universe.
15. God's telecommunication system, though vastly advanced over Man's, is similar in concept. It allows Him to be in His heaven and still be in contact with every part of the universe. This is biblical omnipresence. He also acts through agents and messengers whose actions on His behalf extend His omnipresence in a figurative sense.
16. God's telecommunication system may be facilitated by His "Spirit." the "light" from His presence which illuminates the immensity of space, may allow Him to see and communicate with Men.
17. God's ability to be omnipresent as the Bible describes Him is in no way limited by His corporeality. If Men can communicate over great distances, the ability of God to communicate with the entire universe and go anywhere He desires, or send agents and messengers anywhere on His behalf, is not frustrated by His real, corporeal and personal nature.

The Immutable and Eternal God

The immutability of God is one of the most perplexing concepts in the Scriptures. While the Bible teaches that God does not change, it also contains indisputable evidence that He *has* changed in certain significant and fundamental ways. Careful analysis is necessary, therefore, to understand what it is about God that is unchangeable and what it is about Him that can and does change without violating the biblical attribute of immutability. An understanding of this distinction is not only essential to a knowledge of God, it is critical to resolving the controversy between Mormons and orthodox Christians over the question of whether or not Men can truly become like Him.

Scriptural References to God's Immutability

Malachi 3:6 cites Jehovah's proclamation that, "I am the Lord, I change not; . . ." This declaration is also given in the Book of Mormon to the remnant of Israel on the American continent (3 Nephi 24:6). Moroni 8:18 in the Book of Mormon expresses the same concept with even greater emphasis: "I know that God is not a partial God, neither a changeable being; but he is unchangeable from all eternity to all eternity." (See also Mormon 9:10, 19; D&C 20:17; D&C 76:4.) Thus, the scriptures teach that God is "the same yesterday, and to day, and for ever" (Heb. 13:8; 1 Nep. 10:18; 2 Nep. 2:4; 27:23; Alma 31:17; Mormon 9:9; Moroni 10:19; D&C 20:12; 35:1).

From these and other passages it appears that there is no distinction as to which member of the Godhead is described as being immutable. Like all the attributes discussed in this part, the attribute of immutability applies to each member of the Godhead. It is an attribute that is fundamental to Deity. That immutability can be attributed to each member of the Godhead, including Christ, despite the fact that He changed from spirit to mortality, suffered death and was resurrected, is one of the many issues that require careful attention in this chapter.

Immutability an Essential Attribute of God

The ability to rely upon the continuing benevolence of an almighty being makes immutability an essential attribute of Deity. Thus, in listing and commenting on the various attributes of God revealed in the scriptures as a means for inspiring faith, Joseph Smith taught:

> Thirdly, that he changes not, neither is there variableness with him; but that he is the same yesterday, to-day, and for ever; and that his course is one eternal round, without variation.
>
> * * *
>
> But it is equally as necessary that men should have the idea that he is a God who changes not, in order to have faith in him, as it is to have the idea that he is gracious and long-suffering; for without the idea of unchangeableness in the character of the Deity, doubt would take the place of faith. But with the idea that he changes not, faith lays hold upon the excellencies in his character with unshaken confidence, believing he is the same yesterday, to-day, and forever, and that his course is one eternal round.[1]

The Static Versus the Dynamic View of God

Despite His being unchangeable, God is not static. The real God of the Bible is not Aristotle's Unmoving Mover. He moves and is dynamic in His works and his relationship with Men. He even changed the Law by which they were governed as they learned to obey higher principles (Heb. 7:12).

Most bible scholars today recognize this aspect of God's immutability,[2] but they rarely go far enough in their analysis of the attribute of immutability. They carefully analyze what it is about God that does not change,[3] but rarely examine what it is about God that does. To do that

---

[1] *Lectures on Faith*, 3:15,21.
[2] See, e.g., Elwell, *Evangelical Dictionary of Theology*, s.v. "God, Attributes of."
[3] See, e.g., Morey, *Battle of the Gods*, 210-213.

would raise significant conflicts between classical theism and the teachings of the Bible.

Of course, it is important to understand how God does not change. Some biblical passages are quite specific as to what it is about God that does not change. It is these passages that must be examined first in order to understand the immutability of the true and living God.

In What Way Does God Remain Unchanged?

The principal way in which God does not change, according to the scriptures, is in respect to His purposes or His word. The idea that is made clear in several passages dealing with His immutability is that God does not break His promises. Hebrews 6:17 (NASB) states, "In the same way God, desiring even more to show to the heirs of the promise the unchangeableness [KJV: immutability] of His *purpose*, interposed with an oath." (See Book of Mormon, Alma 42:26 to the same effect.) Doctrine and Covenants 104:2 expresses this attribute of God as follows: "With *promise* immutable and unchangeable, that inasmuch as those whom I commanded were faithful they should be blessed with a multiplicity of blessings."

This aspect of God's immutability is also demonstrated in His character for honesty. Paul wrote to Titus (Titus 1:2, NASB): "in the hope of eternal life, which God, who cannot lie, promised long ages ago." See also Num. 23:19; 1 Sam. 15:29; and Heb. 6:18. It is also seen in His perfect justice (Gen. 18:25). Just as His promises to the righteous may be relied on, if He promises punishment for the wicked who do not repent, they may assuredly count on receiving that punishment. The basic principles of God's immutable justice are painstakingly explained in Ezekiel 18:14-32.

Another aspect of the attribute of immutability is that God does not change His word. That is, all things that He prophesies through His prophets will be fulfilled as He declares them. See Isa. 46:10-11; Mark 13:31; Matt. 24:35; Luke 1:20; 3 Nep. 1:13; and D&C 29:30. Moses 4:30 expresses this principle in the Pearl of Great Price: "For as I, the Lord God, liveth, even so my *words* cannot return void, for as they go forth out of my mouth they must be fulfilled."

The most explicit of the New Testament writers on the subject of God's immutability was James, who wrote: "*Every good thing* bestowed and *every perfect gift* is from above, coming down from the

Father of lights, with whom there is no variation, or shadow of turning" (James 1:17, NASB, literal translation). Here James uses three Greek words to describe God's immutability with precision. They are *parallage*, which means change or variation, particularly in one's nature, and *tropes aposkiasma*. In the latter phrase, *aposkiasma* refers to a shadow cast by variation, usually because of the movement of heavenly bodies. The word *tropes* describes that movement, and means a turning, variation or change, and in some senses a darkening.

These words appear only once in the Bible—in James 1:17. One commentator who has carefully traced the use of these words through ancient literature concludes: "The meaning of the passage will then be 'God is alike incapable of change in his nature (*parallage*) and incapable of being changed by the action of others (*aposkiasma*).'"[4]

Thus, the Bible teaches that God is *steadfast* and faithful in carrying out His word. Indeed, biblical immutability could best be described as perfect *steadfastness* (Dan. 6:26; Heb. 6:18-19). Another synonym found in the scriptures is *"constancy,"* an attribute Men too are commanded to develop (1 Cor. 15:58; Heb. 3:14; 2 Pet. 3:17).

God does not change His mind or the purposes, designs or plans He has announced. He is also immutable in the sense that He will not allow the improper influence of others to change His mind or shift His will in the slightest degree from righteousness. He may be relied upon always to behave consistently with His Godly character.

Such unchangeableness, however, also implies change in other ways. For example, God responds differently to Man's differing behavior in a way that is consistent with His unchanging principles of righteousness by which He governs both Himself and the universe. See, for example, the story told in Jonah 3:4-10. In Jonah 3:4, the prophet said, "Yet forty days and Nineveh will be overthrown." He didn't offer them any alternative. He never added the words, "unless you repent." His promise was certain destruction—period! Yet the Ninevites were hopeful they could be spared if they would repent (Jonah 3:9), and so it happened (Jonah 3:10). This was not what Jonah expected (Jonah 4:1), but God's response was based on righteous principles of justice (Ezekiel 18:21-28), not on the anger of Jonah against Nineveh. Right principles *never* change, no matter what imperfect Men do or say.

---

[4] Joseph Mayor, *The Epistle of James* (Grand Rapids: Zondervan, 1892), 61.

In What Ways Does God Change?

In order to understand the attribute of immutability as it is possessed by God, the passages in sacred writ that describe God as unchanging should be contrasted with the passages that show He has changed in very significant ways. From that comparison, it becomes clear that the Bible does not associate certain types of change with the attribute of immutability as it is possessed by God. Classical theologians will find some of these changes grossly incompatible with their Hellenistic notions about God.

Changes in Knowledge and Wisdom

One very significant type of change in Christ is described in Proverbs 8:22 (NASB) which states, "The Lord possessed me [Wisdom] at the beginning of His way, Before His works of old." This suggests that, although Christ is now omniscient (John 21:17), there was a point in time when He, the Lord of the Old Testament, *acquired* the knowledge He needed to assist His Father in the creation of this earth.

The verb translated "possessed" in this passage is from the Hebrew word *qanah*, which does not mean "had" or "held" or "owned." It means "to acquire." As used here, it implies that Christ did not always possess the wisdom referred to in Proverbs 8. The verse should read, "The Lord acquired me in the beginning of his way, before his works of old." That translation expresses a very important understanding, namely that before the creation there was a change in Christ's knowledge.

There is a similar implication of change or progression in Christ's knowledge in Hebrews 5:7-9, which reads in the NASB:

> In the days of His flesh, He offered up both prayers and supplications with loud crying and tears to the One able to save Him from death, and He was heard because of His piety.
>
> Although He was a Son, He learned obedience from the things which He suffered.
>
> And having been made perfect, He became to all those who obey Him the source of eternal salvation, . . .

This passage indicates that, "in the days of His flesh," Christ *"learned obedience,"* and was "made perfect," setting an example for all Men.

The progression implied in these passages, though it clearly represents a change of sorts, is not mentioned in those verses that declare

God's immutability. The conclusion to be drawn from this is that the acquisition of knowledge and learning which the passages in Hebrews and Proverbs imply is unrelated to biblical immutability. That attribute is the propensity to be steadfast, constant and honest, and is not related to the state or level of one's knowledge or wisdom.

Changes in Bodily Characteristics

In addition to the profound change noted above, Christ experienced another very significant change when He was born of Mary. He changed His *form* from that of a spirit being to that of a physical being, a change that involved entry into a fallen state (Phil. 2:8). Subsequently, He underwent yet another major change of form, from that of a man subject to death to that of an eternal, resurrected being (Luke 24:36-43).

The New Testament is filled with references to Christ's birth, death and resurrection. Yet, these physiological changes are never mentioned in connection with biblical declarations that God is immutable. Obviously, biblical immutability is not about the form of God's body. Again it appears that the attribute of immutability addresses only the steadfast nature of God's personality and character for righteousness.

Changes In Office, Title or Position

The ultimate point of disagreement between Mormons and classical theists in regard to the attribute of immutability relates to the question of whether or not immutability refers to eternal progression. Is it possible for one who once was not God to attain that position and still possess the attribute of immutability? Dr. Beckwith states the classical viewpoint on this question as follows: "God is unchanging (Mal. 3:6; Heb. 6:17; Isa. 46:10b) and has always existed as God throughout all eternity (Ps. 90:2; Isa. 40:28; 43:12b, 13; 57:15a; Rom 1:20a; 1 Tim. 1:17). There never was a time when God was not God."[5]

Is this an accurate statement of biblical theology, as Dr. Beckwith implies through his citations of biblical authority? Not at all. None of the passages he cites addresses the point he makes in his last sentence. Rather, the Bible tells of a very significant change that occurred in respect to Christ's position as Eternal God. It has been mentioned before, but needs careful reexamination in regard to this issue. The

---

[5] Beckwith, "Philosophical Problems," 4.

change occurred in concert with Christ's incarnation and is described by Paul in his letter to the Philippians. Philippians 2:5-7 (NASB) reads:

> Have this attitude in yourselves which was also in Christ Jesus, who, although He existed in the form of God, did not regard equality with God a thing to be grasped,
> but emptied Himself, taking the form of a bond-servant, and being made in the likeness of men.

It will be noted that this passage appears to have a very different meaning in the NASB than it does in the KJV. In this rare instance, the NASB is a more accurate translation of the original Greek. The phrase "He existed in the form of God" means that Christ was a member of the Godhead. He held and exercised the office, position or authority of "Eternal God." He had been acting as Creator and serving Man as the God of Abraham, Isaac and Jacob, the great I AM (Exod. 3:13-14; John 8:56-59) since at least the beginning of this earth.

Note that the passage states unequivocally that He was in a position of "*equality* with God." It does not say He was the *same person* as the Father. Equality is a very different concept than identity. It requires the existence of two entirely separate individuals for them to be equals. The passage teaches that Christ's authority and position in the Godhead was one of complete equality with the Father.

Christ did not regard His position in the Godhead as something that should be held onto jealously, i.e., "grasped" (verse 6). It was necessary at that time for Him to relinquish His duties as a member of the Godhead in order to complete His atoning mission on earth. The Greek word translated "grasped" in this passage is *arpagmos*, which is very rare in secular Greek. It appears nowhere in the Septuagint and only once in the New Testament. Its classical meaning is "robbery," and that is how it is translated in the KJV, but that does not clearly convey the meaning intended here. Later church writers used the word to say, for example, that Peter regarded death on the cross as "*arpagmos*," by which they meant that he saw such a death as "a prize to be grasped eagerly." [6]

It is in this sense that it was used in this passage. Its use in the negative shows that God the Son, in coming into this world "in the likeness of men," did *not* regard His exalted position in the Godhead as a prize to be clutched greedily, as a robber hordes his loot. Instead, He

---

[6] Bauer, *Greek-English Lexicon*, s.v. ἁρπαγμός.

was willing to shed His office and responsibilities to take up His cross. The next verse expresses this concept by saying that He "emptied Himself, taking the form of a bond-servant." That is, He set aside His office or position as Eternal God along with certain of His attributes, like omnipresence, and took on the role of a slave or bond-servant during His mission on this earth. In fact, His willingness to do this, which the Father foreknew, is cited in Philippians 2:9, to be discussed more fully below, as one of the reasons He was exalted in the first place.

The Greek word here translated "emptied" is *ekenose*, the aorist tense of kenos, which means to empty, as in removing something from a container. It could be used of a military officer removing his insignia of rank. It distinctly confirms the understanding that Christ stepped down from His exalted position in the Godhead for the duration of His earthly ministry. The passage is translated by Thayer as follows: "who, although he bore the form of God, yet did not think that this equality with God was to be eagerly clung to [or retained], but emptied himself of it so as to assume the form of a servant, in that he became like unto men."[7]

In orthodox Christian theology, this act on Christ's part is called the "kenosis." Professor Erickson writes perceptively about this event as follows:

> In our interpretation of Philippians 2:6-7, however, what Jesus emptied himself of was not the divine μορφή, the nature of God. At no point does this passage say that he ceased to possess the divine nature. This becomes clearer when we take Colossians 2:9 into account: "For in him the whole fulness of deity dwells bodily." The kenosis of Philippians 2:7 must be understood in the light of the pleroma of Colossians 2:9.[8] What does it mean, then, to say that Jesus "emptied himself"? Some have suggested that he emptied himself by pouring his divinity into his humanity, as one pours the contents of one cup into another. This, however, fails to identify the vessel from

---

[7] Joseph H. Thayer, *A Greek-English Lexicon of the New Testament* (Grand Rapids: Baker Books, 1977), s.v. μορφή.

[8] Here Professor Erickson fails to note that Philippians 2:7 describes what Christ did just before coming to dwell as a man upon the earth, while Colossians 2:9 describes His state in the present tense, and was written in approximately 60 A.D., many years after His death and resurrection.

The Immutable and Eternal God

which Jesus poured out his divine nature when he emptied it into his humanity.

> A better approach to Philippians 2:6-7 is to think of the phrase "taking the form of a servant" as a circumstantial explanation of the kenosis. Since λαβών is an aorist participle adverbial in function, we would render the first part of verse 7, "he emptied himself by taking the form of a servant." The participial phrase is an explanation of how Jesus emptied himself, or what he did that constituted kenosis. While the text does not specify what he emptied himself of, it is noteworthy that "the form of a servant" contrasts sharply with "equality with God" (v. 6). *We conclude that it is equality with God, not the form of God, of which Jesus emptied himself.*[9]

This is an accurate conclusion on Professor Erickson's part. Christ did, in fact, divest Himself, temporarily, of His "equality with God" upon entering mortality. That means during His earthly ministry He ceased to function in the position of Eternal God, i.e., in His capacity as one of the members of the Godhead.

In a sense, one could say that the Son of God was "not God" for the brief period of approximately thirty-three years as Men count time, for He relinquished that *office* in the kenosis. The use of a word (*"kenos"*) that, in classical Greek, meant to divest oneself of the privileges of an office or rank was particularly apt in this regard.[10] Of course, He did so without at any time relinquishing or divesting Himself of His divine nature,[11] as Professor Erickson correctly surmises, and that is the point of this discussion.

Philippians 2:6-7 must now be viewed in the context of God's immutability. The scriptures are clear that He has remained the same yesterday, today and forever. Yet, for a brief period, it was necessary for Christ to step away from His heavenly duties as "Eternal God." What was it that did not change about Him? Clearly, it was His "divine nature." *Holding the position or office of God is not the point on which immutability is measured.* The kenosis of Philippians 2:6-7 proves that whether a person, e.g., Christ, functions in the office of "God" at all times or not is irrelevant to the biblical doctrine of

---

[9] Erickson, *Christian Theology*, 734-735.

[10] See, Bauer, *A Greek-English Lexicon*, s.v. κενόω, and the authorities cited therein.

[11] Contrary to the doctrines of classical theism, the term "divine nature" should not be understood in any metaphysical sense.

immutability. Consistent with the other types of changes noted above, biblical immutability is not about God's office, title or position. It is about His "divine nature," that is, His perfect character and personality.

Origin of the Classical View of Immutability

Despite the clear testimony of Philippians 2:5-7, classical theists believe that God's immutability requires that He has always been God. This view follows irreversibly from their view of the universe. That view is profoundly challenged by the biblical evidence of change in God demonstrated above. The classical view is based on three concepts that were either borrowed from Greek philosophy or developed within the context of Greek philosophy.

The *first* is the idea that God transcends space and time. Coupled with that view is the *second* idea—that He created space, time and matter as an illusion, fabricating all that constitutes the real universe out of nothing. The *third* and last concept that has molded the classic view of God's immutability is the idea that God's presence is necessary to maintain the illusion of reality.

The Idea of God As a Necessary Being

Dr. Beckwith expresses the last concept identified above as follows:

> Moreover, since everything that exists depends on God, and God is unchanging and eternal, it follows that God cannot *not* exist. In other words, He is a necessary being, whereas everything else is contingent.[12]

Elwell expresses the classical idea of God as a "necessary being" as follows:

> [God] was a necessary being. That is, God is not in need of anything outside of his own being for his existence. On the other hand, all other beings are contingent beings. This means that they depend on something or someone outside themselves for their existence.[13]

This idea of the dependent nature of beings other than God is much more than the recognition that Men rely on God's laws and creations, e.g., the earth's bounty and its natural resources. It can only be fully understood in the context of the Greek notion that the real universe is merely an illusion brought into seeming existence by the Supreme

---

[12] Beckwith, "Philosophical Problems," 4.
[13] Elwell, *Evangelical Dictionary of Theology*, 131, s.v. "Being."

Being. Theologically, this concept has been expressed as follows: "Classically, theologians have regarded any being as contingent whose essence does not include its existence. Only God, it follows by definition, is non-contingent." [14]

The term "essence" was defined in Part 1. It is derived from Greek philosophy and relates to the essential nature or description of something by which it can be differentiated from anything else in the universe. According to classical theism, Men do not exist independently of God in any form. Existence, they say, is an attribute of only one being in the universe—God. It is part of His description. If nothing else existed, if everything else in the universe died or disappeared, only God would continue to exist. Thus, as classical theists express it, "only God truly exists."

Likewise, classical theists argue that, because reality exists (or appears to exist), God must exist. The existence of anything as opposed to nothing, they say, is proof of the existence of God.

Origin of The "Necessary God" Concept

The classical view on the necessity of God is in direct conflict with the Mormon concept of Man's basic character as an eternal "intelligence." Classical theism's view arises from the Platonistic idea that God created the phenomenal world, which is not the world of reality but merely one of appearance, by impressing His Thought on Matter. In the Platonistic universe, if such a Being did not exist, everything else would instantly disappear, or at the very least, lose its existing form.

This concept was modified by the Apologists, who took Greek philosophy one step further. They decided that God also created the *Matter* on which His Thought was impressed, and that He did so *out of nothing*. If this were true, it would follow logically that God is absolutely necessary and everything else is contingent. Man, to the classical theist, is nothing more than a fleeting wisp of nothingness that exists, if at all, on the inexplicable whim of a being totally foreign to His creations.

The Biblical Doctrine of God's Necessity

Romans 11:36 (NASB) says that "from Him and through Him and to Him are all things," and Acts 17:28 (KJV) states that "in Him we live and move and have our being." It is understandable that the Greek

---

[14] Harvey, *Handbook of Theological Terms*, s.v. "Contingent."

thinkers of the second century would give such passages a metaphysical interpretation, but such an exegesis was never justified. These words were revealed to the Jews. Given that context, they must have been intended to convey a different concept than the idea that Man is a figment of God's imagination, since that concept never appeared in Judaism except in the Alexandrian community of Hellenized Jews led by Philo.

In these passages, the word "in" is translated from the Greek word *en*, a preposition that can have a variety of meanings. In this instance, its meaning should be taken as *causal* or instrumental. The passages above should be understood as saying "*because of* Him we live and move and have our being." That is biblical doctrine on the necessity of God, and it is significantly different from the Greek doctrine.

Through God's creation, Men enjoy a change of form, from that of bare intelligences to beings capable of perceiving and acting in both spiritual and physical spheres. Man is unquestionably dependent on God for the maintenance of his current physiological condition (i.e., his spiritual and physical form). The passages above remind Man of that dependence and suggest some very deep principles on which the universe itself depends, through God, for order. But in the Bible, Man is the offspring of a God who is literally His Father, a Parent concerned about increasing the capabilities of His children from mere intelligences to resurrected beings like Himself.

No biblical passage expresses Plato's metaphysical notion of the universe that was incorporated into classical theism. God plays an essential *causative* role in the universe, but not the metaphysically sustaining one that the Greek philosophers imagined. He gives Men their daily breath until they can grow to true maturity and gain the kind of independence He enjoys, taking their places beside Him as heirs (Rom. 8:17).

The fundamental basis of Man's personality is uncreated and eternal. It is already self-existent, but would have remained undeveloped without God. The Bible describes a God who develops and enlivens, not one who imagines into reality an illusory form of contingent pseudo-existence.

What If God Did Not Exist?

Mormonism does not indulge contemplation of God's non-existence, but not for the metaphysical reasons given by classical theists.

The reason is that the contingency simply doesn't exist. Hence, neither the Bible nor uniquely Mormon scriptures give any information about what would happen to the universe in the absence of God. One can only speculate on such a situation based on passages that describe God's ongoing relationship to the universe. Presumably, since God created the universe out of eternal elements—matter and intelligence—those elements would not disappear in His absence.

However, the elements might deteriorate in some very unexpected ways. What form the elements might retain without God's organizing influence can only be surmised. Doctrine and Covenants 88:13 indicates that He is the law by which all things are governed. If He were absent, therefore, it is conceivable that the elements would cease to obey what Men regard as natural law, with unimaginable results.

What is certain from scripture is that God will never cease to be God (Book of Mormon, Alma 42:23; Morm. 9:19). The classical theist's statement that "God cannot *not* exist" and the Platonistic ideas about His necessity and the universe's contingency as a figment of His imagination are nothing but metaphysical speculations.

God *will not* not exist! That is the *biblical* absolute. The relationship of God to the universe, true, is one of vast dependence on Him, but it is not that of *logical necessity*, as classical theists believe, based on their adoption of Greek philosophical concepts.

The real universe is very different from that imagined by the Greeks whose ideas were incorporated into Christian theology by the second-century Apologists. The biblical doctrines of God's immutability and His eternal nature allow for an understanding of God's history and the potential that awaits His obedient children that is very different from any imagined in classical theism. On this point, the Bible teaches something very different from orthodox Christianity, as will be further demonstrated below.

Has God Always Been "God?"

Classical theists have had great difficulty explaining the incarnation of Christ and the passage in Philippians noted above.[15] But that is only the icy tip of their dilemma. The Bible does not support the notion that Christ has always been a member of the Godhead. That notion is as unbiblical as the Greek notions mentioned above. It is contradicted in

---

[15] See, e.g., Erickson, *Christian Theology*, chap. 34.

both the Old and New Testaments. While many passages teach that God "has always existed . . . throughout all eternity," no passage teaches what Dr. Beckwith claims—that God (and specifically God the Son), "has always existed *as God* throughout all eternity."[16] What then does the Bible say about the length of time during which God the Son has been "God," i.e. a member of the Godhead?

From Everlasting to Everlasting

Colossians 1:17 states that God "has existed prior to all things, and in Him all things endure together" (NASB, alternative translation). Notably, the passage does not say He "has existed *as God* prior to all things." This is more than a picky distinction or an inadvertent omission in the text; it is the consistent testimony of the Bible. Dr. Beckwith's added terminology, "as God," cannot properly be added to this passage, either by implication or assumption, without contradicting other specific passages in the Old and New Testaments.

Other Old Testament passages are occasionally quoted by classical theists in the effort to bolster their proposition that God has always been God. In so doing, they are not being faithful to the original Hebrew. Psalm 41:13 (NASB), for example, states, "Blessed be the Lord, the God of Israel, From everlasting to everlasting. Amen, and Amen." To the same effect is Psalm 106:48. Psalm 90:2 (NASB) states: "Before the mountains were born, Or Thou didst give birth to the earth and the world, Even from everlasting to everlasting, Thou art God."

The meaning of these passages is deliberately obscured by the word "everlasting" that appears in each. That word is translated from the Hebrew word *olam*, which is intentionally uncertain as to its temporal duration. Literally, it means a long but hidden period of time, "the beginning or end of which is either uncertain or undefined."[17] The most that can be determined about its length as used in scripture is derived from the events specifically mentioned in them. For example, in Psalm 90:2 the time period noted extends from some point before the mountains or the earth were "born." According to most classical theologians, that would be only about six thousand years ago.

Isaiah 43:13 is a more precise statement of the duration of time that Christ has held the office and title "God." It states, "Even from the [first] day I am He; . . ." (NASB, alternative translation). This positively estab-

---

[16] Beckwith, "Philosophical Problems," 4.
[17] Gesenius' *Hebrew-Chaldee Lexicon*, s.v. עוֹלָם .

lishes that Christ, who was that member of the Godhead who acted and spoke throughout the Old Testament, was God from at least the first day of creation.

The term is used in Psalm 104:5 as follows: "He established the earth upon its foundations, So that it will not totter [move out of place] forever and ever" (NASB, alternative translation in brackets). Yet Isaiah states that in the last days, the earth will reel "to and fro like a drunkard, And it totters like a shack, For its transgression is heavy upon it, And it will fall, never to rise again" (Isa. 24:20, NASB). The passage in Psalms does not contradict Isaiah, or vice versa. Rather, the intentional uncertainty of the words translated "forever and ever" in Psalms 104:5 is limited in duration by the last-days prophecy of Isaiah.

Passages in the Old Testament that use the words "everlasting" and "forever" are not necessarily meant to describe a period of infinite duration. Therefore, they cannot be relied upon as evidence that either the Father or the Son has always held the office or position of God. They only express the idea that they have held that position for as long as Man needs to be concerned. Indeed, God may have used the Hebrew word *olam* to express a kind of practical infinity that will be explained in Chapter 18.

Many passages describe God as "the Everlasting God," "the Eternal God" or "the Eternal Father" (e.g., Gen. 21:33; Deut. 33:27; Isa. 9:6; 40:28; Rom. 16:26). This is done without regard to whether the passage is referring to Christ or to the Father (see, e.g., Isa. 9:6). 1 Timothy 1:17 calls God "the King of the ages" (NASB, literal translation). All these may be understood as titles. He is God and He is called Everlasting and Eternal (D&C 19:10).

Hence, either Christ or the Father may be called "the Everlasting God" or "the Everlasting Father" without regard to whether or not they always, throughout *all* infinity, exercised the authority of that office. In fact, it is the position or office that is modified by the word "eternal" in these passages, not the name of the person holding that title. The implication is that it is the *office or position* that is eternal.

Christ's Exaltation to the Office of "God"

Not only is the Bible obscure about the time during which God has been "God," it specifically refers to the exaltation of Christ to the office of Eternal God. Both the Old and New Testaments testify that at some undesignated time in the far distant past Christ was "exalted" to His position in the Godhead. The statement is contained in Hebrews 1:8-9 (quoting Psalms 45:6-7) as follows (NASB):

> But of the Son He says,
> "Thy throne, O God, is forever and ever,
> And the righteous scepter is the scepter of His kingdom.
> Thou hast loved righteousness and hated lawlessness;
> Therefore God, Thy God, hath anointed Thee
> With the oil of gladness above Thy companions."

This event is confirmed in Philippians 2:9 (NASB), which reads: "Therefore also God highly exalted Him [Christ], and bestowed on Him the name which is above every name." The word translated "name" here is the Greek word *onoma*, which means "title." Obviously, the title bestowed on Christ was that of "Eternal God" (cf., 1 Cor. 15:24-28).

Hebrews 1:9 refers to "the Son" as "God," and says "Thy God," referring to the Father (John 20:17), "anointed Thee . . . above Thy companions." As noted above, this passage is quoted from Psalms 45:6-7. The Greek word translated "anointed" here is the equivalent of the Hebrew word used in Psalms 45:7. According to Gesenius, that word means "to *anoint* any one as a sacred rite in his *inauguration* and *consecration* to an *office*" (some emphasis in original).[18]

Who then were Christ's "companions" above whom He was "anointed" (Heb. 1:9) or "exalted" (Phil. 2:9)? The Greek word used in Hebrews, like the Hebrew word translated "fellows" in Psalm 45:7, implies a relationship of peers, companions or partners. The context in the Book of Hebrews is a scriptural demonstration that Christ is greater than the angels. This suggests that His "fellows" or "companions" over whom He was anointed were the angels. As will be seen in the next chapter, that conclusion is consistent with many other scriptural passages.

What is most certainly clear is that He did not hold the office and title of "God" before He was "anointed . . . *above* [His] companions" (Heb. 1:9, NASB). If Christ had been God, a member of the Godhead, before the exaltation or anointing described in the passages cited above, His companions, peers or partners would have been God the Father and God the Holy Ghost. That would mean He was "anointed . . . *above*" the

---

[18] *Gesenius' Hebrew-Chaldee Lexicon*, s.v. מָשַׁח .

Father and the Holy Ghost! It is patent that Christ was never "exalted" or "anointed" above His Father (cf. 1 Cor. 15:27-28). Thus, the Father could not have been one of Christ's peers when He was exalted. Thus, Christ was not "God," a member of the Godhead, before the event described in Psalms 45:6-7, Hebrews 1:8-9 and Philippians 2:9.

Before His exaltation, Christ's peers were the angels, who were the righteous pre-existent spirits of Men (Job 38:4-7), the other children of God the Father who served Him as agents and messengers as will be seen in Chapter 17. Christ was the oldest of these spirits, being the Father's firstborn (Col 1:15), but now He has been exalted over His fellow spirit brothers and sisters and is equal with God the Father and has become the Father of the righteous (Gal. 4:4-7; Book of Mormon, Ether 3:14).

Thus, Hebrews 1:9 documents a time when Christ was elevated from among the ranks of His brothers and sisters (John 20:17) to the office of "God." Before that time, He did not hold the title "God." He was one of the "morning stars" (Job 38:7), being specifically called the "bright and morning star" (Rev. 22:16), a term that likely designates the highest rank among the pre-mortal spirit children of God (cf., Isa. 14:12).

Christ Was Exalted to the Godhead *Because* of His Immutable Righteousness

The passage in Hebrews cited above explains exactly why Christ was exalted to the position of Eternal God, and in so doing it substantiates the testimony of the scriptures that He is immutable in the sense used in the Bible even before He was "God." It was precisely because He was steadfast in righteousness that He was found worthy of that exalted position. Hebrews 1:9, quoting Psalm 45:7, explains that Christ "loved righteousness and hated wickedness" (NASB). The verb is in the past tense, indicating that He had this character *before* He was exalted to the Godhead.

This is the eternal, unchanging nature of Deity upon which Man may confidently rely. It differs significantly from the basis upon which most Men decide between righteousness and wickedness. Some Men choose wickedness because they love it and do not care what happens to them or to others. Others may choose righteousness, but for a variety of reasons. They may have an intellectual understanding that it is to be preferred over wickedness. They may perceive that wickedness will harm them or their fellow Men. They may even choose righteousness because they believe God will punish them if they choose wickedness.

None of these motivations can be relied upon to produce perfect, unchanging, immutable benevolence. Despite the fact that God has the kind of freedom that comes from absolute power, He may be unerringly relied upon to be perfectly benevolent. That is, He will always choose righteousness and reject wickedness. Why? Because it is His personal preference. He *loves* righteousness and *hates* wickedness! That is the characteristic Christ possessed before ever He was exalted to the position and authority of Eternal God. Thus, although He has not always stood in the exalted position of "God" over Man, He has always possessed the kind of character God has. That is the essence of biblical immutability.

Joseph Smith's Teachings About God's History

In the famous King Follett discourse, Joseph Smith taught: "We have imagined and supposed that God was God from all eternity. I will refute that idea, and take away the veil, so that you may see."[19] Few quotations from the first prophet of the latter days have drawn more criticism than this one. Yet the passages discussed above clearly support his statement.

Of course, Joseph's comments should be examined in the context of the point he was making in that famed discourse. He was not denying God's immutability, nor was he contradicting his comments about the attribute of immutability quoted earlier in this chapter. He wasn't even speculating about whether there was a time when God the Father was exalted to His position as "Eternal God." All he taught was that God the Father went through a kenosis the same as Christ. That is clear from his subsequent remarks in the same speech:

> It is the first principle of the Gospel to know for a certainty the Character of God, and to know that we may converse with him as one man converses with another, and that he was once a man like us; yea, that God himself, the Father of us all, dwelt on an earth, the same as Jesus Christ himself did; and I will show it from the Bible.[20]

---

[19] *Teachings of the Prophet Joseph Smith*, 342, et seq.
[20] *Teachings of the Prophet Joseph Smith*, 342.

Thus, Joseph Smith taught that God the Father had been incarnate on an earth just as Jesus Christ was. John 5:19 states: "The Son can do nothing of himself, but what he seeth the Father do: for what things soever he doeth, these also doeth the Son likewise." It follows from this passage that, if Christ experienced a kenosis, the Father must have done likewise, because the Son only did what He had seen the Father do. When and where the Father did the things Christ did here on this earth is not revealed in scripture, but that He did them is strongly implied by John 5:19, as Joseph claimed above.

If Christ were God incarnate on this earth, His Father must likewise have been God incarnate on a similar world (John 5:19). If Christ stepped down from the position of God to occupy the humble position of a mortal man (Phil. 2:6-7, NASB), then His Father must have done the same. If all these things happened as the Bible suggests, it follows that there was a time when the Father ceased to function in the office of God in order to take upon Himself humanity, just as there was a time when Christ withdrew from that position for the same purpose. That was the message Joseph Smith announced in his much-maligned speech, and, as demonstrated above, his message was clearly biblical.

Joseph's Teachings Are Compatible With God's Immutability

Joseph Smith did *not* teach that there was ever a time when either the Father or the Son ceased to be *themselves*, changed their personalities, or altered their fundamental, steadfast character. They are immutable in righteousness, the same yesterday, today and forever. Joseph taught of the Father only what the Bible teaches about Christ: that He was exalted to the position of Eternal God at some time in the distant past, and that preliminary to His mortal incarnation He voluntarily underwent the kenosis described in Philippians 2:6-7.

Since the kenosis involved God setting aside the functions of His office as a member of the Godhead, though not His divine nature, Joseph Smith was technically correct to say that God the Father ceased to be God. Of course, this teaching might have been more pleasing to the philosophers and theologians of his day if he had couched it in more pontifical language. They might have been less offended if he had said that God temporarily ceased to *function* as God, or if he had used the technical terms of Christian theology to say that the Father experienced His own "kenosis," but he was not making narrow theological distinctions at King Follett's funeral. He was announcing some real, down-to-earth truths. His statements must be taken in the limited context in which they were made.

As it regards biblical immutability, Joseph Smith never said that God the Father ceased to have the character of Deity, or that He lost His divine nature during his mortal incarnation, any more than did Christ. He simply explained that God ceased to function in His heavenly calling as God in order to become human, and that His humanity was as real as that of Christ on this earth. This is a doctrine that does not fit the Greek philosophical perspective of God, but it is rooted solidly in the Bible.

Eternal Progression and Immutability

Dr. Beckwith states, "Mormonism teaches that God the Father is a resurrected, 'exalted' human being named Elohim who was at one time not God. Rather, he was once a mortal man on another planet who, through obedience to the precepts of *his God*, eventually attained exaltation, or godhood, himself through 'eternal progression.'" [21]

In this attempt to explain Mormon theology, Dr. Beckwith has added some speculation to his oversimplification of Joseph Smith's comments. Yes, Mormonism teaches that God the Father is a resurrected, exalted human being and that He was once a mortal man on a real, earthlike planet, but that is exactly what the Bible teaches about Jesus Christ. In light of Hebrews 1:3 and similar passages, why should it cause consternation among classical theists when truths about Christ are applied to the Father? It is because they are holding onto the Greek metaphysical concepts noted above. Rather than look to Christ as the true source of information about the Father, they assume that the Father is different from Christ, a metaphysical god described by the Apologists as hardly different from Aristotle's Unmoving Mover.

Professor Erickson writes, "Jesus said, 'He who has seen me has seen the Father' (John 14:9). . . . If we would know what the love of God, the holiness of God, the power of God are like, we need only look at Christ." [22] Why stop with attributes such as love, holiness and power? Christ is the express image of the Father (Heb. 1:3). He is not the Father, for one is not spoken of as the express image of himself. But He is the

---

[21] Beckwith, "Philosophical Problems," 5.
[22] Erickson, *Christian Theology*, 703.

complete revelation of the Father. It should not surprise theologians that they can also learn what the Father *did* by looking at what the Son did.

If then Christ progressed to the point that He was exalted to a position in the Godhead, as demonstrated above, is it impossible to imagine that the Father, at some point in time, did likewise? If Christ and possibly His Father so progressed, but are still considered immutable in the scriptures, it is clear that eternal progression is not incompatible with the concept of immutability as it is expressed in the Bible. To reiterate, immutability relates to God's character for constancy in His word, His justice and His righteousness.

Was the Father Exalted?

Joseph Smith hinted at the exaltation of God the Father in his King Follett discourse when he said, "I am going to tell you how God came to be God." His subsequent remarks, however, contained no details on this subject, only the implication that God became God through eternal progression. Understandably, specific information about the exaltation of God the Father is not given in God's revealed record of *this* world.

However, in Revelation 1:5-6, John says that Christ "made us kings and priests unto *God and his Father*." The NASB translates the italicized portion of this passage, "His God and Father," but a side note admits that the translation should read exactly as it appears in the KJV. The original Greek is consistent with the reality that this passage refers to three generations of Deity: Christ, His Father, and the Father of God the Father. Commenting on this passage, Joseph Smith, in an address given shortly before his martyrdom, said:

> If Jesus Christ was the Son of God, and John discovered [in Rev. 1:6] that God the Father of Jesus Christ had a Father, you may suppose that He had a Father also. Where was there ever a son without a father? And where was there ever a father without first being a son? Whenever did a tree or anything spring into existence without a progenitor? And everything comes in this way. Paul says that which is earthly is in the likeness of that which is heavenly.[23] Hence, if Jesus had a Father, can we not believe that He had a Father also?[24]

---

[23] This teaching is drawn from numerous Pauline teachings. See, e.g., Col. 4:1 and Heb. 8:5. It is also implicit in 1 Cor. 15:46-49, especially when considered in light of Luke 24:36-43.

[24] *Teachings of the Prophet Joseph Smith*, 373.

The guide for Joseph's reasoning here is Christ. If that guide is followed exactly, it can be deduced, even without the aid of Revelation 1:5-6, that God the Father may also have been chosen from among His peers to be exalted to the position of God at some time before He entered mortality. Thus, Joseph Smith reasoned:

> The Scriptures inform us that Jesus said, As the Father hath power in Himself, even so hath the Son power [John 5:26]—to do what? Why, what the Father did. The answer is obvious—in a manner to lay down His body and take it up again [John 10:18]. Jesus, what are you going to do? To lay down my life as my Father did, and take it up again.[25]

All that Christ accomplished He did without affecting the attribute of immutability He possesses. Thus, if the Father did likewise, it would not have violated that attribute in Himself any more than it did in His Son. Neither changed in the steadfastness of their nature, or their immutable preference for good and rejection of evil, as that attribute is described in the Bible. Thus, the exaltation of the Father would not be inconsistent with His being immutable and eternal in the same way Christ bears those characteristics.

Does Christ's "Creation" as a Spirit Refute His Immutability?

In the long distant past, Christ underwent a change related to His bodily form. That change was the transition from His existence as an eternal intelligence to the form of a spirit being, the firstborn spirit child of God (Col. 1:15). This transition from intelligence to spirit being could be called Christ's "creation" or "generation," but it was only a birth, a begetting, from which a spirit body encompassing His intelligence was formed. It was not a fabrication out of nothing.

Dr. Beckwith and other classical theists, however, have interpreted this precept in the context of their own philosophical opinions about the generation of Christ discussed in Chapter 10. They claim that Mormonism teaches there was a time when God was not God, namely before He was created as a spirit.[26] In light of the problems classical theists have had with the issue of Christ's "generation" (see Chapter 10), this criticism suggests that they erroneously think Mormons

---

[25] *Ibid.*
[26] Beckwith, "Philosophical Problems," 6-7.

believe Christ was somehow brought into self-existent consciousness at the time of His birth as a spirit being.

It is difficult, of course, for Men to grasp the thoughts of God (Isa. 55:8), so speculation on any subject not fully revealed in the scriptures must be done tentatively, but there is no reason to see the transition from intelligence to spirit being as fundamentally different in any way from the transition a spirit being undergoes upon physical birth. If incarnation in a physical body did not change Christ's immutable nature (and both classical theists and Mormons agree that it did not), it would be reasonable to surmise that the same is true regarding His transition from an intelligence into spirit form.

Christ pre-existed both transitions, and since the Bible indicates that He is immutable despite His transition into mortality, it follows that His transition into spirit form would be equally irrelevant to His immutability. In other words, it is reasonable to surmise that He has always maintained the same righteous character He now possesses, even before He was born as a spirit. Likewise, one could reasonably conclude that His Father did not change in His righteous nature as a result of either a transition from intelligence to spirit being, or a birth as mortal man, or a resurrection into glory.

Conclusion

God is not static. He changes in many seemingly fundamental ways. He is, however, immutable in a way that gives Men complete confidence in Him and in His word. He is, and has always been, a lover of righteousness and a despiser of wickedness. That is the essence of the attribute of immutability taught in the Bible.

Changes in God's knowledge, form and position have nothing to do with God's immutability as that attribute is described in the Bible. Thus, whether or not God has always been omniscient, corporeal, or held the position of "God," He can still be considered immutable and eternal. This understanding is apparent from the Bible, but it is in direct conflict with the Greek notions of God and his relationship to the universe that were adopted by the second-century Apologists.

Summary

1. While the Bible teaches that God is "the same yesterday, today and forever," it also identifies some significant areas in which He has changed. Therefore, when considering God's immutability, it is important to understand what it is about God that never changes.
2. Both the Bible and uniquely Mormon scriptures teach that God is unchangeable, and that immutability is a characteristic of both God the Father, God the Son and God the Holy Ghost.
3. Joseph Smith taught that the immutability of God was an essential characteristic of Deity.
4. Though God is unchangeable, He is not static. Therefore, while it is important to know how He does not change, it is also important to understand how He does change without violating His immutability.
5. God is unchangeable in His promises, and "cannot lie." He does not change His word. That is, He does not change His plans, purposes or designs once they are announced. He always behaves in a manner consistent with His Godly character, loving righteousness, hating evil, acting both justly and mercifully, and holding steadfast and faithful to His word in the face of opposition. This is biblical immutability.
6. There are ways in which God, as demonstrated by the history of God the Son, can change that do not affect the biblical concept of immutability:

    A. Christ has changed in respect to His knowledge and wisdom. He learned what He needed to know before He created the heavens and the earth (Prov. 8:22).

    B. Christ has changed in respect to His bodily characteristics. He was a spirit being before His mortal incarnation, when He became a physical being. After His death on the cross, He was resurrected, becoming a perfected combination of the spiritual and the physical.

    C. Christ temporarily set aside His position as a member of the Godhead in the *"kenosis"* when He entered mortality, demonstrating that even a change in His official function as "God" did not affect the perfection of His biblical immutability.

7. Classical theists have a hard time with the "kenosis" because of their views, borrowed from Greek philosophy, that God transcends space and time, that He created all reality out of nothing, and that His existence as God is necessary to maintain the illusion Men call reality.
8. The orthodox Christian idea that God's existence is a logical necessity that follows from the presence of the visible universe, and that His existence is necessary to prevent the universe from turning back into nothing, is fundamentally a Greek concept.
9. Mormonism teaches that Man's basic character or personality, his "intelligence," is eternal and uncreated. God created all things out of (1) intelligence and (2) matter. These fundamental building blocks of the universe are real and eternal.
10. The Bible describes a causative role for the Father, consistent with Mormon theology. He is essential to the universe because He is "the law by which all things are governed."
11. Classical theists say "God *cannot* not exist." Mormons say "God *will not* not exist."
12. The Bible clearly teaches that God the Son has not always been a member of the Godhead. At some time in the distant past, before the creation of this earth, He was "exalted" and "anointed" to that position.
13. Biblical passages that say God has been God "from everlasting to everlasting" do not contradict the teaching that, at one time, Christ was not a member of the Godhead.
14. Christ was exalted to the Godhead because of His immutable character. He loves righteousness and hates wickedness.
15. Joseph Smith taught that God the Father went through a "kenosis" to enter mortality as did His Son, Jesus Christ.
16. Joseph Smith did not teach that God the Father ever ceased to retain His divine nature or character. Hence, his teachings are consistent with the biblical understanding of immutability.
17. John 5:19 and other scriptures indicate that what Christ did, as recorded in the Bible, reflects precisely what the Father did.
18. Revelation 1:5-6 speaks of three generations of Deity: (1) Jesus Christ, (2) God the Father of Jesus Christ, and (3) the God who is the Father of God the Father of Jesus Christ.

19. Revelation 1:5-6, as well as common sense based on John 5:19, suggest that just as Christ was once exalted to the position and office of "Eternal God," so God the Father was exalted to His position at some time in the very distant past. That was the teaching of Joseph Smith and it is consistent with the Bible and its teachings about God's immutability.
20. The concept of immutability suggests that Christ, and before Him, the Father, had the same immutable character as intelligences.

17

The Plural and Only God

The last of the fundamental attributes of God to be considered here is classical theism's declaration of orthodox monotheism. The idea that the oneness of the Godhead necessitates the singularity of its persons lies at the heart of the most significant issue in classical theology. It is the question of how Men should understand scriptural references to the "only God."

Classical Theism's Position: One God "by Nature"

The teachings of classical theism on this attribute are expressed by Dr. Beckwith as follows:

> The Bible teaches that although humans at times worship some beings as if these beings were really gods (1 Cor. 8:4-6), there is only one true and living God by nature (Isa. 43:10; 44:6, 8; 45:5, 18, 21, 22; Jer. 10:10; Gal. 4:8; 1 Cor. 8:4-6; 1 Tim. 2:5; John 17:3; 1 Thess. 1:9)....[1]

Dr. Morey expresses his thoughts on the subject as follows:

> While the idols of the heathen are also called "gods" (1 Corinthians 8:5), the authors of Scripture are careful to state that they were "false gods" and that there is actually only one God "by nature" (1 Corinthians 8:6; Galatians 4:8).[2]

The implications and origin of classical theism's use of the term "by nature" in these comments will be discussed later in this chapter. However, it must be noted that the term "by nature" in reference to God appears nowhere in the passages of scripture these men cite, except Galatians 4:8, which uses the term in reference to false gods only. The

---

[1] Beckwith, "Philosophical Problems," 4 (some emphasis in the original).
[2] Morey, *Battle of the Gods*, 182.

372 How Greek Philosophy Corrupted the Christian Concept of God

reference in Galatians implies that Men, who may become the heirs of God (Gal. 4:7), are of the same "nature" as God. The false gods Paul refers to as "them which by nature are no gods" (Gal. 4:8) are thus contrasted with God and Men. In light of passages previously cited on this subject (see, e.g., Rev. 9:20), this is most likely a reference to idols (cf., Gal. 4:9). In any case, Galatians 4:8 does not refer to God as the only God "by nature," contrary to both Dr. Beckwith's and Dr. Morey's implications.

The Scriptures and "the Only God"

That the Bible does not teach the strict monotheism of Greek philosophy, even classical theists admit.[3] The doctrine of the Trinity is a step beyond that belief, though but a small one. That the Bible does not teach the Trinity, however, has already been demonstrated (see Chapter 10). Does that mean the Bible is not monotheistic in its teachings about God? Certainly not. The fact remains that the phrase, "the only God," is undeniably scriptural.

Both the Bible and uniquely Mormon scripture teach that God is "the only God." Many passages to that effect in Isaiah are part of a message denouncing Israel for its idol worship. These passages, of course, must be understood in that context. Exodus 22:20; 2 Kings 19:19; Isaiah 37:20; 1 Timothy 1:7; and Jude 1:4, and 24 each describe God as the "only God," adding sometimes that He is the "only *true* God" (John 17:3), the "only wise God" (1 Tim. 1:17; Jude 1:25), and the "only Lord God" (Jude 1:4). In the Book of Mormon, Ether 2:8 describes Him as the "only God," and in the Doctrine and Covenants He is described as the "only *living and true* God" (D&C 20:19), and the "only *wise and true* God" (D&C 132:24).

If the testimony of Mormon scripture is not enough to convince the reader that Mormonism teaches of "the only God," let the words of Joseph Smith, quoted partially in Chapter 15, be heard on this issue:

> We here observe that God is the only supreme governor and independent being in whom all fullness and perfection dwell; who is omnipotent, omnipresent and omniscient; without beginning of days or end of life; and that in him every good gift and every good principle dwell; and that he is the Father of lights; in him the principle of

---

[3] Erickson, *Christian Theology*, 324, *et seq.*

The Plural and Only God

faith dwells independently, and he is the object in whom the faith of all other rational and accountable beings center for life and salvation.[4]

This theological statement is unquestionably monotheistic in character. Yet, as noted in the previous chapter, Joseph Smith taught a plurality of gods and claimed that God the Father had a Father. Do these teachings conflict, as classical theists claim?

A moment's reflection will force the honest scholar to admit that the Bible does the very thing on which Joseph Smith has been challenged. In fact, Joseph's teaching is in strict accordance to the words of the Bible. Inspired writers have consistently spoken of "the only God" while at the same time naming three persons as God—the Father; Jesus Christ, the Only Begotten Son of the Father; and the Holy Ghost. These teachings were the source of the most trying question that faced the early Church—Who is the God of the Christians? The Arian controversy arose because of these very teachings, and classical theism has been unable to resolve the conflict in a satisfying and biblical manner for nearly two thousand years. How then can they complain of Joseph Smith?

The Apologists tried to resolve the conflict with their doctrine of co-substantiality borrowed from principles of Greek philosophy. But that was not a biblical resolution, and it was filled with its own brand of folly. How can the Bible, like Joseph Smith, teach monotheism in one breath and identify three separate persons as "God" in the next? This chapter will take a thorough look at the biblical answer to that question.

God's Oneness is Figurative

Mormons frequently say that the Father, Son and Holy Ghost are one in purpose. That may be an imperfect way to express the idea, but the point is that their oneness is not literal or metaphysical, but figurative. As noted in Chapter 9, the Father, Son and Holy Ghost are "united as one in purpose, in plan, and in all the attributes of perfection."[5] This explanation is certainly consistent with the Bible's teachings about God, but it has not won acceptance among Evangelical Christians.

One reason for this lack of acceptance is reflected in the metaphysical implications of the classical statement that there is only one God "by nature." The term "nature," as used in Galatians 4:8 (translated

---

[4] *Lectures on Faith*, Lecture Second, 13.
[5] McConkie, *Mormon Doctrine*, s.v. "God."

from *phusei*), refers to "physical origin."⁶ However, as used by classical theists, "by nature" is intended to refer to the fundamental substance or *ousia* of God. The term reflects the Apologists' adoption of Platonistic dualism, the Greek distinction between the *ousia* of God and the *ousia* of created things. This view appears nowhere in the Bible. In fact, as Galatians 4:7-8 indicates, it is directly antithetical to biblical teachings about God and Man.

The other reason classical theologians have not accepted the idea that God's oneness is figurative is their lack of understanding of certain biblical teachings that show the depth and significance of this doctrine and its correlation with other scriptural principles. These principles, to be considered below, include the application of the laws of agency in the Godhead (considered by classical theists, if at all, under the subject of "angelology") and the doctrine of submission (sometimes referred to as "subordination" in classical theology). Both of these doctrines have been difficult for classical theists to resolve.⁷

The Principle of Agency in the Godhead

The Bible indicates that the Godhead operates pursuant to principles of agency that in many ways are similar to the principles of agency common in most human legal systems. In many respects, however, their operation is unique to the kingdom of heaven. There are two basic elements of an agency relationship. The first is that the agent acts on behalf of the principal.

This principle of God's law of agency is exemplified in Revelation 19:10. There John bowed down to worship the being who had been his guide during that extraordinary vision. This being had been speaking to John in the first person throughout the experience, as though he were God. To John's surprise, he was rebuked by this being in the following language: "I am thy fellowservant, and of thy brethren that have the testimony of Jesus: worship God." John's heavenly host then continued, speaking exactly as if he were God.

In most human legal systems the agent acts on behalf of the principal. In God's system of agency, this principle is taken to perfection. The

---

⁶ Thayer, *Greek-English Lexicon*, s.v. φύσει.
⁷ See, e.g., Harvey, *Handbook of Theological Terms*, s.v. "Angelology;" and Erickson, *Christian Theology*, 338, and 698; and Elwell, *Evangelical Dictionary of Theology*, s.v. "Subordinationism."

agent actually speaks as though he were standing in the shoes of the Principal. He delivers the message from God as though he were God.

The messenger's response to John's worship clearly demonstrates that this practice has no metaphysical implications. The messenger and God are not co-substantial, just as the Father and the Son are not co-substantial. The manner of delivery is proof only of the messenger's authority bestowed by the Principal.

Who Are the Agents of God?

The existence of agents of God is most apparent in biblical accounts regarding angels. C. I. Scofield, the noted nineteenth-century lawyer-turned-theologian, made the following comments about angels:

> The Hebrew and Greek words translated "angel" are also used to refer to God, human beings, and messengers. The last use suggests that the spiritual beings are essentially messengers of God. In the Old Testament, the expression "the angel of the Lord" (sometimes "the angel of God") usually implies the presence of Deity in angelic form (Gen. 16:1-13; 21:17-19; 22:11-16; 31:11-13; Ex. 3:2-4; Judg. 2:1; 6:12-16; 13:3-22).... The Greek word *angelos* is used of human beings in Luke 7:24, Gr.; James 2:25, Gr.; and of men or spiritual beings in Rev. 1:20; 2:1, 8, 12, 18; 3:1, 7, 14. In Rev. 8:3-5 Christ is evidently meant. Sometimes *angelos* is used of the spirit of man (Acts 12:15).[8]

This commentary indicates the confusion classical theists find in the study of angels (angelology). But, as Professor Erickson explains, "The primary Hebrew term for angel is מַלְאָךְ (*mal'ak*); the corresponding Greek word is ἄγγελός (*angelos*); in each case, the basic meaning is messenger."[9] According to Thayer, the principle meaning of the Greek is "a messenger, envoy, one who is sent." In modern terms, "one who is sent"[10] is an *agent*. The one sending the agent is the *principal*. This explains why angels are most often mentioned in reference to God, their Principal, as "*his* angels" (e.g., Ps. 104:4). References to angels in the scriptures are nothing more than references to those who are authorized or sent by God to act for Him as His agents.

---

[8] C. I. Scofield, ed., *New Scofield Study Bible—New American Standard* (New York: Oxford University Press, 1988), Heb. 1:4, *note*.
[9] Erickson, *Christian Theology*, 437.
[10] Thayer, *Greek-English Lexicon*, s.v. ἄγγελός.

The Origin of Angels

Classical theists believe angels are specially created beings, entirely different from Men.[11] The Bible teaches that they were created (Ps. 148:2, 5), but says nothing about them being specially created beings different from Men. The classical position on angels is not based on the writings of the Apologists, but was of a somewhat later origin. The first major work on angels is entitled *On the Celestial Hierarchy* by Pseudo-Dionysius, who lived around 500 A.D. Following the Greek philosophical propensity for classification, he developed a hierarchical ranking of angels including seraphim, cherubim, archangels and angels all organized into nine "choirs."[12] Thomas Aquinas adopted a similar scheme in his works *Summa contra Gentiles*, 19, and *Summa Theologica*, 50-64. However, though the Bible mentions seraphim, cherubim and archangels, it never identifies a hierarchy or says that they are beings other than Men.

Angels are always in human form when they appear to Men, though they are most often described as spirits (Heb. 1:14). Since classical theists reject the pre-existence of Man, they have always rejected the understanding that angels are drawn from among the pre-mortal spirits of Men, as well as from among mortal and post-mortal Men.

Thus, classical theists suppose that the mention of "sons of God" in Job 1:6; 2:1; 38:7 are references to angels rather than Men.[13] That position is maintained despite the fact that Hosea 1:10 identifies righteous Israel as "the sons of the living God," and John explains that Christ gave those who believe in Him the "power to become the sons of God" (John 1:12). Paul explains exactly who the "sons of God" are in Romans 8:14. He says that they are "as many as are led by the spirit of God." See also Philippians 2:15 and 1 John 3:1-2.

Thus, there is overwhelming biblical evidence that references to the "sons of God" in the Old Testament identify righteous pre-mortal spirits of Men (cf., Ps. 103:20). So strongly is the pre-mortal spirit of Man identified with this agency that his spirit was commonly referred to as his "angel" (Acts 12:15). That there were also *unrighteous* pre-mortal spirits of Men appears from the mention of evil angels in the Bible.[14]

---

[11] Miley, *Systematic Theology*, 2:490, *et seq.*
[12] Elwell, *Evangelical Dictionary of Theology*, s.v. "Angel."
[13] Miley, *Systematic Theology*, 2:496.
[14] *Ibid.*, 496, *et seq.*

(Such "angels" of course, are *not* angels of God.) Angels are not a different species of creation from Man. They are pre-mortal, mortal or post-mortal Men chosen of God to serve as His agents.

Special Agents of God

Scripture makes specific mention of two angels by name—Michael and Gabriel—of whom one, Michael, is called an "archangel" (Jude 1:9). He is also referred to as "the great prince" (Dan. 12:1). Apocryphal writings name three more—Raphael, Uriel, and Jeremiel.[15]

As Scofield noted above, the most significant Agent of God is often referred to by the designation "the angel of the Lord" (*mal'ak Yhwh*). This title could be seen as nothing more than an indication that the messenger so designated was sent by the Lord. However, there is strong scriptural evidence that, in the Old Testament, this designation was used as a substitute for the name of the Savior.

For example, in Genesis 16:7-14, "the angel of the Lord" appeared to Hagar. In verse 13, she addresses that angel as "God," and is not corrected as John was in Revelation. Again, in Judges 6:12, "the angel of the Lord" appeared to Gideon. In verse 13, Gideon addresses Him, again without correction, as "Lord," and in the very next verse, the passage reveals that it was "the Lord" who "looked upon him."

This designation indicates that Christ, "the God of Abraham, Isaac and Jacob," the second member of the Godhead and the specific deity appointed to represent the Godhead in its administration over Man during Old Testament times, was acting as an *agent*. Though a separate divine individual, He did not represent an authority different from that of His Father. He did not establish Himself as a Principal, nor act on His own authority in the Old Testament. He acted as a very special agent of the Father, an agent who was Himself an equal with the Principal whom He served. Cf., Heb. 1:4-14, esp. in the NASB (N.B., He *became* "much better than the angels," v. 4).

The designation "angel of the Lord" is also used in the New Testament (*angelos Kurios*) at times when it is clear that it could not be referring to Christ or His spirit (e.g., Matt. 1:20, 24; 2:13, 19; Luke 2:9). In those instances, the angel is never identified using the Greek definitive article "the" (ὁ).[16] Also, unlike the Old Testament, nothing in the New

---

[15] *Ibid*.
[16] The single exception is Matt. 1:24, in which the definitive article is used by Joseph to identify the specific angel of the Lord that appeared to him in Matt. 1:20.

Testament suggests that this particular angel was the Lord Himself, or anything other than "an" angel of the Lord.

Still, the Greek designation (*angelos Kurios*) is very similar to the Hebrew title (*mal'ak Yhwh*). It may have been used to designate the same position of special agency. With Christ incarnate on earth, that agency would necessarily have been filled by a different person, most likely a member of the Godhead.

This may explain the Savior's statement in John 16:7: "Nevertheless, I tell you the truth; It is expedient for you that I go away: for if I go not away, the Comforter[17] will not come unto you; but if I depart, I will send him unto you." The implication is that the Comforter was then functioning in the capacity of "angel of the Lord," a position Christ would resume upon the completion of His mortal ministry, thereby freeing the Holy Ghost to act as Comforter.

As Justin Martyr acknowledged, when almost any action is spoken of as being taken by "God" in the Old Testament, it is Christ who is actually taking that action.[18] Christ was the God of Abraham, Isaac and Jacob, the great I AM (Exod. 3:14; John 8:56-59), the presiding deity over Man. In all His actions, however, Christ was in total harmony with the will of the Father. He operated pursuant to the perfect principles of God's agency. As a result, He is often referred to in the Old Testament using words that are normally associated by Latter-day Saints with the Father, e.g., "Lord God," translated from the Hebrew words for "Jehovah" and "Elohim" (see, e.g., Gen. 15:8).

Understanding Passages in Isaiah

In accordance with the principles of agency described above, whenever Christ acted as the agent of the Father, "the angel of the Lord," in the Old Testament, He spoke for His Principal, as though He were the Father, the "only God." This was uniquely His right as a divine individual acting in consonance with His Father as a perfect Agent.

That relationship explains the language used in Isaiah 43:3, 10 and 44:6, and other passages. There Jehovah declares: "I am the Lord your God," "before Me there was no God formed," and "there is no God besides Me." The word "God" used in these passages, just like *Theos* in

---

[17] This word designates the Holy Ghost (John 14:16-17), and is translated from the greek *Paracletos*, meaning "one called alongside to help." See, John 16:7, NASB side notes.

[18] Justin, *First Apology*, 58.

the New Testament, is not a proper noun. It does not name Christ as an individual, but refers to the Principal, namely the Father, and the singular authority exercised by that Principal.

If a proper noun, such as "Joshua," were substituted for the word "God" in Isaiah 43:3, 10 and 44:6, these scriptures would read, "I am the Lord, your Joshua," "before Me there was no Joshua formed" or "there is no Joshua besides me." Notwithstanding the fact that "Joshua" is the Hebrew form of Christ's given name, Jesus, its substitution as a personal pronoun does not communicate the meaning intended in this passage. The word "God" in these passages was not meant to refer to a specific person. It was used to refer to an authority, a position, or an office, of which there is only *one*.

It is irrelevant, therefore, that there are *three* members of the Godhead who could have delivered that message. Each of them would have spoken as the "only God" for there is only one Principal or ultimate authority over Man. Theoretically, Father could have many divine Agents, each of whom, if worthy, could hold the title "God." To Man there would still be only one Principal, only one ultimate authority over the heavens and the earth.

Christ's Submission To The Father

The other element in an agency relationship is that the agent, by voluntary agreement, acts under the direction or control of the principal. This element of God's agency is apparent in the voluntary submission of the Savior to the will and direction of the Father. It was most perfectly demonstrated in the Garden of Gethsemane, when Christ said, "Father, if thou be willing, remove this cup from me: nevertheless, *not my will, but thine, be done*" (Luke 22:42). The expression is even more revealing in Mark 14:36 (NASB). As recorded by that writer, Christ made a reasoned appeal to the Father, saying: "Abba! Father! All things are possible for Thee; remove this cup from Me; yet not what I will, but what Thou wilt."

This was the knowing and voluntary submission of one God to another God. It was not given mindlessly, without any contribution on Christ's part, and it was not given without a full appreciation of what was expected of Him. It was not the forced submissiveness of a slave, but the voluntary acquiescence of an *agent*. It is an example to all who seek to "overcome" and sit with the Son on the throne of His Father (Rev. 3:21).

So complete was Christ's submission to the Father that He told the Pharisees: "*I can of mine own self do nothing:* as I hear, I judge: and my judgement is just; because *I seek not mine own will, but the will of the Father which hath sent me*" (John 5:30). Elsewhere He explained, "*I do nothing on My own initiative, but I speak these things as the Father taught Me*. And He who sent Me is with Me; He has not left Me alone, for *I always do the things that are pleasing to Him*" (John 8:28-29, NASB).

The Savior's submission to the authority of the Father was taught by Paul in 1 Corinthians 15:24-28 (NASB) as follows:

> then comes the end, when He [Christ] delivers up the kingdom to the God and Father, when He has abolished all rule and all authority and power.
>
> For He must reign until He has put all His enemies under His feet. The last enemy that will be abolished is death.
>
> For He [the Father] has put all things in subjection under His [Christ's] feet. But when He says, "All things are put in subjection," it is evident that He [the Father] is excepted who put all things in subjection to Him [Christ].
>
> And when all things are subjected to Him, then the Son Himself also will be subjected to the One who subjected all things to Him, that God may be all in all.

Without obedience to this principle, Christ could not have been an agent of the Father. The time will come when Christ will be the "Eternal Father" to His own kingdom (Isa. 9:6), but this is the Father's kingdom, as the passage above clearly indicates. Here there is but one ultimate authority or Principal—the Father. Christ does not act as a separate Principal or an agent to Himself. By obedience to the principles of agency, power and authority are exercised by Christ in perfect unity with the Father, for whom Christ acts as His Agent.

Paul and the Oneness of "Many Gods"

The resolution of the age-old conflict about the oneness of God is most profoundly given by Paul in 1 Corinthians 8:4-6. In fact, this may be the only passage in scripture that directly addresses this issue.

In his first letter to the Corinthians, Paul answered several questions that apparently had been posed to him by the members in that area. Unfortunately, there is no written record of the questions Paul was

The Plural and Only God

answering, but the presence of certain comments in the letter suggest the subjects in which the Corinthians were interested.

One of the issues Paul dealt with is the eating of things, especially meat, offered to idols. As noted in Chapter 8, offering or dedicating all the meat in the marketplace to idols was a method used by the Romans to persecute the early Church. Paul discussed the subject at length in 1 Corinthians 8.

A side comment, however, occupies verses 4-6. That commentary suggests the possibility that the Corinthians had been speculating about the possibility of additional Gods—not just idols, but other Men who had, at some point in the infinite past, attained Godhood. Paul's remarks are the definitive biblical text for the resolution of this issue and gives the biblical explanation for how many—e.g., three—Gods can be referred to as "one God." Paul wrote as follows:

> As concerning therefore the eating of those things that are offered in sacrifice unto idols, we know that *an idol is nothing in the world*, and that *there is none other God but one.*
>
> For though there be that are called gods, whether *in heaven* or in earth, (*as there be gods many, and lords many,*)
>
> But *to us there is but one God*, the Father, *of whom* are all things, and we in him; and *one Lord Jesus Christ, by whom* are all things, and we by him.

Obviously, the initial subject of this passage is carried over from the previous verse. However, Paul's remarks in verses 5 and 6 are not simply a comment on idols, as Dr. Beckwith's remarks suggest. The first part of verse 5 is Paul's contrast between false idols and the One God mentioned in verse 4. But if this verse related only to false idols, there would have been no reason for Paul to add the parenthetical phrase at the end of that verse.

That phrase, together with the first phrase in verse 6, is best understood as a response to a two-fold problem: (1) speculation about the possibility that *many* individuals in the universe may have attained the title "Lord" or "God," and (2) the resulting confusion in light of the biblical affirmation of "one God." If there were no other Gods or Lords in the universe and the passage was talking only about idols and false gods, the words "to us" in the first part of verse 6 would have been superfluous. Paul would simply have said, "There is but one God."

Paul's remarks make it clear that there are other Gods and Lords in the universe, but that this fact is irrelevant to Men here. "There *are* Gods many and Lords many," he declares, "but *to us* there is but one God." If the first reference were to false gods, the second would have to be taken in the same sense. We cannot assume Paul is talking only about false gods in verse 5, if we are to understand that he is referring to the true God in verse 6.

Paul then goes on in verse 6 to explain how there can be one God "to us," yet many "in heaven" who bear the title "God." The word, *Theos*, translated "God" in this passage and throughout the New Testament, is a word that refers to Deity in general, i.e., "an object of worship." It is not a proper noun. However, in verse 6, Paul used a proper noun, "the Father," to identify specifically He who is, "to us," the "one God." He next shows clearly what it is about the Father that characterizes Him as the "one God." His brief remarks are translated in the NASB as follows: "*from whom* are all things."

If this simple comment is properly understood, it will immediately become apparent that the number of those who hold the title "God" is, and will always be, irrelevant to the issue of whether monotheism is taught in the New Testament. Here the phrase "all things" is translated from the Greek *tà pánta*, which designates the totality of all things collectively.[19] This means that the Father is the source of all power, law, knowledge, authority and materials. He is the sole individual from whom all the essentials for creation, administration and salvation flow. The Bible designates no other being as that source. He is the sole Principal that runs this heaven and this earth.

Paul next described the role of Christ. He is the one "*by whom* are all things" (again translated from *tà pánta*). This means that Christ is the Agent who *exercises* the power, law, knowledge and authority of the Father to create, administer and save Man using everything that flows *from* the Father. Though in all ways Christ is equal with the Father and worthy of being called "God," He is not a separate Principal, but voluntarily submits to the authority of the Father and acts for and on His behalf as the perfect Agent.

---

[19] The Greek is not inconsistent, however, with the possibility that this phrase refers to all things that pertain to this earth and its heavens, i.e., the subject of the Bible's record.

Corporate Aspects of the Godhead's Functionality

The principles of agency employed by God, though certainly not identical, are in some ways like the functioning of a Board of Directors over a modern corporation in which the Chairman of the Board is the sole shareholder. The Father's role is like the sole shareholder. He is the owner, the ultimate authority over the corporation. Christ's agency role in the Godhead bears some organizational resemblance to the position of a Director on the Board of Directors who holds the position of Chief Executive Officer. He has been charged by the Father with executive responsibility over Man (Heb. 1:8-9).

There can be three members of a Board of Directors or a thousand. The sole shareholder seeks to appoint highly qualified individuals, preferably equals, to the Board of his company. In turn, the Board, as a group, exercises a unitary collective authority over the corporation. If one of the Directors is appointed by the Board to act as the Chief Executive Officer or President of the corporation, that does not mean there are no other members of the Board of Directors. The President is the one authorized to act for the Board in taking most of the actions that relate to daily operation of the company. Expressions like those in Isaiah 43 and 44 demonstrate just such a functionality in the Godhead. They emphasize the unity of leadership that would lie behind such a Chief Executive and the Board of Directors He represents.

This is not to suggest that the Godhead operates exactly like an earthly Board of Directors. The analogy breaks down where corporate law, passed by the state, governs the actions of the corporation, its officers, the Board of Directors and the shareholder. Also, both Man's laws and Men themselves are so imperfect it is difficult to comprehend the workings of a perfect governing body like the Godhead. Nevertheless, the analogy may aid in understanding the functionality of a perfect governing body composed of one Principal and two equal Agents.

The Father, the Son and the Holy Ghost function in unity, without the wrangling and dissension that may be found in earthly organizations, and they are free to interact, as Christ's request in Gethsemane implies. Following such interaction, there is perfect submission to the singular course of action prescribed by the Principal. This concept may be difficult to envision without an earthly analogy. Hence the comparison to a corporation. Like a corporation, there is but one Chief Executive, Christ, who represents one Board of Directors, the Godhead, which answers to one Chairman and sole shareholder, the Father. Hence, as Paul explained in 1 Corinthians 8:4-6, "there is none other God but one."

Other Passages Confirm the Father's Authority as Singular

That Christ, as an equal with the Father, does not exercise a separate authority, is graphically demonstrated in Revelation 3:21: "To him that overcometh will I grant to sit with me in my throne, even as I also overcame, and am set down with my Father in his throne." This language indicates that Christ's throne, a reference to His authority, is not separate. It is the throne [authority] of His Father.

In this verse, Christ extends the opportunity to share that authority with all Men, if they are willing to "overcome," an option made possible through His atonement. The full implications of that invitation will be explored in Part 4, but Christ's statement that He is "set down with [His] Father in *his* throne" confirms that the Father is the source of the authority that Christ exercises over Man.

Thus, it is irrelevant to the oneness of God that there is also one Lord, Jesus Christ. That is why Paul did not falter in his statement that there is one "Lord" (1 Cor. 8:6) after he had just stated that there is but one "God" (1 Cor. 8:4). Though Paul doesn't specifically mention Him in 1 Corinthians 8:6, there is also one Holy Ghost. Indeed, it does not matter how many Gods and Lords there are in the Godhead besides the Father. He is the singular source of authority over Man. "To us" there will always be only one God.

Is Biblical Theology Monotheistic?

The Bible never uses the term "monotheism" to characterize its teachings about God. That word is Greek in origin and appears nowhere in scripture. Therefore, Man's focus on that label is of dubious value. The need to use such labels and definitions is not biblical, but was always a Greek trait.[20]

Scripture teaches that this earth is governed through a system in which there is but one Principal—one source of authority over Man. Because of the singular nature of that authority, the system of governance over the universe would best be described as monotheistic. However, there are many (at least three in the Bible) who are identified

---

[20] Hatch, *Influence of Greek Ideas*, 135.

as holding the title "God." These persons are equal with the Father in the attributes of perfection, and hence, one could also label the Godhead as polytheistic.

What the system is labeled, however, is irrelevant. Classification was the obsession of the Greeks. The Bible makes it clear that there is but one *Principal*. The biblical emphasis on one God in the Old Testament made that principle clear to Israel. There was no change in that principal when the New Testament clearly revealed three who hold that title. In both testaments there is but one Principal, and the other Deities in the Godhead voluntarily act as His Agents.

A system in which three persons rule as though they were one is not hard to understand, nor does it require a special label or definition. It is the natural result of perfect agency. Each member of the Godhead is "God," because they are equals, each of whom can act as, or for, the singular source of authority over Men. Further, the Three together are "one God" because they are united in exercising that singular authority.

Failure of the Greek Mind to Grasp the Godhead's Functionality

There are at least four reasons for the failure of the Apologists to grasp the meaning of the passages discussed above. The *first* is the difficulty that the ancient Greeks had in labeling any religious system. They were conditioned to think only in terms of polytheism or monotheism. The first was the popular pagan system they had fought for hundreds of years, and the latter was their own system.

The *second* was the philosophers' notion of a totally singular entity, one Unmoving Mover or Supreme Being, derived from Pythagorus' mathematical observations of the universe. As indicated in Chapter 6, the concern of the Apologists was to fit Christianity into the latter system for the sake of its survival in the late second century.

The problem was that there were elements of truth in the pagan system as well as in the theology of the philosophers. At least two of the Apologists believed that the philosophers borrowed much of their theology from the Hebrews. What was the origin of the pagan system? Did it really have a different source?

All Men are descended from Noah and his three sons and their wives. Whatever understanding of the gospel those individuals had was passed on to their children with varying degrees of accuracy. The Bible traces the descendants of Shem from whom came Israel. The other descendants of Noah generally served God to a lesser degree. Nevertheless, they had some knowledge of Him, and that knowledge shows up to one extent or another in every religious system practiced among Men. The philosophers rejected the false teachings and depravity of the pagan system. At the same time, they threw out any truth that may have remained in that system, including the twisted understanding the pagans had about the existence of many gods in the universe.

A *third* reason for the Apologists' difficulty was the fact that the Greek Supreme Being acted through an agent, the *Logos*. This doctrine appeared similar to Christian teachings, but it was only superficially so. The Greek *Logos* was viewed differently by the various philosophical sects, as well as the Christian heretics. None of them saw him as a separate, voluntarily submissive agent of equal standing with the Supreme Being. Indeed, given their notions about the Supreme Being, that possibility was unthinkable to them.

Some heretical Christian groups viewed the *Logos* as a separate being, but they could not imagine such a view would be consistent with Christ being on a par with the Father. The Apologists saw Him as an emanation of the Supreme Being, but in that view, He was not truly separate at all. Of course, they claimed a belief in the separateness of the Father, the Son and the Holy Ghost, but, as demonstrated in Chapter 10, what they taught amounted to nothing more than metaphysical lip service to that principle. The Stoics and some Gnostic groups conglomerated a host of inferior agents under the designation *logoi* (later conglomerated with the more common Platonistic title, *Logos*). None of their notions, however, were true to the biblical relationship between the Father and the Son, either.

The *fourth* problem faced by the Apologists was that the Hellenized world at the time of Christ was unfamiliar with any successful attempt at management using the principle of agency employed in the Godhead. The rules that govern modern corporations are a relatively recent development, though they are similar to the ideal government envisioned by Plato in *Republic*.

Plato's ideal was never realized in the ancient world. Even the democratic society of Greek city-states had long since given place to dictatorships by the time of Christ. The executive power trips common to the first and second century were very dissimilar to the comparatively high level of cooperation seen in many of today's boardrooms. Leaders then were conquerors and kings, not directors and presidents, and disputes were resolved at the point of a sword, not in courts of law.

Before the time of Christ, governing systems involving more than a single leader had proven unstable. Even in Rome, the republican form of government died with Julius Caesar in 44 B.C., giving way to the rule of an Emperor. If, on occasion, a group of two or three individuals was formed to rule, the system was usually characterized by disunity and dissension due to the imperfect personalities who formed the group. Witness, for example, the result of Diocletian's vain attempt, mentioned in Chapter 8, to install a more corporate form of leadership over the Roman Empire in the late third and early fourth centuries. One member of the group would invariably fight his way to the top by eliminating his competitors. That is exactly the fate Greek thinkers of the time would have assumed for an organization like the Godhead.

Thus, what today would be recognized immediately as a relatively straightforward, though uniquely perfect, governing system, was a major theological problem in the second century. Instead, the actions of Christ on behalf of the Father were mistaken for co-substantiality and the submission of Christ was completely misunderstood. Indeed, Christ's statements in that regard have long presented a source of confusion for classical theists.

The Confused Doctrine of Subordination

Efforts by classical theologians to understand the passages describing Christ's submission to the Father led to a doctrine called "subordinationism."[21] Because they accepted the Apologists' doctrine of co-substantiality, Christ's submission to the Father presented a particularly thorny theological issue. How does one explain the spectacle of one person voluntarily submitting his will to . . . himself?! The effort to understand this phenomenon in a way that would be consistent with co-substantiality has led to a variety of errors and not a few strange and even heretical notions.

The most significant error that arose from the attempt to comprehend the doctrine of submission in the context of a triune God was made by the Arians, who separated the persons of the Godhead, a correct notion, but postulated that the Son was inferior to the Father, an erro-

---

[21] See, e.g., Harvey, *Handbook of Theological Terms*, s.v. "Subordinationism."

neous notion. The confusion that has reigned in Christendom over this doctrine is described by Elwell, as follows:

> The Nicene fathers ascribed to the Son and Spirit an equality of being or essence, but a subordination of order, with both deriving their existence from the Father as primal source. Athanasius insisted upon the coequality of the status of the three Persons of the Trinity, and Augustine that these Persons are coequal and coeternal. Ancient and modern theologians have argued for a subordination in the role of Son and Spirit to the Father and cite in support such passages as Matt. 11:27; John 5:26-27; 6:38; 8:28; 14:28. Some apply a doctrine of subordination of woman to man on the basis of a similar relationship within the Trinity (1 Cor. 11:3). Others argue that passages that seem to teach a subordination of Son to the Father speak of Christ's voluntary humiliation when he assumed human form (Phil. 2:5-8). In his exaltation, however, he returned to the equality of the eternal relationship expressed in such passages as John 1:1; 5:17-23; 10:15, 30; Titus 2:13; Rom. 9:5; 1 John 5:7. The Athanasian Creed declared that in the Trinity "none is before or after another: none is greater or less than another," and the Second Helvetic Confession, the second most influential confession in Reformed tradition, condemns as heretics any who teach a subordination of Son or Holy Spirit.[22]

This quotation describes what has actually been an effort by classical theologians to explain away the doctrine of submission rather than to understand it. Professor Erickson's effort to explain the doctrine of subordination displays the same misunderstanding:

> The function of one member of the Trinity may for a time be subordinate to one or both of the other members, but that does not mean he is in any way inferior in essence. Each of the three persons of the Trinity has had, for a period of time, a particular function unique to himself. This is to be understood as a temporary role for the purpose of accomplishing a given end, not a change in his status or essence.[23]

There is no indication in scripture that Christ's submission to the Father was an isolated incident in time or a limited aspect of His role restricted to the period of His incarnation. There is no logical reason to see it as such, unless one is trying to explain away the inconsistencies between Christ's agency relationship with the Father and the notion of

---

[22] Elwell, *Evangelical Dictionary of Theology*, s. v. "Subordinationism."
[23] Erickson, *Christian Theology*, 338.

co-substantiality. Further, the idea that Christ's submission to the Father was limited to His incarnation is entirely inconsistent with the implications of Revelation 3:21.

Conclusion

The failure of the early Church to grasp the meaning of Christ's submission to the Father resulted in the most fundamental error of that age. They ascribed an equality of being to the Father, Son and Holy Ghost, rather than an equality of *position*.

The fact that the Three are "one" is never explained in the Bible based on Their having the same "substance" or "essence." That is a doctrine rooted entirely in Greek philosophy. The principles of agency are apparent throughout the Bible. Those principles completely and satisfactorily explain the way in which three Gods may be referred to as "one."

The fact that three entirely separate and perfect Deities act in unison to advance the purposes of a singular, almighty source of authority over the heavens and the earth is the biblical truth. Though it was not discerned by the Apologists as the explanation of God's oneness in the face of the New Testament declaration that there are three who bear the title of "God," it should not be ignored by modern theologians as the true biblical explanation of the "only God."

Summary

1. The scriptures refer to the "only God," yet they also clearly refer to three different persons as "God." One of the most significant issues in theology is to determine whether the oneness of God requires a singularity of the three persons in the Godhead.
2. Classical theists rule out any possibility of a plurality of Gods. For them, there is only one God *"by nature."*
3. References by classical theists to one God *"by nature"* use a term that is found nowhere in the Bible, except Galatians 4:8, where it is used in a context that implies God and Man are of the same nature.
4. The doctrine of the Trinity itself goes a step beyond strict monotheism by recognizing that the Bible contains numerous references to three who bear the title "God." This seeming dichotomy is what lay at the heart of the Arian controversy and drove the Apologists to formulate the doctrine of co-substantiality.

5. Uniquely Mormon scriptures, as well as the Bible, refer to the "only God," as did Joseph Smith, who said, "God is the only supreme governor and independent being in whom all fullness and perfection dwell." Joseph also taught the doctrine of a plurality of Gods. Mormons teach that God is one in purpose, plan and the attributes of perfection.
6. Classical theists adopt the principles of Platonistic dualism and make a distinction between the "*ousia*" of God and the "*ousia*" of created things. The latter distinction appears nowhere in the Bible.
7. God operates using principles of perfect agency. The agents of God represent God, their Principal, as though they actually were God (Rev. 19:10). This is not a metaphysical relationship, but one created in a purely legal sense by the laws of God's perfect agency.
8. In the scriptures, God's agents are called "angels."
9. Angels are not specially created beings different from Men. They are Men. The classification of angels by the Pseudo-Dionysius the Areopagite in approximately 500 A.D. reflects the Greek obsession with classification, and is not entirely biblical.
10. Angels are always in bodily form when they appear to Men, and are most often described as spirits. They are drawn from the pre-mortal (e.g., Job 38:7) and the post-mortal spirits of Men, as well as from among mortal and resurrected Men.
11. Some special agents of God are named in the scriptures. Most prominent among these is "the angel of the Lord," whom Bible scholars have correctly identified as the Savior Himself. He became "much better than the angels" upon His exaltation, consistent with the exposition set forth in Chapter 16.
12. Language in Isaiah, chapters 41-45, denying the existence of any God beside Jehovah is to be understood in the context of Christ's agency relationship with the Father. The references to "God" in those verses are correctly understood as addressing the singular office or position of ultimate authority belonging to the Father which that title represents.
13. In the New Testament, Christ repeatedly spoke in terms of complete voluntary submission to the Father, as a perfect agent would speak of his principal.
14. Paul explained the oneness of many Gods in 1 Corinthians 8:4-6. He taught that all things (including all authority) came through the Father, whom he identified as the "one God." Christ, he explained,

is the agent of the Father, and is the one *by whom* all things were done.
15. Using an analogy to corporate law, the Father is like a sole shareholder who is Chairman of a Board of Directors that could be analogized to the Godhead. Christ is the Chief Executive Officer representing this body in the daily operation of the company (universe).
16. There can be one Director or a thousand on a Board of Directors, yet they are the singular governing body of the corporation under the direction of the Chairman and sole shareholder. Likewise, there can be three members of the Godhead, yet only one God.
17. Revelation 3:21 promises that many may sit on the Father's throne with Christ, yet there is but one throne.
18. Efforts to label the system of universal government described in the Bible ran into problems in the Greek mind. Because there is only one Principal, the Father, that governing system is best classified as monotheistic, but the presence of many Gods acting as voluntary agents of the one Principal could be taken as polytheistic, a term that was anathema to the Greek philosophers.
19. The Greeks of Christ's time could not grasp the functionality of the Godhead for at least four reasons: (1) they had difficulty labeling the system, (2) their own system of theology was strictly monotheistic, (3) although their Supreme Being acted through a "*Logos*," he/it was an actual extension of the Supreme Being, not an independent agent, and (4) systems of government involving more than one person acting cooperatively had been unsuccessful.
20. Although Christ's subordination to the Father is clearly taught in the Bible, it was misunderstood by the Church in the third and fourth centuries. The Arians wrongly took it to mean that the Son was inferior to the Father. Classical theologians today take it to be a temporary condition of Christ's mortal incarnation.
21. The Apologists, and the classical theists after them, ascribe an equality of being to the Father, Son and Holy Ghost rather than an equality of position. They ignore the fact that the Bible never explains the oneness of God in terms of their substance or essence. The principles of agency, however, appear throughout the Bible. Those principles represent the biblical explanation of the "only God."

Part IV

Classical Theism Reacts to the Biblical Concept of God:

Philosophical Problems With Eternal Progression

The Lord to Job:

Who is this that darkens counsel by words without knowledge?

Job 38:2

Man and the Infinite

The Greek philosophers, and after them the Apologists who embraced their philosophy, insisted on a vast gulf between God and Man. So vast was this gulf that to them, God was incomprehensible. To them, this situation was not just a condition of the human mind, it was a characteristic of God. Man, in their view, was not simply ignorant, he was in a different reality, making God fundamentally unknowable.

While the Bible places God's thoughts higher than Man's (Isa. 55:8-9), it clearly holds out the hope and expectation that Man can come to know God (John 17:2-3). To the Greek philosophers, however, the idea of knowing God, in the sense of truly comprehending Him, was impossible.[1] They regarded it as part of His transcendency—God was infinite, Man finite.[2]

The belief in an incomprehensible God was a change from the teachings of early Christianity. That is confirmed by Hatch as follows:

> The conception, for example, of the one God whose kingdom was a universal kingdom and endured throughout all ages, blended with, and passed into, the philosophical conception of a Being who was beyond time and space. The conception that "clouds and darkness were round about Him," blended with, and passed into, the philosophical conception of a Being who was beyond not only human sight but human thought.[3]

An Ontological Look at God and Man

This idea of a gulf between God and Man is based on the amalgamation of a number of false Greek doctrines that have been examined

---
[1] See Hatch, *Influence of Greek Ideas*, 239-245.
[2] Philo, *De post. Cain*, 6.
[3] Hatch, *Influence of Greek Ideas*, 239.

in prior chapters. One is the notion of God's transcendency over the real space-time universe (see Chapter 11). Another is the idea that God is God "by nature" (see Chapter 17), and that Man does not, and cannot, share in that divine nature. Ultimately, all these notions derive from the Platonistic idea of duality, God being viewed as pure Mind, and Matter in the form of created things being inferior.

The study of these notions falls within a Greek form of analysis called *ontology*, the term used for what is known in philosophy as the study of "being." Ontology in classical theism is the attempt to analyze, philosophically, the basic nature of an entity or thing. The field of inquiry is based on Plato's and Aristotle's use of the word *ousia*, used to describe the fundamental characteristics of various classes of things (see Chapter 2).

In its application to God, Origen took the notion of *ousia* to the extreme, claiming that God does not have a "nature," but is beyond classification. Man, of course, was never considered by Origen and the other Apologists as beyond classification, which was Dr. Beckwith's point in using the phrase "by nature" in describing God as the Only God (see Chapter 17). The Platonists believed that Man and God are ontologically distinct. Unfortunately, this conclusion has never been challenged by modern classical theists.

There is no biblical basis for this doctrine. The only passage in the Bible that uses the words "by nature" in the context of a discussion about God is Galatians 4:8, which does not distinguish between the nature of Man and the nature of God, but between the nature of God and the nature of idols. That is a common theme in the Bible, but the distinction is always made in a way that emphasizes the *similarity* of Man and God, in contrast to the *dissimilarity* of God and idols.

Thus, in Deuteronomy 4:27-28 (NASB) Moses states that the Lord would scatter Israel among the nations where they "will serve gods, the work of man's hands, wood and stone, which neither see nor hear nor eat nor smell." Paul specifically contrasts the similarity of Man and God with the dissimilarity of God and idols in Acts 17:29: "Forasmuch then as we are the offspring of God, we ought not to think that the Godhead is like unto gold, or silver, or stone, graven by art and man's device."

Yet, it is often said by classical theists that "a Man cannot have God's nature any more than a dog can have Man's nature." [4] That

---

[4] John Stewart, "Bible On the Line" on KKLA (Los Angeles radio station), circa 1991.

statement is a direct contradiction of the biblical statement in Genesis that Man was made in God's image and likeness (Gen. 1:26-27). Thus, classical theism teaches another paradoxical dichotomy. On the one hand, they believe Man is in God's image and likeness in some undefined sense, and on the other hand they believe that God and Man are not even vaguely similar to each other.

Professor Erickson expresses the orthodox belief in an ontological difference between God and Man in these terms:

> God is transcendent; he goes beyond our categories of understanding. He can never be fully grasped within our finite concepts or by our human vocabulary. He can be understood, but not comprehensively. Correlated with God's transcendence is man's finiteness. He is a limited being in terms of both his point of origin in time and the extent to which he can grasp information. Consequently, he cannot formulate concepts which are commensurate with the nature of God. These limitations are inherent in man's being man. They are not a result of the fall or of individual human sin, but of the Creator-creature relationship.[5]

In Part 3, however, it was shown that God is not transcendent as classical theism asserts, though He is certainly on a level that exceeds Man's current state of progression by so much that His status is difficult for Men to grasp. Nor was Man created out of nothing. Mormonism teaches that Man is not limited in terms of "his point of origin in time." The spirits of Men have existed from before the creation of the world as angels, the "sons of God" (Job 38:7), and from modern revelation it appears that, before their creation as the angelic spirit children of God, Men were "intelligences" (D&C 93:29), uncreated personalities who have existed from all eternity as the basic kernel of life.

As to the extent of Man's ability to gain knowledge, it was shown in Chapter 14 that not only God, but Men, have the biological capacity to be omniscient. There is no biblical basis for the claim of classical theism that Men and God are ontologically different.

The Classical Doctrine of Man's "Finiteness"

Notwithstanding the lack of biblical support for their ideas, classical theists have imagined several points about the finite nature of Man

---
[5] Erickson, *Christian Theology*, 247.

which they assert as a basis for distinguishing "finite" Man from infinite God. These points are summarized by Professor Erickson in his *Christian Theology*. Though too lengthy to quote in full, the following are highlights of that list:

1. That man was created means that *he has no independent existence*. He came into being because God willed that he should exist, and acted to bring him into being. Man has received his life from God and continues to experience and enjoy life because of divine provision. *There is nothing necessary about his existence. Man is a contingent being, not an indispensable part of reality.* Nor does man ever come to the point where he is truly independent of God. . . . Man is not at the center of the universe. He exists only because someone far greater brought him into being. . . . *Man is a creation of God, not an outflow from him. Man is not a part of divinity. He has the limitations of finitude.* He does not know all, and is not able to do all. Although the aim of the Christian life is to be spiritually one with God, *man will always be metaphysically separate from God.* . . .

2. Man is part of the creation. . . . *[T]here is a large metaphysical gap within the span of being.* This gap, however, is not between man and the rest of the creatures. *It is between God on the one hand, and all of the creatures on the other.* The origin of man on one of the days of creation links him far more closely with all the other created beings than with the God who did the creating.

3. Man, however, has a unique place in creation. As we have noted, man is a creature and thus shares much with the rest of the creatures. But there is an element which makes him unique, which sets him apart from the rest of the creatures. *They are all said to be made "according to their kind." He, on the other hand, is described as made in the image and likeness of God.* He is placed over the rest of the creation, to have dominion over it. . . .

6. *There are definite limitations upon man. Man is a creature, not God, and has the limitations that go with being finite. Only the Creator is infinite. Man does not and cannot know everything.* While we ought to seek to know all that we can, and ought to admire and esteem great knowledge wherever it is possessed and displayed, our finiteness means that our knowledge will always be incomplete and subject to error. . . . *Finiteness also pertains to our lives.* Whether man as he was created would have died had he not sinned is a subject of debate (see pp. 611-13). We do know, however, that man was susceptible to

becoming subject to death. That is, if he was immortal, it was a conditional immortality. Thus, *man is not inherently immortal. . . . Only God is inherently eternal; all else dies. . . . Finiteness means that there are practical limitations to all of our accomplishments. . . .*

7. Limitation is not inherently bad. There is a tendency to bemoan the fact of man's finiteness. . . . But the Bible indicates that having made man with the limitations which go with creaturehood, *God looked at the creation and pronounced it "very good"* (Gen. 1:31). The human race was limited, *but pronounced good. . . .*

8. Proper adjustment in life can be achieved only on the basis of *acceptance of one's own finiteness.* The fact of our finiteness is clear. We may, however, be unwilling to accept that fact and to accept our place in the scheme of things as creatures of God who are dependent upon him. . . . We ought to be willing to let God be God, not seeking to tell him what is right and true, but rather submitting to him and his plan for us. To pass judgment on God's deeds would require an infinite knowledge, something that we simply do not have. . . . *This means that we need not always be right.* We need not fear failing. Only God never fails or never makes a mistake. It is not necessary for us, then, to make excuses for our shortcomings or to be defensive because we are not perfect. . . . A proper humility will follow if we admit to ourselves our finite creatureliness *and are willing to live accordingly. . . .* We are not God. *We cannot be God. We need not be God. God does not expect us to be God.* Satisfaction and happiness lie in wait for us if we accept this fact, disappointment and frustration if we do not. *We are not beings who should be God but have failed in the attempt. We are what we were intended to be: limited human creatures. . . .*[6]

The Biblical Response to the Orthodox Doctrine of Man's "Finiteness"

Perhaps no other doctrine of orthodox Christianity is as erroneous and misguided as this. While classical theists correctly note many differences that currently exist between God and Man, their doctrine, in effect, denies that the caterpillar will ever become the butterfly. The biblical response to classical theists was given by Christ in the Sermon on the Mount: "Be ye therefore perfect, even as your Father which is in Heaven is perfect" (Matt. 5:48).

---

[6] *Ibid.*, 487-493.

Clearly, Man is expected to become perfect, like God. True humility lies in recognizing how far Man currently stands from that goal. Men are not benefitted, either in their mental or emotional health, by excusing their lack of repentance with the claim that they should be content to remain in their fallen state. God did not make Man as he is now, and He does not expect him to remain in this condition. When God created Adam and Eve, they were "very good," a pronouncement that goes directly against the kind of finiteness described above.

The Bible and uniquely Mormon scriptures (Book of Mormon, Alma 34:14; D&C 20:17, 28) confirm that God is infinite. However, nowhere do they state that Man is finite. In fact, every implication in scripture is contrary to that notion. At the most basic level, the Bible repeatedly refers to God as the father of Man (see e.g., Mal. 2:10; John 20:17; Acts 17:28; Rom. 8:16). It is quite exacting in its testimony that Man is a *literal child* (Rom. 8:16, Greek: *teknon*), *the offspring* (Acts 17:28-29, Greek: *genos*), *of God*. See also, Heb. 12:9. As the literal offspring of God, Man and God should be recognized as being the same *species*.

The Greek word translated "offspring" in Acts 17:28-29 is the root of the current scientific term "genus." It means "descendants of a common ancestor."[7] The "common ancestor" referred to, of course, is God the Father, the Father of the human race. This explains Christ's most common reference to Himself as "the Son of Man." His father was God, the father of Man. As His children, it is the nature of Men to become like God.

Though orthodox Christians vehemently disagree, Mormons believe that the Apostle John's remarks were not limited when he said "Beloved, now are we the sons of God, and it doth not yet appear what we shall be: but we know that, when he shall appear, we shall be like him; for we shall see him as he is" (1 John 3:2). That John had in mind a total likeness to God appears from his statement, "we shall see him as he is." He offers that statement as proof of the promise that "we shall be like him." Only if Men are truly like God could they ever "see Him as He is."

The Principle of Progression

Of course Man, in his current fallen state, and God are very different in certain ways. Many biblical references so indicate, but the differ-

---

[7] Bauer, *Greek-English Lexicon*, s.v. γένος.

ences between Man and God identified in scripture have nothing to do with ontology. They explain that God and Man differ in their *behavior* (see, e.g., Num. 23:19, discussed at length in Chapter 11) and in *degree* (see, e.g., Isa 55:8-9), not in *kind*. They indicate that Man differs from God much as a larva differs from the mature adult in a species. That is the analogy that best expresses the principle of eternal progression.

Man is a long way from God in his progress at this time, but that does not negate the testimony of the scriptures that Man and God are the same species and that Men, conditionally, can eventually become like God. The point to keep in mind at this stage of Man's progression is that, as Men progress, there are no ontological obstacles to God carrying out the promise He made through the Apostle John in 1 John 3:2. Given an eternal length of time in which to accomplish the task God can, and most definitely will make those who purify themselves (1 John 3:3) in every way "like him."

An Infinite Number of Gods

Not only did the Apostle John teach that Man can become exactly like God (1 John 3:2-3), Paul taught that Men can be "fellow heirs with Christ," and "be glorified with Him," provided they "suffer with Him" (Rom. 8:17, NASB; see also Gal. 4:7). Christ taught that "he who overcomes ... will ... sit down with Me on my throne, even as I also overcame, and am set down with my Father in his throne" (Rev. 3:21).

In the latter verse, the symbol of Christ on a throne is one of authority and power. It refers to Christ's position in the Godhead, as one of the Three who function in the office of "God" (see Chapter 17). He has promised a similar position to those who "overcome," symbolized by their sitting on the throne of the Father with Christ. Revelation 3:21 suggests that no matter how many become heirs of God, there will always be a unitary government over the universe. Those who overcome will sit on Christ's throne, but His throne is identified as the throne of His Father.

Only *one throne* is mentioned in this verse, representing the singular authority over the entire universe. If Christ and the Father can "set down" on that throne, and if Men who "overcome" can be offered a seat there as well, it is possible over the eternities that an innumerable host has or may yet "overcome" and be "set down" on that throne with Christ.

The implications of the passages cited above are enormous. Dr. Beckwith is not the only one who has speculated on these themes. Mormons too have indulged in a wide range of speculation on the issues they raise. Regarding that line of speculation and the resulting number of Gods it suggests may exist in the universe (1 Cor. 8:5), Dr. Beckwith states his conclusions as follows:

> It follows from what we have covered that in the Mormon universe there are an infinite number of intelligent entities, such as gods (exalted humans) and preexistent intelligences. If this is denied, however, the Mormon must somehow reconcile a finite number of these beings with an infinite past. For instance, if there is only a finite number of gods in a universe with an *infinite* past, then there was a time when no gods existed (which Joseph Smith denies). For a finite number of gods coming into being cannot be traced back infinitely. Moreover, if there is only a finite number of gods, then the continually repeated scenario of a god organizing intelligences so that they can begin their progression to godhood would have never begun. This is so because in Mormonism one needs a god in order for another to become a god, and no being has always been a god.
>
> Furthermore, if there were only a finite number of preexisting intelligences in the infinite past, then there could no longer be any preexistent intelligences who could become gods, since they would all certainly be "used up" by now. An infinite amount of time is certainly sufficient to use up a finite number of preexistent intelligences. At any rate, in order for Mormonism to remain consistent, it must teach that there is an *infinite* number of gods and preexistent intelligences in an infinitely large universe.[8]

Though Dr. Beckwith has paralleled Mormon speculation on this subject, he does so in the pattern of ancient Greek rhetoric that proved so troublesome to the early Church. His argument makes assumptions with no firsthand knowledge of the universe, and then he insists that Mormons must defend his own assumptions.

For the most part, Mormons should decline the invitation to respond to such arguments if they do not recognize and clearly identify their response as *highly speculative*. It may be that there are an infinite number of gods in the universe, but it is also possible that there are not that

---

[8] Beckwith, "Philosophical Problems," 7-8.

many. So far, the universe has proven to be much more complex than even the most detailed of Man's speculations about it.

A Finite Look at Infinity

Classical theists speak of the infinite as "by definition, limitless."[9] Actually, that is not an entirely accurate statement. Too often the term is applied to the Almighty with little or no comprehension of what it implies about Him. Infinity is a concept that must be better understood if Man is to understand God. It is even more important to understand it if Man is to understand Man.

The distinction classical theists draw between God as infinite and Man as finite is actually theological in nature, but they attempt to use it in a nebulous mathematical sense. Most Men have little or no understanding of the mathematical term, and often they lack any understanding of its use in ancient cultures. To classical theists, the terms "infinite" and "finite" are meant to specify mutually exclusive categories. Because of their lack of knowledge of these terms, they wrongly believe that it is impossible for Man, the finite, to become like God, the infinite. In fact, the Bible never makes that mistake.

The failure of classical theism to grasp this aspect of God's relationship to Man is reminiscent of the group of Greek philosophers who lost their way while hiking in the Alps. One of them took out a map, and after studying it for a long time exclaimed, "Now I know where we are!" "Where?" the others asked. "See that big mountain over there?" came the answer. "We're right on top of it."

To understand an infinite God and Man's position relative to Him, one needs a better map, or at least a better understanding of the map. Though Man's comprehension of the infinite is limited by his mortality, it is possible to break out of that limitation in some measure through mathematical analysis and logic. Modern mathematics has shown that the finite and the infinite are not so far removed from each other as the ancient Greeks supposed.

In dealing with infinities, one must get used to certain concepts that seem paradoxical at first because they are outside the realm of normal experience. However, an understanding of these seemingly paradoxical

---

[9] *Ibid.*, 9.

properties of infinity will aid greatly in understanding some of the statements about God that are made in the Bible.

For example, the number of points on a line of *finite* length, say two inches, is *infinite* regardless of the length of the line. That is because a point is infinitely small, at least in theory. Furthermore, there are as many points on a two-inch line (namely, an infinite number) as there are on a four-inch line (also an infinite number). In practical terms, of course, a point is not infinitesimal, and a different number of them will add up to a two-inch line than it takes to make a four-inch line. This practical difference represents the stepping-off point for mathematical analysis using the rules of calculus. On one side is the practical and on the other side is the theoretical. It is important to understand both the practical and the theoretical aspects of infinity in order to understand the infinite nature of the Universe.

Another unique aspect of infinity is discovered when additional dimensions of space are analyzed. For example, if a two-inch-long line were stretched into two dimensions, it would become a flat plane. That *finite*, four-square-inch plane would be composed of an *infinite* number of two-inch lines, each of which would, in turn, be composed of an *infinite* number of points. That is because, in theory, the width of a line is infinitesimally small and each infinitely thin line is composed of an infinite number of infinitely small points.

If that *finite*, four-square-inch plane were stretched into a *finite* sixteen-cubic-inch cube, it would be composed of an *infinite* number of *finite*, four-square-inch planes, each of which has no height because it is infinitely thin. Those four-square-inch planes would be composed of an *infinite* number of *finite* two-inch lines, which, in turn, would be composed of an *infinite* number of points.

Does this mean there are more points in a sixteen-cubic-inch cube than there are on a four-square-inch plane or on a two-inch line? Here is the paradox: the answer is no! They would all have the same number of points, namely an infinite number. All of infinite space is composed of the same number of points as there are on one little two-inch line—an infinite number!

Not only can infinite space be divided into an *infinite* number of infinitesimal points, it can include an infinite number of *finite* spatial segments (e.g., sixteen-cubic-inch cubes). Each of these segments has at least one finite measurement (length, area or volume), but in infinite space it does not matter how big or how small those finite measurements are. They could even be infinitely large or infinitely small. Thus, in infinite space there can be an *infinite* number of *infinite* spaces! In the real universe this means that there could be an infinite number of "kingdoms," and each of those kingdoms could be infinite in dimension.

Another interesting fact about infinity is that there are larger and smaller infinite numbers. Georg Cantor, the founder of the "arithmetics of infinity," has shown that the number of points in the universe constitute one order of infinity designated by the Hebrew letter $\aleph_1$. That number is actually the second order of infinity. The first order, designated $\aleph_0$, is the number of all possible integer and fractional numbers in the universe. Through mathematical comparison, Cantor has shown that the number of numbers is less than the number of points. Though both numbers are infinite, one infinite number is actually smaller than the other infinite number.[10]

Thus, it is impossible for Man to number all the points in the universe. God has frequently made this very point in describing His creations. See, e.g., Pearl of Great Price, Moses 1:33, 35. Indeed, it is the meaning of God's reference to the sands of the sea as "innumerable" (e.g., Gen. 22:17; Jer. 33:22; Heb. 11:12). The "sands of the sea" is simply an analogy that refers to "the number of points in the universe."

Infinite time is subject to the same type of analysis as infinite space. Any *finite* period of time, like any finite distance, can be divided into an *infinite* number of infinitesimal time segments (usually designated "*dt*" in calculus). These infinitesimal *dt* have the same relationship to measurable periods of time as points have to finite distances. That is, an infinite number of *dt* are experienced in one second, and the same number (infinity) are experienced in a day. Though theoretically infinitesimal, these *dt* accumulate and are subject to the same rules of math as points. Thus, an infinite number of *dt* can have a distinct beginning and a definite end. Everyone has lived through an infinite number of *dt* today, and will live through another infinite number tomorrow.

Just as points are not, as a practical matter, truly of infinitesimal length, so *dt* could actually have a measurable duration for many practical purposes. For example, an eternal being such as God could view

---

[10] George Gamow, *One two three ... infinity: Facts & Speculations of Science* (New York: Viking Press, 1961), 14-23.

a day of Man's time as one *dt*. He would have gone through an infinite number of such *dt*, each with a measurable "beginning" and "end," during His infinite lifetime. These *dt* could actually be much larger, and still there would have been an infinite number of them in any infinite time period. In fact, infinite time, like infinite space, can be divided into an infinite number of *infinite* periods.

Thus, infinite time is so vast that, assuming God progressed from an "intelligence" (D&C 93:29; Abraham 3:22) to His current position as God the Father during an infinite period of time, He could have existed as God for yet another infinite period of time before He created the earth on which Man dwells. Under such circumstances, it would be mathematically correct to say that God was God "from infinity to infinity," notwithstanding the fact that He had previously spent yet another infinite period of time progressing to the point that He became God.

In practical terms, many cultures use much smaller numbers as though they were infinite. In fact, depending on the needs of the culture, infinity can be very limited indeed. Among the Hottentots of Africa, "infinity" was once expressed by the word "many," which was any number greater than three.[11] For purposes of normal, everyday communication, "infinity" is best defined as *any number which exceeds by one the highest number to which anyone in a particular culture could reasonably be expected to count.*

Since God speaks to His children in terms they understand, references to the infinite in the Bible frequently have this less technical, more practical meaning. The word "infinite" is used in connection with God only once in the Bible—to describe one of His attributes, His understanding (Ps. 147:5). The word is not translated from the Hebrew *olam*, discussed in Chapter 16, but from two Hebrew words (*en*, or more precisely *ayin, mispar*) which literally mean "is not numbered."

The same words, translated "innumerable," also appear in Job 21:33, Psalms 40:12 and 104:25, and Jeremiah 46:23. In those passages, they are used to describe things that are numerous, e.g., the animals in the ocean (Psalm 104:25), but definitely finite in both the mathematical and the classic theological sense.

What this means with respect to God's nature should not be taken as any kind of discernable limitation—certainly not one that could be

---

[11] Gamow, *One two three . . . infinity*, 3.

comprehended by Man in his current state. It does, however, have a very practical meaning when it comes to the consideration of Man's ability to become like God. It means that finite Man is not eternally excluded from the possibility of attaining infinite Godhood.

Infinity in Mormon Theology

Mormonism teaches that the universe has existed as long as God has existed. That means the real universe has always existed in some form. If God has created "worlds without number" (Moses 1:33) like the one on which Men now live, it is logical to assume that the universe is populated by an infinite number of "intelligences" and an infinite amount of eternal "element." It also follows that these raw materials have been, and are being, used by God to bring to pass the immortality and eternal life (Moses 1:39) of what could easily be an *infinite* number of Men who have progressed to the point that they are fully mature sons and heirs of God (Rom. 8:14), equal with Him in the attributes of perfection discussed in Part 3 (1 John 3:2).

The universe, however, is by no means crowded by this state of affairs. Applying the principles discussed above, even if there are an infinite number of infinite beings in the universe, each one could occupy an infinite domain without infringing on the infinite domain of any other infinite being. In infinite space and time, there could exist an infinite number of infinite universes, each describable by the infinite terms, "the heavens and the earth," and there would still be room for an additional infinite number of such universes.

Beginnings in Mormon Theology

Dr. Beckwith stated correctly that Mormon theology assumes the existence of a "beginningless universe." [12] As difficult as that is for the Greek mind to grasp, it is the only logical explanation for the existence of any real universe. If one were to identify a beginning in real space-time, the question would have to be asked, "What happened before that?" or "What's on the other side of that?" The answer would always be "more time" or "more space." Still, it would be incorrect to say that there are no "beginnings" in an infinite universe. Any infinite period of time can be divided into an infinite number of finite periods or events,

---

[12] Beckwith, "Philosophical Problems," 5.

each having any given length, even an infinite length, and each with its own beginning and end. (In the case of infinite time periods, either the beginning or the end may be missing, of course.)

Thus, Mormonism unequivocally avers that there was a beginning for the current contents of the universe in which Men exist. That is, there was a beginning for "the heavens and the earth" to which God refers in Genesis 1:1, and there will be an end to these heavens and this earth, at which time they will be replaced by a new heaven and a new earth (Rev. 21:1).

Each intelligence who has been "added upon" (Abraham 3:26) has gone, or may go, through a number of "beginnings." There are four such beginnings/endings specifically identified in Scripture. The first is that of spiritual creation or organization (Abraham 3:22), i.e., birth into spirit form (Isa. 57:16; Zech. 12:1; Heb. 12:9). The second is incarnation, i.e., birth into physical form (Gen. 1:26-27; Heb. 12:9). The third is the transition into the spirit world which Men call "death." Finally there is the resurrection of the fallen and mortal physical form into the perfect and eternal resurrected form (1 Cor 15:51-53).

For each intelligence, an infinite period of time elapses before the first of these beginnings. This is so, no matter when the first beginning happens, because all intelligences have been in existence as long as the universe. After the first beginning, a very long—possibly infinite—period of time elapses before the second beginning occurs. After death, the last beginning will follow within a finite period of time. Specifically, for Men on this earth, the resurrection began with the resurrection of Christ and will end at the end of His thousand year reign (Rev. 20:4-6), which will commence fairly soon by all biblical accounts.

The Number of Gods in the Universe

If an infinite number of intelligences exist in the universe, an infinite number of them could have experienced one or more of the three beginnings described above by now. Yet there would remain an infinite number who still have not experienced any of them. Thus, there will be no end to the "beginnings" that occur in this so-called "beginningless universe." They will occur in an endless cyclical stream throughout infinite time. Man on this earth is currently involved in one of those cycles, one that began, relatively speaking, a short time ago.

However, contrary to Dr. Beckwith's reasoning, the question of whether the number of intelligences in the universe is finite or infinite cannot be determined from the fact that an infinite period of time has already passed. Even if there are only a finite number of intelligences in the universe, there would have been an infinite period of time before God's first creative cycle began. After it started, it would take a very long time, involving numerous cycles, for a large but finite number of intelligences to experience all the "beginnings" described above and reach full maturity. Today could be near the start, in the middle, or near the end of those cycles. In either case, there would be an infinite period of time extending into the past. Thus, Man cannot know the number of Gods and Lords in the universe without some revelation of that fact from God. Paul has already given Man as much information as God considers necessary for him to have. "Unto us there is but one God" (1 Cor. 8:6).

Logical Requisites For Eternal Progression

In the chapter that follows certain philosophical objections to LDS teachings about eternal progression will be examined. These were raised by Dr. Beckwith in the article that has frequently been referred to in this book: "Philosophical Problems With the Mormon Concept of God." In order to understand the errors Dr. Beckwith makes, it is crucial that certain aspects of the doctrine of eternal progression are clearly understood.

It is extremely important to remember that Man is, in fact, infinite in time. This is true, of course, only of Man's "intelligence." His spirit and his physical body had a specific origin in time. However, Mormonism undeniably teaches that Man's basic nature is infinite, and that is a fundamental difference between Mormon teachings and classical theism's view of Man as finite and limited.

Secondly, it is important to understand that Man can become omniscient only through the endowment of God's omnipotence. In order to know the future, Men must be omnipotent, as God is. God is the singular source of all power and authority in the universe. This includes the right to rule over all things as indicated in Revelation 3:21. Men must overcome and sit on God's throne, thereby sharing His power, if they are to be omnipotent and omniscient.

Those on whom God chooses to bestow this boon will have proven themselves trustworthy servants. They will always act in complete submission to Him, just as Christ did (John 5:30; 8:29). This will likely be the case in all that they do, however autonomous their actions may become, the principle being that the perfect follower becomes the perfect leader. It is probable that Men will always remain Agents of God in some respects, exercising the power of His throne in complete alignment with that perfect will which now governs Man (Rev. 22:3-5). They will most assuredly be like God, just as Christ is, for that is what it means to be "joint-heirs with Christ" (Rom. 8:16-17). That is why God requires Men to "suffer with *him*, that we may be also *glorified together*" (Rom. 8:17). But the establishment of a personal kingdom does not necessarily require that Men become separate and autonomous authorities, except unto their own spirit children.

The Function of Free Agency

To allow Men the privilege of eternal progression, God has granted them the blessing (and *test*) of Free Agency, the right to act as their own agents. Ultimately, Men must choose whether they will retain their own agency, becoming a power to themselves (or to someone else to whom they may choose to align themselves), or voluntarily accept God's agency. If God held the strings on that decision, Men would not truly be free to accept God's agency and voluntarily submit to being trusted servants of God. That is why God's presence in the universe *must* be essentially hidden from Men during their probation on this planet.

During their probation, Men have been given unlimited use of certain limited powers, and they may, and often do, exercise those powers in direct opposition to God's will. That is part of the test. They will be called into accountability for misuse of their powers. Based on that accounting, they may be prohibited from becoming like God.

If Men remember the source of their power, acknowledging that they owe all that they are and have power to do, to God, they can obtain greater power from Him. Eventually, they can become, by exercise of His power and authority, truly omnipotent and hence omniscient. These are the essential elements of the attributes of perfection discussed in Part 3.

Conclusion

Man is basically infinite. He is merely going through a finite period of his existence. This existence is a critical part of Man's eternal progression. It is theoretically possible that either a finite or an infinite number of Men have completed it and achieved the ultimate object of progression, to become like God. But, given infinite space, time, matter and intelligences, the number who have attained Godhood could easily be infinite.

Man has the ability to become like God even in the sense of becoming infinite. He can obtain the attributes of perfection, but he must make a decision in this life as to who he will follow. If he follows the Father, Man can learn to be perfect and obtain the infinite attributes of perfection. Otherwise, his progression will come to an end, and he will cease to grow and receive ultimate perfection like Christ.

Summary

1. Classical theism makes God incomprehensible by claiming that, while God is infinite, Man is only finite.
2. Ontology, the study of "being," claims that Man and God have a fundamentally distinct nature. There is no biblical basis for that doctrine. Rather, the Bible compares the nature of God to the nature of idols, stressing the ontological similarity of God and Man.
3. The orthodox idea of Man's finiteness involves (a) a lack of independent existence, (b) status as an inferior created being, though created in God's image (to a limited extent), (c) permanent limitations, and (d) the necessity of realizing that Man cannot be God, ever. Satisfaction and happiness is said to lie in accepting these limitations and living with the realization that Men are "limited human creatures."
4. In contrast to the classical view, the Bible encourages Men to "be ye therefore perfect, even as your Father which is in Heaven is perfect."
5. The Bible and other Mormon scriptures teach that God is infinite, but nowhere describe Man as "finite," or state that he is limited to his current mortal condition. Rather, Man is described as the literal

"offspring" of God, capable of becoming like Him. Man is currently in the process of "eternal progression" toward that goal.

6. If the progression of Men on this earth is archetypical of conditions on other worlds, past, present or future, there could theoretically be an infinite number who have attained to Godhood by now. This possibility necessitates a greater understanding of the concept of infinity and its relationship to that which Men call "finite."
7. The finite and the infinite are not mutually exclusive concepts. In fact, modern mathematics has demonstrated that they are closely interrelated.
8. *Finite* physical measurements—length, width and height—are composed of an infinite number of items having one less dimension—points, lines or planes. Thus, for example, a line of *any* length is composed of the same number of points, an infinite number, and a finite cube contains the same infinite number of points as a line or a plane.
9. An infinite cube can contain an infinite number of finite cubes. In fact, infinite space can contain an infinite number of infinite spaces! Thus, it can contain an infinite number of infinite kingdoms like "the heavens and the earth" created by the Father.
10. It is impossible for Man to number all the points in the universe, because the number of points in the universe has been shown to be infinitely greater than the number of numbers in Man's system of integers and fractional numbers. Thus, to Man, God's creations are numberless, but they are numbered to Him.
11. Time, too, is composed of an infinite number of infinitesimally small segments of time ("dt"). Thus, between any beginning and ending point in time, there are an infinite number of dt.
12. An infinite period of time, like an infinite expanse, can be composed of an infinite number of finite segments of time no matter how long those segments might be. In fact, an infinite time can include an infinite number of infinite periods of time.
13. The arithmetic of infinity demonstrates that, because God has always existed, He could have spent an infinite period of time progressing to Godhood, and yet He could have been God for an infinite period of time before the present day.
14. In practical terms, infinity can be defined as any number that exceeds by at least one the highest number to which anyone in a

particular culture can reasonably be expected to count. For some societies, that number has been as low as four!
15. In the Bible, many references to what classic theists think is infinity are actually references to a practical concept of infinity—a very long, but unspecified period of time. The same is true of things spoken of as "numberless." They only seemed infinite to Men of the culture to which the scriptures were revealed.
16. The practical aspects of infinity do not suggest a limitation of God. Rather, they suggest that it is not impractical for Men to become infinite . . . eventually.
17. Infinite time is not without its beginnings and endings, measured by the beginning and ending of various events (which could be of any duration, finite or infinite).
18. According to Mormon theology, an infinite being, like an intelligence, will go through various beginnings and endings during its infinite existence. One is birth as a spirit being, the next is birth as a physical being, the third is death, and the last is resurrection.
19. Birth as a spirit marks the end of an infinite period in the existence of an intelligence. Spirit life before birth in mortality could also have lasted for an infinite period. Mortality is, by comparison, very brief, followed by a brief time in the spirit world. The last period of Man's existence will, again, be infinite.
20. Under the arithmetic of infinity, if there are an infinite number of intelligences in the universe, an infinite number of them could have experienced one or more beginnings or endings, and still there would remain an infinite number of intelligences left who had yet to experience even the first beginning.
21. Another aspect of the arithmetic of infinity suggests that since the first "beginning" experienced by an intelligence occurs after an infinite period of time, it is quite possible that, despite the passage of an infinite period of time until the present day, only a finite number of intelligences has yet completed all the beginnings and endings that can occur in Man's eternal progression.
22. It is apparent from Mormon theology that Man cannot be considered finite, except insofar as his current existence as a physical being on this earth. Fundamentally, Man is infinite—at least in respect to his or her continuous existence.

23. Man's ability to gain the infinite attributes of perfection depend on his obedience to the singular authority in the universe. Man's willingness to learn from the Father will allow him, eventually, to attain to the same perfect and infinite attributes the Father now possesses.
24. God has indicated His intention to bestow the attributes of perfection on those who are willing to follow Him (1 John 3:2).
23. Free agency is the right to act as an agent for whomever one pleases, whether for oneself or for another. The test of mortality is to determine with whom Men will choose to align their free will. Will they become agents unto themselves, follow Satan or someone else, or become agents of God like Christ? On this decision lies a critical turning point in Man's eternal progression. If Men follow God, who has already obtained Godhood, they can progress to become like Him. Otherwise, they may be prohibited from becoming like God.

19

Answering Philosophical Objections to The Doctrine of Eternal Progression

The continuing influence of ancient Greek thinking and philosophy on orthodox Christianity is well demonstrated by examining a series of objections to "the Mormon Concept of God" raised by Dr. Francis Beckwith, as noted in Chapter 1. These objections are directed at the doctrine of eternal progression by which Mormons believe Men can become like God, their Father in Heaven. One reason they are discussed here is that by now the Greek thinking that underlies them should be easier for the reader to recognize. Another reason is that the goal of eternal progression—attaining the attributes of Deity—should be in better focus. Finally, the concepts of infinity covered in the last chapter should help the reader understand the deeper aspects of this profound doctrine.

Each objection addressed in this chapter is posed by Dr. Beckwith in the form of a supposedly logical Aristotelian syllogism or a similarly composed argument. However, any syllogism is only as good as the premises on which it is based. The premises stated in these syllogisms are based primarily on three types of errors: (1) Greek ideas and notions about the universe; (2) a poor grasp of LDS theology; and (3) a less-than-adequate understanding of the mathematics of infinity. The effort will be to point out the Greek and mathematical errors, and to clarify LDS theology on points that appear to be misunderstood by classical theists.

The Problem of an Infinite Number of Past Events: Can an Infinite Number Be Traversed in a Real Universe?

The first objection Dr. Beckwith raises is what he calls the "Problem of an Infinite Number of Past Events." He has presented this objection syllogistically as follows:

(**Premise 1**) If the Mormon universe is true, then an infinite number (or distance) has been traversed.

(**Premise 2**) It is impossible to traverse an infinite number (or distance).

(**Conclusion**) Therefore, the Mormon universe is not true.[1]

This syllogism clearly demonstrates the difficulty encountered by the mortal mind in grasping the infinite. This was especially true in the days of ancient Greece which provided the philosophical and mathematical basis for this argument. The fact that science has progressed beyond the Greek limitations reflected in this syllogism while theology has not, is why the response to this objection will be aimed primarily at its mathematical errors.

Premise 1 postulates that if the Mormon understanding of the universe is true, an infinite distance or an infinite period of time, has been traversed. That possibility stands in direct opposition to the view of classical theism, based on the Platonistic view of a metaphysical universe, in which the sensory universe was created by God (out of nothing) at the time this earth was organized. Since they believe that God existed in the timeless and spaceless *Pleroma*, it is irrelevant to ask classical theists how long God has existed. To them, there was no way to measure God's existence until He created time as part of the sensory universe.

The idea of a beginning to the universe, however, was not always the thinking of the Greeks. The concept was first formulated by Anaximander in the sixth century B.C.[2] The Stoics were inclined to a doctrine closer to the LDS understanding. They believed that there was no beginning to creation, but that the universe has been going through an infinite number of identical cycles, each of which ends in destruction by fire.[3] This idea, however, has always been a little uncomfortable for Men because they now remember nothing but this finite segment of eternity.

---

[1] Beckwith, "Philosophical Problems," 9.
[2] Hatch, *Influence of Greek Ideas*, 174.
[3] Nash, *Christianity and the Hellenistic World*, 72.

By the time of Christ, most philosophers opted for the Platonistic view of a beginning.

The problem is that the Platonistic view is fundamentally irrational. This becomes apparent when one considers the alternative to a beginningless universe. In a universe that has a beginning, the inescapable question is, What happened before that beginning? Did God exist? Was He active? If the answer to that question is "Yes," as classical theists teach, then there can be no ultimate beginning. The idea that the sensory universe began at some point in the recent past, while God has existed in a *Pleroma* for all eternity, is simply a Hellenistic method of coping with infinite existence.

As noted in Chapter 12, time is always measurable as a chronology of events. If, in the classical view of heaven, there was no time before the creation of the sensory universe, either events would have to occur without any chronological order, or God would have to be doing absolutely nothing. The latter notion is inconsistent with the character and attributes of the God described in the Bible, and the former idea is impossible. Even rational thought would be precluded from a heaven that has activity but no time. Thoughts occur in some order or they do not produce rational consciousness.

Lack of any chronological order in the occurrence of events is the very definition of absolute chaos. There could be no order in such a place. It would be filled with darkness. In that respect, it would be just as Job describes death in Job 10:21-22. But darkness and chaos are not associated with the God of order who is described in the Bible as the source of light (John 8:12).

On the other hand, if God had done absolutely nothing before creation, if He could not even think, it would be tantamount to His non-existence. While He might be there, lying dormant in the darkness, it would be exactly as if He did not exist.

Mormon theology, consistent with the Bible, teaches that God has always existed, that He acts rationally, being a God of order and light. See, e.g., D&C 132:8. Rational, orderly action creates a chronological continuity of events. It follows that God must have existed in a measurable time continuum even before the creation of "the heavens and the earth." The metaphysical conception of the universe adopted by classical theists denies that possibility at the same time it declares the eternal existence of God. Therefore, it is self-contradictory and false.

Can an Infinite Number Be Traversed?

Premise 2 states as fact an entirely Platonistic notion about infinity that is completely lacking in scientific basis. Is it really impossible, as Dr. Beckwith avers, "to traverse an infinite number"? Today, the answer to that question is not even open to argument. As noted in the last chapter, a finite line of *any* length contains "an infinite number" of points. Anyone, by taking the smallest step, traverses an infinite number of points. Indeed, with each additional step, another infinite number of points is traversed. Thus, "an infinite number," as Dr. Beckwith expresses his premise, can be traversed easily, and is, in fact, traversed by mortal Men every day, *ad infinitum*.

In an example used by Dr. Beckwith to prove his **Premise 2**, he hypothesizes a man who plans to drive on Interstate 15 from his home in Las Vegas to the Mormon temple in Salt Lake City. Contrary to Dr. Beckwith's argument, however, during his trip, this man would traverse an infinite number of points. In fact, given the mathematics of infinity explained in Chapter 18, he would traverse an infinite number of points with every finite movement of his car's wheels. When he has traveled a foot from his home, an infinite number of points would stretch behind him. Of course, the same number of points—an infinite number—would lie ahead of him. After this man traverses half the distance to Salt Lake City, there will still remain an infinite number of points in front of him and an infinite number of points behind him.

Of course, notwithstanding the infinity of points in front and behind, the traveler will always be positioned at a specific identifiable point. That point would be in a very different location half way through the journey than it is one foot from his home, but there will always be an infinite number of points between those two points and from either point to the beginning or end of the man's trip.

The infinite number being traversed in the analysis above consists entirely of infinitesimal points. What if the numbers being traversed were composed of *finite* segments? Can a traveler traverse an infinite number of such segments, i.e., an infinite *distance?* This is Dr. Beckwith's real point in **Premise 2**. He is trying to say that it is impossible to traverse an infinite distance.

Again, however, he is incorrect. Given an *infinite period of time*, a traveler can easily traverse an infinite distance. Rationally, any infinite being can traverse an infinite distance. In fact, such a being could traverse an *infinite number of infinite distances!* That is the mathematical error in Dr. Beckwith's syllogism.

The theological error is even more important, however. It is this: Mormon theology teaches that not only God but *all Men* have existed for eternity (in one form or another). Thus, everyone who has ever existed on this planet or who ever will exist, has traversed, or is capable of traversing, an infinite distance.

If Not Men, Hasn't *God* Traversed an Infinite Number?

Dr. Beckwith's theological problems with **Premise 2** do not end with his lack of knowledge about LDS theology. His position challenges the very possibility of an infinite existence altogether. The real issue is not whether an infinite distance can be traversed, but whether or not a being can exist for the eternity it would take to traverse such a distance.

Surprisingly, Dr. Beckwith, speaking on behalf of classical theism, claims not. He says, "If the universe had no beginning, then every event has been preceded by an infinite number of events. But if one can never traverse an infinite number, one could never have arrived at the present day, since to do so would have involved traversing an infinite number of days."[4]

This statement denies the very possibility of infinite or eternal existence altogether. That is a very dangerous proposition for anyone who believes in an eternal God. Apparently, Dr. Beckwith does not believe that God has existed through an eternity of real time. Either that, or he must believe that God is Aristotle's "Unmoving Mover," and therefore has not traversed any distance whatever during His eternal existence. The idea that even God Himself cannot traverse an infinite distance can only be maintained on the basis of Greek metaphysics, in which God exists outside time and space so that He does not traverse distance or time.

Dr. Beckwith's position clearly requires that conclusion. It is confirmed by his recognition that "events" are a more objective measure of time than a specific time period, such as a day. An "event" can be of any duration and is independent of mass and other influences that affect time under the general theory of relativity. Further, "events" are a measure of time that would necessarily exist in the *Pleroma*, if there were

---

[4] Beckwith, "Philosophical Problems," 9.

such a place. Thus, "events" occur in either the Mormon or the metaphysical universe, otherwise there is no God at all.

As long as an "event" is measurable in the perception of any observer, i.e., God Himself, it constitutes a definable way to measure time. To speak of days or years is to use relative terms that change depending on the location and characteristics of the observer. Notably, the Bible itself suggests the existence of a relativistic difference between God's "day" and that of Man (2 Pet. 3:8: "one day is with the Lord as a thousand years, and a thousand years as one day").

For all these reasons, the measurement of "events" is the ideal way to compare the Mormon concept of the universe with the Greek idea of a metaphysical universe. If an event occurs in the real space-time universe, or in the non-spatio-temporal *Pleroma* imagined by classical theism, it could still be defined as a measurable and analyzable quantity, namely the difference between the start and the finish of the event.

The shortest possible event or portion of an event could be defined as dt, an event infinitesimally short in duration. Even in the *Pleroma*, an active God would experience dt that meet this definition. If this active God existed for all eternity before the present day, as classical theists claim to believe, He would have experienced an infinite number of these dt, whether in the real Mormon universe or in the metaphysical Greek universe.

Yet, according to Dr. Beckwith, that is impossible. His position is that it is impossible to traverse an infinite number of dt and thereby arrive at the present day. This position clearly denies the existence of an infinite God, whether in the real universe or the metaphysical universe. That conclusion is unbiblical and thus false.

The only alternative is that **Premise 2** is false. It is possible to traverse an infinite number, whether of points, or of days, or of miles, or of events, and it is possible to do so and still exist at the present day. This is true both mathematically and philosophically, and if God has done it, there can be no theological objection to its accomplishment by Men who have also lived forever.

Conclusion On the Problem of an Infinite Number of Past Events

The existence of God through all eternity is a doctrine of classical theism as well as Mormonism. If there is no mathematical or philosophical barrier to that claim, it follows inexorably that there can be

Answering Objections to the Doctrine of Eternal Progression 419

no valid philosophical barrier to the Mormon concept of Man being eternal also. Indeed, it is possible for an infinite universe, containing an infinite quantity of elements and intelligences, to exist at the present moment, to have existed forever in the past, and to exist forever more in the future. If classical theists cannot establish a philosophical objection to an infinite God, they can have no valid philosophical problems with the Mormon concept of an infinite universe.

The Problem of Eternal Progression With an Infinite Past

Dr. Beckwith's second objection to eternal progression is not presented through a formal syllogism. In this objection his errors are primarily theological. He contends that:

> If the past series of events in time is infinite, *we [Men] should have already reached our final state by now*. Yet, we have *not* reached our final state. Therefore, the Mormon world view is seriously flawed.
>
> The Mormon may respond by arguing that we have not yet reached our final state because there has not been enough time for it to have transpired. But this is certainly no solution, since the Mormon's own world view affirms that an infinite length of time has already transpired. One cannot ask for more than an *infinite time* to complete a task.
>
> We must conclude, then, that since none of us has reached his or her final state—whether it be deity or some posthumous reward or punishment—the past series of events in time cannot be infinite in the sense the Mormon church teaches. For even if we assume that the past *is* infinite, since we have not yet reached our inevitable fate the Mormon world view is still false.[5]

Thus, Dr. Beckwith's argument is that if the intelligences of all Men started the course of their eternal progression an infinite number of years ago, they would all have completed their course by now and either become like God or received some other reward or punishment.

This argument reeks with the simplicity of Greek logic. Unfortunately, the real universe is far more complicated than Greek logic. Dr. Beckwith has forgotten that an infinite period of time can contain up to an infinite number of infinite periods. He has not bothered to consider

---

[5] *Ibid.*, 10-11.

that more than one infinite period may be involved in Man's eternal progression, especially if he is to be infinite—like God.

This argument also shows that Dr. Beckwith is unfamiliar with LDS theology regarding the course of eternal progression. To answer his objection, therefore, it will be necessary to examine more extensively the doctrine of eternal progression in each of its major segments.

Segment One of Eternal Progression: The Intelligence

God's creative work involving Man begins with the spirit birth of an "intelligence." The fact that Men existed in some form before they became the spirit children of God (see, e.g., Zech. 12:1; Heb. 12:9) is information that comes from modern revelation. The exact process involved has not been fully revealed, but in Abraham 3:22 it speaks of spirits as "the intelligences that were organized before the world was."

This is a *personal* use of the term "intelligence." It suggests that intelligences are individual, intelligent personalities that were somehow "organized" into spirit beings. Ontologically, Abraham's words could be interpreted as saying that the spirit body itself is composed of the personal intelligence of the being that is created or "organized." Based on this usage, some LDS theologians have opined that "intelligence" is "spirit element."[6]

Another possibility is suggested by Genesis 7:39 in the JST. There the Lord says to Enoch, "Behold, these thy brethren, they are the workmanship of mine own hands, and I gave them their intelligence in the day I created them."[7] This implies that the workmanship of God, the spirit body, was infused with the personal intelligence of Man on the day it was created. That implies a process similar to physical birth. In that process, the physical body is created by its earthly parents and the heaven-born spirit is infused in the body at some point during the procreative process. The JST passage suggests a similar infusion of spirit body with the personal intelligence.

In the case of mortal men, the infusion of the spirit body into a physical body is not permanent until the resurrection. That was not

---

[6] McConkie, *Mormon Doctrine*, s.v. "Intelligence," and "Intelligences."
[7] The version of Joseph Smith's translation published by an offshoot branch of Mormonism has "knowledge" in place of the word "intelligence" in this passage. See, the "New Corrected Edition" of the "Inspired Version" of the Holy Scriptures published by The Reorganized Church of Jesus Christ of Latter Day Saints (Independence: Herald Publishing House, 1944).

the situation in the original creation. Adam and Eve were created immortal by God (Gen. 2-3). The change from a permanent combination of the spirit and the body to the temporary condition of mortality occurred through voluntary partaking of the fruit of knowledge of good and evil.

The resulting state of mortality, in which all men find themselves subject to death—the separation of the spirit from the body—is not the state in which God intends Man to remain. The resurrection is God's gift to all men (see Rom. 5:12-18; 1 Cor. 15:21-22). It overcomes the problem of impermanent fusion between the physical body and the spirit body and results in the final state originally intended by God (1 Cor. 15:51-54).

Since permanent fusion of the intelligence in both a spiritual and a physical element appears to be the goal of this process, it can be surmised that even if the spirit body is not created directly out of the intelligence, the process employed to create spirit children of God results in a permanent fusion of the intelligence with spirit element.

The same word ("intelligence") is also used in modern revelation in a way that explains something about the characteristics of personal intelligences. See D&C 130:18-19 and D&C 93:21-36. In these passages the word "intelligence" is tied to the impersonal words "knowledge" and "truth." These passages suggest that a principle characteristic of a personal intelligence is its capacity to obtain, possess and use knowledge or truth. Other properties and characteristics of the personal intelligence of Man, with one significant exception, have not yet been revealed.

The one exception is that characteristic discussed in the previous chapter. The personal intelligence of Man is uncreated. D&C 93:29 states, "Man was also in the beginning with God. Intelligence, or the light of truth, was not created or made, neither indeed can be." This passage confirms the personal nature of Man's intelligence and proclaims that it is co-eternal with God.

There is one other aspect of "intelligence" that should be noted here. D&C 93:29 also describes the personal intelligence as "the light of truth." The relationship between personal intelligence and light in this passage and in D&C 88 and 93 generally is difficult to grasp. These passages will have greater import for Men when they have gained a better understanding of the nature of light and matter in the universe. One thing they do suggest, on a scientific level, is that a personal intelligence, like light, has no mass.

Greek Notions About The Intelligence

The similarity of the personal intelligence described above to the Greek notion of pure Mind, as that concept was envisioned by Plato and the other early philosophers, deserves some attention. Because of the metaphysical notions of Parmenides, the concept of "Mind" adopted by the philosophers took a very different turn compared to the LDS concept. However, the similarities suggest that it may have been derived from a related source—an early Hebrew understanding of the personal intelligence.

Although a knowledge of the intelligences of Man was not passed down in the writings currently available from the Jews, according to the Pearl of Great Price it was originally taught by Abraham. Hence, the doctrine should have been known to his progeny, at least until their long period of slavery in Egypt. It does not appear in the writings of Moses, even in the Pearl of Great Price. However, this does not mean the doctrine was unknown to that great prophet.

The Greek philosophers were fascinated with the ideas of other cultures and incorporated them in many of their theories.[8] It should not be surprising to find among the notions of Greek philosophy influences from the nearby province of Palestine. Many kernels of truth taught in the Bible can be found in their philosophies, as both Justin Martyr and Clement of Alexandria noted (see Chapter 2). The concept of "Mind," and the three-fold view of Man taught by Plato (see Chapter 2), are just a few of those ideas. These Greek concepts strongly suggest some understanding of the personal intelligence that comprises the basic element that is Man.

Segment Two of Eternal Progression: The Spirit

Though not physical (Luke 24:36-43), the spirit of Man is material in its ontology. In all scriptural appearances of spirit beings, they are in the form of Men. Perhaps the most graphic record of the appearance of a spirit being to a mortal Man is found in Ether in the Book of Mormon. There, the Brother of Jacob sees the pre-mortal spirit body of the Son, who explains,

---

[8] This is especially true of many oriental notions. See, e.g., *Encyclopaedia Britannica*, 1960 ed., s.v. "Greek Literature, Oriental Influences," and "Greek Religion."

Seest thou that ye are created after mine own image? Yea, even all men were created in the beginning after mine own image. Behold, this body, which ye now behold, is the body of my spirit; and man have I created after the body of my spirit; and even as I appear unto thee to be in the spirit will I appear unto my people in the flesh (Ether 3:15-16).

Thus, to say that the spirit body is in the form of the physical body is to miss the point. The physical body is in the form of the spirit body. The spirit body is the original template for the physical body. The form and appearance of human beings on this earth is after the similitude of Christ's spirit body (Gen. 1:26-27), He being the first spirit child of God the Father (Col. 1:15). A spirit is not a nebulous form that *can* appear as a human being, it is the archetype of the being known as Man. It follows therefore, that what is typical of the physical body may be found in the spirit body.

There are ways, however, in which the spirit body and the physical body differ. One example of these differences, of course, is that the physical body of fallen Man bears within it the seeds of death. It will eventually die, leaving the spirit body to continue, apparently unaffected by disease or decay. (See, e.g., the Savior's description of the spiritual realm in Matt. 6:19-20.)

Spirit bodies are "born." Indeed, the Bible designates Christ as the "first*born*" of the Father (see, e.g., Ps. 89:27; Col. 1:15; Heb 12:23). Acts 17:28 refers to Men as the "offspring" of God using the same term in Greek that is used for literal children of earthly parents. That Men are the offspring of the Father implies a reproductive capacity in the Almighty. That condition is consistent with Hebrews 12:9, which compares earthly fathers to Heavenly Father, describing him as the "father of spirits." Ephesians 3:15 similarly describes the whole of the Father's offspring, both in heaven and on earth, as a "family," using the Greek word that means descendants of a common ancestor.

Segment Three of Eternal Progression: Mortality

In the next stage of eternal progression, the foundations of an earth are laid for the spirit children of God, who look forward to the opportunity to occupy it. Speaking to Job about the foundations of this earth, God explains that "all the sons of God shouted for joy" at the sight (Job 38:4-7). Each spirit is sent down to his or her appointed earth (Heb. 2:6-8) to go through a probation, or test, which culminates in a Final Judgment for all the inhabitants of that earth (Rev. 20:12-13) and gives that spirit an introduction to the physical body. After the judgment, punishment is meted out to the unrepentant (Rev. 20:14-15). An atonement has been provided for all of God's children through Christ's sacrifice. That sacrifice conquered death and allows the repentant to return to God. The earth then ends by fire (Matt. 13:40; 2 Pet. 3:10), and a new earth is established on which the righteous dwell after they have been resurrected (Isa. 65:17; 66:22; 2 Pet. 3:13; Rev. 21:1). This summarizes the essential history of a physical earth on which Men can dwell as mortal beings.

An Adjunct to Segment Three: The Spirit World

Concomitant with the physical earth, the scriptures describe a spirit world to which the spirits of those who die during the earth's history will go to await its completion and the time of their personal resurrection. A description of the spirit world was provided by the Savior in Luke 16:19-31. The Bible suggests that, for those who have not yet embraced the Gospel, the probationary aspects of mortality continue in the spirit world (John 5:25; 1 Pet. 4:6). Thus, it is treated here as part of the third segment of eternal progression.

Segment Four of Eternal Progression: Resurrection and Eternal Life

Some of the glories of the post-resurrection earth are described by John in Revelation, chapters 21 and 22. Others can be surmised from Revelation 3:21. Of course, as the latter passage indicates, these promises are only for those who "overcome."

In Mormon theology, Man is required to "overcome," though it is not possible for him to do so without the atonement and sacrifice of Christ, which makes repentance possible. But the effort to repent is not an easy one. There is no question that the object of the mortal phase of eternal progression is to separate the wheat from the tares (Matt. 13:24-43). The "tares" will have the life they chose, but it is the "wheat" that will continue their progression during this segment of eternal progression and the next.

The object of this phase of progression begins in the mortal segment. It is the effort to achieve perfection—a process by which Men acquire the attributes of perfection discussed in Part 3. This effort is commanded in the Bible, though its completion is not really possible until the resurrection. Christ required, "Be ye therefore perfect, even as your Father which is in heaven is perfect" (Matt. 5:48), but notably He did not include even Himself in this admonition as being perfect like the Father. That was not because of any moral imperfection on His part. It was simply a recognition of His mortality at that time.

After His resurrection, when Christ appeared to the people on the American continent, the Book of Mormon records an admonition to those people similar to the one in Matthew. It reads as follows: "Therefore, I would that ye should be perfect *even as I*, or your Father who is in heaven is perfect" (3 Nephi 12:48). This suggests that resurrection is a crucial part of the process of attaining perfection.

Paul preached extensively on the effort to achieve perfection, and likewise indicated that the goal would not be fully achieved in this life. He explained that the purpose of the Church was to bring Man to "the unity of the faith, and of the knowledge of the Son of God, *unto a perfect man*, unto the measure of the stature of the fulness of Christ" (Eph. 4:13). In Philippians 3:10-21 (NASB), Paul gives a particularly thorough overview of the quest that culminates in the final phase of eternal progression:

> that I may know Him, and the power of His resurrection and the fellowship of His sufferings, being conformed to His death;
>
> in order that I may attain to the resurrection from the dead.
>
> Not that I have already obtained it, or have already become perfect, but I press on in order that I may lay hold of that for which also I was laid hold of by Christ Jesus.
>
> Brethren, I do not regard myself as having laid hold of it yet; but one thing I do: forgetting what lies behind and reaching forward to what lies ahead,
>
> I press on toward the goal for the prize of the upward call of God in Christ Jesus.

Notwithstanding his humble statement above, Paul's subsequent remarks suggest that he had attained to the level of perfection achievable in this life. All that he lacked was the resurrection of which he speaks in the passage above. His words continue as follows:

> Let us therefore, as many as are perfect, have this attitude; and if in anything you have a different attitude, God will reveal that also to you;

however, let us keep living by that same standard to which we have attained.

Brethren, join in following my example, and observe those who walk according to the pattern you have in us.

For many walk, of whom I often told you, and now tell you even weeping, that they are enemies of the cross of Christ,

whose end is destruction, whose god is their appetite, and whose glory is in their shame, who set their minds on earthly things.

Paul next indicates the portion of the effort for perfection that must wait for the final phase of eternal progression. He states:

For our citizenship is in heaven, from which also we eagerly wait for a Savior, the Lord Jesus Christ;

who will transform the body of our humble state into conformity with the body of His glory, by the exertion of the power that He has even to subject all things to Himself.

Those who realize the goal so eloquently defined here by Paul will know eternal life. "Eternal life" is God's life, for He is eternal (Deut. 33:27; 1 Tim. 1:17; see also John 17:3). It is a state in which Men truly know God (John 17:3) because they have become like Him (1 John 3:2). In this phase, Men actually achieve the promises spoken of by Paul in 1 Corinthians 13:12 ("For now we see through a glass darkly; but then face to face: now I know in part; but then shall I know even as also I am known"), and in 2 Corinthians 3:18 ("But we all, with open face beholding as in a glass the glory of the Lord, are changed into the same image from glory to glory, even as by the Spirit of the Lord"). The result of this phase will be realization of the promise contained in D&C 93:28: "He that keepeth his commandments receiveth truth and light, until he is glorified in truth and *knoweth all things*."

An Overview of God's Creative Cycles

The segments of eternal progression are described above from the perspective of an individual intelligence. To answer Dr. Beckwith's second objection to LDS theology, it is necessary to look at eternal progression from the Creator's perspective also. A planet such as the earth has a specific limited size. Its resources are sufficient for a very large, but limited number of human beings. Thus, each earth is designed for the specific number of spirits that will dwell on it during the mortal phase (D&C 104:17). That number is known to God before the world is formed (cf., Jer. 1:5; Acts 2:23; Rom. 11:2; D&C 76:24).

Following a mathematical rationale, it appears from the Pearl of Great Price that God has created an infinite number of spirits already and continues to "organize" new spirits all the time. In Moses 1:37-39, the Lord states:

> The heavens, they are mine, and *they cannot be numbered unto man;* but they are numbered unto me, for they are mine.
>
> And as one earth shall pass away, and the heavens thereof even so shall another come; and *there is no end to my works,* neither to my words.
>
> For behold, *this is my work* and my glory—*to bring to pass the immortality and eternal life of man.*

Moses 1:28 says that the inhabitants of this earth are "numberless as the sand upon the sea shore." This is an allegorical reference to the second order of infinity. Since God has created "worlds without number" (Moses 1:33), the intelligences He has organized into spirits and sent down as inhabitants of all His worlds, collectively, is described in Moses 1:35 as "innumerable . . . unto man." This phrase also suggests that the number of spirits God has created exceeds the first order of infinity (the number of numbers in the universe). See Chapter 18. It follows that there are an infinite number of Men inhabiting the worlds God has created throughout the universe.

With an infinite number of spirits and a limited capacity of persons per earth, God must necessarily create world after world, without end, just as the passage above suggests. When the pattern is completed for one group of intelligences, it begins for another. In fact, the pattern of eternal progression is likely to be on-going simultaneously on other worlds throughout the universe, each world being at a different stage of progression (Moses 1:35).

Mormon scripture teaches that "the course of the Lord is one eternal round" (1 Nephi 10:9; Alma 7:20; 37:12; D&C 3:2, 35:1). These "rounds" consist of the pattern of eternal progression described above. From God's perspective they are cyclical, as each group of intelligences passes through the pattern described above.

Of course, the cyclical nature of God's course does not mean that Men are being recycled in any way. Reincarnation is a false notion, as the Bible firmly declares (Heb. 9:27). Furthermore, the prophetic history of this earth promises a specific end time (see, e.g., 1 Cor. 15:21-24). Such a deadline is not consistent with the open-ended notion of reincarnation.

The end of this world will not terminate God's creativity, nor did its beginning mark the start of His creations. God is an eternal Creator. This earth, and the history of Man on it, are not His first or His only project. Thus, Mormon theology teaches that this earth was not the first and will not be the last of God's creations. His continuing goal is to bring to pass the immortality and eternal life of all Men.

The Duration of God's Eternal Rounds

From the perspective of an individual intelligence, the pattern of eternal progression occurs only once. Therefore, the only way Dr. Beckwith's argument would make any sense mathematically is if all intelligences had left the Intelligence phase of eternal progression for the pre-mortal Spirit phase at or about the same time. Even if that were true, however, Dr. Beckwith's reasoning could still fall short, for it assumes that the pre-mortal Spirit phase has a set finite duration in each spirit.

Actually, only the Mortality phase of eternal progression is given a finite duration in the scriptures. It began with the creation described in Genesis 1 and 2, and ends with the final judgment described in Revelation 20. The other segments of eternal progression are not so defined in the Bible, and could be infinite in duration.

Intelligences may wait through an eternity of time for the opportunity to enter the next phase of eternal progression when they will be formed in the image of God. The time a specific intelligence waits will be longer for some than for others. As demonstrated in the last chapter, infinite time periods can actually end at different times. They are still infinite because, no matter when they end, each period stretches infinitely into the past.

There is no indication in the scriptures of how long the Spirit phase of eternal progression lasts either. It may well last for an eternity before the mortal phase is instituted by laying the foundations of an earth. That conclusion is suggested by the Lord's remarks to Job in Job 38:4-7 when He describes the "sons of God" shouting for joy when the Lord laid the foundations of this earth. As noted above, the last phase of eternal progression is obviously infinite in the future tense. Between these phases, the mortality phase lasts a distinctly finite period of time.

On any day, therefore, the universe is filled with worlds inhabited by beings who are receiving their turn to enjoy mortality. This finite period (mortality) is sandwiched between infinite periods of time of different duration. Mathematically, this arrangement results in a continuum that has and will last for all eternity. These finite periods are all part of God's "eternal round," His infinite cyclical pattern that is capable of producing an infinite number of beginnings and endings, one for each specific group of intelligences ready for their turn on an earth.

Was There a Beginning of Time?

When did these cyclical patterns begin? There is no answer given in the Scriptures. They may have been occurring throughout all eternity. Or there may have been an eternity that passed before they began. If the latter were true, the Lord's cycles may still have begun an eternity ago. Remember that an infinite period of time can contain any number of infinite periods.

Any answer to questions about beginnings must be recognized as speculative. Whatever is speculated, if one assumes that there are an infinite number of intelligences in the universe, the pattern will never cease repeating itself and could have been on-going for all of eternity without all of them reaching their "final state by now."

Dr. Beckwith raises no philosophical objection to this understanding of the universe. He simply asserts that, if Man's past were infinite, Man would have already reached his final state. As demonstrated above, that is clearly false.

Greek Beliefs About the Cycle of Eternal Progression

The early Stoics believed that the world would eventually be destroyed by fire.[9] The idea was of a slow and natural process, rather than the catastrophic judgment described in 2 Peter 3,[10] but one other aspect of the Stoic idea is of interest as it relates to Mormon theology. They believed that, following its destruction by fire, the world would begin again, duplicating the former cycle in endless, eternal repetitions.[11] Further, they believed that this process resulted each time in the deification of all reality, so that all Men and all matter became one again with God in a way that was consistent with their pantheistic notion of Deity.[12]

---

[9] Nash, *Christianity & the Hellenistic World*, 72.
[10] *Ibid.*, 78.
[11] *Ibid.*, 72.
[12] *Ibid.*, 78.

The completely repetitive nature of these cycles (among other details), is not in line with the LDS view, but the notion of an eternal cycle, the end of which is a kind of deification repeating over and over through all eternity, provides an amazing parallel to the doctrine of eternal progression described in Mormonism.[13]

Where, then, did the Stoics get an idea so pertinent to modern LDS revelations on the subject? There can be little doubt that, again, they got the idea from the ancient Hebrews. The doctrine of eternal progression is a fundamental and ancient teaching of the Gospel. There can be little doubt that it was had among the ancient Jews, consistent with the record of Abraham contained in the Pearl of Great Price. The concepts embraced in an apostatized form by the ancient Stoics are a testimony of the modern revelation of the original version of those concepts in The Church of Jesus Christ of Latter-day Saints. The ancient adoption of these concepts was part of the preparation of the Gentiles to receive the Gospel of Jesus Christ in the meridian of time.

The Problem of Achieving Omniscience by Eternal Progression

The errors of Hellenistic thinking are as clearly demonstrated in the last of Dr. Beckwith's philosophical criticisms of Mormon theology as in any of the writings of the Apologists. In postulating his third philosophical problem, Dr. Beckwith makes *a priori* assumptions that are fundamental to the analysis without fully examining them. He also assumes scientific "facts" that are either false or grossly misconstrued, then bases his conclusions on those errors. Finally, he fails to accurately analyze the theology he is criticizing. As a result, his argument is a hodgepodge of error that rivals any made by his predecessors in the second century A.D.

His objection goes as follows:

(***Premise 1***) A being of limited knowledge gaining in knowledge entails the increasing of a finite number.

---

[13] *Ibid.* This aspect of Stoicism was completely out of vogue by the beginning of the first century B.C. There is no evidence that Joseph Smith, whose secular education was limited in the extreme, had any knowledge of ancient Stoic philosophy, nor is there any reason to think that anything in the New Testament that relates to eternal progression was adopted from their beliefs.

(***Premise 2***) Starting from a finite number, it is impossible to count to infinity.

(***Premise 3***) The Mormon view of eternal progression entails a being of limited knowledge gaining in knowledge until his knowledge is infinite (remember the Mormon universe contains an infinite number of things).

(***Conclusion 1/Premise 4***) Therefore, the Mormon view cannot be true, for it is impossible—given premises 1, 2, and 3—for eternal progression to entail that a being of limited knowledge gains knowledge until his knowledge is infinite.

(***Premise 5***) The Mormon doctrine of eternal progression is entailed by the Mormon concept of God.

(***Conclusion 2***) Therefore, the Mormon concept of God is incoherent.[14]

Premise 2 was proven false earlier in this chapter. It is quite possible to count to an infinite number, providing one has had an infinite period of time in which to do so. According to Mormon theology, as Dr. Beckwith well knows,[15] all intelligences have already existed an infinite period of time, and therefore could easily have counted to infinity. In fact, according to the arithmetic of infinity, an eternal being could have counted to infinity an *infinite* number of times by now.

The principle errors in Dr. Beckwith's argument lie in ***Premises 1*** and ***3***. His basic conclusion is that if a man doesn't have it already, he can never acquire omniscience. His first error in arriving at that conclusion is a false assumption. That assumption is found in his statement that Man is "a being of limited knowledge." While this is true during Man's mortal sojourn, the real assumption classical theists make is that Man is limited in a more profound sense than his current level of knowledge. The idea of Man's limited knowledge is based on the Greek doctrine of the incomprehensibility of God, and the idea that God is infinite "Mind," entirely transcendent over Man who is limited by a finite mind.[16]

The false notion that it is impossible for Man to attain a knowledge of God sufficient to become like Him was expressed long ago by Philo of Alexandria. He said:

---

[14] Beckwith, "Philosophical Problems," 11.
[15] *Ibid.*, 6.
[16] See, e.g., Plato, *Republic*, 509; Maximus of Tyre, *Dissertations*, 8:9, 17:9.

> The wise man, longing to apprehend God, and traveling along the path of wisdom and knowledge, first of all meets with the divine Reasons, and with them abides as a guest; but when he resolves to pursue the further journey, he is compelled to abstain, for the eyes of his understanding being opened, he sees that the object of his quest is afar off and always receding, an infinite distance in advance of him.[17]

That *mortal* Men cannot apprehend God's fullness is consistent with Mormon doctrine (Moses 1:5), but, as seen above, there is much more to Man than his current mortal status. In order to understand the ability of Men to become like God in their knowledge of all things, some consideration of Man's previous state and the result of his transition into the current phase of eternal progression will be necessary.

Man's Knowledge in Pre-Mortality

Mormon doctrine teaches that Man has had a veil drawn over the memory of his pre-existence (see, e.g., Book of Mormon, Ether 12:19-21; D&C 67:10, 101:23, and 110:1). He cannot remember what level of knowledge he attained before his incarnation on this earth. This doctrine is demonstrated in the biblical account of Christ, who, although He was God incarnate, had to learn things He obviously would have known from His pre-existence if His memory had not been veiled (Luke 2:52; Heb. 5:8).

How much did Men learn during their pre-mortal existence? Could they have become omniscient before their birth into this life? Christ obviously did (Prov. 8:22). As intelligences and subsequently as spirits, Men certainly had the time (an infinite period) to gain all knowledge. They also had the best teacher—God the Father. With enough time and so great a Teacher (Job 36:22), omniscience would have been the logical, if not certain, outcome.

In some respects Man's knowledge in the pre-existence had to have been infinite. It is unreasonable to suppose that Men waited through all eternity until this lifetime to start their education. They have been learning for an infinite period of time. Of course, on earth Man is limited in his knowledge compared with God (see, e.g., Isa. 55:8-9), but does that mean Man's pre-mortal level of knowledge was similarly limited? If, as seems reasonable, all Men did not apply themselves as well as did Christ, was their knowledge finite or simply incomplete?

---

[17] Philo, *de confus. ling.*, 20.

Answering Objections to the Doctrine of Eternal Progression 433

During Man's infinite pre-mortal existence, there were no limits on his education. Men were theoretically capable of acquiring infinite knowledge. Did they do so?

As noted in Chapter 14, Solomon used a literary form in which Wisdom was embodied and treated as the speaker in Proverbs 8:22, et seq. That passage contains the following clear indication that Men, as the spirit children of God, were exposed to the same wisdom and learning as was the Savior (Prov. 8:31): "Rejoicing in the habitable part of his earth; and my delights were with the sons of men." Thus, Christ was not the only one who learned wisdom in the pre-existence. Verse 31 states that Wisdom's "delights" were also *with the sons of men.*

Obtaining Omniscience

Theoretically, someone with infinite knowledge can always add to that knowledge. One can always add numbers to infinity. God's knowledge is more than infinite, however, it is *complete*. Of Him, the Book of Mormon states "there is not anything save he knows it" (2 Nephi 9:20). But while the knowledge Men acquired during an eternal pre-existence could theoretically be infinite, it is clear from the Bible that Men still have much to learn. For example, they must learn things about the physical world to which they have only recently been exposed. They also need to learn firsthand about the operation of a physical body, including the human brain.

These limitations, however, do not make Man "a being of limited knowledge," as classical theists say. In some areas, knowledge of the infinite past, for example, Man is a being of unlimited knowledge, even though that knowledge has temporarily been veiled from him.

Dr. Beckwith claims: "Mormon theology teaches that all beings are limited in knowledge unless and until they attain godhood (see D&C 130:18-19)." [18] He uses this assumption as a foundation to argue that, for Men to be given infinite knowledge by God, who, in turn, received His infinite knowledge from His Father, begs the question of how infinite knowledge was ever acquired by any being in the first place.[19] As he puts it, "the necessary conditions for the omniscience of *any one* of

---

[18] *Ibid.*, 12.
[19] *Ibid.*, 12-13.

the gods in the series are never fulfilled and can never be fulfilled in principle."[20]

Not surprisingly, Dr. Beckwith does not have a clear grasp of the real universe as it is revealed in Mormon theology. Of course the Father of Man assists His children in their eternal education, but that does not mean He endows them with omniscience like a lightning bolt from the heavens. The Bible teaches that, in this mortal existence, God gives wisdom and knowledge (and joy) to those whom He finds to be "good in his sight" (Eccl. 2:26). His teachings to Men are simple and organized. They come "line upon line" and "precept on precept," so that the least among His children can learn wisdom, while the unrighteous stumble over the truth (Isa. 28:9-13). Ultimately, this means the righteous will obtain the knowledge that, when added to what they already know, will make them omniscient, while the wicked do not receive that knowledge.

Contrary to Dr. Beckwith's use of Mormon scripture in the argument quoted above, D&C 130:18-19 does not say that "all beings are limited in knowledge unless and until they attain godhood." Rather, it says:

> Whatever principle of intelligence we attain unto in this life, it will rise with us in the resurrection.
> And if a person gains more knowledge and intelligence in this life through his diligence and obedience than another, he will have so much the advantage in the world to come.

This is a reassurance that whatever Men learn in this lifetime will benefit them in the resurrection. It does not even address the level of knowledge Men attained during their pre-mortal existence. It certainly does not support Dr. Beckwith's claim that Man is dependent upon an endless series of prior Gods for a supposed instantaneous gift of omniscience. As independently eternal beings, there is no need for that. By learning from God for the eternity that has already passed, they are, like their Father, inherently capable of omniscience.

Dr. Beckwith has made the same error in his ***Premises 1*** and ***3*** as he did in his ***Premise 2***. He neglected to consider the infinite period during which Man has been able to acquire knowledge. In his mathematical counting, he failed to note that infinity times any finite number will

---

[20] *Ibid.*, 13.

always yield infinity. No matter at what rate Men gain knowledge, since they have had an infinite period of time in which to learn, their knowledge must already be, in some respects, infinite. It may not be *complete*, but it is infinite.

How Man Gains Knowledge

The second error Dr. Beckwith makes in **Premises 1** and **3** of his argument is his assumption that Men gain knowledge through a finite, item-by-item process, similar to counting to infinity. He states, "every time one of these beings acquires a new item of knowledge on his or her journey to godhood it amounts to an increase in a finite number of items of knowledge."[21] His idea is that Man gains one item of knowledge at a time, and that each item of knowledge remains in a little cubicle by itself, not interacting with any other item of knowledge obtained by the human mind.

Modern studies of the human thought suggest that these assumptions are quite false. The development of Gestalt psychology following World War I demonstrated that Man's perceptions are determined by context, configuration and meaning, rather than by the accumulation of separate sensory elements.[22]

How Man's brain assimilates and processes knowledge is not completely understood, but the process is far more complex than Dr. Beckwith imagines. Interrelationships between individual items of knowledge give the mind insight into much more than the specific items learned. As knowledge grows, insight expands, so that the brain will often come to a sudden comprehension of a vast array of information extending beyond any single item learned. Such "gestalt" experiences have been well documented, and demonstrate the ability of the mind to learn in ways Dr. Beckwith does not take into account in his reasoning.

When Men regain their memories of the infinite past and all that they have learned during that past, and add to that all they learn in this mortal phase of their existence, the context in which they will view the latter-acquired knowledge is very different from that Dr. Beckwith assumes. It is infinite in nature and omniscience is clearly a likely outcome. Dr. Beckwith greatly underestimates the children of God in arguing that it is not.

---

[21] *Ibid.*, 12.
[22] *The New Grolier Multimedia Encyclopedia, The Academic American Encyclopedia,* (Electronic Version) (Danbury: Grolier, Inc., 1993), s.v. "Gestalt psychology."

Man Can Become Omniscient!

That Men can acquire a knowledge of all things, as Christ did, is not only consistent with scripture, it is suggested by modern scientific discovery. As noted in a prior chapter, researchers at UC Irvine have determined that "the brain's memory storage capacity is effectively unlimited."[23] If unlimited memory is currently available to mortal Men, how can anyone imagine limitations on the brain of a perfect, resurrected human being? If there were such limitations, they would apply as much to the Risen Christ as to any other resurrected being. Thus, if Christ is not limited and prevented by His resurrected human brain from being omniscient, then neither is Man.

Given that *Premises 1, 2* and *3* of Dr. Beckwith's argument are flawed, it follows that *Conclusion 1/Premise 4* is false. It *is* possible for eternal progression to entail that an eternal being with infinite but incomplete knowledge gains knowledge until the sum of all his knowledge is not only infinite, but also complete.

The Coherent Concept of God

Premise 5 of Dr. Beckwith's argument says "The Mormon doctrine of eternal progression is entailed by the Mormon concept of God." This means that the Mormon doctrine of eternal progression is necessarily connected with the Mormon concept of God. If that is true, and Mormons would not argue against that premise, it follows from the failure of *Conclusion 1/Premise 4* that it is *Conclusion 2* that is incoherent rather than the Mormon concept of God.

In order for Men to attain omniscience of the future, however, they need the attributes that make God omniscient. This would require that the veil be removed from their memory of the infinite past, that they learn all wisdom, that they have all knowledge of the past and the present, and that they have the power of God to accomplish all their purposes. Omniscience follows from the possession of these Godly attributes the same for Men as for their Father.

Given an infinite past filled with learning at the feet of God Himself, it is reasonable to conclude that many, if not all, Men are ready to obtain omniscience. All they lack is the knowledge and experience that

---

[23] Steve Emmons, "The Mystery of Memory," *Los Angeles Times*, Tuesday, January 11, 1994, Section E (citing the work of Dr. Gary Lynch, at UC Irvine's Center for the Neurobiology of Learning and Memory).

Answering Objections to the Doctrine of Eternal Progression 437

could only be provided by the experiences of this life, and the power of God. If God exalts Men by allowing them to exercise His Power (Job 36:22), and if they are to be "joint-heirs with Christ" (Rom 8:17) in receiving "all power . . . in heaven and in earth" (Matt. 28:18), it follows that they will have *all* they need for omniscience following their completion of this life, provided they have "purified" themselves "as He is pure" (1 John 3:3). That God, too, obtained His omniscience in this manner is the only coherent concept of God.

Summary

1. Current thinking by classical theists remains deeply influenced by ancient Greek philosophical methods, despite the fact that these methods lead to error as much now as in Aristotle's day.
2. Dr. Francis Beckwith's "Problem of an Infinite Number of Past Events" postulates that it is impossible to traverse an infinite number or distance.
3. In order to believe that an infinite number or distance cannot be traversed, one must accept the Platonistic view that time began with the creation of the heavens and the earth (the sensory universe), and that there was no time before that event.
4. The Greeks, especially the Stoics, originally believed that the universe had no beginning. However, by the time of Christ, most Greek philosophers sided with the Platonistic view that time began with creation of the universe.
5. The Platonistic view is irrational because it fails to recognize that time of some sort exists whenever rational action is taken. If God existed before He created the universe, and He did *anything* coherent, there was subjective time, measured by the chronology of events.
6. The arithmetic of infinity dictates that it is extremely easy to traverse "an infinite number" (of points, for example). The difficulty is in traveling an infinite distance. That feat, however, is possible provided the traveler has lived for all eternity.
7. Mormon theology teaches that Men, along with God, have lived for all eternity in some form. It follows that all Men, as well as God, have traversed an infinite distance.

8. Classical theists do not believe God Himself has traversed an infinite distance or time. That viewpoint is only possible if one accepts the Greek notion of a metaphysical *Pleroma* where God dwells, unmoving, outside time and space.
9. Time would necessarily exist in the *Pleroma*, if there were such a place. It would exist as the measurement of infinitesimal events (dt).
10. The Bible not only indicates that God experiences time; it speaks of that time in relativistic terms, comparing one day in God's time to 1,000 years in Man's time.
11. If God has existed for an infinite period of time, there can be no theological claim that it is impossible to traverse an infinite distance. If there is no theological problem with an infinite God traversing an infinite distance, there can be no valid philosophical objection to the Mormon concept of an infinite universe.
12. Dr. Beckwith's "Problem of Eternal Progression With an Infinite Past" claims that if the intelligences of Men started the course of eternal progression an infinite number of years ago, they would all have completed their eternal course by now.
13. In order to understand why eternal progression is and will forever remain on-going, one must understand that an infinite period of time can contain an infinite number of infinite times. One must also be familiar with the course of eternal progression, known as God's "eternal round."
14. The first segment of Man's eternal progression is his existence from infinity past as an intelligence. Intelligence is described as "the light of truth." It is personal and capable of obtaining and possessing knowledge. The term "intelligence" also appears in scripture with an impersonal meaning: "knowledge."
15. The "intelligence" of Mormon theology is surprisingly similar to the "Mind" in early Greek conceptions about the Mind, Soul and Body of Man. The similarity suggests that, just as Justin Martyr claimed, the Greeks learned what they knew of the truth from the Hebrew prophets.
16. The second segment of Man's eternal progression is his existence as a spirit child of God. It is not clear from the scriptures whether the spirit is formed from the intelligence, which would mean that "intelligence" is "spirit element" (the material out of which spirits are formed), or if "spirit element" is something else and the spirit is

Answering Objections to the Doctrine of Eternal Progression 439

infused with the intelligence. In either case, spirit bodies are "born," making them the literal offspring of God the Father. The spirit body is the original template for the physical body of Man.

17. The third segment of Man's eternal progression is Mortality. Looking forward to this stage of their progression, "all the sons of God shouted for joy" (Job 38:4-7). This phase constitutes a relatively brief "final exam" for the spirit being, as well as an introduction to the human body.

18. An adjunct to the third segment of Man's eternal progression is his sojourn in the spirit world following death. This is a place of continued learning that can involve some continued aspects of a spirit's probation. Here knowledge gained prior to mortality is combined with mortal experience as the spirit prepares for resurrection and eternal life.

19. The last segment of Man's eternal progression is resurrection and eternal life (or some lesser reward or punishment). Not until this phase do Men attain their final state of perfection (assuming obedience to the Gospel in the prior segments). Eternal life is life in a celestial state of glory with God.

20. It appears that God has an infinite and growing number of spirit children. Each world He creates has room for a very large but limited number of them. He has created worlds without number populated by His spirit children, all of whom are going through the same cycle of eternal progression as Man is on this earth. This is God's "eternal round."

21. Only the mortal segment of Man's eternal progression has been given a finite duration in the scriptures. His life as an intelligence was clearly infinite in length, extending from the infinite past until spirit birth. Spirit existence may also have lasted an infinite time. The last segment, resurrection and eternal life, will last for the balance of all eternity, and hence is also clearly infinite in duration.

22. Given the length of the stages of Man's eternal progression, one cannot simply say that an "infinite time" is sufficient for all the intelligences in the universe to complete their cycle. First there may be an infinite number of intelligences in the universe, and second, one must consider which infinite period of time has been completed by which intelligences.

23. Early Greek thinking (among the Stoics) envisioned no beginning or end of the universe, only endless cycles of God's creativity. This doctrine too, though garbled somewhat in the conception of the ancient Greeks, may also have been taken from the teachings of the Hebrew prophets.
24. In Dr. Beckwith's "Problem of Achieving Omniscience by Eternal Progression," he postulates that it is impossible for finite Men to achieve infinite knowledge.
25. The first error in Dr. Beckwith's objection to Man's ability to obtain infinite knowledge is his failure to realize that Men are, in fact, infinite beings by nature, having already lived from infinity past as intelligences and spirit. The idea of Man's inability to understand God comes from Greek philosophy, as was expressed by Maximus of Tyre and Philo of Alexandria, *not* from the Bible.
26. Men had the opportunity to obtain infinite knowledge in their pre-mortal state. Proverbs 8:31 indicates that, besides Christ, "the sons of men" learned wisdom before the earth was formed.
27. Omniscience is not just infinite knowledge, it is *complete* knowledge. God's knowledge is complete. Man's knowledge has yet to become complete. Part of the reason Men come to this earth is to complete their knowledge. The righteous will obtain the knowledge they need to be omniscient. The wicked will not.
28. Men obtain knowledge in a way that is much more complex than the one-item-at-a-time method imagined by classical theists like Dr. Beckwith. The gestalt nature of learning implies a complex interrelationship between items known and new items learned that can result in greater understanding than is provided by a single new item alone.
29. Current medical studies indicate that the human brain is "effectively unlimited" in its memory storage capacity. Thus, even the brain of fallen Man has sufficient capacity to allow omniscience.
30. Mormon theology provides a coherent concept of God, while that of classical theism is demonstrably incoherent.

A Summary of Greek Influences on the Christian Concept of God

Though Greek philosophy has made some positive contributions to Man's intellectual progress, Greek theology was largely fictional and self-made. It was not based on revealed concepts, and many of the assumptions from which its conclusions are derived have long been discarded by science as well as later philosophical thought.

The Apologists of the second and early third centuries, however, had been raised in the educational system of the Greeks and were philosophers themselves. In the second century after Christ, the theological assumptions and beliefs of Greek theology were regarded by the educated peoples of the Hellenized world as fundamental truths. Because there were no Apostles left to correct them, the Apologists unwittingly introduced these beliefs, and the *a priori* assumptions on which they are based, into Christian theology.

Some early Greek beliefs were, in fact, close to the truth. This led Justin Martyr and Clement of Alexandria to say that the Greek philosophers had taken their best ideas from the Hebrew prophets. It also made it more difficult for the Apologists and other members of the early Church to recognize their shift from true biblical doctrine to an acceptance of the basic elements of Greek philosophy, especially when that shift occurred over many years.

In this chapter the focus will not be on the truths taught by the Greek philosophers. Rather, major doctrinal errors found in Greek philosophy that relate to the nature of God will be summarized. Like a festering corrosive, these errors ate away at Christianity, and that effect will also be summarized here. First came the Apologists' adoption of basic Greek doctrines and *a priori* assumptions, then key Christian doctrines were radically affected by dogmatic speculations based on those assumptions. The end result altered fundamental doctrines in the original Gospel of Jesus Christ at many levels.

Erroneous Greek Philosophical Concepts Incorporated into Early Christian Doctrine

The following list summarizes major doctrines of orthodox Christianity that were corrupted by the Greek philosophy against which Paul so carefully warned the early Church (Col. 2:8). To facilitate a more in-depth review, references to pages in this book are frequently provided.

1. Strict Monotheism: The Numerically Singular God

The strict monotheism of Greek philosophy was first taught by **Pythagoras** approximately 530 B.C. He discovered a profound unity in the orderly movements of the heavenly bodies (see pages 36-37[1]). A pure mathematician obsessed with numbers, he saw God in the number "one." His idea of monotheism did not allow for any possibility except a singular God.

This was in direct conflict with the truth about the Godhead revealed hundreds of years later in the New Testament. There, each of three separate persons, the Father, His Son Jesus Christ, and the Holy Ghost, are frequently referred to by the title "God." Because the ideas of Pythagoras about a singular God were so basic to Greek philosophy by the time of Christ, the Apologists could not accept the simple truth that the Father, Son and Holy Ghost are truly separate and distinct beings who voluntarily act in perfect unison to exercise a singular office or authority (373-384).

Though **Justin Martyr** taught their numerical separateness (228-230) and the Bible speaks of three separate persons, the Apologists after Justin insisted that the Father, Son and Holy Spirit were numerically singular in some way (134-143, 228-230). They imagined their singularity to be grounded in the Platonistic idea of "being" (41-47).

---

[1] Page references are to pages in this book. Hereafter, reference to page numbers will be in parentheses with no other designation.

2. The *"Logos"*: Embodiment of the Metaphysical God's "Reason"

Heraclitus coined the word *"Logos"* to represent what he regarded as the law by which God made the universe function (37-38). From his time until the time of Christ, Greek philosophers developed the concept of the *Logos* as an embodiment of God's "Reason," which they imagined to be a rational force that acts positively in connection with God's creative activity (52, 64).

The concept of the *Logos* was defined differently by the various Greek philosophical schools depending on whether they were monistic or dualistic. The **Platonists** taught that the *Logos* was an almost-independent force composed collectively of Plato's "Forms" (42-43). To them, the *Logos* was a kind of intermediary force which they believed to have emanated, as "Thought" or "Reason," from their Supreme God, whom they viewed as "Pure Mind" (40, 52-53). The *Logos* was also seen as revealing God to Man and speaking on behalf of Man to God (222).

The **Stoics** had a different understanding. They used the word *Logos* as a collective term for what they believed to be the rational seeds (*logoi*) that together constituted God (46, 51, 121-122). In each case, the purpose of the *Logos* was to assist a metaphysical God in dealing with a material universe.

The Bible teaches that Christ is an intermediary for the Father (Gal. 3:19-20; 1 Tim. 2:5; Heb. 8:6, 9:15, 12:24), and He was referred to as the true *Logos* in the first chapter of John's gospel (John 1:1-3, 14). This reference and the similarity of functions later served to confuse early Christian thinkers (124-132). **Tatian** spoke of Christ as though He were the Greek *Logos* (131), and beginning with **Melito of Sardis**, the Apologists fully equated Christ with the Greek *Logos* (132-136). He came to be viewed as a kind of embodiment that was not truly separate from the Father (131, 136).

The relationship between the Greek *Logos* ("Reason") and the philosophers' concept of the Supreme God ("Mind"), provided the foundation for the doctrine of co-substantiality formulated by the later Apologists, especially **Athenagoras** and **Irenaeus** (136, 139-140).

3. Dualism: The Absolute Distinction Between Mind and Created Things

Anaxagoras introduced the idea of dualism. Dualism is the Greek philosophical belief that mind or thought is distinctly and absolutely different from matter (40, 41). This belief was later adopted by **Plato** and championed by the **Platonists** (52). This false idea within Greek philosophy created a huge gap between God, whom they regarded as pure Mind, and Men who they believed were created out of inferior and chaotic Matter.

The *Stoics* taught that the human soul was close to pure Mind (51), but that idea did little to bridge the infinite gap between Man and God that evolved from Anaxagoras' philosophy of dualism.

By the time of Christ, the Greek philosophical schools all taught that there was an immeasurable and insurmountable difference between God and Man. **Athenagoras** introduced this notion into Christianity. He taught (a) that God was pure mind, and (b) that everything else was created by this pure Mind out of inferior Matter (134).

4. The Metaphysical Universe: Man's Universe Is an Illusion

Unquestionably the greatest error of Greek thinking ever introduced into Christian theology was the idea that the universe is metaphysical in nature. According to **Parmenides** and the Greeks after him, the sensory or "phenomenal" universe Men see around them is an illusion. Parmenides thought this illusion was caused by mankind's collective thoughts or conscience. According to Parmenides, somewhere outside this illusion lay the real universe, which never changes (38-39).

5. Metaphysical Theism: God Exists in the *Pleroma*, the World of "Forms"

Plato taught that the unreal, illusory universe **Parmenides** advocated was caused by God, who is "Pure Mind." He expanded on Parmenides' belief in a metaphysical universe by introducing the philosophical concepts of (a) theism, (b) the *Pleroma* of God, and (c) the concept of perfect or ideal *Forms* which were subsequently identified with the *Logos*.

It was Plato's idea that God exists in the *Pleroma*, which he believed to be the only true reality. The *Pleroma*, he taught, lies above and outside the unreal, illusory or "phenomenal" universe in which Men exist.

Plato also believed the *Pleroma* contained emanations from God called "Forms" (*Ideai*) that represent an extension of God's perfect vision of every object, concept or ideal in the universe. He believed that the Forms acted on chaotic matter under the direction of God, their objective being to bring the unreal "phenomenal" universe into the same perfect order that Plato envisioned as existing in the *Pleroma*.

According to Plato, Man's world does not actually exist—it is "not being," but is in the process of "becoming." In contrast, he thought the *Pleroma* was pure "being" or *ousia* (40-42). The meaning of the term *ousia* was greatly refined by **Aristotle** (45-47).

By the end of the second century A.D., the leaders of the early Christian Church had come to believe the Father, the Son and the Holy Ghost were a singular "substance" or "essence." To express this concept, they used the word *ousia* in the same way Plato and Aristotle had (190-191).

The idea of Christ's "genesis" as an "emanation" of the Father was an early extension of this concept. It was first stated by **Athenagoras**, though the basis for this doctrine was seen in some remarks by **Justin Martyr** (232-240).

6. God As Transcendent: Existence Outside Time and Space

The imagined and completely unsupportable notion of a metaphysical universe led the Greek philosophers to teach that God exists outside time and space (139-140, 265). By the second century A.D., this was an *a priori* assumption relating to the nature of the universe and God's relationship to that universe. It is found in all Greek philosophy and education after *Plato* (264-265).

The Hebrew prophets, however, never taught this strange notion of the universe, or the resulting concepts regarding the transcendency of God. Metaphysical transcendency appears nowhere in inspired writ, and was not part of the earliest Christian understanding of God (267). Other than **Philo of Alexandria** and the Hellenized Jews in that city (266-267), the Jews vehemently resisted all such Hellenistic teachings and culture as an evil associated with the "Gentiles," and never taught any concept or possibility other than the idea that this world and the surrounding universe are real.

Nevertheless, metaphysical transcendency was adopted by the second-century Apologists, beginning with **Melito of Sardis**, as the foundation for their reasoning about God (131-135). The Greek concepts are clearly the source of the idea that God lives outside space and time, and related metaphysical notions about God (98, 213-214). This will be seen in several of the ideas discussed below.

7. The Supposed Inferiority of Created Things

One of the most significant doctrinal consequences of the Greek concept of metaphysical transcendence was the idea that things in the created realm are finite and therefore inferior. **Plato** taught that the unreal, illusory universe was, by nature, perishable and hence inferior. This notion was adopted by the Apologists, through **Athenagoras** (134-135).

8. The Supposed Incomprehensible and Unknowable God

Aristotle taught that God is pure "Form" without substance (*ousia*) (45). This led to the Hellenistic conclusion that God is beyond all description. That view, together with their idea of God as pure Mind or "being" existing only in the *Pleroma*, led them to the belief that God is unknowable in any ultimate sense (65, 265).

This view of God was first introduced into Christianity by **Melito of Sardis** (132), who followed the lead of **Justin Martyr** in his view of God the Father (129-131). This concept was assumed by the Apologists to be the true nature of God from then on (134-135, 139).

9. The Supposed Incorporeality of God: Mind Without Matter

Another fallout from the doctrine of metaphysical transcendency is the notion of God as incorporeal. For the **Platonists**, God was part of an entirely different sphere from the created universe. To them, He was pure Mind, having no contact with matter (221, 264, 265).

This view was the fundamental assumption and came to be the expressed teaching of the later Apologists, especially **Irenaeus** (136). Because of this Hellenistic belief about the nature of God, and because of the assumption of **dualism** that all matter is part of the illusory and imperfect universe, the idea of God having a physical, material body was unthinkable to any of the Apologists except **Tertullian** (271).

10. Creation and Some Distorted Ideas About God's Omnipotence and Omniscience

The *Platonists* (and *Philo of Alexandria*, who applied their views to Judaism) believed that the universe where Man dwells is the figment of a supposedly transcendental God's imagination. They believed it was created by God impressing His Mind on Matter, through the Forms who acted as intermediaries (52-53, 64). With that premise, it was as obvious extension to conclude that God is omnipotent and omniscient.

The metaphysical transcendence of God (the idea that He exists outside space and time) was likewise used by the Apologists as a basis for explaining the attributes of omnipotence and omniscience. A description of God's power that approximated the Greek view was first given by **Justin Martyr** (129-130), whose views were easily and quickly transferred to the metaphysical concept of God introduced by **Melito of Sardis** (132).

Classical theists today explain God's omniscience on the same basis. They argue that because God exists in the *Pleroma* outside time, He knows the future because (a) He causes it, and (b) He can see it from His special vantage point (315-316).

11. Distorted Ideas About the Omnipresence of God

The *Platonists'* concept of God's metaphysical transcendence held that God exists outside of space, as well as time (265, 266). In contrast, the *Stoics*, being monistic, saw God as a totality of rational seeds of thought (*logoi*) that were present in everything (46, 51, 122). These conflicting ideas syncretized into the basic Greek notion of God's omnipresence.

Following the Platonists primarily, the Apologists, starting with *Athenagoras*, taught that, in one way or another, God was able to leave the *Pleroma* (or cause His *Logos* to do so) and enter the supposed unreal, illusory universe where Man dwells, then return to the *Pleroma* (or withdraw His *Logos*) at will (136). This concept, coupled with elements of Stoic influence, have expanded into the conclusion that God is everywhere simultaneously.

12. God As The "Unmoving Mover": God Differs From Men Because He Never Changes

According to *Aristotle*, that which never changes is God (45). Following *Parmenides'* lead, he reasoned that, if a being were to change or to move, it could only be because some cause greater than that being caused that movement or change. God, he concluded, must be the ultimate unmoving, unchanging Mover. Because Men are changeable beings, Aristotle believed that God was fundamentally distinct from and above all Men.

This concept of God, as being statically unchangeable unlike Man, first appeared in the later writings of *Justin Martyr* (129-130). The idea of static unchangeableness as an attribute of God became a regular part of descriptions given of Him by the later Apologists as early as *Melito of Sardis* (132).

13. The Origin of Christ: No Pre-Mortal Birth for the Firstborn Son of God

The Greek philosophers vehemently rejected paganism (37) and were, at first, considered by the pagans as enemies worthy of death (35). The philosophers' ideas about the *Logos* (see above) were not compatible in any way with pagan notions of procreation among the gods. Thus, it was natural that the Apologists rejected any possibility that Christ's pre-mortal "genesis" was through actual birth (139-140, 232-240). Instead, they struggled with whether and how Christ was co-eternal with the Father and adopted meaningless and unnecessary euphemisms such "genesis" and "emanation" to describe how Christ came to exist before the creation of the heavens and the earth (232-240).

14. Rationalism: Reason Rather than Revelation

Another point of false doctrine advanced by *Plato* and adopted by the Hellenized cultures after him was rationalism. This concept is that Men can learn the truth about God only by thinking (41). Reason, Plato taught, was the only source of truth.

In the second century, this idea undermined the early reliance of Christians on revelation from God as the ultimate source of truth, and led them to conclude that there could be no more new revelation or scripture (134). The philosophical propensity to look for truths about God through reason rather than revelation gradually changed the entire attitude of the early Church toward revelation (170-172), especially as they witnessed the martyrdom of their apostles and prophets without a continuation of knowledgeable and authorized leadership (111-112).

15. Logic More Important Than Empirical Truth

Aristotle organized Rationalism into a form that so delighted the Greeks they became more impressed with the symmetry of an argument than its truth. More care was taken by Greek thinkers to form the syllogistic pattern developed by Aristotle than to ensure the accuracy of the premises on which their syllogisms relied (47). This made it even more popular to rely on reason rather than revelation and empirical sources in theology, and it became easier to make errors in the reasoning process (48).

Conclusion

The foregoing by no means exhausts the doctrines of orthodox Christianity which today remain pervaded by the many erroneous notions of Greek philosophy. Any time the assumption is made that God is a "Being," wholly different and distinct from Man, who exists outside time and space, it should be recognized that Greek philosophy, rather than the Bible, is providing the basis for the resulting doctrine.

Also prominent among these infectious doctrines are classical notions about the inferiority and limited nature of Man. The idea that Man cannot become like his Father in Heaven, despite extensive teachings in the Bible to the contrary, is unequivocally founded on the assumption of Greek philosophy regarding "created things."

It was Plato who taught "that which is, the intelligible, is unoriginated, but that which is not, the sensible [Man and the sensory world], is originated, beginning to be and ceasing to exist."[2] This is the source of the grossly erroneous doctrine of Man's finite origin and limited immortality, not the Bible. The Bible teaches that Men and God are the same species, and that eternal progression is the course that God has made possible for all His children.

Man and God are separated by a mighty gap, as the caterpillar is from the butterfly, but it is not an insurmountable chasm as classical theism claims. This is the monumentally "good news" of the Gospel of Jesus Christ as it was taught in the New Testament! It was believed by early Christianity until the corrupting influences of short-sighted Greek thinkers invaded the early Church through the Apologists. The challenge for classical theism is to return to biblical doctrines on this and other teachings by rejecting the influence of Greek philosophy that has plagued orthodox theology since the second century.

---

[2] Athenagoras, *A Plea for the Christians*, 19.

Scripture Index

Old Testament

Genesis
1 285
1 288
1 292
1 428
1:1 278
1:1 285
1:1 291
1:1 406
1:1-3 289
1:1-3 302
1:2 288
1:2 290-92
1:2 294
1:2 301
1:26 238
1:26-27 226
1:26-27 242
1:26-27 250
1:26-27 261
1:26-27 395
1:26-27 406
1:26-27 423
1:27 291
1:28 238
1:31 238
1:31 397
2 288
2 292
2 428
2-3 421
2:7 291
2:17 238
3:3 238
5:3 250
5:5 238
7:39 420
15:8 378
16:9 327
16:1-13 375
16:7-14 377
16:13 327
16:13 377
17:11 25
17:11 220
18:25 347
21:17-19 375
21:33 359
22:11 327
22:11-16 375
22:17 403
31:11-13 375
32:30 251
48:16 327

Exodus
3:2 327
3:2-4 375
3:2-6 327
3:13-14 351
3:14 25
3:14 220
3:14 243
3:14 378
13:21 327
14:19 327
19:9 228
19:18-20 327
22:20 372
23:20-23 327
24:9-11 251
33:5 228
33:7-11 251
33:20-23 252

Numbers
12:8 252
22:22 327
23:19 259
23:19 260
23:19 276
23:19 305
23:19 347
23:19 399

Deuteronomy
4:27-28 269
4:27-28 275
4:27-28 394
4:28 130
5:4 251
5:4 327
5:31 228
31:28 44
32:1 44
32:4 315
33:27 282
33:27 359
33:27 426
34:10 251

Joshua
5:13-15 228

Judges
2:1 327
2:1 375
2:4 327
6:11 327
6:12 377
6:12-16 375
6:13 377
13:3 327
13:3-22 375
13:18 327
15:14 307

Ruth
2:12 254

1 Samuel
15:29 347

2 Samuel
22:7 333

1 Kings
8:13 333
8:27 332-333
8:32 339
8:34 339
8:36 339
8:39 339
8:43 339
8:45 339
8:49 339

2 Kings
19:19 372
19:35 327

1 Chronicles
10:10 334

2 Chronicles
2:6 332-333

Ezra
5:12 55

Nehemiah
9:6 279

Job
1:6 376
2:1 376
4:17-19 238
10:21-22 415
12:8 44
19:25-27 258
21:33 406
28:24 25
31 55
32:8 256
33:12 238
36:22 432
36:22 437
38 55
38 320
38 323
38:2 314
38:4-7 291
38:4-7 361
38:4-7 423
38:4-7 428
38:4-7 439
38:7 280
38:7 361
38:7 376
38:7 390
38:7 395
38:17 320

38:18.........320	**Ecclesiastes**	45:21-22.......26	**Lamentations**
38:34.........321	2:26..........434	45:21-22......371	3:37..........317
38:35.........321	3:14..........238	46:9-11.......312	
42:5..........55	**Isaiah**	46:10..........25	**Ezekiel**
Psalms	6:1...........336	46:10..........26	18:14-32......347
2:7...........234	6:1-5.........272	46:10.........315	18:21-28......348
11:14.........333	9:6...........327	46:10.........350	20:33-36......252
17:8..........254	9:6...........359	46:10-11......317	**Daniel**
18:6..........333	9:6...........380	46:10-11......322	6:26..........348
36:7..........254	11:10..........34	46:10-11......347	12:1..........377
40:12.........406	14:12.........361	53.............34	
41:13.........358	24:20.........359	55:8-9........272	**Hosea**
45:6-7....360-361	28:9-13.......434	55:8-9........393	1:10..........376
45:7......360-361	37:20.........372	55:8-9........399	8:11-14.......334
57:1..........254	40............332	55:8-9........432	
61:4..........254	40:28..........26	57:15..........26	**Joel**
63:7..........254	40:28.........350	57:15.....272-273	3:4-6.........334
89:27.........423	40:28.........359	57:15.........284	
90:2...........26	41-45.........390	57:15.........301	**Amos**
90:2..........350	41:21-23......312	57:15.........350	8:11...........84
90:2..........358	41:21-24.......26	57:16.........406	
91:4..........254	41:21-24......318	58:8..........367	**Jonah**
103:20........376	41:22..........25	58:9..........228	3:4...........348
104:4.........375	41:25-26......312	60:2...........84	3:4-10........348
104:5.........359	43............383	63:9..........327	3:9...........348
104:25........406	43:3..........379	64:1..........327	3:10..........348
106:48........358	43:10..........26	64:3..........327	4:1...........348
113:5-6.......273	43:10.........371	65:17.........239	**Micah**
123:1.........273	43:10.........379	65:17.........424	6:7...........239
139...........332	43:12b.........26	66............335	
139:7-10......332	43:12b........350	66:1-2........279	**Nahum**
139:7-10......335	43:13..........26	66:1-2........334	1:5...........327
139:7-12.......26	43:13.........284	66:2..........335	
139:17-18......25	43:13.........301	66:22.........239	**Habakkuk**
147:5..........25	43:13.........350	66:22.........424	2:20..........333
147:5.........406	43:13.........358	**Jeremiah**	**Zechariah**
148:2.........376	44............383	1:5...........427	1:12..........327
148:5.........376	44:6...........26	10:10..........26	2:10..........228
Proverbs	44:6..........312	14:22.........279	12:1..........256
1:7............26	44:6..........371	23:23.........337	12:1..........406
8.............349	44:6..........379	23:23-24.......26	12:1..........420
8:12-36.......159	44:7..........312	23:23-24......336	12:8..........327
8:22..........280	44:8...........26	23:24.........324	12:10.........239
8:22..........313	44:8..........371	23:24.........332	
8:22..........322	44:28.........312	27:8...........55	**Malachi**
8:22..........349	45:5...........26	28:14..........55	2:10..........398
8:22..........368	45:5..........371	29:11..........25	3:1...........333
8:22......432-433	45:11.........312	29:11.........220	3:6.........25-26
8:22-23.......314	45:18..........26	33:22.........403	3:6...........345
8:31..........433	45:18.........371	40:15.........371	3:6...........350
8:31..........440	45:21.........312	46:23.........406	4:2...........254
16:4..........279			

Scripture Index

New Testament

Matthew
1:1. 241
1:20. 377
1:24. 377
2:13. 377
2:19. 377
3:16. 255
3:16-17 243
3:16-17 327
3:17. 243
5:48. 397
5:48. 425
6:19-20 423
7:15. 20
7:15. 86
11:27. 138
11:27. 224
11:27. 253
11:27. 388
13:24-43 424
13:35. 290
13:40. 424
19:4. 290
19:8. 290
19:24. 305
19:25. 305
19:26. 305-306
21:12. 333
22:23-33 257
23:37. 254
24:11. 20
24:11. 86
24:21. 290
24:24. 20
24:24. 86
24:35. 317
24:35. 347
24:36. 246
25:34. 290
26:42. 244
28:18. 437
28:19-20 329

Mark
1:10. 255
10:6. 290
10:18. 25
13:19. 290
13:22. 20
13:22. 86
13:31. 317

13:31. 347
13:32. 246
14:36. 244
14:36. 306
14:36. 379

Luke
1:20. 317
1:20. 347
1:34. 305
1:35. 305
1:37. 306
2:9. 377
2:52. 314
2:52. 432
3:22. 255
7:24. 375
10:22. 138
10:22. 253
11:50. 290
13:34. 254
15:12-13 231
16:19-31 424
22:42. 244
22:42. 379
24:36-43 252
24:36-43 . . 257-258
24:36-43 341
24:36-43 350
24:36-43 . . . . 365 fn
24:36-43 422
24:39. 256
24:39. 262
24:41-43 256

John
1:1 37-38
1:1. 388
1:1-3 224
1:1-3 278
1:1-3 443
1:1-14 133
1:3. 279
1:9. 208
1:12. 376
1:14 37-38
1:14. 129
1:14. 224
1:14. 234
1:14. 242
1:14. 270

1:14. 443
1:18. 129
1:18. 234
1:32. 255
3:16. 129
3:16. 234
3:16. 239
3:18. 129
3:18. 234
4:24. 25
4:24 255-257
4:24. 276
4:24. 342
5:17-23 388
5:19. 244
5:19. 314
5:19. 363
5:19. 369
5:19-21 244
5:20 245-246
5:25. 424
5:26. 282
5:26. 285
5:26. 300
5:26. 366
5:26-27 388
5:30. 118
5:30. 244
5:30. 380
5:30. 408
5:37. 252
6:38. 388
6:46. 260
8:12. 415
8:19. 260
8:23. 273
8:25-28 118
8:28 244-245
8:28. 388
8:28-29 380
8:29. 408
8:44. 290
8:56-58 242
8:56-59 351
8:56-59 378
8:58. 243
10:15. 388
10:18. 366
10:30. 115
10:30. 388

14 261
14:7. 253
14:7. 270
14:7-9 224
14:7-9 261
14:9. 331
14:9. 364
14:10-11 261
14:12. 261
14:28. 388
16:7. 378
17:2-3 393
17:3. 26
17:3. 62
17:3 371-372
17:3. 426
17:5. 243
17:20-21 85
17:21-22 62
17:24. 290
20:17. 198
20:17. 398
20:19-20 257
21:17. 322
21:17. 349
21:17 360-361

Acts
1:8. 329
1:9-11 252
1:11. 331
2:1-4 309
2:4. 342
2:23. 312
2:23. 427
3:19-20 327
3:20-21 86
5:28. 337
7:48. 334
7:49-53 334
7:50. 279
7:50-53 335
7:55. 328
7:55-56 251
7:55-56 260
8:9-24 158
10:33. 228
12:15 375-376
13:33. 234
14:15. 279
14:25. 25

15:1........154	11:36.........25	4:4...........252	3:3...........256
15:18.......312	11:36.......271	4:6...........25	3:10-21......425
15:20.......154	11:36.......355	4:6...........271	4:19..........337
17:24.......279	12:5.....85-86	6:16..........334	
17:24.......334	16:26.......359	13:11......85-86	**Colossians**
17:24-25....285			1:15..........131
17:24-25....301	**1 Corinthians**	**Galatians**	1:15..........197
17:24-25....326	1:10..........86	3:8...........312	1:15..........198
17:24-25....332	3:16-17.....334	3:8...........317	1:15..........232
17:24-28....332	4:4...........131	3:19-20......443	1:15..........239
17:27.......337	6:12..........306	4:4-7.........361	1:15..........242
17:27.......339	6:17..........256	4:7...........372	1:15..........252
17:28.......271	6:19..........334	4:7...........399	1:15......260-361
17:28.......355	8..............381	4:7-8.........374	1:15..........366
17:28.......398	8:4............381	4:8............26	1:15..........423
17:28.......423	8:4............384	4:8.......371-373	1:16...........25
17:28-29....398	8:4-6..........26	4:8............394	1:16..........212
17:29.......275	8:4-6..........371	4:9............372	1:16..........278
17:29.......394	8:4-6....380-381		1:16-17.......279
19:27.......334	8:4-6..........384	**Ephesians**	1:16-17.......281
23:6-8......257	8:4-6..........390	1:4............290	1:16-17.......300
	8:5............371	1:5............280	1:17...........25
Romans	8:5......381-382	1:5............312	1:17..........332
1:20...........26	8:5............400	1:11...........312	1:17..........358
1:20..........290	8:5-6..........381	1:22-23.......332	1:18..........239
1:20..........350	8:6............117	1:22-23.......338	2:8............21
2:14-15......208	8:6............338	1:22-23.......341	2:8............83
4:17......291-293	8:6............371	3:9............279	2:8............87
4:17..........302	8:6......381-382	3:15...........423	2:8...........442
4:17..........326	8:6............384	4:5-6...........85	2:16-23.......154
4:17..........337	8:6............407	4:6............324	3:11..........338
5:12..........421	8:10...........334	4:6............338	3:11..........341
6:9...........252	10:23..........306	4:9-10.........332	4:1........365 fn.
6:9...........331	11:3...........388	4:9-10.........337	
6:9...........341	13:12..........426	4:9-10.........341	**1 Thessalonians**
8:14..........376	15:21-22......421	4:10...........336	1:9............26
8:14..........405	15:21-24......428	4:11-14........207	1:9...........371
8:16..........398	15:24-28......360	4:13...........424	
8:16-17......408	15:24-28......380		**2 Thessalonians**
8:17..........198	15:27-28......361	**Philippians**	2:1-4..........88
8:17..........356	15:28..........324	1:27............86	2:13..........290
8:17..........399	15:35-50......257	2:5-7..........351	2:15...........13
8:17..........408	15:44....257-258	2:5-7..........354	3:6............13
8:17..........437	15:46-49...365 fn.	2:5-8..........388	
8:29..........239	15:49..........258	2:5-9..........242	**1 Timothy**
8:29..........312	15:50..........258	2:6............351	1:7...........372
8:30..........312	15:51-53......406	2:6-7......352-353	1:17...........26
9:5...........388	15:51-54......421	2:6-7..........363	1:17..........282
10:14.........117	15:58..........348	2:7............197	1:17..........350
11:2..........312		2:8............350	1:17..........359
11:2..........427	**2 Corinthians**	2:9............352	1:17..........372
11:25..........34	3:18...........426	2:9.......360-361	1:17..........426
		2:15...........376	2:5............26

Scripture Index

2:5........... 371
2:5........... 443
4:1-3......... 160
4:4........... 238
6:20.......... 215

2 Timothy
4:1-4......... 207
4:2-4.......... 20
4:2-4.......... 86
4:3............ 74

Titus
1:2........... 305
1:2........... 347
2:13.......... 388

Hebrews
1:2........... 278
1:3........... 131
1:3........... 252
1:3........... 364
1:4........... 377
1:4-14........ 377
1:5........... 234
1:8-9......... 198
1:8-9..... 360-361
1:8-9......... 383
1:9....... 360-361
1:10.......... 290
1:14.......... 376
2:6-8......... 423
3:14.......... 348
4:3........... 290
5:5........... 234
5:7-9......... 349
5:8........... 432
6:17........... 26
6:17.......... 347
6:17.......... 350
6:18........... 25
6:18.......... 305
6:18.......... 347
6:18-19....... 348
7:12.......... 346

8:5....... 365 fn.
8:6........... 443
9:15.......... 443
9:26.......... 290
9:27.......... 280
9:27.......... 427
11:3........... 25
11:3.......... 278
11:3.......... 291
11:3...... 293-294
11:3.......... 302
11:3.......... 326
11:3.......... 337
11:12......... 403
11:17......... 234
11:28......... 239
12:9.......... 197
12:9.......... 338
12:9.......... 398
12:9.......... 406
12:9.......... 420
12:9.......... 423
12:23......... 239
12:23......... 423
12:24......... 443
13:8.......... 198
13:8.......... 345

James
1:17.......... 348
2:25.......... 375
2:26.......... 252
2:26.......... 256

1 Peter
1:2........... 312
3:8............ 86
4:6........... 424

2 Peter
1:20........... 12
1:20.......... 290
2:1............ 20
2:1............ 86
3............. 429

3:4........... 290
3:7........... 238
3:8........... 418
3:10.......... 424
3:10-12....... 238
3:13.......... 239
3:13.......... 424
3:17.......... 348

1 John
1:1........... 290
2:13-14....... 290
2:22.......... 155
3:1-2......... 376
3:2....... 398-399
3:2........... 405
3:2........... 412
3:2........... 426
3:2-3.......... 62
3:2-3......... 198
3:3........... 399
3:3........... 437
3:8........... 290
4:1............ 20
4:1............ 86
4:2-3......... 155
4:9........... 234
5:1........... 234
5:6........... 155
5:7........... 244
5:7........... 388

Jude
1:4........... 372
1:9........... 377
1:24.......... 372
1:25.......... 372

Revelation
1:5-6..... 365-366
1:5-6..... 369-370
1:20.......... 375
2:1........... 375
2:8........... 375
2:12.......... 375

2:18.......... 375
3:1........... 375
3:7........... 375
3:14.......... 198
3:14...... 232-234
3:14.......... 238
3:14.......... 240
3:14.......... 290
3:14.......... 375
3:21........... 62
3:21.......... 379
3:21.......... 384
3:21.......... 389
3:21.......... 391
3:21.......... 399
3:21.......... 407
3:21.......... 424
4:11........... 25
4:11...... 278-279
8:3-5......... 375
9:20.......... 130
9:20.......... 269
9:20.......... 275
9:20.......... 372
13:8.......... 290
17:8.......... 290
19:9-10....... 341
19:10......... 374
19:10......... 390
20............ 428
20:4-6........ 406
20:12-13...... 424
20:14-15...... 424
21............ 424
21:1.......... 239
21:1.......... 406
21:1.......... 424
22............ 424
22:3-5........ 408
22:8-9........ 327
22:16......... 361
22:20......... 228

Book of Mormon

1 Nephi
10:9.......... 427
10:18......... 345

2 Nephi
1:26.......... 315

2:4........... 345
2:10.......... 315
9:20.......... 314
9:20.......... 433
18:8.......... 332

27:23......... 345

Jacob
5:7-17......... 34

Mosiah
4:9........... 309

Alma
7:8........... 304
7:20.......... 427
13:3.......... 314
13:7.......... 314

26:35........309	**3 Nephi**	9:10..........345	3:14..........361
30:13-15......314	1:13..........317	9:19..........345	3:15-16.......423
31:17.........345	1:13..........347	9:19..........357	12:19-21......432
34:14.........398	12:48.........425	**Ether**	
37:12.........427	24:6..........345	2:8...........372	**Moroni**
42:26.........347	**Mormon**	3:6-17........251	8:18..........345
42:23.........357	9:9...........345	3:14..........338	10:19.........345

Doctrine & Covenants

3:2...........427	38:1-2........323	88:13.........271	93:29.........404
19:10.........359	45:25......... 34	88:13.........357	93:29.........421
20:12.........345	50:27.........309	88:37.........287	93:29-30......242
20:17.........345	63:59-60......338	93 421	101:23........432
20:17.........398	67:10.........432	93:2..........208	104:2.........347
20:19.........372	76:4..........345	93:21-36......421	104:17........427
20:28.........398	76:24.........427	93:24.........314	109:332.......332
29:30.........317	84:46.........208	93:26.........314	110:1.........427
29:30.........347	84:102........315	93:28.........426	130:18-19.....421
35:1..........345	88 342	93:29......... 61	130:18-19 .433-434
35:1..........427	88 421	93:29.........197	132:8.........415
38:1-2........318	88:11-12......332	93:29.........395	132:24........372

Pearl of Great Price

Moses	1:33..........405	1:39..........405	3:22..........197
1:5...........432	1:33..........427	4:30..........317	3:22..........404
1:28..........427	1:35..........403	4:30..........347	3:22..........406
1:31-35 ...289-290	1:35..........427	**Abraham**	3:22..........420
1:33..........403	1:37-39.......427	3:21-22.......242	3:26..........406

Subject Index

— A —

Adam / Eve - 116, 156, 238, 398, 421
Adoptionists / Adoptionism - 170, 189, 193-194
Aeons - 59, 155, 160, 162-165, 199, 227-228
agents / agency - 53, 125, 341, 361, 374-375, 377-380, 382, 385-386, 408
Alexander of Alexandria - 18, 195-196
Alexandrian Fathers - 17, 46, 173
allegory / allegorical - 75-76, 114, 165, 236, 263
Ananus - 90
Anaxagoras - 36, 40, 52, 75, 297, 444
Anaximander - 414
Andronicus, Livius - 71
Angel of the Lord - 229, 232, 254, 327, 377-378
angels - 64, 128-129, 133, 222, 233, 246, 360, 361, 375-376
Anicetus - 101
Ante-Nicene Fathers - 14, 17
Anteros - 181
anthropomorphism / anthropomorphic - 253, 254, 262, 307
Antoninus Pius (Titus) - 71, 93, 109, 129
Apelles - 119
Apostolic Fathers - 14, 17, 94, 101-102, 110, 117, 126, 263
Apostles, fate of - 91-93
a priori assumptions - 206-211, 213, 215, 250, 280, 307, 330, 400, 430, 441-442, 445
Aquinas, Thomas - 306, 376
Arian controversy / Arianism / Arians - 46, 118, 141, 145, 148, 170, 173, 176-177, 182-183, 188-189, 192-200, 373, 387
Aristides - 15, 17, 93-94, 102, 143, 145, 263
Aristobulus - 76
Aristotle / Aristotelian - 36, 44-48, 50, 69, 70, 72, 87, 99, 130, 132, 135, 210-211, 228, 309, 394, 445-448
Arius - 187-188, 194-201
Arrius Antoninus - 179
asceticism - 79, 154, 160-161
Athanasius - 14, 183, 193, 200-201
Athenagoras - 16, 17, 115, 121, 134-136, 142, 218, 227, 235, 238, 240, 269, 270, 273, 443-447
atheists / atheism - 106, 118, 120-121, 124, 128, 134, 143, 145, 177, 180
Augustine - 19, 75, 167, 201, 207, 218, 280, 305-306
avomoios - 199

— B —

bara - 291
Bardesanes / Bardaisân - 160-162
Barnabas / *Epistle of Barnabus* - 1, 17, 113, 124
Barth, Karl - 218, 226
Basilides - 115, 158, 160, 162-163, 167, 297
Beckwith, Francis J. - 22-24, 29, 217, 263, 304, 306-307, 311, 313, 319, 325, 331, 350, 354, 358, 364, 366, 371, 381, 394, 400, 405, 407, 413-414, 416-420, 426, 428-431, 434-435
being / not being / becoming - 3839, 41, 47, 134, 164, 293, 295, 307, 312, 393, 442, 445-446, 449

beginnings / beginningless universe - 23, 405-407, 414-415
Berkhoff, Louis - 218

— C —

Cainites - 159
Callistus - 142-143, 189
canon - 172
Cantor, Georg - 403
Carpocrates - 158-159, 163
Carvilius, Spurius - 71
catholicism / catholic - 147-148
Celsus - 107, 268-269
Cerdon - 165
Cerinthus - 155, 159, 245
Christ, always God - 358-359, 361
Christ, baptism of - 327
Christ, bright and morning star - 361
Christ, co-eternal with the Father - 197-198, 448
Christ, compared to Greek Logos - 127-128, 131, 443
Christ, created/uncreated - 194, 198, 366
Christ, creator - 299
Christ, different from Jesus - 155
Christ, emanation of the Father/"genesis" - 51, 136, 236, 240, 445, 448
Christ, equal with the Father - 198, 239, 361, 377
Christ, Eternal God - 350, 360
Christ, exaltation of - 359-360
Christ, firstborn of the Father - 194, 197, 232, 234, 242, 361, 366, 423
Christ, immutable - 198, 346, 350, 353, 361, 366-367
Christ, kenosis of - 352-353, 363
Christ, knowledge acquired - 349
Christ, likeness to the Father - 131, 198, 364
Christ, omnipresence of - 331, 341
Christ, omniscience of - 313
Christ, only begotten - 270
Christ, origin / genesis of - 232-241
Christ, pre-existence of - 194, 197, 209, 236, 242, 254, 327, 361, 367
Christ, progression of - 197, 349
Christ, rational force - 232
Christ, relationship to the Father - 124-128, 133, 197, 229, 245, 351
Christ, relationship to Man - 198
Christ, resurrection of - 251, 256
Christ, separate from the Father - 125-129, 133, 137, 142-143, 193, 196, 228-230, 239, 243-246, 261, 269, 442
Christ, spatio-temporal location of - 327
Christ, steadfastness of - 361, 363
Christ, throne of - 384
Christian *gnosis* - 169
Christian Research Institute - 22, 28
Claudius Apolonaris - 16, 18, 120
Clementines - 156
Clement of Alexandria - 16, 18, 60-61, 107, 115, 169, 422, 441
Clement of Rome - 15, 17, 94-95
Commodus - 180
confessor - 182
conscience, self-/center of - 213, 220, 225-228, 243-247, 325, 327-328, 330, 367
Constantine - 147, 186-188, 199-200
Corinthus - 158
co-substantiality / consubstantiality - 140-143, 146, 176, 189, 191, 193, 196, 220, 224-227, 229-233, 238, 241, 243, 246, 271, 306, 337, 373, 375, 387-389
Council of Arles - 183
Council of Carthage - 182
Council of Constantinople - 201
Council of Trent - 11
created / uncreated - 197, 234, 237-240, 263-264, 374, 394, 444, 446, 449

Subject Index

creation, "all things" - 279, 281, 290
creation, *ex nihilo* - 103, 115, 168, 234, 237, 279, 288, 290-294, 296, 298, 300, 354-355, 366, 414
creation, immediate/direct - 279
creation, mediate/derivative - 279, 292
creation, out of pre-existing materials - 167, 288, 291-292, 295-296
creation, reality/time/space - 278-280, 282-283, 285-286, 299-300, 315, 354
creeds - 177
Cyprian - 16, 18, 118, 182-184

— D —

daemons - 64, 221-222
Dark Ages - 84, 87, 89-90
Decius - 181-184
Demiurge / *Demiurgus* / Demigod - 43-44, 136, 155, 159, 164-166, 199, 245
Democritus - 40, 296
Diatessaron - 113, 161
Didaché / *Teaching of the Twelve Apostles* / *Teaching of the Apostles* - 113
Dio Chrisostom - 77-78
Diocletian - 184-187, 387
Dionysius of Alexandria - 18, 191-193, 198, 216, 231, 237
Dionysius of Rome - 18, 191-192, 216, 329
Dionysius Thrax - 70
Dionysius the pseudo-Areopagite - 169, 376
Dioscorus - 182
docetes / docetic / docetism - 116, 137, 157-158, 160-161, 163-164, 166
dogma / dogmatism - 148, 214-216, 242, 331
Domitan - 91-92, 207
dualism / dualistic - 40-41, 44, 52-53, 121, 134, 160, 165, 221, 264, 296, 298, 374, 394, 444, 446

— E —

Easter - 101, 147
Ebionites - 100, 154-156
Edict of Milan - 188, 199
Egyptian school (Gnostics) - 160-162, 165
Einstein, Albert - 308-309
element, eternal - 405
Elkasaites - 157
Encratites - 161
energy - 307-309
Epictetus - 52, 87
Epiphanes - 159
Epiphanius - 156
Epistle to Diognetus - 15, 17, 126
Essenes - 155-156
eternal progression - 350, 364-365, 399, 407-409, 413, 419-428, 430, 432, 449
eternity / everlasting - 265, 284, 358-359

— F —

fables - 20, 207
Father Basil - 75
Festus - 90
Forms / World of Forms - 42-47, 52-53, 64, 159, 222, 319, 444-447
free agency - 52, 59, 318, 408

— G —

Gaïus - 172
Galerius Maximus - 184-186
Gallus - 183
Gestalt psychology - 435
Gnostics / Gnosticism - 19, 20, 50, 57-59, 63, 76, 111-112, 132, 137, 154-155, 157-162, 164-166, 168-170, 172, 188, 199, 215, 223, 227, 234, 239, 287, 297, 386
God, always God - 358-359
God, cannot *not* exist - 357

God, compared to corporation - 383-384, 386-387
God, compared to Greek God - 126, 128, 132-133, 136, 443
God, corporeal/incorporeal - 23-24, 64, 97, 131, 206, 214, 250-251, 253, 257, 263, 265-268, 270-271, 275-276, 307, 309, 311, 318, 321, 324-325, 331, 340-342, 367, 446
God, creator - 25, 40, 42-43, 63-64, 263, 278-279, 298, 354, 428
God, emanations from - 158, 165, 199, 245, 386, 445
God, eternal - 26, 37, 64, 270, 282, 284, 357, 359, 361-363, 366, 417, 428
God, eternal round - 428-429
God, exaltation of - 365-366
God, "fills" the universe - 324, 336-338, 342
God, honesty of - 347
God, immanence of - 272-273, 337-338
God, immutable - 23, 26, 64, 345, 349, 354, 357, 361-363, 365, 367
God, impalpable - 98-99
God, impassible - 98-99, 125, 135, 270
God, incomprehensible - 65, 79, 97, 132, 135, 141, 163, 214, 223, 226, 231, 270, 307, 393, 446
God, infinite - 23, 259, 276, 280, 307, 393, 398, 401
God, invisible - 63, 135, 260, 270
God, kenosis - 362-363
God, location/place/presence - 23, 225, 261, 325, 327, 336, 339-340,
God, Man/father of Man - 260, 280
God, Man to become like - 80, 126-127, 381, 396, 405, 409, 424-426, 432, 434, 436, 449
God, Man to return to - 79
God, matter co-eternal with - 162
God, nature - 371, 373-374, 394

God, necessary/sustainer/author of natural law - 25, 26, 288, 325, 331, 354, 356
God, no qualities - 64
God, no sensory organs - 269, 274-275
God, not God-when? - 353
God, *nous*/Mind/wisdom - 40, 52, 58, 63, 136, 145, 190, 221, 227, 241, 245, 307, 324, 394, 422, 431, 443-444, 446
God, office/title/position of - 224, 270, 350-353, 354, 358-363, 379, 385, 389, 399
God, omnipotent - 23, 25, 304, 307-309, 318, 341, 362, 407-408, 446-447
God, omnipresent - 23, 26, 324-330, 332-333, 336-339, 343, 447
God, omniscient/omniscience of - 23, 25, 311-314, 317, 320, 322, 325, 336, 341, 407-408, 437, 446-447
God, oneness of - 229-230, 265, 371, 373, 380-381, 384-385, 389, 442
God, Only/many - 23, 26, 162, 371-373, 379, 381-382, 384, 389
God, of order - 415
God, personal - 24, 220-221, 324-325, 327-328, 330, 339
God, presence of - 327-328, 336, 342, 354
God, promise/word/purpose - 347, 367
God, self-sufficient - 145
God, size of - 333-334
God, spirit body of - 255
God, steadfastness/constancy - 348, 363, 366
God, transcendent/transcendency of - 43, 64-65, 79, 98, 190, 194, 209, 211, 217, 221, 223, 231, 250, 261, 263-266, 268, 270-273, 276, 287, 296-299, 311, 326, 334, 337, 354, 394-395, 431, 445-447, 449
God, unbegotten - 129, 135, 221, 234, 270
God, uncontained - 135, 221, 270

God, uncreated - 134, 234
God, undying - 221
God, ultimate truth - 169
God, with wings? - 253-254
Gordian III - 181

— H —

Hadrian - 106, 108, 145
Hatch, Edwin - 56, 168, 172, 205, 213-215, 221, 223, 227, 240, 267, 298, 393
heavens and the earth, the - 278, 288-289, 294-295, 298-299, 405-406
Heracleon - 158, 164-165
Heraclitus - 35, 37-40, 42, 45, 50, 75, 87, 132, 443
heretical sects, number of - 90
Hermas - 17, 102-103, 113, 295
Hermogenes - 167-168
Hippolytus - 16, 18 77fn., 111, 115, 167-168, 170, 181, 298-299
Holy Ghost, Comforter - 378
Holy Ghost, God's "Wisdom" - 138-139
Holy Ghost, separate from the Father - 142
homoousia / Homoousians - 199-200
homoousious - 190-192, 199-200, 216, 224, 231
Hosius, Bishop - 200
Hottentots - 404
Hydroparastatae - 161
hypostasis - 190-191

— I —

idioms / idiomatic - 289
idols / idolatry / idol worshippers - 274-275, 283-284, 325, 372, 381, 394
infinity - 276, 284, 326, 400-401, 407, 413, 418-419, 427, 429, 433
infinity, arithmetic of - 401-404, 406, 413, 416, 427, 431
infinity, practical - 359, 404

Ignatius of Antioch - 15, 17, 93, 96-99, 100, 145
intelligence / intelligences - 44, 197, 355-357, 366-367, 395, 404-406, 419-422, 427-428
intermediaries - 52-53, 165, 221-222, 234, 298-299, 447
Intermediate, the - 164
Irenaeus - 16, 17, 92, 103, 108, 111-113, 115-117, 121, 134, 136-138, 142, 147, 155, 160, 164-166, 168, 224, 227, 245, 287, 295, 296, 330-331, 443, 446
Italian school (Gnostics) - 164

— J —

James, the Lord's brother - 90
JSV - 305, 420
Judaizers - 154
Julius Caesar - 387
Justin Martyr - 15, 17, 35, 44, 93, 103, 108-110, 112, 118, 120, 123-124, 126, 128-131, 136, 143, 160, 166, 168, 193-194, 209, 223, 228-229, 230, 232-236, 237, 239-240, 243, 245, 269, 294, 296, 298, 378, 422, 441-442, 445-448

— K —

King Follett - 362, 364-365
Kronos - 281

— L —

labels - 79, 216-217, 313, 384-385
lapsed - 182-183
Lawrence - 184
Leonides - 180
Libanius - 75
libellus - 181-182
Licinius - 187-188, 199
logical impossibility - 226, 231, 305-306, 316-317, 338, 357
logoi - 46, 51, 122, 222, 236, 386, 447

Logos - 37-39, 44, 52, 121-122, 135-136, 141, 163, 189, 192, 194-195, 198, 222-224, 227-228, 235, 239-240, 245, 298-299, 386, 443-444, 447-448

Logos-power - 131, 237

Lucian - 106

Lucian of Antioch - 187-188, 195, 199

Lucius Verus - 120

Lyceum, the - 69, 72

— M —

Macrianus - 184

Man, created in God's image/offspring of God - 223, 242, 250, 356, 394-396, 398-399, 423, 449

Man, eternal - 356, 397, 409, 421

Man, finite - 395-397, 401, 405, 409, 431, 449

Man, joint-heirs with Christ - 356, 372, 399, 405, 408, 437

Man, pre-existent knowledge veiled - 433

Man, pre-existence of - 376, 432-433

Marcia - 180

Marcion / Marcionites - 101, 113, 137, 158, 160-161, 165-167, 183

Marcus / Mark (Gnostic) - 158, 164-165

Marcus Aurelius Antoninus - 52, 120-122, 124, 129, 132, 143, 177-179, 180, 227, 239

Mars' Hill - 334

Mathetes - 15, 17, 126

Maxentius - 187

Maximian - 184-186

Maximilla - 171

Maximin - 186-187

Maximin the Thracian - 181

Maximus of Tyre - 65, 265

Melito of Sardis - 16, 17, 76, 121, 132-134, 443, 445-448

Menander - 158, 160

metaphysics / metaphysical - 39-42, 45, 73-74, 79-81, 97-98, 114-115, 122, 124, 126-127, 132, 136-138, 141, 145, 164, 189, 207, 209, 211-212, 216, 224, 227, 230-231, 236, 238, 240-241, 244, 246, 261, 263-264, 270-271, 279-280, 286, 293, 295, 296, 299, 311-313, 319-320, 326-327, 331, 337, 339-340, 342, 356-357, 364, 373, 386, 396, 414-415, 417-418, 444, 446-447

Militades - 120

Minucius Felix - 16, 18, 121, 140

Modalism / Modalists - 170-171, 189-191, 193

Monarchianism / Monarchianists - 170, 173, 188-189, 195

monism / monistic - 38, 45, 121, 240, 308

monotheism - 36, 41, 155, 189, 193, 216, 371-373, 382, 384-385, 442

Montanists / Montanism - 170-172, 180

Montanus - 170-171

— N —

Naasenes - 159

necessary vs. contingent - 23, 355, 357, 396

Neoplatonism - 78-79, 240

Nero - 91-93, 120, 207

Neurobiology - 321

Nicaea / Nicene - 30, 46, 118, 146-147, 177, 189, 199-201, 231

Nicolaitans - 159

Nietzsche - 286

Novatian - 18, 182

— O —

Oedipodean intercourse - 107, 124

ontology / ontological - 393-395, 399, 420, 422

Ophites - 159

Oriental school (Gnostics) - 164

Subject Index

Origen - 16, 18, 60-61, 107, 115, 157, 173, 180-182, 190, 240, 242, 280, 330, 394

orthodoxy - 147, 173

ousia - 41-47, 63-64, 160, 190-191, 224, 229, 231, 297-298, 312, 389, 394, 445-446

— P —

pagans / paganism - 34, 36, 75, 79-80, 100, 108, 111, 118, 128, 153, 234, 274, 385-386, 448

pantheism / pantheistic - 51, 220-221, 324-325, 328, 331-332, 342, 429

Papias - 15, 17, 93-94, 102

Paraclete - 171

paradox / paradoxical - 207, 231, 306, 330-331, 339, 395, 401

Parmenides - 35, 38-42, 52, 142, 264, 294, 320, 331, 422, 444, 447

Paul of Samosata - 188, 192-194, 195

Peripatetics - 50, 130, 210

persona - 191, 225

phenomenon / phenomenal world - 39, 41-42, 52, 115, 134, 264, 294, 355

Philo of Alexandria - 50, 63-65, 76, 114, 130, 132, 139, 222, 263, 266, 293, 356, 431, 445-446

Plato - 35-36, 39-45, 47, 52, 60, 68, 69, 70, 72, 74, 84, 120, 134, 136, 159, 169, 206, 222, 235, 238, 264, 273, 284, 294, 319, 356, 386, 394, 444-446, 448-449

Platonists / Platonism - 44-47, 50, 52-53, 56-57. 64, 69, 76, 79, 108, 121-122, 133-136, 141, 155, 159, 162-163, 168, 189, 198-200, 221, 240, 245, 264, 293-295, 298, 307, 319, 355, 357, 374, 394, 414-416, 442-444, 446-447

Plato's Academy - 69, 72, 265

Pleroma - 41-42, 58-59, 142, 163-164, 212, 231, 263, 265, 271, 273, 284, 286-287, 293, 312, 316, 319, 414-415, 417-418, 444-447

Plotinus - 79

Plutarch - 264-265, 273

Polycarp - 15, 17, 91, 93-94, 96-98, 100-102, 111-113, 117, 127, 147, 163, 165, 178

Pontianus - 181

Pothinus - 122

Praxeas - 171-172, 189

prayer - 325, 330, 342

pre-existence / pre-existent / pre-mortal - 43-44, 60, 62, 197, 206

Principal, One - 374-375, 377-380, 382-385

principatus patris - 193

Prisca - 171

problem of evil - 53-57, 59-62, 97, 153, 166, 234, 239

process theology - 312, 314, 329-331

Proclus - 171

Protestant Reformation - 11, 85

psychic - 164

Ptolemy (Gnostic) - 158, 164

Ptolemy Philadelphus - 72

Pythagoras / Pythagoreans - 35-37, 39, 41, 50, 56, 59, 64, 108, 157, 265, 385, 442

— Q —

quantum theory/structure of vacuum - 286, 287

Quintilianus, Fabius - 71

— R —

rationalism / rational / rationalistic - 41-42, 80, 207, 210, 242, 314, 319, 332, 340

reincarnation - 427-428

revelation - 170-171, 448

rhetoric - 70-73, 75, 79, 100, 115, 400

Rhodon - 119

Rusticus - 124

— S —

Sabellians / Sabellianism - 170, 190, 192, 216
Sabellius - 190-193
Sacrament, water - 161
Saint Ambrose - 75
sands of the sea - 403, 427
Satornilus / Saturninus - 158, 160-161
schism - 183, 195
semi-Arianism - 200
Septuigent (LXX) - 72-73, 285
Serpentarians - 159
Sethites - 159
Severa, Octacilia - 181
Severus, Alexander - 71, 181
Severus, Caracalla - 180
Severus, Septimius - 180
Simon Magus - 76, 158, 160
Skeptics - 50, 74
Smith, Joseph - 27, 179, 180, 207, 242, 289, 299, 305, 331, 346, 362-366, 372-373
Socrates - 35, 70
sola Scriptura - 11-14, 216, 231
sons of God - 280, 361, 376, 395, 423, 428
Sophists - 70, 77
soul - 43-45, 63-64
spiritual body (*soma pneumatikon*) - 257-259, 262, 309, 328, 331
Stephen of Rome - 183
Stoics / Stoicism - 46, 50-52, 57, 60, 62, 108, 120-123, 135, 221-222, 235-236, 298, 386, 414, 429-430, 444, 447
submission / subordination - 193, 240, 244, 261, 374, 379-380, 386-389, 408
substantia / substance - 190-191, 225, 232
summum genus - 47, 297
syllogism - 47, 195, 413-414, 417, 419, 448-449
Syrian school (Gnostics) - 159-162, 165-166, 239, 443

— T —

Talmud / Oral law - 73
Tatian - 16-17, 112, 115, 119, 122, 128, 131-132, 160-161, 229, 236-237, 297-298, 443
telecommunications - 321, 336, 340, 342
Temple / Temple of Solomon - 333-335, 340
temples made with hands - 334-335
Tertullian - 16, 17, 85, 91, 103, 112, 115, 118, 166, 170-171, 176, 180-181, 183, 190, 225, 271, 446
Theodotus - 164, 189
theophany - 253
Theophilus - 16-17, 121, 138-140, 142
Thyestean banquets / ritual child-murder - 107, 124
traditor - 185
Trajan - 92, 94, 100, 106, 123, 177, 180, 207
Trinity / Trinitarianism - 46, 138, 173, 189, 192-193, 200, 225-228, 230-231, 238, 243-244, 246, 306-307, 372

— U —

Unmoving Mover - 45, 99, 130, 228, 232, 269, 346, 364, 385, 417, 447

— V —

Valentinus / Valentinians - 101, 113, 158, 160-164, 223
Valerian - 181, 184
Vulgate, Latin - 285

— W —

Whitehead, Alfred North - 312, 329
"Who is the god of the Christians?" - 123, 129, 139, 145, 177-178, 373
Wisdom / Sophia - 139, 159, 163-164, 194, 222, 227, 280-281, 313

— X, Y, Z —

Zyphyrinus - 171